"Rigorously researched. . . . Thick, accusative, and critical, *Wrapped in the Flag of Israel* is indeed a must-read for all."
—ANNE DE JONG, *American Anthropologist*

"Engaging and insightful. . . . The book makes an important contribution to the literature, demonstrating that throughout the history of Israel, the Jewish immigrants of European descent have retained their privileged socioeconomic position and maintained claims to cultural superiority over communities coming from Asia and the Middle East. *Wrapped in the Flag of Israel* is an important ethnography of Mizraḥi women and an excellent addition to anthropology of Israel."
—YULIA EGOROVA, *American Ethnologist*

"Lavie's study is solid, scrupulously researched and documented and has the ring of truth that comes from the personal experience of a researcher who has had to live through her fieldwork situation in a manner that few anthropologists experience. . . . Lavie has created a text whose insights and analysis extend far beyond her admirable Israeli study."
—WILLIAM O. BEEMAN, *Anthropological Quarterly*

"An important and provocative book that deserves to be widely read well beyond anthropology. The central question it addresses—the relationship between the rise and fall of social protest movements in Israel, and the wider conflict in the Middle East—is of crucial importance not only for people interested in the region, but for all those with a concern with progressive politics more generally. . . . *Wrapped in the Flag of Israel* is recommended to researchers, postgraduate students, and undergraduates who are interested in Israel/Palestine, political protest, discrimination, and the anthropology of the state."
—TOBIAS KELLY, *Journal of the Royal Anthropological Institute*

"Lavie raises important questions about victimhood and agency pertinent to the study of the subaltern. . . . This book is not just a unique contribution to understanding gender and race in state bureaucracy and the operations of nationalism in the Middle East; it will interest anyone studying the disenfranchised and their everyday life, something that almost always involves

T0373062

'bureaucratic torture.' ... *Wrapped in the Flag of Israel* exposes how inhumanity can be normalized and can thrive in any modern liberal democracy."
—SEALING CHENG, *Asian Anthropology*

"Lavie's meticulous ethnographic work and pointed theoretical analysis explain the hopelessness of social protest and problematize the concept of agency in the context of intra-Jewish conflict in Israel; in this Lavie also addresses the ramifications of Mizraḥi marginalization on the wider Israeli-Palestinian conflict."
—SHOSHANA MADMONI-GERBER, *Cultural Studies*

"Lavie illustrates how asking difficult, troubling questions that disturb taken-for-granted silences can be an important strategy of resistance. In doing so, *Wrapped in the Flag of Israel* offers theoretical and political insights that extend beyond Israel's undeclared borders."
—SIMONA SHARONI, *Journal of Palestine Studies*

"Incredibly insightful conceptually but also powerful politically. It does not merely challenge conceptual frameworks and academic canons but actively undoes them through shifting and diverse modes of writing."
—ADI KUNTSMAN, *Journal of Middle Eastern Women's Studies*

"Lavie has written a brave and scholarly auto-ethnography using an extended case study method, of a social movement in contemporary Israel. ... With theoretical sophistication and granular accounts of day-to-day struggles of her own and other single mothers' efforts to survive and gain access to resources and entitlements as Israelis ... This is a painful account well worth reading. Social workers from many nations who are involved in difficult macro- and mezzo-practice would find illuminating the many elements of social movement activity and peer-group support that Lavie characterizes and theorizes so powerfully."
—BARBARA LEVY SIMON, *Affilia: Journal of Women and Social Work*

"Lavie offers an unflinching political analysis and cultural critique of the struggles of Mizraḥi single mothers and their relationship with the domestic policies of the state of Israel and the politics of the Israeli-Palestinian

conflict. . . . The Award Committee recognizes Lavie's innovative approach to academic writing that combines critical theory, auto-ethnography, and memoirs to animate the lives of women in a community that has long been disenfranchised, particularly in light of limited scholarship on the topic."
—ASSOCIATION OF MIDDLE EAST WOMEN'S STUDIES
2015 Book Award Competition, Honorable Mention

"[Lavie's] compelling account defies conventional labels for ethnography by combining elements of auto-ethnography, memoir, testimonial, cultural critique, extended case study, Bakhtinian contrapunct, and the reflexive essay style of critical race feminists. . . . [A] courageous intervention of substantive, theoretical, and methodological significance."
—FAYE V. HARRISON, professor of African American studies
and anthropology at the University of Illinois at Urbana-Champaign
and president of the International Union of Anthropological and
Ethnological Sciences

"Contributes whole new dimensions to transnational feminist theory and feminist of color theory."
—PAOLA BACCHETTA, professor of gender and women's studies at
the University of California, Berkeley

"Lavie's work marks the first English-language ethnography . . . on single motherhood outside North America. It is also the first ethnography to explore the complex interplay between gender, race, and bureaucracy in the Middle East. . . . [A] must-read for scholars of the state, race, gender, class, religion, [and] the Middle East."
—SUAD JOSEPH, Distinguished Professor of Anthropology and
Gender, Sexuality, and Women's Studies at the University of
California, Davis

"Lavie's analysis of the fusion of bureaucratic and religious power is without equal in the classics of political anthropology."
—MARTHA MUNDY, professor emerita at the London School of
Economics

"This a powerful, indeed an exceptional, book on the fate of Mizraḥi single mothers in today's Israel . . . without the romanticism and idealism within which Israeli middle-class Jews love to bedeck themselves and present themselves."

—DON HANDELMAN, Sarah Allen Shaine Professor Emeritus of Sociology and Anthropology at Hebrew University of Jerusalem

"Lavie's ethnography fills a chasm in the anthropology of Israel that documents inter-ethnic hierarchies and how these are impacted and enforced by the state. . . . She situates the Mizraḥim not only in relation to their own subordination within Israel, but also in relation to the on-going inability of the Israeli government to forge peace with Palestine."

—ANJA RYDING, *Allegra Lab Online Book Reviews*

"At the crossroads between a coursebook, a piece of writing about life and a feminist manifesto, *Wrapped in the Flag of Israel* . . . [is] both an enlightening insight into Israeli intra-racism and an original and valuable connection between two seemingly unrelated concepts: bureaucracy and torture."

—SORINA GEORGESCU, *Hypercultura*

"Rarely one encounters a comprehensive, nuanced, insightful, and realistic exposition on Israeli society packaged in such a slim book. *Wrapped in the Flag of Israel* is such a research and book. The work is extraordinary, imaginative, and creative; it is a fruitful presentation of the anthropological imagination's tremendous abilities to see a social world encapsulated in a drop of 'fieldwork.' Indeed, this is a tour de force of the unique abilities reserved to anthropology's insight production."

—MEIR AMOR, *Arab Studies Quarterly*

"Far from traditional anthropology, Lavie's work is a contribution to the legacy of women of color feminist works of auto-ethnography and documentations of affect in poetic and scholarly prose. . . . Readers will encounter worlds of knowledge placed in proximity, affinity, and opposition, resulting in a dynamic narrative and an informative, academic text. . . . A masterwork of transnational feminist studies and critical theory, a teachable

work of feminist anti-Zionism from the perspective of a Mizraḥi welfare mother and critical scholar—the like of which does not exist."
—BROOKE LOBER, *Feminist Formations*

"Lavie makes an important contribution in challenging traditional methods of ethnographic research and emphasizing the necessity of subaltern auto-ethnography, particularly in the study of marginalized groups. . . . While we should not disregard studies that emphasize the positive potential of mobilization, Lavie makes an important step in explaining a case where such mobilization was not only unsuccessful but never had the possibility of creating change. Scholars of social movements should follow her lead."
—LEONIE FLEISCHMANN, *Peace and Change*

"[Lavie's] unflinching exposure of intra-Jewish racism and its political consequences is unmatched."
—SALLY BLAND, *The Jordan Times*

"Smadar Lavie offers a bracing alternative to the 'Jewish Disneyland' image of Israel in her book *Wrapped in the Flag of Israel*. The book documents the lived experience of women in Israeli society—from the feminist-of-color movement to the politics of funding NGOs to the role of the bureaucracy of the state. Using a combination of deep anthropological research and the personal narratives of Mizraḥi single mothers, Lavie effectively challenges preconceptions about Jewish Israeli society, and in so doing, exposes the lopsided structures of power and privilege between Ashkenazi and Mizraḥi Jews in Israel. Understanding Israel's intra-Jewish racism and its impact on families is crucial to any just solution for the people of Israel/Palestine."
—REBECCA VILKOMERSON, executive director of Jewish Voice for Peace

"The book. . . . is Lavie's ensuing analysis. . . . of the infrastructure that put. . . . single mothers in their precarious position. Lavie's book is a political book, in the sense that it addresses the socio-political head on, refusing to accept. . . . the divinity of the state as a given. . . . The book thus deals. . . . with the very historical, political, social, and cultural realities that lie at the basis o. . . . Zionism and Mizraḥi women, and the wider socio-politics of Mizraḥim in Israel. Lavie offers a masterful analysis of the historical Mizraḥi support of the Right."

—YAACOV YADGAR, *Journal of Modern Jewish Studies*

Wrapped in the Flag of Israel

Expanding Frontiers:
*Interdisciplinary Approaches
to Studies of Women,
Gender, and Sexuality*

SERIES EDITORS:
Karen J. Leong
Andrea Smith

Wrapped in the Flag of Israel

Mizraḥi Single Mothers and Bureaucratic Torture

REVISED EDITION

Smadar Lavie

With a new afterword by the author

University of Nebraska Press
Lincoln and London

Library of Congress Cataloging-in-Publication Data
Names: Lavie, Smadar, author.
Title: Wrapped in the flag of Israel: Mizraḥi
single mothers and bureaucratic torture / Smadar Lavie;
with a new afterword by the author.
Other titles: Expanding frontiers.
Description: Revised edition. | Lincoln: University
of Nebraska Press, 2018. | Series: Expanding frontiers:
interdisciplinary approaches to studies
of women, gender, and sexuality | Includes
bibliographical references and index.
Identifiers: LCCN 2017038815
ISBN 9781496205544 (pbk.: alk. paper)
ISBN 9781496207487 (epub)
ISBN 9781496207494 (mobi)
ISBN 9781496207500 (pdf)
Subjects: LCSH: Single mothers—Israel—
Social conditions—21st century. | Single mothers—
Israel—Economic conditions—21st century. |
Mizraḥim—Israel—Social conditions—21st century. |
Mizraḥim—Israel—Economic conditions—
21st century. | Feminists—Political activity—
Israel. | Social movements—Israel. | Israel—Social
conditions—21st century.
Classification: LCC HQ759.915 .L38 2018 | DDC
306.874/32095694—dc23 LC record available at
https://lccn.loc.gov/2017038815

Set in Merope Basic by E. Cuddy.

For Shaheen

CONTENTS

NOTE ON TRANSLITERATION

In transliteration of Hebrew, Yiddish, and Arabic words I have adhered more or less to the standards of the *International Journal of Middle Eastern Studies* (IJMES). Because the Arabic words in this book are mainly slang, I have transliterated them from their phonetic Arabic using IJMES Hebrew to English transliteration rules. Hebrew and Arabic have more or less a similar alphabet. I have refrained from using lines above vowels to demarcate long-vowel pronunciation, as is normally standard under IJMES.

For individual persons' names, I use the transliteration they personally use in news media and publications. Most often these transliterations do not conform to the IJMES standard.

I have used the following system:

HEBREW RADICAL	ENGLISH TRANSLITERATION
א	a
ב	b
ב	v
ג	g
ד	d
ה	h
ו	v
ז	z
ח	ḥ
ט	t
י	y
כ	kh
כ	k

HEBREW RADICAL	ENGLISH TRANSLITERATION
כ	kh
ך	k
ל	l
מ	m
ם	m
נ	n
ן	n
ס	s
ע	'
פ	f
פּ	p
ף	f
ף	p
צ	ts or tz
ץ	ts or tz
ק	k
ר	r
ש	sh
ת	t

Wrapped in the Flag of Israel

Introduction

Marching on Jerusalem with Israel's Single Mothers

On 2 July 2003, Vicky Knafo, a forty-three-year-old single mother of three, started her march on Jerusalem wearing a black baseball cap and wrapping herself in the Israeli flag—a made-in-China rectangle of white cloth sporting twin blue stripes and the blue Star of David at its center. Her 205-kilometer (around 125 miles) pilgrimage ascended to the capital from Mitzpe Ramon, a tiny Mizraḥi desert town perched upon a windswept plateau and overlooking a spectacular cirque. Remote and isolated, Mitzpe also has one of the highest unemployment rates in the State of Israel.[1]

Vicky is part of the 50 percent majority of Israel's citizens—the *Mizraḥim* (Easterners or Orientals, Hebrew), Jews with origins in the Arab and Muslim World and the margins of Ottoman Europe.[2] Mizraḥim also constitute the majority of Israel's disenfranchised. Their parents immigrated to Israel mainly in the 1950s from places such as Morocco, Libya, Egypt, Lebanon, Yemen, Iraq, Iran, Pakistan, Turkey, Bulgaria, former Yugoslavia, and India.[3] Mizraḥim are often mistakenly called *Sephardim*, derived from the Hebrew word *sfaradim* (Spaniards). *Sephardi* (adjectival form) is a religious term named after a type of *nosaḥ*. Nosaḥ is the set of liturgical melodies for chanting the Torah, the layout of text in Jewish prayer books, and the traditions and customs associated with both holidays and everyday life. The Sephardim are descendants of the non-Yiddish-speaking Jews who were expelled from Spain and southern Europe in 1492, and they constitute only one group of Mizraḥim. English-language media outlets use *Sephardim* rather than *Mizraḥim*, so *Sephardim* has become the default international term. Diasporic Jews also use the term *Sephardim*, as opposed to *Mizraḥim*.

1

Most non-Yiddish-speaking Jews originating in Asia and Africa refer to themselves with a designation of their family's country of origin—Moroccan, Persian, Yemeni, Bulgarian, Indian, Greek, Turkish, and so on. If observant, they pray in synagogues that chant the nosaḥ of their communities of origin. Officially, the Israeli government terms Mizraḥim "descendants from Asia-Africa," or ʿEdot HaMizraḥ (Bands of the Orient, Hebrew) (Lavie 1992).

In the early 1980s, the coalitional term *Mizraḥim* was coined by activist-intellectuals such as Shlomo Swirski (1989) and David Hemo in the Hebrew periodical ʿIton Aḥer (1988–1994). In the 1990s, the term was developed further by the Mizraḥi intelligentsia in academic-political exile in the United States, or by the Israelis who founded the Mizraḥi Democratic Rainbow NGO in 1996. From its inception, it has been used as a political term by Jews from the Arab and Muslim World to refer to themselves (Ducker 2005).[4] They vehemently reject the identity descriptor "Arab Jews," designated for them by diasporic anti-Zionist Mizraḥi intellectuals.

Palestinians comprise about 20 percent of Israel's citizenry. In Arabic they are called ʿArab Thamaniya Wa-Arbaʿin, or "'48 Arabs"—shorthand for those who stayed in Palestine after the 1948 *Nakba* (catastrophe, Arabic)—the expulsion of most Palestinians from their homeland to carve out the State of Israel. The expulsion was a direct result of Zionism—a fin de siècle European ideology of Jewish nationalism with a main goal of colonizing Palestine to establish a Jewish state (Davis 2003; Krimsky 1977; Masalha 2001; Massad 2006; Morris 1987; Pappe 2006). To this day, the erasure of Palestine continues, even in everyday Hebrew speech. The government and popular culture term Palestinians "Arab citizens of Israel," or "Israeli Arabs." In Hebrew, until the early 2000s, they preferred to be called "Palestinian citizens of Israel," "Palestinians residing in Israel," or, in short, "Palestinian Israelis." As talk about the Nakba has become more prevalent in the Israeli public sphere, the Hebrew appellation has shifted to ʿArviyei Arbaʿim veShemone ('48 Arabs, Hebrew) among a few progressive Hebrew speakers. In colloquial Hebrew, most Israelis use the generic shorthand ʿAravim (Arabs, Hebrew plural) rather than "'48 Arabs" or "Palestinian citizens of Israel." Throughout this book, "'48 Arabs" will refer to Palestinian citizens of Israel.

The remaining 30 percent of the state's citizenry are the *Ashkenazim*, who originated in Central and Eastern Europe and spoke Yiddish. Even as a demographic minority, they control the division of power and privilege in the state. While their first organized immigration wave arrived in Palestine in 1882, most came after the Holocaust (Lavie 2007). Official Israeli Hebrew terminology endows them with the appellation *Kehilot Ashkenaz* (Ashkenazi communities) (Ducker 2005; Lavie 1992). Their correct social science name is AHUSALIM (plural). AHUSAL (singular) is a Hebrew acronym for Ashkenazi, *ḥiloni* (secular), *vatik* (old timer), socialist, and liberal (Kimmerling 2001). The Zionists who perpetrated the Nakba were mainly AHUSALIM. In colloquial Hebrew, when Israelis say "Ashkenazi," they mean AHUSAL. AHUSALIM reject both terms, preferring to call themselves "Israelis." Throughout this book, I use the colloquial "Ashkenazi" for the scientific AHUSAL.[5]

AHUSALIM-Ashkenazim ought not to be confused with the *Russim* (Russians, Hebrew) — post-Soviet Ashkenazim who emigrated from the European parts of the former Soviet Union to Israel in the early 1990s. Russim constitute about 10–12 percent of the state's citizenry and are the visible and vocal post-Soviet immigrants to Israel. Despite the distinction between Russim and Ashkenazim, there is a continuity between old and new Eastern European immigrants. Many second-generation Russim seem to be well integrated with the Ashkenazim. As such, they are careful to distinguish between themselves and the *Kavkazim* (people from the Caucasus Mountains in Inner Asia, Hebrew plural masculine), or immigrants who arrived in Israel from the Asian, Muslim-majority republics of the former USSR, and the *Gruzinim* (Jews who immigrated to Israel from Georgia, Hebrew plural masculine). Neither have Yiddish-speaking origins. Kavkazim and Gruzinim constitute about 2–4 percent of Israel's citizenry. AHUSALIM and Russim count Kavkazim and Gruzinim with the Mizraḥim.

Overall, approximately 85 percent of world Jewry is Ashkenazi, but only a small percentage of them live inside the State of Israel. Conversely, only 15 percent of world Jewry is Mizraḥim, yet a great majority lives inside the Israeli state (Swirski 1989).

Ironically, the term *Mizraḥim* only made it into the Israeli public sphere when Mizraḥi intellectuals preoccupied with scholarship about identity politics disseminated the term via Ashkenazi-controlled print and electronic media. From the mid-1990s on, in nonliturgical, everyday Hebrew, self-identification as Moroccan, Persian, Yemeni, Bulgarian, Indian, Greek, or Turkish became replaced by the catchall term *Mizraḥim*. Official discourse camouflages the fact that the majority of Israel's citizenry is of Mizraḥi origin. The Israeli Central Bureau of Statistics devised an all-inclusive demographic category, called *yelidei ha-Aretz*, referring to those Israeli Jews "born in Israel." If one does not know the identity of the parents and grandparents of those "born in Israel," then the proportions of Mizraḥim and Ashkenazim seem more equal than they actually are. When younger Jewish Israelis are described as born in Israel, they lose their historical diasporic roots, which still define racial-ethnic zones of privilege. Because Mizraḥi families had much higher birth rates than the Ashkenazim until the middle of the 1970s, it is evident that the majority of Jews born in Israel are Mizraḥim (Ducker 2005). Moreover, the Bureau of Statistics classifies children of mixed marriages by the father's ethnicity. It is more common for Ashkenazi men to marry Mizraḥi women than the reverse.

Indeed, many Ashkenazim excuse the ethnic-racial gap between them and the Mizraḥim by stating that there is a very high rate of mixed marriages between Ashkenazim and Mizraḥim. Ashkenazim point to these mixed marriages as evidence of the disappearing color-class bar between Mizraḥim and Ashkenazim. The legend of prevalent mixed Ashkenazi-Mizraḥi marriages is a key component in the Zionist mythology regarding the ingathering of the Jewish diasporas in the State of Israel. Mizraḥim and Ashkenazim most often marry across their own ethnic groups. Mizraḥi-Ashkenazi marriages, though more common than they once were, still constitute less than a third of Jewish marriages in Israel (Blumenfeld 1997; Okun and Khait-Marelly 2006; Shahar 1988). Identifying these disparities, or their occlusion in the census, greatly clarifies the patterns of discrimination within the Jewish population (Lavie 2011a).[6]

To address the discrimination they face, Mizraḥi women have only one social movement that advocates specifically for their predicament—*Aḥoti* (Sistah, Hebrew)—For Women in Israel. In 2000, it morphed into a feminist NGO. A member of Aḥoti's executive board at that time, I received a daily

LISTSERV digest with important news items. On 3 July 2003, I was perusing these emails and learned about Vicky Knafo. One was from a fellow board member who had been driving south to Mitzpe for an artists' workshop. The town has become a fashionable retreat for artists, yogis, and New Agers because it is the perfect combination of natural beauty and cheap housing. While these creatives have only recently floated south to Mitzpe, the townies have always dreamt of moving north, to the Tel Aviv metropolitan area, for jobs and lives not stuck in the middle of nowhere. The board member reported that at dusk, she spotted a flag-shrouded bleached blonde marching northbound on the forlorn highway. Another e-mail was from a co-founder of Aḥoti who kept regular communication with Mitzpe's women. Vicky had called her from the road, panting: "I'm marching on Jerusalem for tens of thousands of Israeli single moms. Enough's enough. Up to 29 June, we were big-time *Likudnikim* [Likud party supporters, Hebrew] and voted for Bibi [Benjamin Netanyahu]. He gonna hear from me no more! Please help me find places to refill water and spend the night."[7]

We Sistahs were the first to join her march, to protect her legally and physically from the police who would try to arrest her for blocking traffic. We also worked to get her story to a press ravenous for news. These were the days of the *hudna* (ceasefire, Arabic), the temporary truce between Israel and Palestinian Ḥamas. No nationalist violence for the evening news. So when Vicky appeared on TV, dozens of poverty-stricken single mothers from Israel's Mizraḥi ghettos and barrios started their own marches on Jerusalem. Ilana Azoulay was one of them. From 'Arad, another desolate desert town, she pushed the wheelchair of her crippled son, who cradled an old three-legged Chihuahua in his lap.

———

Wohl Rose Park is Israel's largest rose garden. It is also the symbolic center of Israel's three government branches. The park bears the name of its chief funders, Vivian and Maurice Wohl. Maurice (1923–2007) was an Eastern European Jew, London real estate magnate, and "charmingly eccentric" commander of Order of the British Empire (*Daily Telegraph* 2007). From the park's peak, one can look down to the Supreme Court and Government Min-

1. Ilana Azoulay and her son take a break on their march from ʿArad to Jerusalem. Meir Azulay, 2003.

istry offices. Also visible is the Knesset (Israel's parliament), and, at the far edge of the park, the huge bronze menorah that is the emblem of the state (Handelman 1990). Because of the park's position, protest movements use it as an ideal staging ground for demonstrations. Protesters with grievances against the Knesset settle themselves on the hillside opposite the Knesset building. The same with the Supreme Court. The most popular slope faces the buildings that house the offices for the Ministry of Foreign Affairs, the Ministry of Internal Affairs, and the Finance Ministry, among others. Officials in these ministries enact policies that directly target disenfranchised Israelis.

On 9 July 2003, a passerby enjoying the garden's serenity would have had her ears perk up. At first, distant sounds—police sirens, the low roar of motorcycles, a static of hoarse, high-pitched shouts—all set to a metallic background beat. Then expanding—horses whinnying, cell phones ringing, dogs yipping and howling, camera shutters clicking. The sounds would grow steadily louder until a caravanserai of hundreds became visible, trudging down the road from the visitors' parking lot. The cavalcade's outer ring—a retinue of police mounted on motorcycles, scooters, or horses overseeing a tight group of slow-driving 4x4s, "Press" signs taped to their back windows. The next layer in—marchers from all walks of Israeli society, from young women in tight shorts and spaghetti-strap tank tops to show off their belly buttons to ultra-Orthodox men in black frocks and fur-covered hats. Finally—the tender center—mothers, all sunburned, their hands locked with their children's. Demonstrators blew whistles and horns, banged spoons on soup kettles, and rhythmically chanted rhyming, antigovernment slogans. Dogs of all kinds—tongues hanging out the sides of their mouths from the heat—wove through the marchers' legs and pulled their owners toward other dogs or horses and away from the harsh police sirens. In time, the passersby would become one with the crowd, on the slope facing the Finance Ministry.

That evening, Jewish owners of Jerusalem's sporting goods stores came out and donated igloo-style tents for the mothers to sleep in. Jewish restaurant owners donated leftovers. Jewish Jerusalemites gave blankets and sleeping bags. Over the next few days, hundreds of citizens donated food and clothes. Some wrote checks.

> On the soil of the homeland, in the city of Tel-Aviv, on Sabbath eve, the 5th day of Iyar, 5708 [14 May 1948], the members of the People's Council, representatives of the Jewish community of Eretz-Israel [the land of Israel, Hebrew] and of the Zionist movement declare the establishment of a Jewish state in Eretz-Israel [i.e., Palestine], to be known as the State of Israel. (Declaration of Establishment of State of Israel 1948)[8]

And again, on the soil of the homeland, in the divided city of Jerusalem, on the ninth day of Tammuz, 5763 (9 July 2003), during the momentary respite of the hudna, the impoverished single mothers of the State of Israel declared the establishment of a shantytown in Wohl Rose Park, to be known as *Knafoland* (Hebrew).

How ironic that the linguistic formation of a Hebrew name added to the English word *land* found its way into colloquial Hebrew from Palestine liberation-struggle vocabulary. The formation was first used in the term *Fataḥland*, or the land of FATAH—the Arabic acronym for the PLO (Palestine

Liberation Organization). Fataḥland referred to the 1972–82 PLO-controlled southeast Lebanon border zone with the State of Israel. In Hebrew, *land* has become a suffix used in the same way Americans use the word *gate*, to suggest a scandal or controversy, as in *Watergate*, echoed in *Irangate*.[9]

Knafoland had its ups and downs. But on the whole, it grew in size and popularity with the media and the public until 19 August 2003, when a Palestinian suicide bomber blew himself up in Jerusalem, diverting media and public attention back to the Israel-Palestine conflict. Shortly thereafter, Knafoland dissipated and disappeared.

"Reaganomics," Ḥok HaHesderim, and the Oslo Boomtime

Israel's middle- to lower-class single mothers are not the same as North America's or Europe's. Most Israeli single mothers were married by their early twenties and birthed their children into a legal union shortly thereafter. Thus, when the mothers divorced, they had limited professional experience and little property to divide with their ex-husbands.

The State of Israel has never had viable mechanisms to collect child support from deadbeat dads. For this reason, in 1972, the Knesset passed the Child and Spouse Support Law, meant to strengthen the enforcement of a law by the same name passed in 1959. The Child and Spouse Support Law of 1959 had no real method of enforcement. The 1972 law amends this oversight by instructing the National Security Bureau (NSB) — similar to the U.S. Social Security Administration (SSA)[10] — to pay minimal subsistence to divorced mothers unable to collect court-ordered child support. The 1972 law also orders the NSB, if possible, to deduct minimal subsistence from the paychecks of a deadbeat dad. This assumes, however, that the father has a regular salaried job. It is quite difficult for the NSB to deduct these sums from fathers who are self-employed, or who work irregular part-time jobs. To avoid the deduction, some deadbeat dads resign from their employers, only to turn around and become independent consultants who perform the same job. To top it all off, the 1972 law was not put into full effect until after the Knesset passed its 1992 Law for Single-Headed Families. These efforts in 1992 to enact the 1972 law coincided with the influx of immigrants from post-Soviet states. Conveniently, among these immigrants was a high concentration of single-headed families from European post-Soviet states.[11]

Israeli taxpayers, therefore, must make up the shortfall (see Reger 2011). For 2010 alone, the debt of nonsalaried deadbeat dads to the NSB was 267,000,000 New Israeli Shekels (NIS), or $75,423,728 (Reger 2011).[12] As of 2010, Family Courts determined minimum subsistence for a mother and two children to be 1,250 NIS, or about $300 a month. For comparison, in 2010, an average two-bedroom rental in the center of Israel, where most employment is located, was $800 a month.[13] Moreover, the 1997 Israeli Supreme Court appeal verdict 4445/96 in *Shaul Bar-Noy v. NSB and ʿAliza Bar-Noy* ordered Collection Court to be more compassionate toward deadbeat dads — salaried or otherwise — than to other kinds of debtors. So much for the feeble five-year attempt at helping single mothers get child support. Today, when a bereft mother, even with the backing of the NSB, attempts to collect a child support debt, she finds it almost impossible to obtain.

Some mothers can rely on their families for financial assistance. These are almost always Ashkenazi. Mizraḥi single mothers — the majority of single mothers — cannot rely on their families for extra income. Thus, they turn to welfare.

In 2003, the State of Israel decided to slash welfare allowances for single mothers with its amendment to *Ḥok HaHesderim* (Arrangements Law, Hebrew). This is why Vicky started her march.

Ḥok HaHesderim is the Israeli version of the U.S. Consolidated Omnibus Budget Reconciliation Act of 1985 — a "Reaganomics" initiative to deregulate and downsize government, reduce spending, decrease taxes for the upper classes, and ease inflation through monetary control. In the same year, Zionist Left Labor prime minister Shimon Peres and right-wing Likud finance minister Yitzhak Moday copied the U.S. law to deal with the mega-inflation plaguing the Israeli economy (Knesset 2009). The Israeli simulacrum, however, lacked oversight. The Knesset Finance Committee rarely deliberates the dictates of the neocon Finance Ministry experts. These experts are products of Israeli universities' economics departments, heavily influenced by the ideologies and methods of Milton Friedman, the University of Chicago guru of neoconservative economics.[14] Instead, the Finance Committee rubber stamps the experts' decrees. Today, Ḥok HaHesderim has become a permanent part of Israel's Budget Law. It consolidates diverse deregulatory budget cuts into a single annual Finance Committee–backed amendment the Knesset votes into law (Rolef 2006). The vote usually occurs in the wee hours.

The privatization-deregulation of Israel's centrist government economy started in 1985. But it accelerated after the 1993 Oslo Peace Accords signed by Prime Minister Yitzak Rabin of Israel and Yasser ʿArafat, the head of the Palestine Liberation Organization (PLO). The peace architects — upper-class Ashkenazi politicians and entrepreneurs — broke up labor unions as they did away with the concept of sustained, salaried work. They worked in concert with the affluent Tunis leadership of the PLO that landed in Ramallah to form the Palestinian Authority (PA) and rule over the West Bank and Gaza right after Oslo. Aside from managing huge sums of U.S. and Western European funds, and private money pouring into the peace economy, both sides cut financial deals with each other for their own benefits (Berger 1996; Bichler and Nitzan 2001; Hashai 2002). Together, they formed a tight-knit clique the Hebrew media dubbed the "Beilin-ʿAbed Rabbo Flying Circus" after two high-profile members: Yossi Beilin, prominent member of the Meretz Zionist Left party and former holder of high-powered government positions, and ʿYasser ʿAbed Rabbo, a "pro-peace" member of the PLO executive committee and former PA minister of Information and Culture under Arafat.[15] The descriptor "flying" referred to how the clique flew lavishly to Europe and the United States to encourage international investors to pour money into the peace economy. "Circus" referred to the clique's peace performances that delighted Western European and North American politicians, financiers, and press (Shelah 2002). The Flying Circus completely ignored their lack of support among the majority of Israelis — the Mizraḥim — and the majority of Palestinians — the Islamists. The new PA economy parroted the Israeli economy, built on cronyism and monopolies (Leibovitz-Dar 2002). Investment capital, funneled through Israeli entrepreneurs, funded enterprises run by ʿArafat's coterie (Bergman and Ratner 1997; Korin-Leber 2002; Schwartz 1997).

Israeli university professors advised the peace clique that the Israeli-PA economic boom ought to emulate the high-tech assembly lines of Bangalore (Helpman and Trachtenberg 2000). The clique also made major use of outsourcing (Plotzker 2001). Factories in Israel closed and moved to places like Jordan and Honduras (Zomer 2001), leaving Mizraḥim and '48 Arabs jobless (Greenstein 2000). "The top tenth of people hold two thirds of the financial capital in Israel" (Lavie, Z. 2003; see Sinai 2002), the media exhorted, pointing out the widening disparity between economic classes. News reports reiterated the common knowledge that "the average pay an Ashkenazi gets is 40 percent higher than the average pay of a Mizraḥi . . . and is larger than the income gap between Whites and Blacks in . . . the U.S." (Barne͑a and Shiffer 1999; ͑Eshet 2000; Regev 2006).

The Palestinians of the West Bank and Gaza were hit by unemployment as well. The Palestinian Authority created very few jobs for Palestinians because the PA continued to be a market for Israeli-produced goods. Israeli employers imported guest workers from the Philippines, Thailand, Bolivia, Ghana, Romania, India, Bulgaria, China, Ukraine, Peru, Moldova, Niger, Burkina-Faso, Turkey, Columbia, and Belarus, to name a few. These guest workers took over lower-tiered jobs Palestinians used to do before Oslo (Zilberg 2002). The workers were cheaper because they were not subject to Israeli minimum-wage regulations. Plus, they were not likely to become involved in anti-Israeli guerrilla actions.

The Oslo Accords also failed to halt the expansion of Israeli settlements in the West Bank and Gaza. Rather, because of the boomtime, the center of Israel—inside the pre-1967 armistice lines—became a high-priced real estate bubble. Concurrent with the Oslo Accords was a huge influx of Ashkenazi post-Soviet immigration. Post-Soviets caused housing costs to skyrocket, pushing out Mizraḥi families from the ghettos and barrios in the gentrified center (Lavie 1991).[16] These families needed to remain near the center—near major employers and better schooling. Their best bet was to move a dozen or so kilometers (or around 7.5 miles) to the east, into the large-scale West Bank settlements less than a half-hour drive away from the state's economic core. West Bank settlers can drive to work, or take heavily subsidized, frequent public transportation, along a well-maintained system of "apartheid roads" (B'Tselem 2004; McGreal 2005). While Israeli law does not preclude non-Jews from using these roads, the many roadblocks and military checkpoints effectively bar West Bank Palestinians from using them.[17] Mizraḥim therefore became the main population to fill the large settlement expansions invigorated by the boomtime.

Losing their jobs and land to the Oslo peace process stirred civil unrest among the Palestinian people. To maintain control, the PA police force, coerced to follow orders from the Israeli Defense Force (IDF), oversaw the everyday lives of West Bank and Gaza Palestinians. No wonder the second Al-Aqsa Intifada broke out in October 2000 (Greenstein 2000). Israeli troops and tanks once again waged war on Palestinian civilians, who responded with increased suicide bombings. These bombings often occurred in loosely policed public buses, open markets, and in ghettos and barrios—where Mizraḥim, ultra-Orthodox Jews, post-Soviet immigrants, and guest workers resided or frequented (see Rappaport 2003; Shadmi 2004a, 2012). Public panic penetrated all levels of Israeli society. To Tel Aviv natives, the ultimate indicator of this panic was easily available parking in the normally bustling downtown area.

The Hudna

The Ḥok HaHesderim amendment took effect on 29 June 2003—the same day the Israeli government and Ḥamas declared the hudna ceasefire.

In Islamic terminology, the term *hudna* means a truce between two factions or tribes in conflict that both belong to a larger umbrella group or tribal alliance. In 2003, Haifa University anthropologist and Bedouin expert Joseph Ginat plucked the concept from the 628 CE Treaty of Hudaybiyyah between the Prophet Muḥammad, representing the state of Medina, and the Quraish tribe, who controlled Mecca. Ginat cut-and-pasted this concept in his long-term role as the Israeli regime's consultant on Arab and Muslim affairs (Erlich 2005; Ginat 2006).[18]

A temporary relief in the middle of the Al-Aqsa Intifada, 2000–2005. The IDF pulled back from the centers of Palestinian towns and villages. Suicide bombings in Israel stopped. But the hudna also meant no Grand Guignol for an anxious foreign press corps. So when the Israeli media glommed onto Knafoland, the foreign press—ranging from CNN, Reuters, and AP to smaller outfits from Nigeria and the Philippines—followed right along. And wherever the foreign press went, SHATIL went as well. SHATIL is an acronym for *Sherutei Tmikha veYeʿutz leIrgunim* (Support and Consulting Services for NGOs,

Hebrew), a subsidiary of the New Israel Fund (NIF). Originally founded as a tax shelter for the heirs to the San Francisco Levi's Jeans empire, NIF is now the U.S.-based funder of almost all Israeli human rights and civil society NGOS.[19] SHATIL acts as a public relations and organizational structure consultant for NIF grant recipients. The most valuable resources SHATIL has are its lists of cell phone numbers for all national and international news correspondents. The end result is that NIF, through SHATIL, has near-complete control over the international media portrayal of Israeli NGOs and of social movements. For Knafoland and other Mizraḥi movements, SHATIL was especially instrumental because it offered access to English speakers well versed in communicating with the media. Though it is not mandatory for NIF grant recipients to use SHATIL, it is strongly encouraged by NIF itself. Most recipients comply with SHATIL's oversight for fear of losing their funding.

During the day, international reporters would camp out in their own enclaves next to Knafoland. At night, they would cross town in a caravan of 4x4s to Palestinian Jerusalem, to the venerable bar inside the American Colony Hotel. Located on the seamline between East and West Jerusalem, the American Colony Hotel is a historical landmark, and its bar the preferred watering hole for diplomats, politicians, and foreign correspondents. The American Colony Hotel is also rumored to teem with CIA agents who prefer to engage in high-style subterfuge.

Knafonomics: Vicky and I

In June 2003, Israel's NSB mailed single mothers notices about slashing their monthly income assurances, income augmentations, and rent aid. The notices also informed them about the retroactive debt to the NSB they had incurred for the period between January, when the Ḥok HaHesderim amendment entered into law, and June, when enforcement of the law started. Distraught mothers packed the lines at the NSB and at government bureaus for rent assistance, food donations, and job placements. They had no choice, as even those mothers with jobs had little if any hope of paying their monthly expenses with this debt looming over them. Media charts and graphs consistently show that for every dollar an Ashkenazi male earns, a Mizraḥi male makes only seventy cents. A Palestinian male makes only fifty cents. Women in the

State of Israel as a whole make only 63 percent of what their male analogues are paid. There are no statistics available that detail the income gap between Ashkenazi, Mizraḥi, and Palestinian women (Regev 2006; Tzimuki 1999).

Vicky's march started because she could no longer pay her bills. Her half-time job paid her about 1,217 NIS (about $280) a month.[20] The 2003 amendment cut 1,304 NIS (about $300) from her monthly income welfare supplement of 1,983 NIS (about $456), reducing it to 679 NIS (about $156). The retroactive debt swallowed that paltry sum completely.

Up until June, I was making about 1,200 NIS (about $276) a month as a base-level hourly visiting adjunct associate professor at Beit Berl, a kindergarten and elementary-schoolteacher's college on the margins of Israel's center. NSB income augmentation boosted that up to 3,200 NIS (about $736). In June 2003, my augmentation was cut to 447 NIS (about $103). In July of that year, I was laid off for the summer and got neither a paycheck nor any welfare support. I should have received full income assurance from the NSB. I received nothing.

Like Vicky's, my assurance was eaten up by my retroactive debt to the NSB. But I had access to privileges that Vicky never had. I had an Ashkenazi father, and my parents raised me in a largely Ashkenazi working-to-middle-class neighborhood less than ten miles south of Tel Aviv. My mother's marriage strategy (see Blumenfeld 1997; Shahar 1988) spared me the intergenerational poverty that had affected her own childhood in a Jerusalem slum, and that of her mother—my Yemeni granny who had been forced into child marriage at age eight. I had access to superior education (see Okun and Khait-Marelly 2010, 384). Yet my biography was not supposed to include an encounter with welfare. I should have arrived in Knafoland as a University of California researcher. But that route had closed.

Between 1999 and 2007, I was stranded in Israel. In February 1999, I fled from Berkeley to Tel Aviv to save my nine-and-a-half-year-old son. Between 1993 and 1999, I lived through an acrimonious divorce. Its California chapter ended when my violent ex-husband convinced a California Family Court to grant him full custody of our son.[21] I did the only thing I could to save him from further violence. I took him to live with my family in Israel. Within a week, my ex-husband filed child abduction charges against me in Israel.

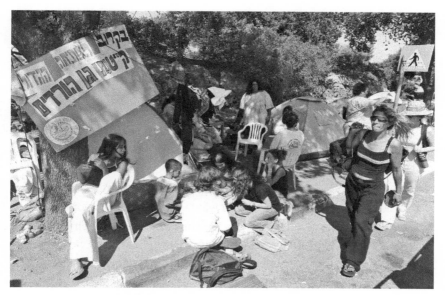

2. Everyday life in Knafoland. Lior Mizaḥi, 2003.

The Israeli courts strictly observe the Hague Convention on the Civil Aspects of International Child Abduction, even disregarding the convention's allowable exceptions that specify the rare conditions permitting the abducted child to stay in the country where he or she has been brought. The return rate of children abducted to Israel from the United States is much higher than in other countries that are signatories to the convention (see Bruch 1988–1989, 2000a, 2000b, 2003; Levy 2007; Schuz 2004). When our trial began, we had to submit both our Israeli and U.S. passports to the court. International law recommends that a child abduction trial at all levels of courts should last no longer than one year, to provide a swift remedy in the best interest of the child (Schuz 2002, 2004). But in our case it took two years to decide, because the court chose to ignore the evidence we presented. In a precedent-setting 2001 decision, the Israeli Supreme Court cleared me of any child abduction charges (see Israel's Supreme Court Verdict 5253/00; Schuz 2008).

According to the Hague Convention on the Civil Aspects of International Child Abduction, child abduction constitutes a legal emergency. Courts are to respond to abduction cases with no delays—a recommended duration of up to three months from pleadings to judgment in each level of court. Most child experts believe that lengthy Hague proceedings threaten the best interest of the child (Rhona Schuz pers. comm.; see Edleson et al. 2010, 170–71; Weiner 2008, 368n176, 366–69, 378, 398–99). Israel has three levels of court for abduction cases—Family Court, District Court, and the Supreme Court (Schuz 2002, 2004). Shaheen and I expected to spend a maximum of nine months in litigation through all three levels. But every time the court made a decision, my ex-husband appealed the decision to the next court level. With each appeal, the court greatly exceeded a reasonable timeframe to reach its decision. Perhaps the courts did not want to decide in my favor because of their overly strict adherence to Hague convention (see Bruch 1988–1989, 2000a, 2000b, 2003; Edleson et al. 2010, 234–37; Levy 2007; Schuz 2004). But the courts had no choice, as my son's circumstances constituted an "intolerable situation" (see Edleson et al. 2010, 3; Weiner 2008, 378). Altogether, Shaheen and I spent twenty-five months in anxious limbo until the Supreme Court decided in my favor.

Recognizing the Israeli court decision, the U.S. State Department instructed me to go to the U.S. Consulate in Tel Aviv and get new valid U.S. passports for Shaheen and me. I did so, but as Israeli citizens we needed Israeli passports to leave or enter Israel. The Israeli authorities would not give these back to us. Why? Under international custody law, after a minor lives in a country for two years, the minor's domicile changes to that country (Schuz 2001, 2004). Now that we had been living in Israel for two years, and the Hague matter was behind us, I should have been granted automatic custody so that I could become Shaheen's legal parent (Rhona Schuz, pers. comm.). But I was not. So to get our Israeli passports back, I now had to ask the Israeli family court for Israeli custody of Shaheen.

Why did our original case not get a decision until twenty-five months afterward? Was it because the courts were waiting for my son's domicile to change? I had been fully cleared of child-snatching charges by all levels of the court. So after the domicile change, why was I not granted automatic custody, as recommended for a parent who is the physical custodian of a child (Bruch 2003; Levy 2007; Rhona Schuz 2004, pers. comm.)?

For almost six more years, the Tel Aviv family court refused to make a decision to grant or withhold custody. I therefore had to resign my tenured associate professorship at the University of California, Davis — a position I had held since 1994 — just as my promotion to full professorship was in process. I could not fill my role, standing at the front of a classroom in Davis, writing on a blackboard. In Israel, my color and politics excluded me from academic positions that paid a living wage.

When Israelis look at me, they detect no trace of my blond-haired, green-eyed father. Inscribed into my phenotype are my Yemeni race marks — olive-chocolate skin and dark brown eyes, wide eyelids, high cheekbones, prominent collarbone and wrist bones, narrow waistline with wide hips, short torso and Asian height. This split-second typecasting made it hard for people to believe I was my father's daughter. In my childhood 'hood, my Ashkenazi classmates called me *kushi sambo* (sambo nigger, Hebrew slang), and their parents called me *sheinale schwartzale* (nice little black, Yiddish feminine) — both to my face. In my teen-danger years, male Mizraḥi youth on street corners or on buses would whistle and catcall me, saying "Hey, Yaman!" (Yemen, Arabic). I took these as compliments because I did not know any better. In Israel, my phenotype always trumps my privilege. To all, I am a dark female form. A Mizraḥi woman. And in the fauna and flora of Israel's professors, Mizraḥi women are a rare species.

Nonacademic Israelis — most of whom are Mizraḥim — use the term "Ashkenazi Academic Junta," or "the Academic Junta" to indicate their estrangement from the impenetrable networks of the Israeli academic elite (Blachman 2005; Zarini 2004). Despite this negative label, the benefits of a tenured academic position cannot be denied. Israeli university pay scales and benefits packages are equal to those of court judges — both are completely paid using public funds, as all Israeli universities are public. Professors also enjoy the glamorous public image of the cosmopolitan academic lifestyle, due to regular travel to North America and Western Europe for conferences and sabbaticals. In general, tenured university professors are much more equitably compensated for their work, as compared to those who earn money through backbreaking physical labor or minimum-wage service jobs, such as Vicky Knafo's part-time position as cook on an Israeli army base.

Iris Zarini (2011) counted 1,032 women professors among the estimated 5,000 associate and full professors in Israeli universities and community colleges, and in government services, such as hospitals or agricultural research facilities.[22] Mizraḥi women number 37 out of these 1,032. Of these 37, almost all are married to wealthy and well-placed Ashkenazim. Only 6 of these 37 are in the nonapplied humanities and social sciences. Zarini (2011) reports that all 37 self-identified as Zionists. I do not. My scholarship and publications have been critical of the thin veneer of universalist humanism that conceals Zionism as a racialized, colonialist ideology and practice.

Since my 1970s adolescence, I have participated in demonstrations, community outreach, and education, first in Israel, and then in North America and Western Europe, that call for a just solution to the Israel-Palestine conflict. For me, this includes the right of return for Palestinians expelled in 1948 from Palestine to make room for the State of Israel. I have always supported the establishment of one secular state, Israel-Palestine, between the Jordan River and the Mediterranean Sea. A *masorti* (traditional, Hebrew) Jew, I have a long historical memory of anti-Jewish persecution and legal discrimination in colonial and postcolonial settings where Christianity or Islam were intrinsically tied to the regime. The State of Israel's Zionist doctrine of "maximum land, minimum non-Jews" toward Palestinians demonstrates how Judaism, when intrinsically tied to the state's definition does the same.

I was a Mizraḥi anti-Zionist woman professor. In Israel, a pariah. No jobs for me. Perhaps it was safer for the State of Israel to keep me there as a welfare mother. That way, I could not go back to the comforts of tenured professorship to write up in a timely manner an ethnography from the data I collected between 1990 and 1995 on the interplay between Ashkenazi-Mizraḥi racism and the Israel-Palestine conflict. Titled "Hebrew as Step-Mother Tongue: The Lives and Works of Arabic-Speaking Jewish and Palestinian Authors and the Rupture of Israel's Eurocentrism," the book was about the lives and words of authors, both Mizraḥi and Palestinian, who cross borders by writing Hebrew literature and poetry even though their native tongue is Arabic. The book was to focus on their life histories, including family, kinship, and their problematic sense of belonging in the Ashkenazi intellectual milieu. These authors tried to avoid the "burden of representation"

(Hall 1988, 27) of their own communities of origin by avoiding writing about Ashkenazi Zionism's negative effects. This was to be one of the first ethnographies to critically apply the U.S.-Mexico Chicana border theory and the U.S. paradigm of feminism of color to the anthropology of the Middle East. My scholarship analyzed Zionism from a Critical Race Theory perspective, and from the vantage point of both Palestinians and Mizraḥim (Lavie 1992, 1995, 1996, n.d.;[23] Lavie and Swedenburg 1996b). In the mid-1990s, a scholar without Israeli university affiliation or U.S.-European Zionist positionality could not have carried out such an empirical project, derived from people's daily lives, without rousing fear in the Ashkenazi Zionist regimes of knowledge. No Israeli academic institution would give me the time and space of a full-time position to think, research, write, and publish.

Jobs like secretary or supermarket cashier were out of my reach. "Overqualified and with too many Google hits," deemed prospective employers. Stranded and jobless, I became a single mother dependent on the government welfare bureaucracy to survive. To stay sane, I joined the effort to build the Mizraḥi feminist movement. I gamely ethnographed everything. I became my own informant.

Unlike mine, Vicky's encounter with Israel's welfare bureaucracy was foreseen. Even as early as the 1920s, the Jewish Socialist Zionist Labor Movement—already colonizing Palestine—was creating the beginnings of what would be Israel's bureaucratic infrastructure (Shapiro 1993; see Handelman 2004, 39–40). So by the 1948 declaration of Israeli statehood, the bureaucracy had enjoyed almost thirty years of growth. In the 1950s, the regime settled new Jewish immigrants from the Arab and Muslim World into the far-flung corners of Palestine where Palestinians exiled during the Nakba once lived (Willner 1969). These immigrants—mainly observant Mizraḥim—were forced into downgraded economic mobility, as they were suddenly cut off from their customary sources of employment and resources. To accommodate this influx, the state greatly expanded its bureaucratic infrastructure into a system that provided monetary supplements, housing, and government-sponsored employment in exchange for their docile loyalty. The system's all-encompassing grip left new citizens with no alternative but complete reliance on the bureaucratic infrastructure (Handelman 2004; Marx 1976).[24]

The regime's overarching goal was to secularize the Mizraḥim while, paradoxically, Judaizing the newly formed State of Israel (see Giladi 1990; Krimsky [1919] 1977, 119; Lavie 1992; Madmoni-Gerber 2009; Shohat 2001). To maintain these contradictory goals, the regime endeavored to block any possible communication, and thus any possible collaboration, between the Mizraḥim and the Palestinians. The regime feared a Mizraḥi-Palestinian coalition arising out of a common culture and mother tongue—Arabic.

So while I came to Mizraḥi feminism as an intellectual, Vicky became a feminist leader through the vicissitudes of life. We both belonged in Knafoland. Yet, I hesitated to take Shaheen, then fourteen years old, and our dog, Baḥit (Barkley, Hebrew feminine), to the encampment. Still in litigation over Shaheen's custody, I was hyperaware of Family Court informers infiltrating the protest. If we stayed overnight at Knafoland, informers could accuse me of jeopardizing Shaheen's quality of life. The Family Court would have license to take him, place him in government boarding school, and ship him to his father in California. All without due process. Ultimately, Shaheen and I decided to go to Knafoland together for half a day, every other day. While there, I was one of the Aḥoti board's representatives. I was a welfare mother with no welfare. I was an ethnographer and autoethnographer.

On Ethnographic Data

In 1990, when my son was one year old, I shifted my center of research from Egypt to Israel-Palestine. I continued my relationships with the Mzeina Bedouin I had studied since 1975 because these relationships had gone beyond research. The Mzeina became family to whom I still keep close today. The change in my research focus seemed like an exciting switch at the time. My American colleagues were starting to shift their focus inward, to study the exoticisms of their own culture rather than those of faraway places. I, too, wanted to shift from "fieldwork" to "homework" (Lavie and Swedenburg 1996a). My research among the Mzeina had addressed the cultural conflicts and conjunctions in modernist colonial systems, and it was set in a context where postcolonial nation-states clashed with indigenous cultures in a transnational setting (Lavie 1990; Lavie, Hajj, and Rouse 1993). The "Hebrew as Step-Mother Tongue" project was to explore similar problems yet in a complex, urban, postmodern setting. The Mizraḥi-Palestinian borderlands provided a setting where articulating and living through the cultural concept of nation was itself under racialized scrutiny from experiential, political, and literary perspectives.

My shift in research sites was also practical. I was a young mother in Berkeley. I was without any communal or familial support. Many of my female colleagues had forsaken children in favor of achieving tenure. They had little sympathy for the balancing act I was struggling to maintain. They did not even know about the turmoil at home that I kept private. If I were doing research in Israel, I could at least get communal and emotional support, as well as childcare, from my family and friends.

I understood that research and publication of scholarship critical of Israel-Palestine was a career risk. In 1990, I was a U.S.-based scholar. The pro-Israel lobby was and still is highly influential in North American universities. I knew that studying intra-Jewish racism in the Homeland of the Jews could alarm the lobby. And, at that time, I could not count on any allies in the burgeoning field of Palestine studies. The field was not yet nuanced enough to consider any conflict other than the simple Israel vs. Palestine divide. Nevertheless, I thought my tenure-track position would provide safe harbor for "Hebrew as Step-Mother Tongue." At any rate, my tenure was to be decided on my research on the Sinai Bedouin of Egypt. No pro-Egypt lobby meddling with academic freedom.

Funded by scholarly grants, I had conducted my first segment of ethnographic research in Israel between 1990 and 1994. Soon after I arrived in Israel in 1999, I embarked on another segment of my research, lasting until 2007. This time, I was funded mostly by the NSB's income augmentation checks and the pittance I received as an adjunct professor at Beit Berl. Beit Berl is the historical bastion of the Labor Party, so between classes I made forays into its stacks. I collected data, including archival research in both official Ashkenazi state archives and the private archives of Mizraḥi independent scholars and activists unaffiliated with Israeli universities. I also made use of the rich book and periodical collections of Beit Ariela, Tel Aviv's main public library. I read and collected articles from all of Israel's Hebrew dailies and weeklies, in print and electronic forms. Many of the references in this book have been published only in Hebrew, and not by major Israeli presses. These texts were not translated into English because there is a translation block between the Hebrew and English with regard to grassroots Mizraḥi scholarship (see Lavie 2006b).

I also conducted fieldwork, that is, homework, and compiled notes as I participated in and observed events in literary salons; social movements; the welfare system; family, labor, youth, criminal, civil, and collection courts; civil society NGOs and their funding agencies, when possible; dance clubs; street demonstrations and marches; cafés; housing projects; neighborhoods; schools; concert halls; tourist sites; universities; film screenings; panel discussions; and the like. I spoke with intellectuals, activists, and members of various Mizraḥi and '48 Arab communities. In addition, I subscribed to and analyzed many popular e-group correspondences and Internet sites affiliated with Israeli NGOs and protest movements throughout the duration of the research and into the present day.

I took photographs, as is customary, for my 1990–94 research stint. But for my 1999–2007 segment of research, I have very few photos. This time around, I was not an ethnographer coming to spend a well-defined period of research in "the field." I was a full participant in the events I documented. If I were to hold a camera and hunt for optimal photographic angles, I'd completely alienate myself from my fellow participants. In settings like food and clothing lines, they feel ashamed of their situations. They do not wish to be photographed.

Finally, I kept a personal diary, my auto-ethnographic logbook. Without this diary, I may have had a hard time believing that I lived through all that I did.

Wrapped in the Flag of Israel's Bureaucracy: A Road Map

Knafonomics is not unique to the sociopolitical context of Mizraḥi single mothers. Throughout the world, single mothers of color and their children share this story of victimhood when the nation-state sacrifices their human dignity to global neoliberal restructuring. Yet, there is a scholarly lacuna in the study of single-headed households in anthropology, let alone in literature about single mothers outside Western Europe and North America

(Carey 1993; Kingfisher and Goldsmith 2001; Lockhart 2008; Parmar and Rohner 2005; see McClaurin 1998). *Wrapped in the Flag of Israel* examines state welfare bureaucracy as a system of torture for its single Mizraḥi mother clients. It might seem strange to equate bureaucratic entanglements with torture, but according to the *Merriam-Webster Online Dictionary*,[25] the first definition of torture is "anguish of body or mind" or "something that causes agony or pain." Epidemiologist Nancy Krieger (2005) draws direct lines between chronic bureaucratic entanglements, hypertension, chronic pain, and death. As well, it might seem strange for an anthropologist to study the victims of state racism, who, at the same time, espouse right-wing, chauvinistic ideologies and practices, especially in the Middle East (see Bacchetta and Power 2002). Anthropologists tend to study subjects they are personally comfortable or familiar with. In urban settings, the groups studied are often progressive and left leaning.

To study bureaucracy as a system of torture, *Wrapped in the Flag of Israel* starts with the model for bureaucratic logic Don Handelman outlines in his groundbreaking book, *Nationalism and the Israeli State: Bureaucratic Logic in Public Events* (2004). Handelman challenges Max Weber's secular model of bureaucracy as a rational system (Weber [1948] 1991, 196–98) by positing bureaucracy as a cosmology. Based on Handelman (2004), I argue that bureaucracy forms a *divine* cosmology. *Divine*, in this context, refers to religious trappings in only the most general sense, including rituals that must be enacted, symbols that must be heeded, and dictums from higher authorities that must be followed without question.

I further argue that bureaucracy is composed of two types of divine cosmology, intertwined and operating simultaneously. I term the first type, the "Divinity of the Jewish State." This divinity emanates from its very definition—the Promised Land, the homeland of the Jewish people. No longer imaginary, it is a sovereign state with an army to guard its territorial claims.[26] Jews religiously conceive themselves as "the chosen people" (Frank 1993; Novak 1995), and their religiously conceived "chosen land" (Lustick 1988; Schweid 1985) is Eretz Israel, or historic Palestine. I term the second type of divine cosmology the "Divinity of Chance."[27] This divinity is defined by the goals the faithful have when they go on pilgrimage. A welfare mother petitioning a bureaucrat is like a pilgrim beseeching the jawbone of a saint. Mother and pilgrim are bound by the strict script of religious ritual on the one hand, and by serendipity on the other. A mother trying to track down her income augmentation might consult a bureaucrat at the NSB, the post office clerk, an appointed bank official, a caseworker at the municipal welfare office, or others. All the while, she is constantly praying for a miracle. None of these avenues is guaranteed to succeed. She has no choice but to subject herself to this godly roulette. It is godly because both mother and bureaucrat conceive themselves as integral parts of the miraculous ingathering of the Jewish diaspora in the Promised Land. This is the land of divine bureaucracy governed by *etsba' Elokim* (the finger of G-d, Hebrew),[28] where citizenship is one guaranteed miracle, so long as you can prove five generations of Jewish mothers. The other guaranteed miracle for Israeli Jews is an IDF draft notice to report for duty at age eighteen.

In addition to this pair of divinities, bureaucracy has at its foundation a calcified amalgamation of the categories of gender and race, a pair of criteria that, in the case of Israel, have become foundational classifications. Handelman does not deal with these. Gender and race together form the foundational phenomenological essence of bureaucracy that has become a primordial truism—"GendeRace." Among Israeli Jews, race and class completely overlap (Shenhav and Yonah 2008; Yitzhaki 2003). GendeRace, thus, does not obscure the mechanisms of Israeli intra-Jewish class discrimination. Bureaucracy, acting as a divine cosmology, amalgamates the intersectional, constructionist concepts of gender and race, and then calcifies them into a primordial truism.

This book explores the conundrum of protesting against a state that one is strongly obliged to deeply love. While the Single Mothers' March on Jerusalem could be conceived as an act of agency, I argue that the mothers' totalistic love for the State of Israel nullified the agency imminent in that act of identity politics. Scholars who study protest movements often showcase this agency and write that these movements will almost always eventually obtain hoped-for results (see Bevington and Dixon 2005; Epstein 1991; Giddens 1985; Tilly 2004). For Mizraḥi protest movements, this keyboard radicalism fails to apply.

The Single Mothers' March is a case study that reveals the interrelationships between racialized mothering and poverty among immigrants and refugees in conflict and postconflict settings. I argue that these sets of interrelationships exclude agency. The root cause of these interrelationships is the gendered and racialized logic of the Israeli state's bureaucracy. State bureaucracy is divine. Compelled by this logic, bureaucrats utilize ritual practices to enact procedural torture. To elucidate my argument, I utilize my dissonant take on the "Manchester Extended-Case Study" method for the autoethnography of myself—a single mother on welfare. Whereas anthropology traditionally employed the method of citing examples from ethnography in apt illustration of general ethnographic and analytical statements, the Manchester Extended-Case Study was based on the opposite logic: "the idea was to arrive at the general through the dynamic peculiarity of the case. Rather than a prop, the case became in effect the first step of ethnographic analysis" (Evens 2006, 46; Evens and Handelman 2006, 1). The "Manchester School of Anthropology," as it became known, focused on case studies "from which the anthropologists have been prepared to draw inferences and to formulate propositions about . . . social and cultural phenomena in general" (Evans and Handelman 2006, 3; see Mitchell 2006, 25). Adherents of this school concentrated on analyzing conflict and contradiction as key to social order and processes (Evens 2006, 45; Evens and Handelman 2006, 3). This kind of analysis required "a very detailed and intimate familiarity by the observer of the behaviour and cognitive orientations of the actors in the events being described. The restriction on the coverage such detailed investigation requires necessarily imposed limitations on the extent to which the observer is able to describe the whole 'culture' or whole 'society' of the people being studied" (Mitchell 2006, 26).

Wrapped in the Flag of Israel uses the toolset of the Manchester Extended-Case Study method to present bureaucracy as a system of torture, through detailing the lives of Mizraḥi single mothers as "a series—emerging through time, invoking different context of social practice, creating variance in continuities and discontinuities, evoking inconsistencies in self-preservation—all the while staying close to 'lived realities,' that is, close to the scale at which people in interaction, by themselves, shaped their own lives. . . . [T]hrough the extended-case method, social (and moral) order [becomes] more complex, less rigid, less integrated, more contradictory, more indeterminate" (Handelman 2006, 99; see Evens 2006, 45; Evens and Handelman 2006, 1; Mitchell 2006, 38–39).

Anthropologists are good storytellers, and their main method of conveying stories is through the use of narrative continuity. While ethnographers try to illuminate the discontinuities and inconsistencies of social life, they do so through a continuous, hermetically sealed narrative bearing logic with few, if any, seams. *Wrapped in the Flag of Israel* does not attempt to create an ethnographic narrative continuity where there was none (see Tedlock 1983; Tyler 1987). The only throughline that the book provides is my simultaneous existence as Mizraḥi single mother on welfare, former university professor turned feminist-of-color activist, and media personality.

Further, the Manchester Extended-Case Study toolset described and analyzed situations performed through discursive articulations (see Scott 1991, 794; Ortner 1995, 188). I argue that bureaucratic torture, lived by single mothers of color in the Knafo case study, never leaves its prediscursive domain to become discourse (Thrift 2008, 1–26). The mothers cannot reconcile the fact that their beloved nation-state is also the administrator of their pain. As such, this book does not provide an ethnographic narrative. Rather, it offers a chaotic rendition of Mikhail Bakhtin's (1981) "contrapunct" (see McLean 2004, 18), hoping not to "preclude analysis of the workings of the system and its historicity" (Scott 1991, 779).

It is interesting to note the role of the Manchester Extended-Case Study in Israeli anthropology. In the mid-1960s, Max Gluckman formed the Bernstein Research Project in Israel (van Teeffelen 1977, 2). The students accepted into this program were all Ashkenazi.[29] The new Israeli anthropologists who came out of this project used the Manchester Extended-Case Study to discuss possible modes of postconflict integration for Mizraḥim and '48 Arabs as the subaltern citizens in the state's Ashkenazi hegemony. In the process, the anthropologists made social and financial gains as they secured their junta lifestyles through the appropriation of Palestinian and Mizraḥi cultures (see CAAIA 2004).[30]

Tightly related to the Manchester Extended-Case Study method was Gluckman's "Peace in the Feud" (Gluckman 1955). Though separate, they are united through Gluckman's own optimistic character and its impact on Gluckman's social analysis (Kapferer 2006, 149; Kempney 2006, 199). In short, in Peace in the Feud Gluckman recognized a paradoxical equilibrium of violence and containment resulting from a society regulating its own conflict resolution. According to Gluckman (1955; 1968), these mechanisms arise from tradition.

My Manchester-style treatment of the Single Mothers' March on Jerusalem does not align itself to Peace in the Feud. Unlike in the Manchester Extended-Case Study, the Single Mothers' March on Jerusalem was not resolved with consonant harmonious chords, bringing Peace in the Feud. It ended with the discordant blast of a suicide bomb that left 23 dead and over 130 wounded. No peace in Israel's intra-Jewish racial feuds. No peace between Israel and Palestine. No closure. No equilibrium (see Gluckman 1968).

The Manchester Extended-Case Study called for societal processes that were to bring about conflict resolution. But these single mothers, even when marching as a group, were unable to articulate the decomposition of their bodies and spirits incurred by the bureaucratic torture they must withstand day in and day out.

As Toine van Teeffelen astutely observed, "Israeli anthropological writings . . . [were] not a comment on Zionist ideology, but an expression of it" (1977, 9). Dating back to the earliest Mizraḥi and '48 Arab antiracist movements, Israeli anthropology deployed the Manchester case study as an arm of governmentality to design pacifying policies of co-optation (Lavie 2005, 8). This was done through in situ execution of Gluckman's Peace in the Feud model stemming out of his "case study" approach. This book is an attempt to counter Israeli anthropology's insistence on harmonious finales. I posit that conflict resolution is not a foregone conclusion as Gluckman believed.[31]

I have started this book with the beginnings of the Single Mothers' March in correlation with the ceasefire between the IDF and Ḥamas. Chapter 1 proceeds to detail the larger backdrop for the Single Mothers' March by first outlining the typology of single mothers in Israel. Following that comes an ethnolinguistic discussion of the Hebrew term ḥad horit (single parent, feminine adjective) and a historical overview of Mizraḥi women in Mandatory Palestine, and then Israel. The chapter ends with a review of the reasons why Mizraḥi single mothers paradoxically support right-wing, anti-Arab politics even as they protest against the economic policies of the right-wing government. The main reason the Mizraḥim support the Right is the foundational role of the Zionist Left political parties that established and maintained the intra-Jewish racial formations of Zionism.[32] Other reasons stem from the Mizraḥi sense of belonging to the Zionist state. This sense often results in Mizraḥim setting themselves apart from those who share their phenotype and regional heritage, but who are not Jewish—the Palestinians and the citizens of neighboring Muslim states. While intra-Jewish racial formations divide Mizraḥim and Ashkenazim, the theological binary classification of the world as Jews vs. *goyim* (non-Jews, Hebrew; enemies, colloquial Hebrew) unites Mizraḥim and Ashkenazim as Jewish citizens of Israel—the self-proclaimed homeland of all world Jewry in the midst of the Arab World.

Chapter 2 lays out the process that makes the agency of identity politics impossible for Mizraḥi single mothers to enact. It first explains how the Israel-Palestine conflict eclipses Mizraḥi identity politics because Hebrew and international media construct hermetically sealed, binary oppositions out of the conflict. If the international media covers intra-Jewish rifts, these have to do with the conflict between the secular Jews of the Ashkenazi minority (30 percent) and the well-organized lobby of the Mizraḥi and Ashkenazi ultra-Orthodox—another minority (10 percent).[33] It is not the purpose of this book to explore the well-studied observant versus secular rift among Jews in the Israeli state (see, for example, Atzmon 2011; Leibman and Katz 1997; Sobel and Beit-Hallahmi 1991; Yadgar 2011). Rather, chapter 2 delineates a model stemming out of the Divinity of the Jewish State fused with the Divinity of Chance. This pair of intertwined divinities explicates GendeRace as the touchstone for bureaucratic pain as well as the denial of identity politics. To capture and convey the torture of bureaucracy, I argue for employing the ethnographic writing and theorization styles of World Anthropologies and feminist-of-color essayists, rather than relying on the U.S.-UK academic model of presenting ethnography and anthropological theory. The chapter ends with an explanation of why I write my autoethnography utilizing the mode of victim narrative. I do this intentionally, and against the tendency of postmodernist and postcolonial studies to bestow agency upon victims that silences their victimhood.

Chapters 3 through 5 present three separate takes on the narration of the Knafo protest: (1) subaltern theory of the interrelationships between bureaucracy and torture, (2) dissociated social analysis, and (3) an autoethnography of a welfare mother.

Chapter 6 describes the end of the Knafo protest and its relationship to suicide bombing. It includes an epilogue connecting the summer 2011 mass protests in Israel and how they have played out like a rerun of the Knafo protest of 2003, though on a much larger scale.

The road map has been laid out for you. Nonetheless, it is a tough journey. This book lacks the modernist Romanticism of the upper-middle-class, postcolonial scholar, who saves a culture through text that imbues its actors with agency. Many scholars insist that anthropology has progressed past its (post)colonial idealism. But what follows proves this not to be the case. Colonial idealism is still at the very heart of scholarship, because funding for research and publications is mostly situated in North American and Western European institutions that set the research agenda. Anthropology students learn from their mentors that they must have the optimistic "pretense of coherence" (Narotzky 2006, 143) to appease senior colleagues who review their grant proposals. Once let through the gate, an anthropologist can gather data and publish the kinds of refereed journal articles and book manuscripts that garner merit and promotion.

As luck would have it, I was a welfare mother in the lines when I conducted my research. There was no safety net. I could not quit and go back to the lifestyle of a tenured professor. But even though I became a nonentity for the movers and shakers of the discipline, I did not stop being an anthropologist. Rather, I had found complete freedom away from the academic corporation and the trends that it sets. I could study my subject and write it up the way I saw fit. This book refuses the contours of academic sentimentality that often come with booklength ethnographies. No happy endings. Only jagged edges.

CHAPTER 1

Left Is Right, Right Is Left

Zionism and Israel's Single Mothers

On 14 May 2004, I received an email from Seteney Shami, my Berkeley grad school classmate. She worked for the Social Science Research Council (SSRC) as the program director over the Middle East, North Africa, and Inter-Asia sections.

Dear Professor Lavie,

I am writing to ask you if you would be willing to contribute two articles to the forthcoming Encyclopedia of Women in Islamic Cultures. EWIC will be the first ever encyclopedia on this subject. The project is a five-year effort to bring together hundreds of scholars world-wide, to write critical essays on women and Islamic cultures....

The goal is to survey all facets of life (religion, society, economy, politics, the arts, sports, health, science, medicine and so forth) of women in cultures where Islam has made significant contributions. The Encyclopedia of Women and Islamic Cultures is envisioned as a broad based, interdisciplinary, cross-cultural, transhistorical, and global project....

[W]e are requesting from you [an article] on Zionism . . . which risk[s] going unwritten. . . . The catch is that, should you accept, the articles need to be completed very quickly. I could offer you a deadline of June 15 for the first draft . . . since this volume of the encyclopedia is scheduled to come out in Nov. 2004.

It was absurd for me to accept this invitation, even though I wanted to. EWIC's project head was Suad Joseph, the founder of the Association for Middle Eastern Women's Studies, former president of the Middle East Studies Association of North America, and, from my graduate school days until today, a mentor, role model, colleague, and dear friend.

Academic writing rarely pays any money. Often publishers expect academics to front their own money for their own research and production, taking the costs as a business loss. Academics must continuously publish in peer-reviewed journals not only to stay at the forefront of their respective fields but also to keep their institutional positions, including the perks, such as generous benefits packages, travel funds, and a staff of inexpensive student labor. High-profile professors attract students, meaning a larger enrollment of tuition payers. Tenure-track professors can take the pressure to publish for granted. I could not. All I had was an hourly teaching position at Beit Berl College that did not pay for rent and utilities, let alone food and transportation. How could I find the time for the copious research required for an encyclopedia entry? I was in survival mode. I had lines to stand in at the NSB, the job placement bureau, the Tel Aviv social welfare bureau, and NGOs for food handouts, among others.

I devoted my nigh nonexistent spare time to community outreach. I was already overwhelmed. I had used my own apartment as the location for the first meeting between Aḥoti and Anwar (Lights, Arabic), a '48 Arab feminist NGO. We wanted to work through the animosity and suspicion between '48 Arab and Mizraḥi feminists. Mizraḥi feminists viewed Palestinian feminists as "kissing ass" with well-funded Ashkenazi feminist NGOs. Palestinian feminists viewed Mizraḥi feminists as right-wing Arab-haters with no funding for joint projects.

Esther Hertzog, Hanna Beit Halahmi, and I built the Coalition of Women for Mothers and Children, the broadest coalition in Israel's feminist history. It included veiled Islamists, ultra-Orthodox Jewish women from the West Bank settlements, and everything in between. We fought against Israel's Family Courts and their Family Court Services welfare experts. The courts always favor ex-husbands in child custody cases, even when the fathers are violent abusers. Welfare services ship children who resist court-ordered placement with their abusers into government boarding schools to break them (see Tzur 2001).[1]

Rafi Shubeli and I built the Mizrahi-Palestinian Coalition Against Apartheid in Israeli Anthropology (CAAIA). We also organized Israel's first-ever Mizrahi-Palestinian conference at Beit Berl College on the topic of "Ashkenazim" for the Mizrahi Democratic Rainbow. The conference made it onto the popular 7:00 a.m. national radio news—quite a rarity for media dominated by the Israel-Palestine conflict. Huge numbers of activists, scholars, and students turned out. Also unexpected were dozens of retired Ashkenazim, irate at the news, who showed up to remind us that without the education they bestowed upon us, we could not have put on such a conference. In case we had forgotten.

I dove into these movements for my sanity and because I thought I was enacting personal and communal agency. I still believed our NGOs could foster social change. With hindsight, the Palestinian-Mizrahi coalitions were doomed to fail, just like almost all Israeli-Palestinian collaborations. One notable exception is the partnership between the IDF and the PA's security apparatus. Palestinian-Mizrahi initiatives were short-lived because underneath the activism was the binary: the continued existence of the State of Israel means the erasure of Palestine. To Palestinians, we were citizens of Israel, the entity that erased them in 1948 and continued to colonize them. That we were Mizrahim was irrelevant. We Mizrahi activists were part of the occupation machinery. In addition, we faced accusations of treason from Mizrahim because we dared to collude with the enemy. The Palestinian activists who met with us faced similar pressures from their own communities.

On top of my activism, I was a single mother. *Had horit.* I had to take care of Shaheen. That meant dozens of court hearings over his custody, fighting for his scholarships by filling out endless forms, navigating labyrinthine phone menus, and staging impromptu sit-ins at schools and offices. These all took a toll on my body. While I attempted to manage my health crises, I never considered stopping. Rest meant no money, no food, no method to reconcile how far I had fallen.

I could not take on Seteney's project, let alone meet her deadline. It would take a full-time research project to provide an alternative history that would rescue the entry from the Palestine-Israel binary. But I could not think of anyone else who could do it.

So I wrote back and agreed to write the entry, anyway. But life took over, and I did not have the time and space necessary to begin. It wasn't until September 2005 that I heard anything more:

From: Isabella Gerritsen
Sent: Tuesday, 20 September 2005 14:37

Dear Dr. Lavie,

This letter serves as an advance reminder in order to bring to your notice that the deadline is approaching for your article. . . . [W]e need the cooperation of our authors to meet their deadlines. . . .

My new deadline was 1 November 2005. It took a whole month for me to find the time to reply:

Dear Isabella,

I hope I can get the deadline extended until 1 December. I've been overextended to the max with previous deadlines. I'm thankful for your consideration. Please resend the instructions for authors. I can't locate them on my hard disk.

    Smadar

In October 2005, the Family Court finally recognized me as Shaheen's legal mother. We got back our Israeli passports and were free to travel outside Israel. Free at last, but at the cost of my NSB income augmentation. I immediately went job hunting, but no allowances are permitted for single mothers traveling abroad to job interviews. Once in the poverty cycle, always in the poverty cycle. Thankfully, my travel costs were paid by the inviting institutions. Yet, to the regime, I was a born-again jet-setter.[2]

A couple months later, I lucked into a scholar-at-rescue grant. Fellow colleagues found a private source who donated funds to hire an assistant for my community advocacy. In return, I promised to write up my Mizraḥi research results for future publication in academic journals. I finally had a sliver of time to start my research for the EWIC entry. Over the following months, Isabella and I went back and forth, pushing the deadline a few months at a time. Every time I sat down to haggle extensions with Isabella, I put on the diplomatic gloves of academicspeak to guide my fingertips — fanciful intervals in my coarse life. Eventually, we settled on a deadline of the end of July 2006. "No more excuses after that," I wrote.

But on 12 July, Israel started the 2006 Lebanon War. As usual, most of the demonstrations were in Tel Aviv. I felt obliged to join the protest, even though I got into arguments with the usual Ashkenazi BCBGs[3] — dubbed "the Regulars" or "the 250" by Mizraḥi activists. These were always the same Ashkenazi faces who came to every demonstration against Israel's military atrocities toward Palestinians. Less than a handful came to our Mizraḥi demonstrations, however. Predictably, I sparked arguments by pointing out the Mizraḥi-ness of most IDF and civilian victims in Lebanon 2006 and in the suicide bombing preceding the hudna.[4]

Would Ḥezbollah missiles target Tel Aviv? Out of my hands. I had the EWIC deadline to deal with.

From: Smadar Lavie
Sent: Tuesday, 18 July 2006 09:21

ALMOST done . . . . The anti-war demos are slowing me a bit, but in sha Allah, will be completely done with the draft over the weekend.

I had to get out of the humid Tel Aviv inferno. My skin longed for the cool, dry nighttime desert breeze. My mind, the quietude to focus. On the morning of 30 July, I made my mandatory weekly caseworker visit at the job placement bureau. The usual — no job for an overqualified University of California professor. Afterward, I borrowed my mom's car and drove south to Mitzpe Ramon.

Past Beer Sheba begins the gradual ascent to Mitzpe through the Negev Desert. Wide, dry riverbeds span the yellows and beiges of windswept limestone plateaus. Waves of heat blur the landscape to the edgeless horizon. And slicing through it is a lone strip of black asphalt—the same road Vicky Knafo walked upon, wrapped in the flag of Israel.

Every now and then, dark dots pop up in the distance, hugging the road. Only when close do they grow into the craggy metal and plywood shacks of the Negev Bedouin. Most drivers in their air-conditioned cars zoom past these "unrecognized settlements," as the Israeli regime has termed them. At high speeds, the shacks are easy to blink away. So much the better to ignore the ongoing, syncopated Nakba amidst the vast expanse of desert lyricism.

Yes! I made it all the way to Mitzpe! And at dusk. How romantic. And to Sigal, a fellow Aḥoti member. I hadn't seen her since 2004. How generous of her to invite me to her cramped apartment when I told her I needed a time-out from Tel Aviv. Even with her haphazard schedule as an hourly maid at Mitzpe's only hotel—a high-end boutique spa.[5]

Mitzpe's Aḥoti branch has been a hub of Mizraḥi feminism, even before Vicky's march. Vicky was not even Mitzpe's first newsworthy Mizraḥi feminist single mother. In 2000, Ḥavatzelet Ingber—she got her Ashkenazi last name from her ex-husband—led a rebellion against the closure of a military-uniform sewing workshop. Many Mitzpe women worked there as seamstresses. The workshop was a sweatshop that demanded unreasonable hours and even required employees to bring their own toilet paper and coffee from home. Worse, the women endured months of delinquent paychecks. Still, it was their only employment option in remote Mitzpe.

No one expected Mizraḥi women to rebel against their employer. So the media took interest. Donations poured in from Israel's center, and, with the funds, the women purchased the sweatshop and made it into their collective. Two years later, the collective fell apart. The women lacked management training, and they clashed with Mizraḥi men who took their goods to market. The government also strangled the collective with bureaucratic red tape. Were it to succeed, it would have posed a threat to Israel's "free-market" industry model.[6]

In the Ingber revolt and the Knafo march, Mitzpe's single mothers had their moments as shining examples for the rest of Israel's Mizraḥi single

3. Seamstresses and their families protested the closing of Mitzpe Ramon's military-uniform sewing workshop. They maintained tire fires outside to dissuade collection teams from taking away factory equipment to cover the factory owner's debts. Meir Azulay, 2000.

mothers. But neither movement lasted, leaving these women once again completely dependent on paltry NSB allowances.

Once again, they were *ḥad horiyot* (single mothers, Hebrew plural). Before venturing into when and how I completed the EWIC entry, let me first explain the byzantine etymology of the Hebrew term for a single mother, *ḥad horit*, and the classification of Israeli Jewish single mothers.

Ḥad Horit: Notes on the Hebrew Etymology of Single Motherhood

Ḥad horit (single parent, feminine adjective) is the Hebrew term used to refer to a single mother. It is shorthand for *em ḥad horit*, or "single parent, mother." The prefix *ḥad* (uni-) is notable here, as it is used in Hebrew to mark something singular or an outlier. Examples include *ḥad mashmaʿi* (unambiguous and unilateral), *ḥad peʿami* (single-use), or *ḥad sitri* (one-way street). *Ḥad* usually connotes formal language or terminology.

If used in casual conversation, the staccato utterance, "ḥad horit," creates a hiccup in the conversational flow. Here is an example:

The August morning was already sticky with sweat. I stood in line in front of the Tel Aviv NSB—a sleek high-rise at 17 Yitzhak Sadeh Street, towering above car dealerships and body shops. Exactly on the border between Southside Tel Aviv's "Black City," with its Mizraḥi ghettos and barrios, and Central Tel Aviv's posh "White City," a UNESCO world cultural heritage site where Ashkenazim live (Rotbard 2005).[7] I still hadn't gone through the first security checkpoint, where everyone was X-rayed and checked for knives, guns, and other weapons. The man in front of me, his face still crusted over from the night, turned and said:

"Aren't you the Berkeley professor on welfare?"

"Yup."

"What 'hood?"

By referring to "'hood," he already assumed I was from the Black City, or Southside Tel Aviv.

"Tel Ḥayim, east of Yad Eliyahu."

"We're neighbors," he said. "I'm from Yad Eliyahu. The bus was late today, and then when it came, three of 'em showed up."

"I know. I was on the third. The a/c didn't work, so I almost fainted from the smell. Let me tell you—American deodorants work much better."

We chuckled.

"So why are you here?" he asked. "On TV they said your dad's Ashkenazi. Can't he help you get a normal job?"

"He's dead. I work by the hour, and it doesn't pay the bills. On top of that, it's summer, so the college let me go. I'm on an allowance, and it didn't arrive."

"What kind of allowance?"

"Ḥad horit." Up until now, the conversation flowed easily. But now, a pause.

"Ah . . . ," he moaned. "*Ḥad horit . . . du raglit. . . ,*" he kvetched. *Ḥad horit, du raglit* literally means "single mother, bipedal."

Then he paused again before resuming the previous conversational rhythm:

"I'm here for my allowance, too. Disability. I cut my finger at the plant." He raised his right hand and showed me his chopped pinky. "They decided to replace me with someone younger, even though I can work now. The allowance and my wife's salary don't pay the bills, either."

I proceeded to ask him one of the most common questions among Israeli Jews: "What's your origin?"

"My folks came from Syria in 1951. My wife is Persian. Her family made their way outta the South, but my family's still stuck there."

I had this kind of conversation many times. When "ḥad horit" was mentioned, the same awkward pauses happened, and then, the same spontaneous sing-song of "ḥad horit, du raglit."

Du raglit (two-legged) is itself a term loaded with meaning beyond the dictionary definition. Unlike *ḥad*, the prefix *du* (two) does not force the listener to take notice. It is more commonly used in casual speech, such as in *du kiyyum* (co-existence), *du komati* (double-decker), and *du sitri* (two-way street). *Du ragli* (masculine, and thus the default term), is shorthand for *ḥayot du ragliyot* (plural), a zoological term denoting bipedal animals.

Just prior to the 1982 Lebanon War, Prime Minister Menachem Begin applied "du ragli" to the Fataḥland Palestinian guerrillas who took Israeli schoolchildren hostage in the Galilee to demand the release of their fellow guerrillas from Israeli prisons.[8] Begin refused and sent the IDF to attack the school. In the ensuing battle, the guerrillas killed twenty-two schoolchildren, all Mizraḥim. This incident became known as the "Maʿalot massacre."

The Maʿalot massacre was not the first time that Begin referred to Israel's enemies as "du ragli." During the tenth session of the Knesset in 1951, he spoke against the idea of German Holocaust reparations, referring to the Nazis as "du ragli" (Aviv 2007, n115).

After the Maʿalot massacre, "du ragli" spread into common use in Hebrew slang to refer to all Palestinians. At the onset of the first Intifada (1987–1993), Prime Minister Yitzhak Rabin ordered the IDF to shoot nonviolent Palestinian demonstrators in the legs. His justification: the demonstrators were "du ragli"—that they were wild and dangerous animals, disorderly and in need of culling.

The Typology of Israel's Single Mothers

While the appellation "ḥad horit" connotes deviance, it does not differentiate among the various kinds of single motherhood in Israeli society. In my two decades of research, I have discerned three types of Jewish single mothers in Israel: hip alternative single mothers, post-Soviet single mothers, and postdivorce single mothers, most of whom are Mizraḥim, in line with Israel's demographics.

The Hip Alternative Single Mother: Under the label of "hip alternative single mother," there are three subtypes. The first is usually an older, well-to-do, single Ashkenazi heterosexual woman whose biological alarm clock is ringing. With strong encouragement from her family of origin, she chooses to undergo fertilization treatments to have a child. Oftentimes, the woman finds an Ashkenazi gay man in the same position to donate sperm and enter joint custody. The second subtype is a lesbian couple. Since each woman can have a child, each can claim single-mother status—and many of the benefits thereof, such as coupons for schoolbooks, rent assistance, and other such aid. In so doing, however, they forego the legal option of the mutual adoption and guardianship of each other's children. The third subtype is a single mother who is part of an alternative family assembled by support group.

To consider adults as full human beings, Israeli society requires them to be parents. Psychology-trained "reproductive facilitators" have formed support groups that allow women and men not interested in marriage to "shop" each other for their preferred gene pool. Group members pair uteruses and sperm with each other for the ideal match. Single lesbians or heterosexual women are often paired with a gay man or gay couple to create a family unit. Often the mother still declares single-mother status because of the benefits. Single women and lesbian couples in the "hip alternative single mother" category enjoy a higher level of education and are financially viable, enabling them to pass with flying colors the psychological tests for state-funded fertilization programs. Married couples are automatically entitled to the programs, with clear preference toward the production of Jewish babies (Carmeli and Carmeli 2010; Kanaaneh 2002, Nahman 2013). None of these mothers marched on Jerusalem with Vicky Knafo.

The Post-Soviet Single Mother: The great influx into Israel of post-Soviet single mothers is due mainly to the early 1990s collapse of the Soviet economy, and the sizable monetary and taxation benefits Israel endows upon Jewish immigrant families (see Bushinsky 2005; Curtiss 1994). But

Israeli authorities were not inclined to allow single-headed families to immigrate. To circumvent this obstacle, post-Soviet single mothers—both *Russiyot* (Russian, Hebrew plural feminine) and *Kavkaziyot* (Kavkazi, Hebrew plural feminine)—with children out of wedlock, married the estranged fathers of their children for the benefits. Then the mothers traveled to Israel by themselves, paid the father part of the immigrant allowance in cash, and declared to the absorption authorities that the husband could not immigrate with her for any number of reasons. Others obtained fictive marriages in order to get pregnant, signed up for immigration, arrived in Israel by themselves, and then divorced the fathers of their children. Still others arrived as part of a married couple, enjoyed the Israeli incentives for Jewish immigrants, and only then divorced. Oftentimes, the husband would return to the former Soviet Union, and the single mother, unable to collect child support, would go on to collect a welfare allowance on top of her immigrant benefits.

Only at the height of post-Soviet immigration to Israel in 1992 did the Yitzhak Rabin-led government pass the Law for Single-Headed Families that started to half-heartedly enact the Child and Spouse Support Law of 1972 that supposedly remedied the Child and Spouse Support Law of 1959 that vaguely ordered fathers to pay support to mothers and children after divorce. In addition, the 1992 law increased the NSB allowances for single-headed families up to half of poverty-level income. It also created a special office in Israel's Housing Ministry to provide rental aid to these families. The Israeli absorption authorities passed the law despite knowing that 35 percent of post-Soviet single mothers are actually *Pravoslavim* (Russian Orthodox Christians, Hebrew plural). To immigrate to Israel and become citizens, they presented fake documents that allegedly proved five generations of Jewish mothers. Perhaps the absorption authorities were less concerned with Jewishness than with increasing Israel's whiteness, or "eugenic capability" (Falk 2006; Malka 1998; Nahman 2013; Stoler-Liss 1998). It was quite opportune that this influx of white immigrants came just before the Knesset passed its 1992 law that gave teeth to the Child and Spouse Support Law of 1972. The new law directly benefitted the surge into Israel of white post-Soviet single-headed families.

Post-Soviet single mothers made up about a quarter of Knafoland. They mainly kept to themselves. The Russian Knesset members who visited the encampment advocated only for these mothers. It is not within the scope of this text to discuss post-Soviet racism toward first-, second-, and third-generation Mizraḥim, or Mizraḥi racism toward post-Soviets.

The Postdivorce Single Mother: The majority of postdivorce single mothers, like the majority of Israelis, are Mizraḥim. They often have their first child very young — in their early to mid-twenties. And they usually have three to four children spaced about two years apart from each other. While married and mothering their young children, they either work part-time jobs or stay at home as full-time housewives. Their husbands' salaried employment usually provides most of the household income. Therefore, the mothers' postdivorce ability to independently generate income is severely limited. Child support is next to impossible to collect from deadbeat dads.

At this point, postdivorce single mothers can be divided into two groups: those who rely on their family of origin in lieu of child support, and those who have no choice but to become welfare mothers. Mothers in the first group are most often Ashkenazi. Their families have the ability to transfer intergenerational wealth down to the single mothers and their children. Mizraḥi single mothers largely lack this resource. So they must turn to state welfare.

———

Back to Mitzpe. The next day. With a broad smile, I stepped up to the security checkpoint at the Mitzpe Public Library on Ben Gurion Avenue and waited while the guard inspected my books, papers, and laptop. Afterward, I strode through the doors, ready to finalize the EWIC entry.

The library was mine, almost. Only a bearded Russian surrounded by Israeli law codices shared the large library hall with me.

"What project are you working on?" I asked, collegially.

"I plan to sue the government for the cultural neglect of Mitzpe."

"Thank you," I said, not wanting to enter that conversation. I hastily settled on a spot across the room, where I arranged four desks for all my research materials. No other noise interrupted the quiet whir of the central air conditioner. I worked in a frenzy until noon.

At noon, the library closed for the customary siesta. So I went down Ben Gurion Avenue about half a block to the public swimming pool—Israel's least expensive at 10 NIS (around $3)—to swim some laps until the library opened back up at 3:00 p.m. Despite their steep entrance fees ($15–$40), public pools in Israel are completely mobbed in the summer months. But Mitzpe's pool was always sparsely populated. So I was unprepared to find it packed with families.

As he searched my bag, I asked the security guard:

"Why is this place so packed today? I've never seen it this full."

"Folks from the North came here to get away from the war. Flora said the pool should be free as long as the war goes on." "Flora" meant Moroccan-born Flora Shoushan, Mitzpe's mayor and longtime Aḥoti member. Her husband and Mitzpe's previous mayor, Sami Shoushan, handed the mayorship to her for a better government position. And at that very moment, her brother Amir Peretz was orchestrating IDF troops in Lebanon in his position as Israel's defense minister.

Families sat in the shade and huddled around picnic lunches. With the pool too full to swim my laps, I waded into the water, my ethnographer's ears ready:

"Looks like Ḥezbollah has the upper hand."

"The IDF thought they'd wipe the floor with Ḥezbollah and be done with 'em. That's why they sent in the elite Ashkenazi boys right after the air force crushed South Lebanon."

"The war's stretched, and I don't see an end. They already sent the infantry to get their hands dirty—these days, Mizraḥim and Russians, the brara ["imperfects," Hebrew slang for riffraff]."

"They said online that the IDF told them to break into Lebanese groceries and take bottled water if they were thirsty. Can you believe it?"

"My neighbor's son rang and said his platoon only had outdated minefield maps. All the good maps were back in ha-Bor ["the pit," Hebrew, common slang for the IDF's war room]. No updated copies for the brara at the front. Unbelievable."

"The government has abandoned us not only on the battlefield but also in their bomb shelters. They're corrupt—all of 'em."

"What can we do? Nothing. Work if we're lucky. Pay taxes either way."

Almost all were from the economically depressed agricultural co-ops and development towns on the Israel-Lebanon border. In contrast, their mainly Ashkenazim kibbutznik neighbors could stay put in the North. Whenever there are border flare-ups with Lebanon or Syria, the whole kibbutz retreats into well-equipped, air-conditioned underground shelters funded by the government.

My ears made the connection: the North Mizrahi margins flee to their relatives in the South Mizrahi margins.

At 3:00 p.m., I gathered my things and returned to the library to continue writing until 7:00 p.m., when the library closed.

For the week, I followed the same work routine. Almost done! I completed a draft and emailed it to Isabella, who passed it onto Professor Julie Peteet, associate editor of EWIC, responsible, with Associate Editor Seteney Shami, for article solicitations on the Middle East region.

I spent my evenings with Aḥoti members or hung around with Sigal's family and friends—all hourly workers like her. We passed the time munching sunflower seeds as we channel-surfed the TV for news from the front. The women who worked at the hotel compared notes on their extended work hours—quite the opposite from their normal sporadic schedules. Wealthy Ashkenazi families from the Galilee's *mitzpim* (observation points, Hebrew plural, for highly exclusive gated communities towering above Galilean Palestinian villages)[10] had fled their homes in style to flood the hotel spa.

We roared with laughter as we gossiped about the families' daily forays to the alpaca and llama ranch just outside town. Summer days were too hot to hike the cirque, leaving the ranch as Mitzpe's only viable tourist attraction. The ranch exhorted itself as the "one and only ranch of its kind in the world" and enticed visitors with a promise that "a beautiful South American herd of alpacas and llamas will host you for a fun family experience." This was literal. Not widely advertised—but universally known—was the herd's propensity to freely engage in copulation, no matter who was present. Upon entrance, signs warned parents that their small children might ask questions about what they saw.

One evening, Sigal turned to me and asked, "How goes the writing?"

"Almost done. Thank G-d for the quiet of the library and your generous hospitality."

"Just you wait. I'll return the favor. I'll need to shop for clothes in Tel Aviv for Rosh Hashanah. Anyway, what are you writing about?"

"The history of Mizraḥi women in Palestine during the Yishuv."

Yishuv (settlement, Hebrew) was first used in the 1880s to refer to the period of the Ashkenazi settlement of Palestine between 1882 and 1948.[11]

"It's for an encyclopedia on women in Muslim cultures," I added.

"Muslim cultures?!" another woman blurted out. "Do Muslims have culture?"

"Why would they care about Jews?" asked another.

"And why Palestine?!" exclaimed a third. "It's Israel!!"

"Why don't you read for us at the end of Tisha B'Av," suggested Sigal. "We'll have a pot luck and you can lecture."

Tisha B'Av is the annual fast day commemorating the destruction of both the First and Second Temples in Jerusalem. It is a national holiday and a day of fasting.

So on 3 August 2006, at dusk, we gathered in the apartment of Luna, a Tunisian single mother of four. Though she was fasting, she could not turn down the hotel's request to show up and work extra hours. So she was still dressed in her maid attire along with the head cover that signified religious observance.

Luna's apartment had the typical layout of a housing project: a small living room and dining area opening onto a balcony. A short, narrow corridor led to two small bedrooms and a bathroom and toilet crammed in between. Just like Sigal's. Family photos hung on the walls opposite a large print of the snowy Alps in all their grandeur. A ceiling fan twirled above us, and twin fans oscillated in the corners of the room, pushing dry, hot air.

Luna's second-floor balcony overlooked the wolf-toothed cliffs at the cirque's edge. Partially blocking the view were two "frogs"—Israel's hulking, green-painted, cast-iron dumpsters. As we waited for the sun to set so that we could break our fast, the skies alternated mauve, orange, strawberry red, then blurred into gray before blackening to night. In the twilight, sickle-horned Nubian ibexes loped elegantly toward the frogs to graze on the reeking trash.

In all, six women sat in a circle to hear me read. Luna, Varda, Iris, Ortal, and my host, Sigal, were born in Israel to North African parents. None were originally from Mitzpe. They relocated following their ex-husbands, who obtained blue-collar jobs at the IDF officer school nearby, the town's biggest employer. Iris was an unemployed remnant of the sewing collective started by Havatzelet Ingber. Ortal worked as a part-time cook in the officer school. Varda, Ortal, and Iris had joined Vicky Knafo's march in 2003.

The sixth woman, Ludmilla, was an Ashkenazi whose family fled Russia to Azerbaijan after World War II. Because she and her husband technically immigrated to Israel from an Asian republic, the Israeli authorities offered them housing in Mitzpe instead of the center. She held a job at Mitzpe's elementary school as an hourly data-entry worker. But the school had closed for the summer, so she was jobless. Her husband—an unemployed classical violinist—was the bearded man I shared the library with earlier that week. As we started eating, Ludmilla told me about his crusade to convince any government office in Jerusalem to bring a piano tuner to service the lone public piano in Mitzpe's *Beit Ha'am* (people's home, Hebrew for community center)—a vestige of Israel's socialist era.[12]

In front of those women, I trembled inside. It was one matter to write an academic book and have other scholars read and comment on it. It was another matter altogether to deliver a talk to real people huddled around you in a hot, stuffy room. These women were my small audience, and I wanted to keep things civil. How would these right-wing Likudniks accept my text? It went against the Ashkenazi Zionist credo drummed into their heads in school. I sure hoped they didn't throw me in with the Ashkenazi Left "peacenik" feminists and kick me out of town. Even if I kowtowed to them, could I handle the typical Israeli habit of interjecting an opinion,[13] welcome or not? My text was in English. I had to translate on the fly. Even so, whenever possible, I relied on the terms the women learned in school and carefully injected new meanings to get my point across.

Could I make it to the end?

Nevertheless, with pauses and hesitations, I began to read.[14]

———

On Zionism

Zionism is a European ideology of Jewish nationalism whose main goal was to colonize Palestine in order to establish a Jewish state. It can be seen as an ethnic by-product of the rise of European nationalism in the mid-nineteenth century. Most of its founding figures were non-observant Jews. Theodor Herzl, the father of Zionism, detested religious and traditional Judaism. So disdainful was he of Judaism that he refused to have his son circumcised.[15]

The Jewish state in Palestine was supposed to redeem the persecuted Eastern European Jews by importing European cultural technology. At the same time, the state planned to reinforce its conception of European superiority by casting native Palestinians as "primitive." From the late nineteenth century on, Zionism motivated most of the Ashkenazim who immigrated to Palestine. In Israeli schools, we called this period the Yishuv. Its motto: Palestine is a land without people that is to be settled by a people without a land.

The piece I just completed at the Mitzpe public library is about pre-1948 Zionism's treatment of Mizraḥi women in Palestine. While the prevalent assumption is that most Mizraḥim first arrived in the State of Israel in the mass migration of the 1950s, the reality is that there were Mizraḥim living in Palestine well before that time. For hundreds of years, the Mizraḥim immigrated back and forth between Palestine and the Arab World, as well as Persia, Turkey, the Balkans, Greece, southern Italy, and India. Until 1948, however, the Ashkenazim constituted the majority of Jews in Palestine.

Finding information about Mizraḥi women who lived in Palestine under the late Ottoman or early British empires is next to impossible. It is also difficult to find information about Jewish women who immigrated to Palestine from Muslim countries to become laborers for the European Zionist colonization of Palestine. My research assistant, son, and I reviewed thick stacks of women's personal memoirs, novels, scholarly monographs, coffee table books, periodicals, and magazines at the main Tel Aviv library and the library at Beit Berl College. Very few of these materials were written by Mizraḥi women, with the great majority of them written about or by Ashkenazi-Zionist women. To find any information about Mizraḥi women, we used tweezers to pick out relevant paragraphs or disparate sentences, and even then, had to infer some of our findings.

"Mizraḥim" is a coalitional term activists have been using since the 1980s, and scholars since the 1990s. Culturally translated, it might be conceived as Jewish "people of color," originating mostly in the Muslim World. The period I cover here is from the late nineteenth century, just on the eve of the British colonization of Palestine, until its end in 1948, with the establishment of the State of Israel and the Nakba. In Arabic, *nakba* means "catastrophe" and describes the 1948 expulsion of approximately 750,000 of the 900,000 Palestinians from their homes located in the newly proclaimed State of Israel.

During the period between Ottoman and British rule, Mizraḥi women who lived in Palestine were divided into four major groups. The first and largest group of immigrants was from Yemen. Overall, they were strictly observant. The other three immigrant groups were Jews from the Balkans, from Persia, and those known as *Sephardim* (Spaniards, Hebrew). Sephardim were descendants of Jews who were expelled from Spain in 1492, and arrived in Palestine from then on, through Mediterranean countries. The Ottomans, and later the British, considered them the elite of Palestine's Jews. There also was a very small group of Jews who immigrated to Palestine from the Maghreb (North Africa, Arabic). It might be hard to imagine this, as Maghrebi Jews have been the largest ethnic group in Israel since the 1960s. Among these non-Yemenis, the working classes were strictly observant, while the elite were more lenient in following religious dictates. Very few were secular.

The history of Ashkenazi Jewish women's colonial settlement of Palestine is entangled with both the outside colonizers and the indigenous Palestinian population. That history is also intimately woven with the history of the Mizraḥim, mainly Yemenis. During the nineteenth century, European Jews started feeling safe enough to relocate from the ghettos and acquire nonartisanal professional skills. Yet by the end of the nineteenth and the beginning of the twentieth century, radical shifts occurred in Eastern Europe's Jewish ghettos. Jews were once again limited in terms of their livelihoods and freedom of movement. These renewed restrictions were accompanied by large-scale persecution and waves of pogroms, first in 1881–82, and then in 1903–5 as part of the Russian Revolution.

Ashkenazi immigration to Palestine, mainly by nonobservant Jews, coincided with a period of economic depression all over southern Arabia, particularly in Yemen. As a colonialist movement, the Ashkenazim realized that Palestine had already been colonized by the Ottomans, and that the British were likely to take it over as a result of the Ottomans' gradual decay.

So the Ashkenazim had to demonstrate to the Ottomans and British that they were not simply another competing colonialism reliant on indigenous Palestinian manual labor for agriculture, infrastructure construction, small industries, and domestic work. Rather, they had to demonstrate self-sufficiency, and to do that, they had to demonstrate a sizable source of manual labor to exploit for their colonial enterprise. Most Palestinian manual labor was already earmarked for the British. In 1882, five years before the first World Zionist Congress in Basel, Switzerland, Socialist Ashkenazi Zionist emissaries organized the E'eleh ba-Tamar (Ascendance via palm trees, Hebrew, a phrase borrowed from the Song of Songs [7:9 in the King James Bible]), the first wave of Arab-Jewish labor migration from Yemen to Palestine. Most of the migrants were pious young families. As the southern Arabian economic crisis intensified, several organized waves of Yemeni Jewish labor migration followed. Anthropologist Scott Atran has defined the Ashkenazi Zionist colonial mission in Palestine as "surrogate colonialism." The Ashkenazim brought in their own brand of Arabs—Yemeni Jews—to build their own European franchise in Palestine independent of indigenous Palestinian labor. Zionist settlers termed the Yemenis "natural laborers," and endowed themselves with the appellation "ideological laborers." Surrogate colonialism helped usher in the 2 November 1917 Balfour Declaration affirming the inalienable right of Ashkenazi Zionists to a Jewish homeland in Palestine.

To understand our oppression as Mizraḥi women today, we must learn about Mizraḥi women's histories in the Yishuv. Mizraḥi women in Palestine lived through multiple axes of oppression. They faced colonization by the Ottoman Empire and then the British. They faced surrogate colonialism from the ruling classes that shaped Israel's Ashkenazi-Zionist economic and cultural hegemony, as well as the Ashkenazi middle classes. They faced oppression from Mizraḥi men in their own communities. These women's histories are volatile, so Zionists have devoted tremendous efforts to erase them. "Post"-Zionist Israeli feminists contain and repackage these histories to still be critical of Zionism, but not challenge its racial foundation.

Before 1948, about 450,000 Jews from Yiddish-speaking countries, mainly in Central and Eastern Europe, immigrated to Palestine. Most of them were Zionists. Many were Holocaust survivors, disillusioned with any form of religiosity. In addition, there were 150,000 Mizraḥim made up of the few families who had always lived in Palestine and the immigrants who arrived in Palestine during the Yishuv from the Balkans or from Muslim countries. About 40,000 of these were Yemeni.

The Palestinians referred to the Yemeni Jews as *Yamaniyun* (Yemenis, Arabic). They referred to the rest of the Mizraḥim not from Yemen as *Yahud* (Jews, Arabic). The Jews who immigrated from Yiddish-speaking countries were called *Shiknaz* (Ashkenazim, Arabic). The Yishuv-era Mizraḥim used *Shiknaz* to coin the name for European Jews.

As the Yishuv commenced, Ashkenazim founded *moshavot* (farming colonies or plantations, Hebrew plural), mainly on lands Baron Edmund de Rothschild bought for a pittance from Palestinian landowners or from Bedouin sheikhs. Near these colonies lived the Yemeni families who worked for the farmers. Later on, many groups of Ashkenazim lived in agricultural cooperatives, either sharing among themselves all land and labor, and raising their children collectively, such as in the *kibbutz*, or sharing the land through individual household production units, such as in the *moshav* (farming co-op, Hebrew). Due to the collective peasant nature of their colonization of Palestine, most Ashkenazi settlers allied themselves with the socialist parties of the Yishuv. Despite touting socialist ideals, the settlers did not practice these ideals outside their Ashkenazi circles.

Most Sephardim lived in cities where the population was a mixture of Jews, Muslims, and Christians, as in Jerusalem, Jaffa, Haifa, Tiberias, and Safed. Later on, the Ashkenazi Zionists went on to establish cities for Jews only that were typified by the international Bauhaus style of German architecture. The first one was Tel Aviv. Members of right-wing parties lived in these cities and towns as small business owners and small-scale entrepreneurs. But they were the political minority. Socialist Zionist parties governed city and town life as well.

In the mid-1940s, about 2.5 million Jews lived in Muslim countries such as Morocco, Tunisia, Algeria, Iraq, Syria, Lebanon, Turkey, Iran, and Afghanistan; or in other countries with mixed Muslim and non-Muslim populations, such as Yugoslavia and Albania; or in mainly Christian countries such as Greece and Bulgaria, whose Jewish communities did not speak Yiddish. Between 1949 and 1962, about 1.4 million of them immigrated to Israel, mainly from the Muslim World. Most were observant Jews.

After the 29 November 1947 UN resolution calling for the division of Palestine into two states, relations became extremely strained between the Arab World's majority Muslim populations and its Jewish communities. Jewish neighborhoods all over the Arab World suffered Muslim riots protesting against the Zionist colonization of Palestine. After 1948, the protests were directed against the Nakba over its destruction of Palestinian villages, and in several cases, the massacre of those who refused to flee. The Nakba dispersed Palestinians to Lebanon, Syria, the West Bank of the Hashemite Kingdom of Jordan, and the Egyptian Gaza Strip. The Zionist master narrative portrayed these riots as "pogroms," thus exploiting the linguistic terminology and imagery of the long history of European anti-Semitism. Many of these riots, however, sprang from the anticolonialist liberation movements of the Arab World, insurgencies directed at the French and British colonialists. These movements perceived Arab Jews as collaborating with the colonial regimes, partly because the British had facilitated the surrogate colonization of Palestine by the Zionist movement.

When the mass migration of Mizraḥim arrived in Israel, the Ashkenazi Zionist establishment viewed them as a fifth column because of their historical embeddedness in Arabic language and cultures. Right after the establishment of the State of Israel, Mizraḥim were coerced or co-opted to go through a de-Arabization and secularization process in order to become Israel's good-enough, non-Ashkenazi Zionists. Because Mizraḥi families tended to be larger, Mizraḥim overnight became the majority of the Jews in the state—but without majority privileges. In order to camouflage this population disparity, Zionist demographers created a new census category: "Born in Israel," that included the Mizraḥim. "Born in Israel" has gradually become the largest category of Israeli citizens.

The Division of Zionist Women's Labor

The population of Jewish women in Palestine was divided into three major labor groups: *ḥalutzot* (pioneers, Hebrew), *gvarot* (ladies, Hebrew), and *'ozrot bayit* (domestic laborers, Hebrew).

Before they immigrated to Palestine, the majority of Ashkenazi women were housewives. With the founding of the *moshavot*, they became ladies. The Yishuv is remembered for its "pioneer" single women who immigrated to Palestine mainly from Russia after 1904, and who were members of the agricultural cooperatives. Historical records demonstrate, however, that many of them relocated to the cities. In 1911, they founded the Tnu'at ha-Po'elet (Women's Labor Movement, Hebrew). Its members were not feminists. In their articles and memoirs, many state that they just wanted to resemble the pioneer men. A few originated in the Eastern European upper middle classes, and had actually been educated to become ladies. As daily unskilled laborers, the ḥalutzot competed mostly against Palestinian men and Yemeni Jewish men and women for jobs in agriculture; small industries, such as textiles, clothing, or canneries; and manual labor, such as road pavers or stonemasons. Ḥalutzot specialized as cooks for pioneer men in large collective kitchens in the rapidly growing Yishuv towns and cities. The women's knowledge of Ashkenazi food gave them a marked advantage over any Arab worker.

During the Yishuv and well into the 1960s, Ashkenazi women experienced high rates of unemployment. This continues now in the form of middle- and upper-class Ashkenazi women's underemployment. Unemployment provided the leisure time for these women to pursue charitable activities, including the establishment of charities and other volunteer organizations with a mission to civilize Mizraḥi women. Thus these charities became disseminators of Ashkenazi patriarchal ideologies and practices within Mizraḥi communities. In general, such charities characterize the nonobservant upper-middle and upper classes. But in Palestine's Yishuv, these charity volunteers came mainly from the middle classes because the Ashkenazi-Mizraḥi racial divide bestowed upon Ashkenazi women a symbolic upgrade in class status. The dynamics of this underemployment and dissemination continues to the present.

Many Palestinian Jewish women, or those who emigrated to Palestine's Yishuv from Muslim countries, worked as domestic servants. The Ashkenazi Zionist Labor Party apparatchiks, whose wives were busy with public charities, favored Yemeni women as cleaners and launderers. The gvarot named these workers *teimonichkas* (little Yemeni women, Yiddish) or *rumiyas*, after the fragrant herb *rumiya*, used by Yemeni Jews for the *havdala* (the ritual ending the Sabbath and demarcating the beginning of another week). Later on, Yemenis made "Rumiya" into a common name for baby girls. The Sephardi elite preferred Balkan Jewish immigrants as ʿozrot bayit. Jews who resided in the western neighborhoods of Jerusalem, mainly German immigrants, preferred the Palestinian domestic laborers from the nearby villages. All domestics who worked for Ashkenazim had to develop a reasonable command of spoken Yiddish.

Aside from the severely disabled and the very old, all members of the Yemeni family worked outside the home. The women worked in the fields and did domestic work for the farmers' wives. Some used Jerusalem as their home base and journeyed to the moshavot as seasonal laborers who lived, roofless, in the fields. Others lived in barns and slept with the livestock. Some built wooden shacks that became the base for today's Yemeni ghettos. No Yemeni working women were allowed to live inside the residential zones of the Ashkenazi colonies. In the summer they peeled almonds and harvested grapes, and in the winter they fertilized the grape vines and harvested oranges. Most women worked even while pregnant and nursing.

The moshavot relied on child labor by Yemeni girls, and, less frequently, by Palestinian girls. The girls' workdays usually exceeded twelve hours, and usually they were not given any time off, including for Sabbath. A common Ashkenazi term for a working Yemeni girl was *behemat bayit ktana* (little domestic beast, Hebrew). Their salaries were meager, and they received almost no food from their employers, since Zionism predisposed "natural laborers" as genetically frugal. Ashkenazi employers, both men and women, battered Yemeni female laborers of all ages. Because of the pleas issued by Zionist labor leaders criticizing the sexual abuse and rape of Yemeni domestic workers, we know that some Ashkenazi employers used to rape their Yemeni women workers.

The phrase from Yishuv Mizraḥi speech, *zmorot yeveshot* (dry twigs, Hebrew), became a key metaphor for the exploitative subordination of Yemeni women to their Ashkenazi masters. It encapsulates an incident that happened in the colony of Rehovot in 1913. At the end of the workday, Yemeni women agricultural laborers used to gather dry twigs from the vineyards and orchards for cooking or heating water. The colonies' farmers thought of these twigs as their private property. Yemeni women laborers argued that collecting this firewood was one of the very few benefits their agricultural labor entitled them to. When farmers caught these women gathering twigs, they punished them with fines taken from their paltry weekly pay.

One February dusk in 1913, a farmer, Jonathan Makov, son of Polish single mother and feminist leader of the moshavot, Batiya Makov, came to his fields to make sure his workers labored until the very last minute of daylight. He noticed three women collecting twigs. Not only did he beat them, he also tried to tie them up. The women resisted, ran away, and hid in the vineyard. One of their Palestinian male co-workers chased and caught them for the farmer. The farmer tightly roped their wrists and ankles together and fastened the rope to his donkey's tail. Then the Palestinian worker beat the donkey and the women with a stick to drive them faster toward the colony center. The pace was too fast for the women to stay on their feet. They were dragged all the way, the worker walking behind to prevent the women from escaping. When they all arrived at the colony plaza, Makov rushed to ring the bell to summon both Ashkenazim and Yemenis. He wanted make an example of these women for the crowd. There was a public outcry against him, ultimately landing him in court. Although he was found guilty of a crime, his penalty amounted to a ten-cent fine. The Makov incident led to the unionization of Yemeni laborers. Yet no evidence can be found that women were members of the union.

Marriage and Motherhood

Palestinians and Mizraḥim once shared many similarities in kinship and marriage practices. During the Yishuv and the massive immigration of the 1950s, however, each Mizraḥi group married within itself. Ashkenazi groups were the ones who married across the various Yiddish-speaking ethnicities.

In the 1950s, mixed Mizraḥi-Ashkenazi marriages accounted for 14 percent of Jewish marriages in Israel. Come the late 1990s, the percentage doubled to 28 percent. This is no pittance. But when conducting ethnographic research, most of the Ashkenazim I spoke to hailed the ethnic problem as solved. "Almost everyone is mixed-marriage these days," some said with assurance. Implicit in this statement is the assumption that the Mizraḥi has forfeited her heritage for a standardized, transparent Ashkenazi Israeliness.[16]

During the Yishuv era, *walad ʿam* (paternal, parallel cousin, Arabic) marriages, or marriages within the father's and mother's extended families, were quite common among Palestinian Jews or Jews who immigrated to Palestine from Muslim countries. So were marriages of older men to minor girls. In the medical and psychological discourse of the Yishuv's experts, however, such marriages were diagnosed as disorders, grouped together with syphilis, gonorrhea, tuberculosis, alcoholism, drug addiction, and other mental or neurological ailments. No such category was designated for *badal* (exchange, Arabic) marriages. Common among Yemenis, this kind of marriage involved a brother and sister from one family marrying a brother and sister from another family. The swap saved on bridewealth and dowry. Polygyny was prevalent among Mizraḥim, mainly among Yemenis, but there is no documentation of British or Ashkenazi preventive or educational measures against it. Many Mizraḥi widows did not remarry. Burdened with many children, they worked extra hours as maids and seamstresses in addition to their daily jobs.[17]

Ashkenazi Zionist family ideologies and practices were based on the putative science of eugenics, imported from Germany and the United States.[18] They were popularly articulated in the high-circulation monthly magazine *Ha-Em ve-ha-Yeled* (Mother and child, Hebrew). The gynecologists, pediatricians, psychologists, and pedagogues of the labor union's public health care system wrote for this magazine. These specialists also gave radio advice talks and educated the new generation of the Yishuv's family care experts. They were all preoccupied with the quality of the Jewish race, how to improve it, and what policies ought to be designed as preventive measures so that the Jewish race would not degenerate as it expanded its demographics.[19]

For the betterment of the Jewish race, Ashkenazi Zionist family experts reinvented motherhood as *pulḥan ha-imahut* (motherhood rite of passage,

Hebrew). Only those at the crux of the Zionist ethos were able to be part of this. Others thought eugenically incapable of participation included Palestinians, Sephardim, Jewish immigrants from the Balkans and Muslim countries, and the ultra-Orthodox Ashkenazim whose majority was anti-Zionist. On the model of the "ideal laborers," the experts advised the Ashkenazi mother to strive to be the ideal mother, since she was defined as *Ha-Em ha-ʿIvriya* (the Hebrew mother, Hebrew). In the colonies, cities, and towns, most Hebrew mothers quit work for the sake of this rite of passage. The Mizraḥi mother, on the other hand, was termed *Em Zara* (alien mother, Hebrew), perhaps because she would counter the Zionist eugenic project.

Most Em Zara could not afford the communal childcare centers to which nonworking city and colony Hebrew Mothers sent their children. Most daughters of Em Zara became daily laborers at the age of twelve or thirteen. Hebrew texts about child-rearing practices also called on Hebrew Mothers to volunteer and reprogram Alien Mothers so that they would (re)produce better citizens. This trend peaked by the end of the 1940s, during the large-scale immigration of Jews from Muslim countries to the newly founded State of Israel. The *Ha-Em ve-ha-Yeled* team of experts defined one of the new state's missions as purifying each Arab-Jewish ethnic group of its morbidity so that these groups would not hamper the collective healing of the whole Jewish people. Nevertheless, Mizraḥi mothers were called to offer their large Arab families and high birthrates as reservoirs of soldiers, culminating in the futuristic hoped-for appointment of a Yemeni chief of staff.

The Zionist mother was called upon to raise a baby with a lucid mind, tough stomach, and formidable muscles. Zionist child-rearing ideology referred to the traditional Arab and European modes of parenting as "pediarchy" — raising self-absorbed babies through around-the-clock attention. In opposition, 1930s Zionism prescribed for mothers the ideology and practice called "anti-pediarchy." This counter-method required the parents to be rough with the child. Mothers were instructed to be firm, limit the length and duration of nursing, wean their babies from diapers and toilet-train them early, particularly baby girls, in order to prepare them for the precision required in the arduous life that lay ahead. Mothers were required to beat their children, yet the beating was to be executed in a controlled manner. This was in order to inoculate the child with morality and prepare him for war—not one of offense, but rather of defense.

Another reason for Mizraḥi babies being fit only for second-class national service—that is, serving as the rank-and-file of the military and lower classes, but staying excluded from the ranks of political, economic, and cultural power—stemmed from their childcare arrangements. Unable to afford the price of professional daycare centers, their working mothers left them with older kin or close neighbors. This was conceived as retrograde, since the babies were not socialized into the contractual relationships that Zionist educators assumed were part of the baby-caregiver relationship in a professional day-care center setting. Further, Mizraḥi women's aura of motherhood was doubly taken away from them. First, they had to work as the domestic servants who facilitated the Ashkenazi mothers' participation in the motherhood rites, including placing their Ashkenazi children into antipediarchic kindergartens. At the same time, Mizraḥi women worked as maids who cleaned these Ashkenazi kindergartens and cooked the children's daytime meals.

Education

The few Sephardi girls who belonged to the elite went to British or French schools. Working-class Arab-Jewish girls relied on the Yishuv's Ashkenazi Zionist school system. Their education was gender segregated. Records show that in the Yemeni ghettos, the Yishuv's educational wing allocated far fewer classrooms for girls than for boys. If the girls continued onward to high school, the education they received was mainly vocational. Many studied to become seamstresses, and some studied knitting and weaving.

From a handful of educators' memoirs, we know that few Yemeni girls attended kindergarten. The documents reveal that during the day, the teachers educated the moshavot's girls. After their afternoon nap and dinner, they would open the kindergarten between 8:00 and 10:00 in the evening so that the Yemeni girls, returning from their workday at the farmers' homes or fields, could play with the dolls. Mizraḥi girls received inferior education, if any at all. Many were pulled out of the elementary schools to go to work because of their families' extreme poverty. Almost all teachers were Ashkenazi women who conceived of their own work as a feminist act. They also thought that the indoctrination of their Mizraḥi pupils into Zionism would advance the girls and liberate them from the bonds of Arab backwardness. But the results were diametrically opposed—Mizraḥi mothers were always already considered incapable of raising proper Zionist children.

Despite the scarcity of schools in Mizraḥi enclaves, the leadership of the Yishuv's educational wing strongly feared that the large Mizraḥi families, lacking constructive European learning environments, might debase the whole Yishuv population. The welfare and educational officials therefore cajoled the Mizraḥi families and, when cajoling failed to work, used bureaucratic and even physical force to compel the families to enroll into boarding schools or kibbutzim any children above the normative two-child family. For boarding schools or the kibbutzim in the educational system, this forced boarding provided a stable source of income paid by the Jewish Agency welfare authorities and, after 1948, by the Welfare Ministry of the Israeli state. The Ashkenazi educators made sure that the boarded Mizraḥi children would not intermingle with the superior Ashkenazi children. Rather, Mizraḥi children would receive separate and inferior education in order to provide the Zionist apparatus with the next generation of blue-collar laborers.

As for academic education, the Hebrew University was founded in 1925. On its board of trustees there were no Mizraḥim, let alone Mizraḥi women, even though Sephardi elite women were part and parcel of the Jerusalem socialite cosmopolitan colonial scene. I could not find any evidence as to the percentage of Mizraḥi women among either its students or faculty during the British Mandate—presumably there were none. In 2006, for every four Ashkenazi undergraduate university students there was one Mizraḥi student and 0.2 Palestinian citizens of Israel. No gender distribution data concerning Mizraḥi or Palestinian university undergraduates are available. Between 2002 and 2004, Iris Zarini, my student and Aḥoti member, conducted a survey of the almost seven hundred women professors in Israeli universities. Only eighteen of these women professors were Mizraḥi, and almost all admitted that they owed their careers to their well-connected Ashkenazi husbands and parents-in-law. None were Palestinian. Information about Mizraḥi and Palestinian women faculty is officially unavailable.[20]

Cultural Appropriations

The Yishuv era was characterized by a bustling Ashkenazi Zionist literary scene. Romantic epics were a popular genre in this scene. Some of the classics focused on Yemeni women's dual lives as hard-working laborers and as insatiable sex bombs trapped in the Judeo-Islamic honor-shame scheme. The Ashkenazi male authors—mostly members of socialist parties who funded their publications—conducted their "field" research for such epics on their own maids. The maids, in turn, felt obliged to furnish their probing masters with folk stories, methods of traditional healing, and intimate details of their own and their community members' lives, just so they would not be fired. Ashkenazi Zionist women authors preferred the format of short stories that focused more on their own lives, with Mizraḥi women servants as background characters.

In 1906, Lithuanian Jewish sculptor Boris Shatz founded the Bezalel Art Academy in Jerusalem. In their efforts to create authentic Israeli art, the Shatz circle invented many themes featuring grotesque exotica of Yemeni Jewish women's harsh lives. Early Ashkenazi Zionist artists conceptualized the figure of the Yemeni woman as a Jewish imitation of the indigenous Muslim Palestinian woman. They also borrowed motifs from Yemeni Jewish and Palestinian Muslim women's embroidery, pottery, and basket weaving. The art of the Shatz circle sold for extremely high prices to collectors who were also donors to the Zionist settlement project in Palestine.

Concurrently, Ashkenazi Zionist souvenir dealers used some of their own Ashkenazi contacts, such as rabbis' wives, and also subcontracted the services of Yemeni women with large community networks—often wives of Yemeni rabbis. These women themselves subcontracted Yemeni embroiderers, potters, and basket weavers working from home for meager pay. The middlewomen sold the finished goods to souvenir dealers, who in turn either sold them in Palestine or, more often, exported them as Zionist mementos to European and American Jews. Yemeni embroidery thus became one of Zionism's showcases and its claims for authenticity.

As in the case of the mock-indigenous art, in the first decades of the twentieth century, Ashkenazi Zionist classically trained musicians and choreographers invented new dances and songs based on traditional Mizraḥi and Palestinian folk dances and songs. These were major mechanisms to socialize immigrants into the newly invented national society of the Yishuv. Many of the melodies were appropriated from traditional Yemeni and Sephardic women's songs or Palestinian wedding songs, but then Ashkenazi composers copyrighted them for royalty purposes. Many of the dance steps were appropriated from Yemeni and Kurdish women's ceremonial dancing.

Through the histories of Mizraḥi women and the Ashkenazim who dominated them, I present pre-1948 Zionism as a surrogate set of colonial and imperial ideologies and practices. Intricately positioned along the Israel-Palestine divide, these histories best demonstrate Zionism's racial formations and the sophistication of its power structure over Mizraḥim. Mizraḥi women, situated as they were between the rock of Ashkenazi Zionist economic and cultural oppression and the hard place of Palestine's war for independence, were forced to unlearn their Arab culture and Orthodox Judaism as Zionism was superimposed on their communities. Nevertheless, these communities welcomed the 1948 founding of Israel on the land of Palestine and hoped to be integrated into it. The Zionist foundational narratives set the scene for the atrocities suffered by Mizraḥi women after the establishment of Israel, culminating in the kidnapping of their babies to be sold for adoption and unconsented medical experimentation.[21] Today, disenfranchisement, poverty, Arab phenotype, Arabic accent, and Arab name discrimination are still integral to the lives of Mizraḥi women.

———

When I finished reading the EWIC entry, no one talked. Only the twirl of the fan blades. I felt the women's gaze on me. There were no pages to retreat behind. Unlike the scholars who would read the encyclopedia entry, my audience on this night was staring me in the face. As I translated the text for them, I skipped the portions that they already knew, such as information on the specifics about the kidnapping of Mizraḥi babies sold for adoption. The women probably knew more about these than I did. The content that they did not know so well—and what the women thought of it—was what caused me to tremble.

Averting my eyes, I stared at the half moon knifing through the open balcony doors. Still anxious, and without the postperformance glow. Throughout the talk, the women freely interjected "Israel!" every time I mentioned Palestine. They sparked up arguments to protest or support points I raised, using examples from their own lives. To my surprise, my advocate was Ludmilla. "Let her talk! Let her talk!" she shushed in her Slavic-accented Hebrew.

But now—silence.

Luna arrived from the kitchen with cold Diet Sprite. As she passed out plastic cups, she muttered, "I don't believe any of it. Can't be that bad. Ashkenazim and us—we're all Jews with warm Jewish hearts. Goyim—the rest of 'em."

Iris, louder: "Yes, it's that bad. It's worse, even. They planned it. They run like clockwork. These Europeans—so cold and calculated. *Ash-ke-natzim!*" "Ashkenatzim" is bigoted Israeli slang combining "Ashkenazim" and "Nazis." Iris pronounced it slowly, every syllable a hammer stroke. "Troublemakers in Europe back then, troublemakers here right now."

"How dare you! Don't touch my Shoah!" exclaimed Ludmilla. "What chutzpah! Were your parents in the camps?" She paused. "Partisans?" she needled.

Silence again.

"Their model is not German. They're Socialists. Bolsheviks. Stalinist mentality. Stalinist mentality," Ludmilla hissed. "I believe everything the professor said because it's just like the Soviet mind, and because my husband told me how every morning, she would bring bags of books and papers to write up her research. Four desks full! All in Hebrew, and published here— that's how you know it's the truth!" Ludmilla took another pause, suddenly aware of her gushing. The fans rumbled. "Jews need to stop being victims! In the Middle East, it's the law of the jungle—all of us here accept it. You don't." She turned to me and pointed. "But that's nature—the Jews' right to survive in the jungle. When in war, act like it's war."

Ortal: "These Ashkenazi leftists raise their self-esteem, saying 'I'm helping the weak. I'm loving the *'Aravim*. I'm generous. I'm wonderful.' What an ego trip! But what about us? Why do they hate us?"

"They hate us alright, but advanced us," said Sigal. "We're no longer *'Aravim*. We no longer veil. No killing daughters for honor. Our men no longer marry several wives. Thank G-d we live in a Jewish state. So what if the Ashkenazim birthed it?"

Iris: "Yes they hate us because we vote Likud. Of course we vote for the Right. They didn't do these crimes to us. It was the Labor Party and the rest of 'em Left. That's what she lectured about."

"Likud screwed with us too," said Sigal. "But we must support them. They're not wishy-washy with peace mumbo-jumbo. Look here: when the Left is in power, there are wars with the 'Aravim — '48, '56, '67, '73 . . . even now, with Flora's brother. He's Labor. With Likud and the Right, there's quiet. The 'Aravim are afraid to come out of their cubbyholes. The Right doesn't talk peace. They're honest. When in war, act like it's war."

Why Mizraḥim Support the Right Wing

The majority of Ashkenazim are non-Orthodox Jews who vote for the Israeli political Left. The Left agrees on a land-for-peace settlement for the Israeli-Palestinian conflict but is divided among three factions. When Vicky Knafo marched in Jerusalem in 2003, the first faction, the Zionist Left bloc, consisted of the Labor Party and the Meretz Party. The bloc's affluent constituency has customarily been composed of the Ashkenazi economic-political upper classes — industrialists, bankers, developers, and high-tech businessmen (Reider 2006; Shubeli 2006).

The Kadima centrist party joined the Zionist Left bloc in 2005, two years after the Knafo struggle folded. It was started by then Likud chairman and prime minister Ariel Sharon and was joined by supporters of his 2005 plan to disengage from negotiations with the Palestinians and unilaterally withdraw from the Gaza Strip. This action was only a partial reason for the party's founding. In 2001, Sharon's son criticized the high number of Mizraḥim in the Likud Center. The Center decides the composition of the Likud candidate list for Knesset members. He also complained that Likud's fate had fallen into the hands of *Indiyanim* (Indians or Native Americans, Hebrew plural; primitives in colloquial Hebrew) (Shmueli 2001). On the other side of the political spectrum, a mustachioed Moroccan, Amir Peretz, was elected as party head of Labor in 2005, partly as a reaction to the social problems the Knafo protest addressed. The

Ashkenazi-dominated Labor Party officials, such as former party head and Israeli president Shimon Peres, joined Likud's Ashkenazi leadership to form Kadima as a refuge from the "Mizraḥization" of the Labor Party. Since the Ashkenazi Zionist Left kept moving to the right, the Kadima Party had been considered a leftist party. Kadima had no socialist roots, but, because its leaders promoted the idea of a land-for-peace swap with the Palestinians, it was viewed as leftist.

In the 2013 Knesset elections, Kadima lost twenty-six of its twenty-eight seats to Yesh 'Atid (There is a future, Hebrew), led by Ashkenazi celebrity Yair Lapid, former actor, journalist, author, and TV news anchor. Yesh 'Atid adopted Kadima's neoliberal agenda, including its wariness of the "Mizraḥization" of Labor and Likud. Most voters from affluent Ashkenazi enclaves flocked from Kadima to Yesh 'Atid.[22] But no matter which Zionist "Left" party is in power, it will consistently carry out right-wing domestic social and economic policies.

A second faction of the Left is the post-Zionists. They recognize the reality of the 1948 Nakba and conduct active demonstrations against Israel's 1967 occupation of the West Bank and Gaza. They do not differ from the Zionist bloc when it comes to its Ashkenazi upper-class interests.

The third faction, the anti-Zionist Left, is also of the Ashkenazi upper classes but traces its roots back to the European new Left of the 1960s. It favors transforming Israel from a Jewish state, where Jews have advantageous privileges of citizenship, into a secular state with equitable citizenship for all inhabitants, including the '48 Arabs. A minority within the anti-Zionist Left believes that one state, Palestine-Israel, ought to be formed from Israel, the West Bank, and the Gaza Strip. None of these leftist movements have managed to attract the Mizraḥim.

On the eve of the 1967 war, Michael Selzer (1967)[23] argued that all factions of the Ashkenazi Left had aryanized the Jews, much more than those of the Right had, by co-opting the then-fashionable counterculture discourse of peace and love to make solidarity overtures to the Palestinians. But the Left, while romanticizing the Palestinians, could not digest its own Jewish Arabs—the Mizraḥim—as part of the conflict between Israel and its neighbors. Selzer pointed out that the Ashkenazi Left had treated Mizraḥim as the inassimilable excess of what it termed "the peace discourse" (1967, 94).

To connect peace discourse with the Israeli Left is an extreme irony. So many post- and anti-Zionist Ashkenazi leftists can trace their political and familial lineages to the socialist MAPAI,[24] the precursor to Israel's Labor and Meretz parties. This is the same party largely responsible for the colonization of Palestine from 1882 onward, the 1948 Nakba, the Retributional Operations of the 1950s to the early 1960s, the 1956 Suez War, the 1967 Six-Day War, and the first settlements in the West Bank and Gaza, the 1968 Karameh Operation, the 1987–93 crushing of the First Intifada, the 2006 Lebanon War, and Gaza 2008. And though waged under the Menachem Begin Likud government, the 1982 Lebanon War was orchestrated by his defense minister, Ariel Sharon, whose political lineage can be traced back to the Labor Party. All the while, it is this very Zionist Left that has presented a veneer of peacemakers with socialist ideals to facilitate its doctrine of aggression. The only lasting peace agreement between Israel and any of its Arab neighbors was signed by the right-wing Menachem Begin government in 1978.

Selzer concluded that unless the political Left dismantled Israel's intra-Jewish apartheid system by de-aryanizing Israel's Ashkenazi domination and hegemony, there would be no armistice, let alone peace, between Israel and the Arab World. And indeed, it was the Zionist Left who initiated the expulsion of Palestinians from their homes and the 1950s mass migration of Mizraḥim into newly formed Israel. It was the Left that forced Mizraḥim into downward mobility. Until 1977, the Zionist Right did not have enough supporters to be a major influence on the settlement of Palestine, and then Israel. Selzer went on to say that the Left had not "realiz[ed] how significant it is that the Ashkenazim have shown themselves incapable of living with their own Jewish brethren of Arab background" (1967, 94).

Statements opining the differences between Ashkenazim and Mizraḥim were common from the Zionist Left leadership during the 1950s mass migration of Mizraḥim. According to Moshe Etziyoni, a judge on the Israeli Supreme Court in 1959:

4. Dov Ariel, a transit camp manager and Labor Party apparatchik, supervised Yemeni Jewish laborers in 1959. In this photo, they stood in the fields of Nuris, a Palestinian village whose residents were expelled during the 1948 Nakba. The Israeli regime settled the Yemeni Jews in the Palestinians' place. Central Zionist Archives.

An Ashkenazi thug, thief, pimp, or killer will not receive sympathy from Ashkenazim (if such an ethnic group even exists). He would not dare ask for sympathy. But among the primitive band, the Moroccans, this is very possible.

And according to Zalman Shazar, third president of Israel, in 1951:

We will pay a high price. We have allowed this scourge of Mizraḥi immigrants with no speck of high school education. They cannot take so much schooling, so much studying. So be it. We can let them into elementary schools. But what will happen to the quality of education? And the fate of the Yishuv? How do we continue serving as the guiding light for the goyim? Will the Israeli Yishuv survive without Jews like us—Europeans and Anglo-Saxons?[25]

No wonder that the Mizraḥim voted in 1977 almost as a bloc, leading to Menachem Begin's election as Israel's prime minister. They voted to protest the left wing's Zionist racial formations and its inability to acknowledge Mizraḥi humiliation and discrimination under Ashkenazi Socialist Zionism during the Yishuv, and under subsequent Left Labor Party governments since 1948. In 1959, Begin served as head of the right-wing Ḥerut Party and operated far outside the liberal-Socialist Zionist consensus. He became a revered figure among many Mizraḥim when he made a solidarity visit with the rebels of Wadi Salib, an overcrowded Haifa slum where North African Jews had risen to protest the squalid conditions. Because of this visit, and especially because Begin was the first politician to acknowledge that discrimination against Mizraḥim was based on their non-Ashkenazi ethnic origins, the Mizraḥim became long-term voters for the Likud Party, successor to the Ḥerut Party. The Wadi Salib rebellion was the first event to shape post-1948 Mizraḥi consciousness.

Menachem Begin won in a landslide in 1977, due in part to early 1970s civil unrest sparked by the Mizraḥi Black Panthers, a protest movement that took its name as a symbolic gesture to the eponymous Oakland, California, movement. The Black Panthers were also in coalition with the budding late-1960s new Left anti-Zionist Ashkenazi movement. Starting in Jerusalem's pre-1967 border-zone slums, their demonstrations swept through almost all Mizraḥi ghettos in Israel's urban centers. These were suppressed by brutal police force, following the instructions of Prime Minister and Labor Party leader Golda Meir. Some Panthers were shot dead at short range by police snipers. Others were co-opted into establishment positions, and those who remained activists are still denied meaningful employment and housing by the Israeli regime. One mysteriously disappeared.[26] Just when they were about to embark on coalitional relationships with European new Left and radical socialist groups, Israeli officials confiscated the passports of their delegation members. Israeli scholars and the public believe that the Black Panther movement led directly to the fall of the Labor Party and the transfer of power to Begin and the Right. The Israeli political Right has held power since 1977, except for short periods, and has carried out a policy originally initiated by the Labor Party—

settling the West Bank and Gaza through colonial outposts under the ideology of Eretz Israel.

A new generation of Mizraḥi politicians aligned themselves with the Likud Eretz Israel ideology and practice and rose into lower-level municipal politics as mayors. Then some went to the Knesset or obtained ministerial portfolios. But this new cadre of Mizraḥi politicians was still subservient to those with Ashkenazi lineage in the Likud, who were popularly called *nesikhim* (princes, Hebrew), due to their legacies from the old-family cadre of historical Ḥerut. The Mizraḥi politicians advanced the political agenda of the nesikhim rather than that of their own Mizraḥi communities. Even so, they enjoyed repeated reelection.

Nevertheless, there were good reasons for the lower-class Jewish majority of Israel to keep voting for the political Right. Many Mizraḥi families wanted to escape the Mizraḥi ghettos, especially when the cities in central Israel started turning into real estate bubbles that made housing there utterly unaffordable.[27] In pursuing its goal to settle Eretz Israel, the Likud continued the Labor Party's policy of creating viable single-family dwellings for lower-middle-class Israelis.

It was the Labor government that started devising a plan in which the only housing upgrades available for poor people were in large-scale West Bank settlements like Ariel, Maʿale Adumim, or the newer expansion of Jerusalem's neighborhoods to deep inside post-1967 occupied Palestine. Here, upscale-for-the-poor projects bore names such as Pisgat Zeʾev (the Wolf's Peak, Hebrew)[28] or Neve Yaʿakov (the Oasis of Jacob, Hebrew). Since the mid-1980s, however, the right-wing governments of Israel not only invested in these settlements but also initiated project renewal in the Mizraḥi ghettos throughout the country. Although the project did not support enough new housing, it did establish community centers and significantly improve the infrastructure, particularly electricity and sewage. Furthermore, it was during the right-wing Israeli regimes that Mizraḥi culture, as long as it avoided connecting its own Arabness with that of the Palestinians, embarked on a renaissance (Abargel and Lavie 2009).

One of the slogans chanted in many demonstrations by all varieties of the Israeli political Left is "Fund the 'hoods," that is, the Mizraḥi slums and development towns, "not the settlements," meaning Israeli communities in the West Bank and Gaza. Rafi Shubeli (2006) argued that the evocation of this catchphrase is illusory. He asked: Since when has the Israeli Ashkenazi Left fought for the Mizraḥi poor or tried to provide a viable alternative to the avenues for upward mobility provided by allegiance to the Right? Ironically, the kibbutzim, the showcases of enlightened Socialist Zionism, had exploited Mizraḥi development towns by hiring underpaid menial laborers with no rights (Chetrit 2004). Shubeli noted that the Ashkenazi Left habitually depicts the Mizraḥim as the atavistic chauvinistic masses.

The Left almost always chants, "Fund the 'hoods, not the settlements," in the context of the military occupation of the West Bank and Gaza without acknowledging the fact that the Mizraḥim are the silent majority of the West Bank and Gaza settlements. They do not chant that slogan in the context of the racism and poverty typical of lived experience in Israel's slums, not of Palestinian Nazareth or mixed Palestinian-Israeli upper Nazareth, let alone skid row in South Tel Aviv. They would only head south to Black City for inexpensive foie gras shish kebabs rolled into Iraqi pita-bread. Shubeli concluded that by using such a slogan, the Left inflamed one public, the Mizraḥim, against the other, the Palestinians, in order to downplay the more stark division between the majority settlers who are the Mizraḥim, and themselves (compare to Barʿam 2003; Leibovitz-Dar 2002).

In Israel today, there is virtually no political Left as it is usually conceived. In fact, it is reasonable to question whether the Left has ever had a true foothold during the Yishuv and the subsequent Israeli state (Sternhell 1999). Even though the Labor Party (usually seen as leftist) *was* Israel until 1977, almost all political parties in Israel, including the Labor Party, offer various flavors of the political Right. Yet, politicians and the media invoke the binary logic of Left versus Right politics to win elections and garner public support. This same binary logic informs Israel's bureaucratic system. All aspects of nuance are screened out. Once again, almost all issues raised in the public sphere are ultimately reduced to us versus them, Left versus Right, whether such distinctions are applicable or not. They often are not. But that does not stop Israelis—Ashkenazim and Mizraḥim alike—from believing in the Left-Right binary. Thus, in Israeli society, Ashkenazim are almost always presumed to belong to the Left, even if they enact neo-con legislation and policies. Mizraḥim, on the other hand, are almost always suspected to be right-wing, even when they join the protests of the post- or anti-Zionist Left against the state's injustice against Palestinians.

Why Mizraḥi Feminists' Hands Are Tied

Israeli feminism arose in the 1970s among middle-class Ashkenazim, many of whom had immigrated to Israel from English-speaking countries. In the mid-1980s, the tight space these women had carved out for feminism in the public sphere was usurped from them by the gvarot of the Ashkenazi elite. Upper-class Ashkenazi feminists had the wealth, leisure, and Zionist pedigree to conduct full-time feminist advocacy through their fathers, husbands, or other kinship ties.[29] It was an uphill struggle for the early Mizraḥi feminists to carve out a place for their agenda in the little space left for civil society devoid of militarism or the liberal feminist agenda.

In the mid-1980s, feminist activists Ilana Sugavker (Shazor), whose parents immigrated to Israel from Mumbai, and Hanna Cohen, daughter of Iranian immigrants, founded the Tel Aviv Mizraḥi Women's Group. Its initial members were Yemenis Yonit Mansour, Yael Zadok, and Ronit Dagan-Timsit; Iraqis Ilana Shamai, Rutie Gur, Irit Daloumi, and Shosha Goren; Iranian Zehava Goldstein; and Egyptian Vicki Shiran, who throughout her life acted as the leader for Mizraḥi feminism. Their goal was to bring immediate aid and long-term empowerment and social justice to disenfranchised women in their communities. They were inspired by the distinct voices of U.S. feminists of color who had emerged in the 1970s, arguing that white feminism could not transcend the racism, ethnocentrism, and privilege that typified the Western public sphere and its liberal feminist movements.

All members of the Tel Aviv Mizraḥi Women's Group were Zionists, but criticized the upper-class and Anglo-Saxon influences on Israeli feminists. They criticized the classism and racism faced by Mizraḥi and '48 Arab women as well (Shiran 2002; see Shiran 1991, 1996; Shohat 1988). They pointed out that the Ashkenazi Left feminists who controlled the major feminist NGOs in Israel had chosen to strategically focus on Israel-Palestine binarism, in English, and for North American-Western European consumption, rather than improving the daily lives of the majority of Israel's women. The Israel-Palestine binary was and still is the cornerstone of Ashkenazi feminist NGOs' international fund-raising (Lavie 2011a). In 2000, the group was joined by more Mizraḥi feminists, mainly from Jerusalem and Haifa, to found Aḥoti. Aḥoti is the only feminist movement in Israel that currently draws its membership from all segments of society, including intellectuals, artists, small-business owners, fired factory workers, and homeless welfare mothers (Shiran 2002).

Almost all Israeli feminist NGOs are funded by the New Israel Fund (NIF) and Women-to-Women USA-Israel, a subsidiary of the New York-based National Council of Jewish Women.[30] These foundations espouse an enlightened, left-leaning form of Zionism and have influenced the scholarly political, cultural, and social agendas of Israeli feminism and gender and women's studies university programs.

Almost all Israeli social movements have undergone "NGO-ization"—a process by which grassroots social movements transform into "'safety valves' by channeling popular discontent along constitutional, peaceful, and harmless ways . . . [In the process] the exploited and oppressed [are divided] into sections and identities." It is a process by which social movements turn into "self-help communities . . . absolving the state from all social responsibilities" (Chachage Seithy L. Chachage 2004, quoted in Sangtin Writers and Nagar 2006). By offering activists job opportunities at a time of job scarcity, NIF and SHATIL have been responsible for much of the NGO-ization in Israel. Activists hired to be professionals often conformed to role expectations, forcing them to depoliticize. In the Israeli feminist arena, NIF metes out its funds into part-time positions offering fragmented hourly pay, without benefits or labor rights. These positions have mainly been held by Mizraḥi and Palestinian women. In contrast, NGO leadership has been composed mostly of Ashkenazim with full-time salaries and benefits.

The efforts of NIF and SHATIL have also enacted a Durkheimian division of protest labor. Durkheim ([1893] 1984) classified how different labor hierarchies cohere into a social order. Through its funding policies, NIF has created a pool of protest labor organized into a gendered-ethnic-national hierarchy. NIF and Women-to-Women USA-Israel funded the progressive-liberal feminist elite's protest over human and civil rights violations against West Bank and Gaza Palestinians, and even '48 Arabs. The protest employed the language of cosmopolitan human rights, including the discourse on the struggle of indigenous First Nations. NIF did not object to the NGOs' use of terms like "racism" and "apartheid" to describe the discriminatory ideologies and practices of Israel against Palestinians.[31]

On the other hand, NIF and SHATIL have relegated Mizrahi NGOs to the role of substituting for severely truncated state welfare programs. Ahoti has used its NIF funding on projects like helping women reenter the job market through workshops for starting small businesses. Women would learn, for example, how to sell their home cooking in a tight, highly professionalized catering market. Or they would find out how to sell their embroidery in an exploitative ethnic crafts market already dominated by the more exotic (and more in-demand) embroidery and weaving made by Bedouin women's collectives. If a Mizrahi NGO would not submit itself to SHATIL's reorganization suggestions, NIF would threaten to withhold funding. As Racheli Avidov (2004) argued, NIF has transformed Mizrahi feminism into a depoliticized subcontractor of mainstream Ashkenazi feminism.

For example, in 2002 and the first quarter of 2003, I worked with Vicki Shiran on Ahoti's long-term budget. We went to present it to NIF's Jerusalem offices on 6 January 2003. From 1:30 to 3:30 p.m. we defended the budget proposal in front of the woman official in charge of funding Mizrahi NGOs. Though the budget was not rejected outright, the official refused to fund our consciousness-raising to educate our communities on feminism of color. "Too divisive for Israel's feminist movement," she said. Ironically, she herself was an Ashkenazi Jewish immigrant from Latin America and veteran activist against Latin American authoritarian regimes.

NIF tied Ahoti's hands financially. But Ahoti also tied its own hands as well. Its metropolitan ideologues and activists were factionalized along the same lines as the Ashkenazi Left: Socialist Zionists, Post-Zionists, and Anti-Zionists. Yet, they avoided publicly exposing these factions or their beliefs on the Israel-Palestine binary. They dared not invade this Ashkenazi elite turf, and not only because NIF would not fund them. As a group,

Mizraḥi feminists had not called for a just solution to the Palestine problem by, for example, illuminating the conjuncture of the military occupation's cost with the lack of money for enough mammogram machines in public health clinics in the unemployment-ridden Mizraḥi ghettos. They did not point out that the early Ashkenazi-Zionist eugenic ideologies and practices against Mizraḥim connect to the treatment of Palestinians (Abargel and Lavie 2009; Lavie 2007). If the Mizraḥi communities they advocated for and served found out about their political opinions, they would have likely rejected Aḥoti's attempts to conduct projects for women in the 'hoods. The community was concerned only with harsh Mizraḥi life, with limited access to nutritional stability, employment, housing, and education. And like all Israelis, they were constantly preoccupied with issues of war and military security. Therefore, Mizraḥi feminists agreed among themselves that silence on Palestine was the only strategy.[32]

———

After the talk, Sigal and I helped Luna gather her dishes from the table. We then walked back to her apartment. We chose the scenic route along the promenade on the edge of the cirque. We ambled, tired from the fast, the large meal, and the arguments. The lopsided moon's rays lit the craggy cliffs above the plateau but left the cirque's searing depths in thick darkness. The crisp and cool desert breeze came from the north and caressed our southbound backs.

Sigal and I said nothing to each other. The sustained silence between us implied neither a deep bond of friendship, nor absolute strangerhood. Were we still sisters to the struggle? Did she and the others think I was one of those Ashkenazi leftists? Would they abandon Aḥoti in our future projects? Would it be my fault?

Without warning, Sigal blurted out:

"Why do you speak in favor of the 'Aravim? It's over with. Do you really love them? When the time comes, and they slaughter us, you won't get a pass because you call yourself an 'Arab Jew' and think you're one of them. They are the enemy. G-d bless Mitzpe, far away from the Qassam missiles in Gaza, let alone Ḥezbollah's Katyushas from Lebanon. You know, the missiles can reach Tel Aviv, where you and the chi-chi sisters live. But Ḥamas and Ḥezbollah won't dare attack."

She forced out a chuckle.

"Suicide bombers don't come to Mitzpe," she continued. "Too piddly. The media won't come this far to cover them. News has to be within an hour's drive. Two hours, max."

I paused before answering. I didn't want to start an argument. After all, she was my host. "I really don't know. I think we can't separate the Mizraḥim from the Palestinians."

"Sure we can," she shot back. "We are Jews. They are goyim."

There was nothing I could say to shake her from that belief. So I said nothing. Right and Left. Us and the bureaucrats against the goyim. Gone was social class. Gone were race and ethnicity. Only the absolutism of the binary. From the cradle to donning military fatigues at age eighteen, all Israeli citizens tracing Jewish lineage learned that their most vital responsibility to the state was in creating new generations of Jewish citizens. Judaism *is* citizenship. Sigal believed this as a product of the state's formal and informal education system. I, too, was a product of that system. But through the privileges of my Berkeley education, I was able to get outside the system and become an ethnographer and community leader with "strategies." But here, no strategies. Sigal and I were entrapped in lethal webs of welfare bureaucracy.

We walked the rest of the way home in silence.

———

On 5 December 2005, the State of Israel marked International Volunteer Day and expressed its gratitude to volunteers worldwide.[33] So it was appropriate that I handle my own volunteerism to the international scholarly community—my EWIC entry. It had been about four months since I had sent Isabella and Julie my final draft. I shot a short email to Suad to see what was up with the volume:

From: Smadar Lavie
Sent: Tuesday, 5 December 2006 09:32

To: Suad Joseph
Subject: Encyclopedia

Written to Seteney. She's on maternity leave. Julie didn't answer. Has she relocated?

What's going on with the entry? I put a year's work into it—80 books and about 50 volumes of periodicals.

Thanks

Smadar

At the end of 2007, Brill published my entry in Volume 6 of the Encyclopedia of Women in Islamic Culture, the supplement reserved for all articles from various volumes that missed their deadlines. It was quite generous for the EWIC editors to facilitate the publishing of these late arrivals.

CHAPTER 2

Protesting and Belonging

When the Agency of Identity Politics Becomes Impossible

Figurations of Agency

After divorcing her husband, Zeina Sawaʿed, Bedouin citizen of Israel and single mother, relocated to a housing project in the largely Mizraḥi town of Tiberias, on the shores of the Sea of Galilee. She moved from her ancestral Palestinian village nearby. The village had zero tolerance for a single mother, let alone one without a caftan and veil. Inspired by Vicky Knafo, she embarked on her own 170-kilometer (around 105 miles) march on Jerusalem. She was impressed by the scene and returned to Tiberias to bring her three children back with her to Knafoland. On 22 July 2003, in front of eager cameras and microphones, Zeina pitched her tent in Wohl Rose Park (Sinai 2003).

The Hebrew media usually portray Mizraḥi single mothers with a stereotype: bleached blonde hair, skinny jeans, smoking expensive import cigarettes—proof of their loose morals and wastefulness. But not so with Zeina. She fit the stereotype, yet became the press corps's darling—the unveiled, liberated, blonde Bedouin in skinny jeans, brandishing oh-so-eloquent Hebrew.

"I represent four hundred Arab single mothers," she proclaimed. "Arab and Jewish women now unite and fight the budget cuts" (Greenbaum 2003).

Whenever she spoke, Zeina referred to herself as "Arab," rather than "Palestinian." Israeli Jews use "Arab" to refer to the Palestinian citizens of the state. Israeli official discourse has ingrained this term, and thus the denial of Palestine, into the fabric of mundane conversation.

To reporters questioning her about her possible identification with Palestinian nationalism, Zeina proclaimed her Bedouin-ness. Her shrewd and careful identity crafting played into the Israeli public's romantic image of the Bedouin, based on Abrahamic mythology—nomads who stake no claims to permanent land. This romance has no bearing on reality, however (Lavie, Hajj, and Rouse 1993).

"Our men serve in the IDF and sacrifice themselves for the State of Israel's security," Zeina declared (see Kanaaneh 2009, 10, 61).[1] Unlike the majority of Israel's Palestinian citizenry, Bedouin are required to serve in the IDF. "So where's our fair share? I'm a single mother. I marched here for my allowance. I want it back."

Unfazed by her deft maneuvering, the media pelted her with Intifada questions. Though she did not directly answer their questions, she still became their favorite. Was it because of her "novelty factor"? Or was it because of the media's tendency to seek the familiar binary comfort of the Israel-Palestine conflict?

On 24 July 2003, six busloads of '48 Arabs, mainly veiled women, came to support Zeina. On 8 August, a thirty-vehicle Ta'ayush (Life in Common, Arabic) motorcade descended the hill to Knafoland. Ta'ayush is the mainly Ashkenazi leftist-cum-'48 Arab NGO that organizes food convoys for refugee camps in the PA—even through Israeli blockades (Shadmi 2003).

"Support the slums, not the settlements," exhorted the ever-present Ta'ayush banners (Kim 2002; see Shubeli 2006).

Soon after the Ta'ayush motorcade departed Knafoland, Zeina and her children were sent away from the encampment. I asked Vicky about it. She didn't respond. But I didn't push her to talk. I wanted the silence to prompt her answer. Luckily for her, a Tokyo TV reporter pulled her out of the tent for a photo-op in the waning sun. That left me in the tent with Ilana and her Chihuahua—Knafoland's mascot.

Ilana broke the silence: "Bibi ain't gonna hear from me. He don't wanna talk anyway. But the peace circus in the Knesset—they talk to me. Ashkenazim, all of 'em! Lefties, all of 'em! They wanna toss out Bibi, and they gonna use us. They want peace—whatever! Their peace is our poverty. Our jobs cost too much. Them and the media—all Ashkenazim! Lefties! Arablovers! They're out to get Bibi. All they want is Jews doing bad things to Arabs and feeling guilty about it. They want the Bedouin. She's their pet. She gets the spotlight. What about us? Y'see—I'm a Moroccan. She's an Arab. These Ashkenazim—self-hating Jews! They wanna help her, not me! She ain't here no more. At least Bibi ain't no Arab-lover."

I immediately called the Aḥoti board and founding members to tell them about Zeina's expulsion. All of them immediately jumped to comment on the opportunism of the Ashkenazi Left (Barʿam 2003; Leibovitz-Dar 2002). "Since when did the Left support the Mizraḥi slums?" many said. So Aḥoti made a strategic decision not to intervene on Zeina's behalf, even though most members are pro-Palestinian.

"We work with right-wing women, like Ilana and Vicky, on projects to better Mizraḥi women's lives," many said. "We *cannot* risk alienating them." Just as Ashkenazi feminist NGOs depended on Israel-Palestine binary-focused projects for backing, Aḥoti depended on the participation of Mizraḥi women to receive funding for its initiatives.

Almost all Mizraḥim share Vicky and Ilana's right-wing stance because they conceived the Zionist Left regime as the historical perpetrator of their disenfranchisement. The Left also initiated Oslo economics that outsourced the single mothers' jobs to the Arab World or brought to Israel cheaper Third World women to replace them (Zomer 2001). Thus, they had stood with the Right. And they continued to stand with the Right, even though the Right hurt them economically.

But what about Zeina and her children?

———

"If we're cute, we'll get nothin'," said Ayala Sabag, challenging Vicky and Ilana.

At end of July 2003, Ayala Sabag led her own group of single mothers, all from the Jerusalem ghettos and barrios, to Knafoland. Ayala is a Moroccan and the sister of the late Seʿadya Martziano, cofounder of the Jerusalem Black Panthers. After establishing her presence at the camp, she started to take her cohort of mothers to affluent sections of Jerusalem, where American Jews live. For several nights, always in the wee hours, they shut off electric circuit boxes and water switches to ornate apartment buildings, hoping to garner the attention of the international media.

"The rich need to feel what we feel when we can't pay bills," she stated.

The actions of Ayala and her coterie were all done without the consensus of the mothers in Knafoland. Vicky, Ilana, and most other mothers felt pressure to self-censor their images to fit into SHATIL's ideal form of protest— nonviolent and nonaggressive. Ayala threatened this image, and therefore threatened the mothers' continued support from SHATIL's PR staff. So Vicky and Ilana asked her to leave. Aḥoti had to respect the single mothers' stance against Ayala even though we supported her actions and were very suspicious of SHATIL.[2]

———

On the whole, the single mothers in Knafoland decided courses of action by discussing to reach a consensus, rather than casting simple majority votes. We in Aḥoti tried to guide the mothers' decisions and mediate their internal conflicts. Oftentimes we disagreed with them but still strategically concurred with their decisions.

In the case of Zeina, we resented the feminists of the Ashkenazi Left. We agreed with Ilana about them. Ashkenazi Left feminists are perceived internationally for their activism on behalf of Palestinians, at times risking their own lives for the causes of peace and human rights. But, they also choose to avoid facing the long history of their communities' racial, social, and cultural discrimination against the Mizraḥim. In so doing, Ashkenazi feminists alienate Israel's Jewish demographic majority because they do not think its problems are important compared to the perennial Israel-Palestine conflict (Lavie 2011a). We watched how they used the Palestinian plight to obtain generous funding and media coverage. Zeina was the perfect candidate for their benevolence.

The Left's Ashkenazi feminists responded to Israel's grave human rights violations during the First Intifada (1987–93) and the al-Aqsa Intifada (2000–2005). In her writings, Gila Swirsky (2002), one of the founders of Women in Black and the Coalition of Women for Peace, vividly evokes the brave feats of Israeli peace activists demonstrating in solidarity with the Palestinians of the West Bank during the al-Aqsa Intifada—endangering their own lives as they distributed food to besieged villages, preventing with their bodies

5. A Mizraḥi police officer oversees an anti-occupation protest in Jerusalem led by Women in Black. Members of the Ecumenical Accompaniment Programme in Palestine and Israel demonstrate alongside them. EAPPI.

the uprooting of olive trees, or exposing themselves to physical and verbal violence from right-wing Israelis as they marched to crown Jerusalem with peace. Ashkenazi feminists have demonstrated more often than men; because of the combination of their gender and class privilege, it is less likely that the IDF soldiers on active duty policing the West Bank, most of whom are Mizraḥim, would attack them to stop the demonstrations (Keshet 2006). Still, Ashkenazi feminists ignored the plight of their disenfranchised Mizraḥi neighbors; rather, they could be found just across the street, in favor of what Swirsky describes as "TV crews from all over the world" who documented their "street theatre" protests against the occupation. These photographed well for the media in search of simplistic Palestine-Israel binarisms. Concurrently, as Swirsky aptly put it, these feminists continued to wonder why their groups remained "largely invisible to the Israeli public" (2002, 238).[3]

The Ashkenazi Left took for granted the loyalty of the Mizraḥim to the state. Indeed, Mizraḥim continued to vote for the Right regardless of which party was in power. Similarly, Ashkenazi feminist scholarship and activism continued to ignore these class and race divisions within Israel (Lavie 2010).

Aḥoti dealt with practical issues plaguing the Mizraḥi majority: access to due process, the inalienable rights of Mizraḥi parents to their children, personal and communal safety, health, education, jobs, housing (see Tzimuki 1999). We were not mainstream. The mainstream thought of Knafoland as a freak show despite pouring its charity onto the mothers. The Knafoland mothers' figurations of agency, however, catered to their own desires to belong to Israel's mainstream. In so doing, the mothers short-circuited their own protest, making the agency of identity politics impossible.

Protesting and Belonging: An Argument in Six Parts

Because the Israeli regime always already has a web of bureaucratic entanglements to preempt civil disobedience, the Knafo protest, like all Mizraḥi protests, was doomed to fail. Scholarly literature on protest movements often cites how the movements' transformational effects can remain ambiguous, delayed, ephemeral, contradictory, and difficult to trace for extended periods of time. Eventually, however, hoped-for social change comes about (see Bevington and Dixon 2005; Epstein 1991; Giddens 1985; Tilly 2004). But this chapter discusses why Mizraḥi social protest movements do not advance the Mizraḥi cause as these scholars would optimistically assume. In the case of the Knafo protest, any instance of success that mothers may have had was illusory. They did not obtain any policy changes they sought, and throughout the following years, their day-to-day realities have worsened. In fact, many draconian additions to Ḥok HaHesderim since the 2003 amendment have further cut their NSB monetary support, and postprotest public hostility toward Mizraḥi single mothers actually increased.

I explicate the reasons behind the failure of Mizraḥi protest movements and the ways I choose to ethnograph it through a six-part processual argument. It starts with Knafoland as a case study springing forth from Israel's majority citizenry, located at the crux of the binary Israel-Palestine conflict. Nevertheless, this same majority is completely ignored in any international peace talks (Lavie 2011a). I then use Knafoland as a springboard for a general discussion on bureaucracy as both a system of torture and a tool of divine control over the citizenry in a self-defined, ethnoreligious state.[4] The State of Israel defines itself as a Jewish State and a homeland for all world Jewry (see Israel Ministry of Foreign Affairs 2008)—the "chosen land" (Lustick 1988; Schweid 1985) for the "chosen people" (Frank 1993; Novak 1995). The State of Israel is divine, and government bureaus are its sacred pilgrimage sites. Also divine is the indeterminacy of success the mothers can expect to achieve in any bureaucratic encounter. The foundational typecasting of the mother by her gender and race weaves the Divinity of the State and the Divinity of Chance together as it effects the logic of bureaucratic torture. Mizraḥi single mothers have no recourse but to submit themselves to this torture that makes the agency immanent in identity politics impossible to enact.[5]

As I attempt to capture and theorize the somatics of situations with minimal possibility for agency, I encounter the limitations of the U.S.-UK anthropological formula for articles and monographs espoused by major journals and scholarly presses (Boskovic 2008, 2). I then argue for both the "World Anthropologies" methodological toolkit (Narotzky 2006, 143; Ribeiro 2006, 364) as well as multiple genres of testimony (McClaurin 2001, 61; Smith and Watson 2011) to accurately capture the elusiveness of bureaucratic torture.

A Primer: Notes on Religion and Secularity in the Homeland of the Jews

Before turning to the argument itself, it is helpful to briefly shed light on the Divinity of the Jewish State. I do so through exploring the lesser-known Ashkenazi-Mizraḥi rift via the more visible intra-Jewish rift between "Orthodox," or strictly observant Jews, and "secular" Jews in the State of Israel. I put these terms in quote marks to denote their common usage in news media.

On 13 December 2011, *Haaretz*, the understated broadsheet read mainly by the Ashkenazi elite, exhorted: "Like Iran and Afghanistan—The Mark of Israel on the International Index on Freedom of Religion—Zero" (Bar Zohar 2011). This headline is in striking contrast to how the State of Israel presents itself as a phoenix of U.S.-European modernity in the middle of the Muslim, Arab World. How does a U.S.-European democracy not have freedom of religion built into its nationalism?

Modern, metropolitan nationalism is connected to secularity, liberty, and equality (Van Der Veer 1996, 7). If this nationalism is enacted by a colonial power, the colonialist legitimates its rule "under the rubric of progress and rationality" (Van Der Veer 1996, 3). Is modern colonialist rule, therefore, by definition, secular rule? Gauri Viswanathan argues that modern colonialist nationalism assumes secularity by compacting "aspirations, goals, and agendas," through a process of "selection and filtering that irons out the contradictions embedded in the construction of national identity from the fragments of religious, racial, cultural, and other forms of self-identification" (1996). Sabah Mahmood concurs, arguing that it is not possible to separate an assumption of secularism from the workings of modern, colonialist power on Europe's Others (2010).

Ashkenazi Zionism was a colonialist movement. Its goal was to create a secular democracy, defined, however, as a Jewish democracy—where Jews are favored as citizens in a land carved from British-Mandated Palestine in 1948. Israel's claims to be a modern, secular, and Jewish democracy may seem incongruous to an outside observer. But written into the laws of the land are regulations based on halakha, the collective body of Jewish religious laws: no public transportation runs from Friday at dusk until Saturday after three stars are in the sky (i.e., Shabbat observance);[6] businesses cannot obtain a kosher license if they operate on Shabbat;[7] Jews cannot marry non-Jews inside the State of Israel. And while the practice is not technically written into civil law, almost all Israeli Jewish boys undergo the religious ceremony of circumcision at eight days of age, performed by a licensed mohel (circumciser, Hebrew), sacramentally trained, but not medically educated. Mohel circumcision has transcended the halakha to become the badge of Jewish male citizenship. Every city and town in Israel has a rabbinical council that regulates the above and more. Rabbinical court decrees regulate many aspects of Jewish family law.[8]

Hussein Agrama's theoretical framework of the secular normativity of the modern postcolonial nation-state, using Egypt as a case study, might serve as a useful comparison to Israel's secular claim. He asks where one can "draw the line between religion and politics (*and a presupposition that there is a line to be drawn*) [emphasis mine]. The identifiable stakes [of secular state sovereignty] are the rights, freedoms, and virtues that have become historically identified with liberalism, such as legal equality, freedom of belief and expression, and tolerance, as well as the possibilities and justifications for peace and war" (Agrama 2010, 501; see Agrama 2012, 28). Egypt's blurred lines between the shari'a, the Muslim parallel to halakha, and the state's secular rule are analogous to Israel's, with near zero tolerance for religion other than the state's sanctioned religion (Bar Zohar 2011). But, while Egypt's law of the land is based on the shari'a, Egypt does not boast its status as *the* Muslim state" or "Homeland of the Muslims." Nevertheless, like Egypt, Israel is an instance of authoritarian democracy (see Pratt 2007). In both, there is an incongruence between secularism's ideals—liberty, equality, and religious neutrality—and the impossibility of a democracy based upon a religious foundation.[9]

The ruling Ashkenazi minority, including the intelligentsia, would like to portray Israeli society and state as a democracy that is rational, secular, and egalitarian, yet Jewish-centric. Because this minority controls Israel's public image, the state enjoys a liberal portrayal on the international stage. State PR officials, along with Ashkenazi feminists and intelligentsia, encourage international media coverage of the secular elite's skirmishes with the exotic ultra-Orthodox minority. Such stories bolster the enlightened Jewish State's commitment to progressive secularity in the face of fundamentalist religious primitivity. Articles about topics like the ultra-Orthodox Jewish demand for women to sit at the rear of buses—and featuring the Ashkenazi feminist protests against the practice—appear in publications with well-heeled readers, such as *Haaretz* and the *New York Times*. Despite the attention-grabbing headlines, hostilities between Israel's secular and ultra-Orthodox Jews represent a clash between minority groups.[10]

Left out of the limelight are the majority of Israel's Jews, who are neither secular nor Orthodox. They are the *masortim* (traditional, Hebrew plural masculine) or *shomrei masoret* (keepers of the tradition, Hebrew plural). Masortim view themselves as neither strictly observant, nor absolutely secular. They do not adhere to strict halakha. Rather, they cherry-pick the Jewish customs that they conceive of as vital to tracing a direct lineage to the intergenerational preservation of the Jews as a people, a nation. Many keep partially kosher and avoid either pork or seafood or both. Some light candles before Shabbat dinner and perform the kiddush (blessing of the Shabbat wine), but still use electrical lights and appliances, a taboo for the Orthodox. Masortim may drive cars on Shabbat, but only to nonwork events, unless there is a pressing deadline they need to meet on Sunday. They attend synagogue services on High Holidays and whenever it is convenient. Most masorti men do not wear a *kippah* (Hebrew term for yarmulke, Yiddish). Married masorti women do not cover their hair. Israeli masortim are not organized and should not be confused with the Masorti Movement—a synonym for organized Conservative Judaism, a major branch of Judaism in North America and Western Europe. The majority of masortim, like the majority of Israeli Jews, are Mizrahi. The forced secularization of their parents in the 1950s was only partially successful (see Yadgar 2010).

According to the Israeli Central Bureau of Statistics (Romanov et al. 2011), the population breakdown of Israel's Jews is: 44 percent secular, 27 percent masorti, and 29 percent religiously observant, subdivided into 21 percent Orthodox and 8 percent ultra-Orthodox. MeMizraḥ Shemesh (Eastern Sun, Hebrew), a grassroots NGO training cadres of young Mizrahi leaders with roots in Israel's barrios, has statistics showing that 40 percent of all Israeli Jews identify as masorti, and the majority of them are Mizrahim.[11] My qualitative research seems to corroborate the MeMizraḥ Shemesh figure of masortim at 40 percent. My research also estimates around 30 percent secular and 20 percent Orthodox. Ultra-Orthodox are 10 percent of the Jewish population. The most extreme ultra-Orthodox groups—anti-Zionist and Ashkenazi—are less than 1 percent. One such a denomination is Neturei Karta, which has a representative in the Palestine National Council and has even met with and supported Mahmoud Ahmadinejad's hate speeches against the State of Israel. Such groups have always been fashionable for anti-Zionist scholars to tout, with the media following suit. Neturei Karta may be a reification of the complete, utopian disjuncture between the ideology and practice of Judaism and that of Zionism and the Israeli state (see, for example, Boyarin and Boyarin 1993). Most Israeli Jews view these groups as extraterrestrial. In spite of their divisions, secular, masorti, and Orthodox Jews all agree on their loathing of ultra-Orthodox Jews' legal right to ignore the IDF draft. Their post-high school Torah studies fulfill their civic duty to fight for the nation.

How can Israel's Central Bureau of Statistics claim that 44 percent of Israel's Jews are secular while MeMizraḥ Shemesh claims that 40 percent are masorti? The great disparity between these figures cannot be bridged. Only one can be correct. My own research correlates with the MeMizraḥ Shemesh figures. In fitting with how the state portrays itself, it might be fair to ask if the Bureau of Statistics numbers are yet another way to push forward the discord between secular and ultra-Orthodox, obscuring the Ashkenazi-Mizraḥi rift.

This primer is not meant to encompass all of the scholarship on the rift between Orthodox and secular Jews (see, for example, Atzmon 2011; Leibman and Katz 1997; Sobel and Beit-Hallahmi 1991; Yadgar 2011). Rather, it pulls in enough information on the subject to give proper contextualization to the six-part argument that springs forth from the Divinity of the Jewish State of Israel.

The Palestine-Israel Binary

The global public typically knows about intra-Jewish strife through the binary of ultra-Orthodox Jews versus the secular minority. On the international media scene, however, these stories are reduced to interesting cultural anecdotes, rather than full-fledged news. This is the opposite of how the international media depicts stories about either the Jewish State versus Arab neighboring states that are its enemies, or the Palestinian-Israeli conflict. These latter two dominate any news coming out of Israel for international consumption. News presenters and politicians are able to greatly influence Israel's public portrayal by reducing the daily lives of Israeli citizens to fit neatly into the Palestine-Israel or Muslim World-Jewish State binaries. In the case of Palestine, the State of Israel is the dominant side of the binary.

Policy change is unlikely unless parties outside the binary become involved. In the past, pressure from the international community has been able to coerce the Israeli regime to amend some of its policies, so getting international attention remains the best way for a protest movement to achieve any positive change. Much of the Israeli media, however, is controlled by the Ashkenazi elite (Horev 2007). Much of the U.S.-European media is controlled by the pro-Israel lobby (Lavie 2011b; Mearsheimer and Walt 2007). They work in concert to cover the Israel-Palestine binary to the exclusion of other newsworthy stories, preventing any news item about intra-Jewish racism from escaping into the worldwide media stage.

Inside Israel, the Hebrew media does narrate stories such as the Knafo protest—but only as isolated oddities. These stories never cohere into a statement about structural intra-Jewish apartheid (see Madmoni-Gerber 2009).[12] The international media largely ignores these stories, and thus, Israel's Mizraḥi majority.

The Ashkenazi Minority Mainstream

Sami Shalom Chetrit, a CUNY professor and veteran-in-exile of the Mizraḥi struggle, told the Hebrew press about his thoughts on Vicky Knafo:

> I woke up in the morning and heard Vicky on the radio, panting . . . I was moved . . . A couple of hours later I turned on the TV and saw her marching, but with a flag. I got my head back into bed right away. . . . this flag . . . got me paralyzed . . . The mental dependency of these people on the state is unyielding. . . . The tragedy of the desire to belong. Don't forget me, don't neglect me, and at the same time, I want to protest as well. You can't do both. It's schizophrenic. (Chetrit, quoted in Salʿi 2003)

Chetrit points at the second reason for the failure of Mizraḥi protests—the desire of Mizraḥim to belong to Israel's mainstream (Lavie 2011b). This is exactly why Vicky wrapped herself in the flag. Indeed, it worked. The Israeli public gushed at the mothers and donated tents, food, toys, books, second-hand clothes, professional services, and even money. But the mothers and their supporters from all sectors of Israeli Jewish society could not translate this pandering into any lasting systemic change.

Mizraḥi social protest movements are not typical minority resistance movements. Mizraḥim are a majoritarian group that cannot exercise majoritarian rights. The ruling Ashkenazi minority has racialized and disenfranchised Israel's demographic majority as it largely defines Israel's mainstream (Bitton 2011; Blachman 2005; Ducker 2005; Gamlieli 1965; Giladi 1990; Hertzog 1999; Horev 2007; Lavie 1992, 2006a, 2011a, 2011b; Madmoni-Gerber 2009; Malka 1998; Shahar 1988; Shenhav and Yonah 2008; Shiran 1991; Shohat 1988, 2001; Stoler-Liss 1998; Yitzhaki 2003; Zarini 2004). A racialized, minoritized majority, Mizraḥim strive to enter the Ashkenazi mainstream to gain improved housing, schools, job opportunities, and health care (Lavie 2011b). In the past, the mainstream forced Mizraḥim to shed anything Arab because the Ashkenazi regime conceived their Arabness as dangerously primitive (Lavie 1992; Shohat 2001) and forced them to secularize. Most modern-day Mizraḥim gladly let go of their Mizraḥi heritage—if previous generations have left them with any. They seek to become second-rate Israelis, equating their parents' involuntary shedding of Arab language and heritage to the willful shedding of *Yiddishkeit* (Eastern European shtetl Jewish way of life, Yiddish) by Ashkenazim. The goal of these Mizraḥim is to achieve the Ashkenazi "Israeliness"—a dehistoricized provincial simulacrum of Euro-American white popular culture.

Ashkenazi Israeli intellectuals commonly equate "Israeliness" with what they conceive as "enlightened Israeli secular culture." But they are able to overlook the fact that Judaism is their access to Israeli citizenship in a state that defines itself as a homeland to "the Jewish Nation." They do not recognize masortim as having mainstream "Israeliness." Most Mizraḥim, however, view a departure from the Orthodoxy of their parents and grandparents to become masorti as a route to enter the Israeli mainstream. As Mizraḥi masortim enter the mainstream, Ashkenazim lament the erasure of their "enlightened Israeli secular culture."[13] Ironically, some Ashkenazi intellectuals are attempting to bridge the gap between their secularity and their Jewish citizenship by reacquainting themselves with Jewish traditions. They study Scripture to revive what they conceive of as Jewish spirituality. This secular Ashkenazi-centric trend of the last two decades has become a source of amusement for masortim and the Orthodox, not to mention the ultra-Orthodox.

These days, Mizraḥim who have made it into the mainstream self-censor discrimination and humiliation to become "brown-skinned gringos" (Gómez-Peña 1996, 8)—but without the historical Ashkenazi privilege. When a Mizraḥi becomes a "brown-skinned gringo," he or she undergoes *hishtaknezut* (Hebrew), or Ashkenazification, derived from the verb *le-hishtaknez* (to become an Ashkenazi, Hebrew). Ashkenazified Mizraḥim shed their ethnic markers, such as dress style, extended family commitments, accent, surnames, political views, and musical tastes as they attempt to move upward in socioeconomic class. Most notably, Mizraḥim deny the history of discrimination that they and their parents experienced in order to fit into the Ashkenazi middle-class mainstream, that is, to embody "Israeliness." Thus, a Mizraḥi undergoing Askhenazification casts away his or her Middle Eastern past in favor of a united Jewish Israeli front. It is interesting to note that "to Ashkenazify" is a Hebrew word in common usage, but there is no analogue for becoming a Mizraḥi.

Mizraḥi activists refer to mainstream Mizraḥi leaders who deny, and thus refuse to hear about, intra-Jewish race relations as suffering from "Mizraḥi kapo syndrome" (see Ortner 1995, 175). Kapos were Jewish concentration camp prisoners whom the Nazis employed as brutal low-level camp managers in return for subsistence-level privileges. For the sake of intra-Jewish unity, the raison d'être of the Jewish State's survival in Palestine, the Ashkenazi mainstream and its Mizraḥi kapos judge anyone speaking about intra-Jewish race relations guilty of *le-hitbakhyen* (whining and being a crybaby, Hebrew). The term *le-hitbakhyen* is usually deployed by those articulating what is known as "the Israeli discourse of pluralist enlightenment" as part of its "Israeli (i.e., Ashkenazi) universalism vs. Mizraḥi ethnic particularism" analysis of Israeli society. Good examples for the evocation of this verb are in the context of affairs such as the kidnapping of Mizraḥi babies from the 1930s to the early 1970s and their subsequent selling for adoption to Ashkenazim (see Madmoni-Gerber 2009; Zeid 2001), or the Ringworm Children Affair (see Belhassan and Hemias 2004; Topol 2005), when about 150,000 Mizraḥi children, mainly of North African origin, were irradiated with high-dose X-rays without their parents' consent or knowledge. Members of Israel's Mizraḥi majority find it next to impossible to present a case for racial discrimination in court (Bitton 2011). Their cases are almost always disarmed and stripped of legitimacy by accusations of le-hitbakhyen.

Bureaucratic Logic Denies Majoritarian Agency

State bureaucracy entraps Mizraḥi protesters in its lethal webs (Handelman 2004; Hertzog 1999; Marx 1976). Ilana Feldman's comprehensive study (2008) focuses on the bureaucracy that governed Gaza, Palestine, until 1967. She points out the junctures where the colonial regime's rules, regulations, and procedures grate against the population not recognizing the regime's legitimacy and sovereignty. I posit that this is where agency of Gaza's Palestinian majority can spark to resist colonial and postcolonial bureaucracy (Feldman 2008, 17, 320). The gap between the regime and the population it governs allows for this agency (15). Unlike the Gazans under Egyptian rule, Mizraḥim *do* have a "felt organic connection between government and population" (15). United with the Ashkenazim through the self-identification as "chosen people," Mizraḥim insist on protecting their Jewish refuge from the goyim. Thus, the Mizraḥim and Ashkenazim together have recast themselves as the unified last line of defense for the Jewish "chosen land," an ethno-religious state formation—Israel. The Mizraḥi majority therefore cannot exercise rights held even by legally recognized minorities such as North African Muslims in France (Scott 2007), Latinos in the United States (Anzaldúa 1987), even Palestinian citizens of Israel (Torstrick 2000).[14]

Any slight possibility of majoritarian agency is ruthlessly dominated by and edited through the logic of bureaucratic categories. Handelman (2004) posits a model of the logic underlying state bureaucratic ideology and operation. Bureaucratic logic in Handelman's model is monothetic (2004, 5–6, 19–38), or based on one classificatory criterion. He further argues that to understand the foundation of bureaucratic logic, one needs to dig into the processual ritual logic of Victor Turner (1969)—the religious logic that Foucault deploys to theorize his operational model for the modernist, rational Panopticon (Foucault 1977). This same ritual process mediates the interplay between obedient ethno-religious citizenship and chauvinistic ethno-religious nationhood, making them prone to institutional bureaucratic torture.[15] The interplay transcends the citizenship-nationhood conjuncture into "communitas" (Turner and Turner 1978). Handelman, therefore, returns to classificatory schemes that crystallize into a collective mind devoid of agency (Durkheim and Mauss 1963, 65). These schemes cohere into the social organism that functions on the constrictive societal grid of organic and mechanic solidarity (Durkheim 1961), with no time or space for agency.

The state bureaucracy continuously adjusts its screws to impede the maneuvers of resistive identity politics. Thus, Mizraḥi social movements tend to be short-lived and lead to no lasting change.[16]

The regime uses the mirage of Mizraḥi and Ashkenazi Jewish unity to narrate how all Jews should fight on a single front so Israel—the little David—can survive surrounded by Arab goyim Goliaths. In reality, the regime uses this false unity to mask how it uses bureaucracy to crush, marginalize, contain, and buy out individuals or groups within social protest movements. Nevertheless, the regime does acknowledge protest movements—but only those that showcase "the chosen people's" national unity, devoid of race, class, or religious observance.[17] Movements that do not showcase this national unity are ignored. Eventually, all Mizraḥi movements become sucked into the Palestine-Israel binary and then disappear from the public sphere.

I participated in the Mizraḥi single mothers' movement as a single welfare mother, Aḥoti member, and ethnographer. A scholar of agency during my two decades at the University of California (Lavie 1990; Lavie and Swedenburg 1996a, 1996b), I searched for it (Abu-Lughod 1990; Mahmood 2001; Ortner 1995; Spivak 1988)[18] while stranded in Israel. I found none. This book, thus, cannot align itself with the U.S.-European progressive academic mold designated for the subaltern—even that of docility as a form of agency (Mahmood 2001). Rather, it describes how Israel's state bureaucracy denies Mizraḥi single mothers their agency. Since discursive articulations often spring forth from the enactment of agency, the mothers cannot transform bureaucratic pain into discourse. I therefore do not intend to preach "agency" just to show that anthropology is a politically engaged discipline. There are situations where agency is impossible.

Love Thy Country—Gender and Race Wrapped in the Flag

Mizraḥi protests, such as the Knafo march on Jerusalem, fail because Mizraḥi protesters cannot break the bond connecting their love for the Jewish State with the somatic pain inflicted upon them by the state's bureaucracy. Unlike the unity of all Jews as the "chosen people,"[19] Israeli bureaucratic logic *does* differentiate between Mizraḥim and Ashkenazim when it selects victims. Women who are middle- to upper-middle-class and higher Ashkenazim have financial and social resources that allow them to circumvent bureaucratic entanglements (Danet 1989). Bureaucratic logic's main classificatory criterion is a calcified amalgamation of gender and race—"GendeRace." I use the neologism "GendeRace" here as a practical solution, factoring in the complicated relationship between the analytical categories of "gender" and "race."[20] GendeRace also connotes the bizarre amalgamation of gender and race in a nation-state that unifies this amalgamation into a finite classificatory category. At the same time, the state presents itself as a Jewish democracy, offering equal, deracinated, and ungendered citizenship to all.

Gender and race are parts of Renato Rosaldo's model of mobile culture as a "busy intersection" (1989, 17). Jasbir Puar (2005, 121–22) argues that the intersectionality model has become too structured and ought to be treated as a nomadic assemblage. In contrast with both, a Mizraḥi single mother marching on Jerusalem, wrapped in the flag, reifies "the intersection" (see Collins 1990; Combahee River Collective 1983; Crenshaw 1991; Harrison 1997)[21] as the set of phenomena immanent in the GendeRace essence. Even though she moves through time and space, she can only move through the time and space allotted by the regime. Because she loves her Jewish homeland and fears that genuine resistance will weaken her homeland's stand against the goyim, she can enact only a figurative simulacrum of resistance. The regime merely lays its web in wait for her to entangle herself.

I am taking Diana Fuss's "risk of essence" (1989, 1; Lavie and Swedenburg 1996a, 164) despite the tendency in contemporary scholarship to avoid foundational analysis. Fuss argues that "too often, constructivists presume that the category of the social automatically escapes essentialism" (Fuss 1989, 6; Lavie and Swedenburg 1996a, 164). Michalis Bartsidis (2011) states that "the social is always already a process of becoming a metaphysical essence." Ted Swedenburg and I argue that one learns to culturally construct race and gender differences as one simultaneously naturalizes them into essences (Lavie and Swedenburg 1996a). Nature itself is a calcified cultural construction (Walter Benjamin, in Buck-Morss 1989, 161, 422). When gender and race become part of the national cohesive grand narrative, they go through a process of essentialization-naturalization (see Taussig 1993; Lavie and Swedenburg 1996a, 165). Amalgamated, they calcify into a finite category that assumes a naturalized fixity of social structure and organization (Lavie and Swedenburg 1996a, 164; see Firth 1961, 1972, 236–40; see Handelman 1990, 78). Among Israeli Jews, race and class are in complete correspondence (Shenhav and Yonah 2008; Yitzhaki 2003). No Israeli scholar writing in Hebrew would dispute the fact that the Mizraḥi majority is comprised mainly of the lower middle class and down, while the Ashkenazi minority is largely middle class and up. There is a translation block between the Hebrew and English with regard to Mizraḥi scholarship and activism. Many of the materials on the Israeli fusion of race and class are available to the Hebrew reader, but are not translated into English (see Lavie 2006b).

GendeRace, thus, does not obscure the mechanisms of Israeli intra-Jewish class discrimination. The Ashkenazi-Mizraḥi distinction is a gendered and racialized formation always already including class. It is resilient enough to withstand historical challenges such as the upward mobility of Mizraḥim after 1967, when West Bank and Gaza Palestinians replaced them as bluecollar laborers, and the mass immigration of Ashkenazim from the former Soviet Union in the early 1990s (Lavie 2011a). One might argue that even though 1990s post-Soviet immigrants to Israel are classified as Ashkenazim, they still fall prey to bureaucratic torture. But, from the 1990s on, the lobby of Russian Knesset members has continued to argue that Holocaust survivors who do not enjoy German reparation money,[22] or those who fought against the Nazis in World War II—that is, Ashkenazi post-Soviet citizens from the European part of the former USSR—deserve preferential treatment. The lobby thus cuts through bureaucratic red tape for its European Jewish constituency. Russian Knesset members rarely extend their support to immigrants from the Asian parts of the former USSR, who are considered Mizraḥim (Ben Yefet and Maduel 2011).

It is this GendeRace essence that racializes the state's Mizraḥi Jewish demographic majority into a disenfranchised minority. Moreover, the Israeli regime normalizes GendeRace into transparency. The regime uses the "chosen people/chosen land" divine decree to enact and simultaneously deny this transparent GendeRace essence. Bureaucracy devoid of agency amalgamates the intersectional, constructionist concepts of gender and race, and then calcifies them into a primordial truism that prohibits identity politics.

Even though a Mizrahi single mother moves through time and space, she can only move through the time and space allotted by the regime. The success she finds as she moves through bureaucratic time-space is dependent upon the Divinity of Chance, the serendipity overseeing any bureaucratic encounter. If she accomplishes any of her goals at a bureau, it is akin to a miracle. The mother does not know, and has no way of knowing, which actions correlate with success or failure.

———

At dusk, she kissed the mezuzah, the door-mounted frame containing the *Shmaʿ*, the ultimate kernel of Jewish prayers: "Hear, O Israel, the LORD our G-d, the LORD is One." For good luck. She slammed the door shut and waited for the bus. Her hand in her pocket clutched the amulet the neighborhood's rabbi prepared for good luck (and for a modest charge). Luck so the bus to the NSB would arrive on time. Luck so her journey to pick up her income assurance check would be fruitful. In the bus, she joined other barrio mothers on pilgrimage to the NSB. The chi-chi side of town.

At the end of their ride, they poured out to begin their slow trek through the lines. She took a number, praying for any combination of *khamsa* (the number five in Arabic), for the five-fingered talisman. That, or a derivation of *ḥai* (the number eighteen and the word *alive* in Hebrew).[23] For good luck. Then she stood. Waited. Took a few steps forward. Waited. Waited. Stepped. Waited. Was ordered to go into another line. Waited. Another line. Another. To calm herself, she dug through her bag for her *tehillim* (psalms, Hebrew), wrapped in a sandwich bag for protection. For good luck. With enough, she would be rewarded with a seat in front of the caseworker's office to rest her back. With even more luck, she may even sit before a female caseworker who would not ask for sexual favors. At last, she walked into the office, kissing the mezuzah on the doorpost. But her pilgrimage did not end.

"No 'Y,'" said the clerk, pointing to a spot on the printed record. "There is a 'B.' A mistake. Go to the unemployment bureau and get the 'Y.' Then return."

6. The building that houses the National Security Bureau in Tel Aviv at the intersection of Yitzhak Sadeh and HaMasger Avenues. Yitzhak Sadeh Avenue bisects all of Tel Aviv and is the unofficial separating line between White City and Black City. Esti Tsal, 2013.

Her fingers tightened around her amulet. Half of her listened to the clerk, and the other half chanted *Shmaʿ Israel, Hear O Israel, Shmaʿ Israel* in her head.

"Get a low line number there and come back here before 4:00 p.m. tomorrow. With luck, you will see me again."

Not enough luck to evade *etsbaʿ Elokim*. The finger of G-d. With no allowance, her postdated checks for water, electricity, and rent would bounce. So after leaving the room, she began to pray: "Shmaʿ Israel, Hear, O Israel, the LORD our G-d, please deliver the allowance soon, before collection court sends me a summons to debtor's prison. Shmaʿ Israel. How can Jews do this to other Jews?"

Government bureaus are where the Divinity of Chance meets the Divinity of the State.

Why does she put up with this never-ending cycle of torture? The answer is her love for her Jewish homeland. She fears that genuine intersectional resistance will weaken her homeland's stand against the goyim. Thus, she can enact only a simulacrum of resistance.

A dark female form, wrapping herself in the flag, she is always already entrapped in the regime's bureaucratic web.[24]

World Anthropologies, Autoethnography, and the U.S.-UK Anthropology Journal Formula

The U.S.-UK anthropological journal formula and its "northern conventions of research, writing, and thinking about the world" (Gledhill 2005) has low tolerance for an ethnographer who doubles as an indigenous "key informant" that theorizes rather than just tells stories to "his" anthropologist. This formula also applies to book-length anthropological monographs published by scholarly presses. The anthropologist should not have near-complete overlap between her ethnographic experience and personal and communal biography, as I had for nearly a decade. I did not join Mizraḥi single mothers as a participant-observer. I was a welfare mama for real—my own informant (Lavie 2011a). Unlike the formula prescriptions for cultural studies-cum-feminist scholarship, I do not avoid the victim narrative. I was a victim and have no qualms about narrating my own victimhood and that of the other mothers.

One might point out U.S.-UK anthropology's diversity in forms of theoretical argumentation styles and contents, and in various genres of ethnographic writing. But this diversity, let alone an ethnographer having a near-complete overlap between her ethnographic experience and personal and communal biography, rarely appears in the top-tier U.S.-UK journals or scholarly presses. For example, despite her class privilege, Ruth Behar used herself as a "key informant" through creative writing about disenfranchised Latina women (Behar 1993). She was clearly an anthropologist coming from American elite–Ivy League universities, so she did not threaten her upper-middle-class colleagues. Even so, her more creative body of writing rarely appears in top-tier anthropology journals such as *American Anthropologist, American Ethnologist, Current Anthropology, Cultural Anthropology*, or the *Journal of the Royal Anthropological Institute*.[25] Autoethnographer Zora Neale Hurston never published her story of being an independent scholar living in dire poverty in top journals or academic presses.[26] She died virtually abandoned and destitute at age sixty-nine. How ironic and tragic that she achieved acclaim for works such as *Their Eyes Were Watching God* (1937) only years after her death. Gloria Anzaldúa died at age sixty-two from lack of adequate medical care. Her monumental autoethnography, *Borderlands/La Frontera* (1987) was published by Aunt Lute, a small underfunded feminist press, because larger university presses deemed it incomprehensible. The University of California posthumously bestowed upon her a long-deserved PhD.[27]

The ethnographic writing I employ in this book is that of World Anthropologies (Boskovic 2008; Gledhill 2005; Ribeiro 2005; Ribeiro and Escobar 2006). The rigid U.S.-UK formula standardizes the explication of the stuff of life. World Anthropologies allows for a range of nonstandardized arguments illuminated and interconnected from within their "epistemic murk" (Taussig 1986). Perhaps the narration of these intrinsic interconnections from within the "murk" is what leads to the stymieing of World Anthropologies essays and books during the anonymous review process of major U.S.-UK journals and scholarly presses (Bogopa 2010; Boskovic 2008). The World Anthropologies Network (WAN) Collective (2005), in fact, argues that the U.S.-Euro-centered decolonization of anthropology has actually led to further colonization of the discipline because it was mainly unidirectional. Theory was formulated and articulated in U.S.-European metropolitan universities, but the data came from postcolonial situations, either in the Third World or in "Third-Worlded" (Koptiuch 1991) Western metropolises (Ribeiro 2005; Ribeiro and Escobar 2006; Reuter 2005; Koizumi 2005; Lavie 2006c; San Juan 2002; WAN 2005; see Harrison 2008, 11).[28]

Thus, U.S.-UK elite Ivy League anthropologists created a body of scholarship—one that superimposes itself upon other anthropologies, rather than dialogues with them (McClaurin 2001, 50–51, 59; Ribeiro 2006, 372–73; Ribeiro and Escobar 2006, 2–3; WAN Collective 2003, 266–67).[29] "'World Anthropologies' . . . calls for a reconceptualization of the relationships among anthropological communities. Monological [and unidirectional] anthropology needs to be replaced by . . . anthropology . . . [that] opens the way to a more creative and egalitarian environment" (Ribeiro 2006, 364). Further, "categories that shape local knowledges should be treated as part and parcel of a historically formed discursive framework during coflictive . . . times and spaces" (Narotzky 2006, 143). World Anthropologies calls for engagement with local categories of knowledge, not as data to be ethnographed in English-language metropolitans but as theory that refuses to adhere to a U.S.-UK "pretense of coherence" (Narotzky 2006, 143). Within the contemporary U.S.-UK anthropological framework, however, there is quite a bit of theoretical and ethnographic emphasis on the incoherence of culture. But much of this scholarship merely takes the concept of incoherence and plugs it back into the U.S.-UK formula (see, for example, Clifford and Marcus 1986; Fabian 1983; Fox 1991; Marcus and Fischer 1986; Navaro-Yashin 2009; Tedlock 1983).

Not only does this book refuse to preach the agency designated for the subaltern by the U.S.-UK formula; it also presents subaltern theorization and autoethnography as testimony (Mihesuah and Wilson 2004; Smith 1999). In the U.S.-UK formula, one moves an anthropological argument by sprinkling "voices from the field"—choice snippets from the fabric of the ethnographic materials—to substantiate the argument with authenticity. I refuse to reappropriate informant vignettes as I generalize my model for the GendeRace of divine bureaucratic torture.

Writing with Anger

The subaltern subject writing the U.S.-UK formula is expected to produce dispassionate scholarship. This book refuses to do this. On the contrary, I employ humor, irony—and, yes, anger—as literary devices to relay my ethnographic findings.

Thirty years ago, Audre Lorde wrote a classic essay, "The Uses of Anger: Women Responding to Racism" (Lorde 1984, 124–33), advocating for the articulation of raw anger in academic texts: "the anger of exclusion, of unquestioned privilege, of racial distortions, of silence, ill use, stereotyping, defensiveness, misnaming, betrayal and cooptation" (124). She then argued that anger in academic language should retain emotional power because it was "a liberating and strengthening act of clarification" (127). Finally, she discussed the multivocal orchestration of anger as text: "women of color in America have grown up within a symphony of anger, at being silenced, at being unchosen, at knowing that when we survive, it is in spite of a world that takes for granted our lack of humanness. . . . And I say *symphony* rather than *cacophony* because we have had to learn to orchestrate those furies" (129).

Lorde spelled out the reason academic audiences gave for resisting articulations of racialized-gendered anger: "It is very difficult to stand still and to listen to another woman's voice delineate an agony I [the Anglo audience] do not share, or one to which I myself have contributed" (1984, 128). Lorde wrote this three decades ago. In 2013, perhaps women-of-color scholars in North America might be able to express anger in their scholarly texts. But when similar scholarship comes from outside North America or Western Europe, the hegemonic gatekeepers label it "polemic," and therefore unfit to publish. Even though I am a feminist of color outside of North America and Western Europe, I still follow Lorde's guidelines as I write about the magical realism and horror of Israel's divine bureaucracy.

Capturing and Conveying Elusive Bureaucratic Torture

This book is not only a scholarly exploration of the interrelationships between bureaucracy and torture; it is also an experiment in various modes of ethnographic writing. To overcome the elusiveness of bureaucratic torture, this book must transgress the boundaries of scholarly language as it attempts to attain mimetic redemption from nondiscursive suffering.

I now have the time and space to reflect back on my nine years as a disenfranchised single mother who also had access to privileges, such as education and training in literary and rhetorical skills. How do I provide accurate discourse for my own somatic pain and the pain of the mothers who stood with me in line? What writing techniques can I employ? Writing up the somatic injuries of bureaucracy is elusive. Is language capable of capturing these injuries? Further, the documents and events that inflict the nondiscursive torture are in Hebrew, often articulated via bureaucratic code words and the slang used to cope with them. How can I translate these codes and concepts to an English-language reader? Pedantic, literal translation is inadequate to convey the whole gamut of sensory experience, including unspoken shades of meaning. Even with my privileges, I'm lost.

I could provide the reader with a word-for-word translation, relying on endnotes to explain the possibilities for the various shades of meaning. But then I would be stripping my text's ability to flow naturally, as the Hebrew original did. The literal translation would also remove the pain and anger from the mothers' voices to fit in with the less emotive Northern U.S.-UK model of academic scholarship. A literal translation would create a "scholarly construction . . . [lending itself to be] supported by a corporate institution which makes statements about the Orient, authorizing views of it, describing it, by teaching about it, settling it, ruling over it" (Edward Said, quoted in Smith 1999, 2).

Hebrew-to-English translation involves the interpretation of Hebrew code words that carry meaning and weight not apparent in dictionary definitions or from Wikipedia entries. These code words can take the form of either "bureaucratese" or plain terms, such as certain family and town names. I address this problem by using Clifford Geertz's "thick description" (Geertz 1973), a method of interpreting not only the act itself grounded in the meanings that stem out of sets of symbols. Rather, "thick description" goes deeper to explicate a whole system of symbols, so as to place a particular act within its larger societal context.

I did not employ "thick description" for social analysis as Geertz had intended. He thickly described his ethnographic "I have been there" of the Balinese cockfights from his home base at the University of Chicago. I wrote about welfare mothers because I was a welfare mother. During my nine years wedged between and among the cogs of Israel's bureaucratic machine, the only home base I had was my own body. I use "thick description" purely as a tool for translation to avoid Geertz's colonialist detritus (Lavie 2006c; Robinson 1995).[30] As I translated the Hebrew, I initially attempted to provide an interpretation of the codes within the culture itself, to explain the intrinsic meanings. I then tried to build conceptual and cultural bridges to provide an anchor for the English-language reader. I avoided literal translation with annotations, because that would strip the text of its everyday flow and colloquial embeddedness. Such a pedantic translation, while accurate philologically, would remove the pain and anger from the mothers' voices to fit in with the U.S.-UK model of dispassionate academic scholarship. Emily Apter states, "The translation zone defines the epistemological interstices of politics, poetics, logic, cybernetics, linguistics, genetics, media, and environment; its locomotion characterizes both psychic transference and the technology of information transfer" (2006, 6). Sanford Budick and Wolfgang Iser remark, "A translation is a species of extended metaphorical equivalent in another language of an 'original text'" (1996, 207), and add, "Quite extraordinary feats of translation are necessary to disentangle a given theoretical formulation from its linguistic and cultural roots, assuming anyone should wish to do that. In fact, it may be impossible to do it" (211). The principles of Apter, Budick, and Iser guided me in my translations. For example, when I translated the words of the single mothers from Mizraḥi ghettos and barrios, the English resembled the fast-paced staccato rhythm of the inner city.

In chapter 5, I include "thickly described" interpretations to accompany Hebrew-to-English translations, divided by horizontal lines. But "thick description" alone cannot make nondiscursive pain into discourse. I still grope for words that emulate within you, the reader, the tactile discomfort experienced by the mothers. In my attempt to overcome the impediments to writing up bureaucratic torture, I employ three takes in sequence, each take employing and integrating different genres of writing. Take 1 presents a general model of the interrelationships between bureaucracy and torture. As I do so, I explicate the conundrum of a deracinated, ethno-religious "chosen people" who colonize their "chosen land." In Take 2, I write with the so-called scientific objective gaze that includes a structured distance between actual women's voices and the scholarly writing process that reduces them to concepts to be evaluated and peer-reviewed (Strathern 1987; see Lavie 1990, 34–38). In these first two writing modes, I purposely avoid cutting and pasting "voices from the field" into the theory as nodal "I have been there" points of proof. Academic press peer-reviewers expect ethnographies to have these voices sprinkled in as grounds for the production of theory, so vital to being hired, quoted, and promoted in the university system. I hope to avoid appropriating these women's lives and words to glorify my theoretical model of bureaucratic torture. But, as much as I wish to abdicate my ethnographic authority over this text, I cannot escape it.

Only in Take 3 do the "voices from the field"—voices from my homeland (Lavie and Swedenburg 1996b)—appear, so as not to reappropriate them for theory's sake (Handelman 2016). Here, I present the diary I kept during the Knafo movement. Take 3 follows Lorde's guidelines. The diary is a multigenre subaltern autoethnography—a collage of handwritten descriptions and dialogue, printouts of official documents and emails, newspaper clippings, classic quotes from feminist-of-color theory, poetry, and even Kabalistic curses.

Joan Scott (1991, 794) posits that experience is always already in transformation into discourse, making it representational. Nigel Thrift (2008, 1–26), on the other hand, discusses everyday experiences that do not lend themselves to representation. While Scott's notion of experience-turned-discourse is grounded in vectors of difference, such as race or gender, Thrift discusses nonrepresentational embodiment without delving into such vectors. Sherri Ortner (1995, 188) is in agreement with Scott about the relationship between discourse and its representation in text. Ortner thus suggests that conventional ethnography suffices. The ethnographic data in Take 3 point at nondiscursive phenomena that must be represented by multiple nonconventional modes of narrative in order to be made graspable. In Take 3, these narrative fragments appear nonchronologically and with purposeful repetitions and overlaps. My hope is to create a textual contrapunct (Bakhtin 1981; see McLean 2004, 18) where seemingly cacophonic melodies of

7. Pisgat Ze'ev (The Wolf's Peak, Hebrew), one of Israel's largest neighborhoods, located in North Jerusalem, deep into the West Bank. It was built on Palestinian lands expropriated by Israel after 1967 and was annexed to the Jerusalem municipality to create a Jewish residential continuum from the West Bank to the old pre-1967 center of West Jerusalem. Most of its residents are Mizraḥim. In the background is a Palestinian village. Esti Tsal, 2013.

experience best analyze the historicity and workings of Israel's bureaucratic system (see Scott 1991, 779).

I use each of these three takes until it collapses from an inability to convey the nondiscursive immediacy, confinement, and totalism of bureaucracy as divine experience. By using multiple and different genres of writing, I hope to evoke the constant tension that forces Mizraḥi single mothers to bracket their lives so that they don't disrupt the ruthless phantasmagoria of the "chosen people in the chosen land."

I want you, my reader, not only to comprehend the text. I want you to survive it.

CHAPTER 3

Take 1

The GendeRace Essence of Bureaucratic Torture

Israel is not the only nation-state that prioritizes its neoliberal agenda over its disappearing middle class. Single mothers of color and their children are in the vanguard of the losing side in the globalization battle, be it in Israel or elsewhere. Social work practice, policy, and research focus primarily on the circumstances that lead to single mothers' reliance on welfare, the policies that maintain their disenfranchisement, and the possible actions to break them out of the poverty cycle. This is the case from both functionalist and political-economic modes of analysis. It is not my intention to analyze Israel's welfare bureaucracy as either a Marxian or functionalist case study to illustrate the neoliberal collapse of the welfare state.

This chapter examines the role of bureaucracy as an inflictor of pain on welfare mothers. Scholarship rarely reifies bureaucracy as a system of torture. Rare and limited in scope as well is the ethnographic literature about single mothers outside North America and Western Europe (Carey 1993; Kingfisher and Goldsmith 2001; Lockhart 2008; Parmar and Rohner 2005; see McClaurin 1998). This chapter analyzes the welfare encounter as a "ritual in its own right" (Handelman 2005). It conceives single mothers' repeated journeys through long lines at bureaus as divine peregrinations with their own cosmological order, conjoining the divinity of Israel, the ethnoreligious Jewish State, and the Divinity of Chance, the serendipity that governs whether the divine authority of the bureaucrat grants them the ability to accomplish each of their daily goals.

Underneath the Knafo protest is the bureaucracy whose role is to assist impoverished Mizraḥi single mothers meet daily needs. Don Handelman

(2004) posits a model of the logic underlying the state's bureaucratic ideology and operation. He argues that bureaucracy's categories are liminal time-spaces governed by the same singular logic that governs ritual processes (Handelman 2004, 5–6, 19–38, 201–7; 2005). His ethnographic data are drawn from his lifelong research on Israeli bureaucracy and the national ceremonies that Israeli society designs and performs to enact the Israeli state.

Ilana Feldman's 2008 study of the pre-1967 Egyptian bureaucracy in Palestinian Gaza offers a secular, political-economic portrayal. Despite Feldman's departure from Handelman's ritual analysis, both argue that bureaucracy is a repetitive, authoritarian discourse of "belief in it for itself" (Feldman 2008, 15–16). Feldman relies on the rational secularity of Weber (311–12) and Foucault (303–4). Moreover, she maintains that Palestinians have not abdicated their agency because they understand that the Egyptians who govern their daily lives through bureaucratic procedures are an occupying force. Unlike Feldman, Handelman challenges Max Weber's model of rational, secular bureaucracy that assumes a transparency of reason allowing for the participants in the bureaucracy to assume a set of causality relationships that will almost always be true. In Handelman's model, participants cannot make assumptions when dealing with bureaucratic logic. Bureaucracy is a labyrinthine world the outsider cannot comprehend without specialized insider knowledge of the rules. Categories change. Rules change. The application of rules to categories also changes. A world unto itself. Arbitrary (Handelman, pers. comm.). Thus, my reading of Handelman's model of bureaucracy is as a divine cosmological order (Handelman 2004, 27; see Handelman 1990, 78, 220). He rules out the possibility of citizens' agency against the bureaucracy that governs their daily lives. Israeli bureaucrats and their clients cling to bureaucracy—the State of Israel's unifying Jewish national cult. They must cooperate against the surrounding enemy Arab goyim—against any goyim, for that matter. And despite their differences, both Handelman and Feldman do not address bureaucracy's gendered and racialized formations.[1]

My approach springs forth from Handelman's even though he does not focus on the differentiation between Ashkenazim and Mizraḥim, as I do. Also, Handelman conceives of bureaucracy as a performative discourse, whereas this chapter explicates bureaucratic torture as a *pre*-discursive set of phenomena. Therefore, this chapter offers my own subaltern read of scholarship on pre-discursive phenomenology and how it dialogues with discursive structures at the crux of the interplay between symbols, meanings, and actions.[2] Nevertheless, Handelman's bureaucratic model is highly applicable to my own Mizraḥi ethnography.

Classificatory Schemes of Bureaucratic Logic

Handelman argues that studying bureaucratic logic is not about studying bureaucratic institutions. It is about studying resilient schemes of classification, each scheme entailing its own singular logic. Handelman digs past poststructuralist flows and fluxes into the logic that lies underneath Foucault's Panopticon[3]—a Turnerian ritual process (Turner 1969) that mediates the interplay between citizenship and nationhood, transcending their conjuncture into communitas. The citizenship-nationhood ritual transcendence into communitas (Turner 1969) is what facilitates the ruthlessness of the state's reductionist panopticon.

Handelman calls for a return to Émile Durkheim and Marcel Mauss and their classic anthropological theory of classification based on logical reductionism of the "collective mind" (Durkheim and Mauss 1963, 65). These schemes of classification construct the social organism functioning on the Durkheimian societal grid of organic and mechanic solidarity (Durkheim 1961).

This book's ethnography focuses on the events surrounding the Knafo protest. Underneath those events is the bureaucracy whose role is to assist impoverished Mizraḥi single mothers to meet their daily needs. Rarely do middle- to upper-middle-class and higher Ashkenazi women deal with bureaucracy in person. To circumvent bureaucracy, they are able to employ three general methods. They may hire attorney and accountant services to cut through the red tape of bureaucracy for them. Alternatively, they may call upon an attorney that their family keeps on monthly retainer for matters of all sorts. Or, they can also use their social networks to "pull strings" because higher-up bureaucrats tend to be their neighbors, former classmates, or otherwise associated with them or their families (Danet 1989).

In the bureaucracy I lived through and studied—the bureaucracy Mizraḥi single mothers face—the abstractness of Handelman's schemes is reified by officials, clerks, and long lines of subjects dependent on these schemes for survival. The schemes and their reifications are founded upon the phenomenological essence of gender fused with race—one of the foundations of Zionism from its onset in 1880 (Lavie 2007; chapter 1 of this book).

Urban daily life in Israel fits into the Jamesonian model of late capitalism (1991), on its flexible regime of accumulation (Harvey 1990). The Oslo Boomtime is the perfect example. The logic of late capitalism is founded upon mobile, classificatory criteria (see Puar 2005; Rosaldo 1989). Late capitalist criteria for the *vie quotidienne* are not finite and are constantly being redefined. Bureaucracy allows for the creation or addition of categories, ad infinitum, as long as these categories are differentiated and separated from one another within a given logic of abstraction. Israeli bureaucratic logic, however, does *not* come with postmodernist flows and fluxes, as it should. The juridical principles that dictate the interplay between bureaucratic decrees and court procedure require the binary—guilt or innocence. Therefore, Handelman argues that bureaucratic logic is monothetic (2004, 5–6, 19–38). Each categorical scheme inside a bureau is based on a single classificatory criterion.

Each classificatory criterion, in turn, is used by the overarching bureaucratic system to create liminal time-spaces populated by two kinds of participants—in my ethnography, the bureaucrat and the single mother. Both enact the two divinities immanent in the bureaucratic encounter: the Divinity of State—the sanctity of the chosen people in their chosen land, and the Divinity of Chance. The bureaucrat is stationary inside a bureau. At low levels, bureaucrats are usually Mizraḥim, and often women, since the pay is low, but the benefits package is excellent. Mizraḥi activists also dub these low-level bureaucrats "kapos," just like they dub Mizraḥi mainstream politicians. Only when climbing upward in the hierarchy do Ashkenazi bureaucrats appear.

The single mother depends on the bureaucrat. She rushes from bureau to bureau. She waits in long lines at each one. When she steps through the limen into the bureau time-space,[4] she attempts to accomplish certain linear goals, narrow in scope and vital to her and her family's survival.

If unemployed, she hopes to receive income assurance and job referrals. Both unemployed and underemployed mothers may also attempt to obtain government rent subsidies and food stamps for daily living, referrals to charities for food, clothes, furniture, medical co-pays, and medications, textbook vouchers for their children, and the like. After conducting her business, she must exit the space for the next single mother. If her goal is not accomplished, she must keep returning and returning, day after day, until the goal is accomplished and a cyclical interval for her visits is established— once a week, twice a month, and so on. But even this modicum of stability is deceptive, as occasional and arbitrarily imposed changes to bureau regulations can disrupt the cycle, once again requiring her to visit the bureau daily until she can reestablish a new routine. In any case, the mother will return to perform her suffering in front of the bureaucrat in order to enact the same ritual. She thus enacts Mircea Eliade's "Myth of the Eternal Return" (Eliade 1971; see Turner 1973). Government bureaus are the sites of her repeated sacred pilgrimages. Thus, from the single mother's perspective, regulatory changes are in the hands of divine authority.

Negative Communitas: Bureaucracy's "Tough Love"

To survive, the single mother must traverse through many liminal time-spaces inside the state's welfare bureaucracy. These time-spaces are arranged into the linear tracks of two systems—vertical and horizontal (Handelman 2004, 21). A vertical system is a straight up-and-down hierarchy of officials and clerks in a specific ministry, bureau, or court. A horizontal system is the arrangement in space of neatly compartmentalized vertical systems in the wider governmental landscape—the architecture of a regime. Thus, the single mother's most important tool in slogging through bureaucracy is the ability to taxonomize in accordance with bureaucratic logic. Each vertical system can have its own procedural logic independent of any other vertical system. The bureaucrat is only one part of a single hierarchical verticality, usually at the lower end. The decisions of any one bureaucrat are completely contingent on the hierarchical logic inherent in that specific verticality. Any exception presented by a single mother is seen as an anomaly and therefore a disruption (Handelman 2004, 19–38). Bureaucratic logic forces the fuzzy intersectional paradigms of identity politics into these vertical and horizontal systems. So, like Lévi-Strauss's deep structure, bureaucracy is totalistic, entailing its own transformation and self-regulation (Lavie 1983; Lévi-Strauss 1967).

Handelman mentions, but does not problematize, the theological decree underpinning secular Ashkenazi Zionism—the "chosen people" living in the "chosen land" (Frank 1993; Lustick 1988; Novak 1995; Schweid 1985). The biblical Holy Land is Palestine, and the "chosen people" came from Europe to colonize it, informed by fin-de-siècle ethics of eugenic superiority (Falk 2006; Lavie 2007; Malka 1998; Stoler-Liss 1998). "Chosen people" and "chosen land" are totalistic fictions that belong in Zionism's nonnegotiable divine order. After the Nakba, the Ashkenazim found themselves a European minority in the middle of the Arab World. To justify their claim to a Jewish homeland and bolster their Jewish demographics, they engineered a mass migration of those they considered "bad human material" (Gelblum, quoted in Segev and Weinstein 1986, 159–61; see Tsur 1997)—namely, Jews from the Arab and Muslim World. "Chosen people–chosen land" is the cosmological principle superimposed upon the Mizraḥim, who willingly accept it as an axiom (Lavie 2011b). This heavenly conundrum may illuminate Handelman's argument regarding the anti-Weberian logic of Israel's bureaucratic machine.

Most often, ceremonial ritual liminality leads to communitas, resulting in positive catharsis (Turner 1957, 1969; Turner and Turner 1978). Based upon Handelman's analysis, I argue that the limen of the bureaucratic encounter generates communitas.

But, so crushed by the system that they march on Jerusalem, Mizraḥi single mothers can only obtain "negative communitas" (Edie Turner, pers. comm.) from the bureaucratic times and spaces they routinely inhabit.[5] Eventually, the moms may manage to achieve catharsis by progressing from line to line to line, accomplishing small goals like reconnecting electricity and water. But the relief from these hard-fought wins is fleeting.

Handelman outlines how the Israeli regime controls its citizens via the torqueing relationship between the national-emotional "chosen people–chosen land" and the regime's bureaucratic grip on every facet of citizens' lives (2004, 203–4; see Ortner 1995, 176, 190). I posit that his argument is

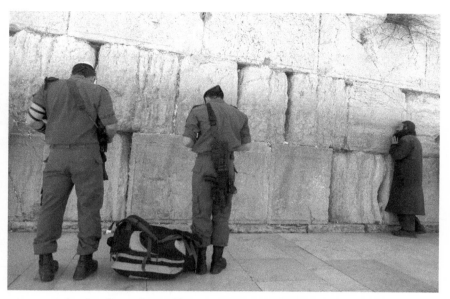

8. Two armed and uniformed IDF soldiers and an ultra-Orthodox Jewish man pray at Jerusalem's Western Wall, one of the Jewish faith's most sacred sites. Lior Mizraḥi, 2013.

limited to the subaltern, racinated citizens of the state. The Mizraḥi majority and Palestinian minority citizens of Israel have no choice but to submit themselves to the "tough love" of the state's bureaucracy to get any state welfare.[6]

The Palestinians, at least, do not buy into the illusion of "tough love" and have thus organized to claim their minority rights. In 2002, for example, fifty-six Palestinian NGOs were registered with Ittijah, the Union of Arab Community-Based Associations in Israel. For the Mizraḥi victims of bureaucracy, love for the Jewish nation hampers efficient organization and actions for social change to redeem their citizens' rights. This love for and dependency on the state prevents Mizraḥi single mothers from speaking about the pain they suffer from bureaucracy. Yet, the pain is present, and it wears down the strength of those who suffer it. Because the torture is elusive, there is no remedy.

While at the University of California, I focused on the Arab-Israeli borderzone (Lavie 1992, 1995, n.d.; Lavie and Swedenburg 1996a, 1996b) and the hybridity and tactical essentialism at the intersectional crux of Mizraḥi identity politics. I argued that agency sparks at the borderzones, where identity and place grate up against each other and are forced into constantly shifting configurations of partial overlap (Lavie 1992; Lavie and Swedenburg 1996a, 1996b). When in front of a welfare bureaucrat, however, I couldn't state that I existed at the intersection of my identities as a former UC professor, single mother, repatriated citizen from hip Berkeley, Mizraḥi identified with an Ashkenazi father, anti-Zionist, and semi-observant Jew. The bureaucrat would most probably eject me from the office. To him or her I would be yet another Yemeni welfare mama. There are no borderzones in Israel's bureaucratic logic (Handelman 2004, 35), thus no agency. Ultimately, a mother's compliance is always already dictated by the history of protest movement failures torqued with her love for the Jewish State, not by the negotiated multiplicities of identity politics.

So, to withstand the bureaucracy, in order for my son and me to survive the day-to-day, I went back to the lessons learned at my parents' knees growing up in Israel. Like the intergenerational transmission of trauma, those lessons were the essential unspeakable (see Cho 2007, 164). But they were vital, nonetheless: *Be tenacious. Be demure. Keep returning to the officials. Nudge 'em. Nudge 'em again. Keep your mouth shut. Suffer. Eventually, you'll get stuff done, even though the system may not make sense.* Bizarrely, these essential lessons echoed Chomsky's innate set of logic principals (Chomsky 1978) as well as the study of the deep unconscious implicit in structures that have their own deductive, a priori rationale (Lévi-Strauss 1967; Levy 1976, 62–63; Saussure 1959). This is bureaucratic logic.

The Plus-Minus Model of Torture

Elaine Scarry's *The Body in Pain* (1985) is still the classic text on the regimes of pain and torture inflicted by politics, and on the manners of healing.[7] In it, Scarry attempts to codify traumatic pain and post-traumatic healing. Scholarship on traumatic pain does not designate bureaucracy as a possible locale of trauma. Likewise, the scholarship of bureaucracy does not discuss the somatization of bureaucratic logic into physical pain. The relationship between the two remains an unexplored conceit. Pain resists objectification in language and is articulated in verbal fragments (Scarry 1985, 6). Articulating pain transforms the physical into the discursive. The experience of pain can become discourse (see Scott 1991, 787–97) when direct relationships exist between the inflictor of torture and the inflicted suffering pain (Scarry 1985, 35; see Scott 1991, 787–97).

In cases involving torturers and tortured, such as rapists and rape victims, or SHABAK[8] interrogators and detained Palestinian guerillas, the inflictor and inflicted share a plus-minus relationship. The inflictor knowingly and willingly causes pain. The inflicted understands the inflictor's role in the torture and is aware of the methods of torture (Scarry 1985, 35, 48). According to Scott's model for the evidence of experience (1991), torture can transform and progress from a pre-discursive reality between inflictor and inflicted into a relationship that has potential to become a narrative (1991, 794).

Likewise, Scarry outlines the three simultaneous phenomena in the structure of torture: the infliction of pain; the objectification of the subjective attributes of pain, producing discourse; and the translation of the objectified attributes of pain into a mimetic insignia of power (1985, 51). This process that Scott and Scarry outline is unlikely for the Mizraḥi single mother.

The Zone of Repulsion: Plus-Plus Relationships of Pain

Bureaucratic logic throws asunder the plus-minus relationship between inflictor and inflicted. The bureaucrat, or the inflictor, and the dependent single mother, or the inflicted, share a plus-plus relationship. The bureaucrat is unaware of the infliction of pain because she or he is there to assist the single mother in accomplishing her goals at the bureau. The single mother cannot objectify the torture because she comes to the bureau searching for the solace of practical solutions. Full understanding of their inflictor-inflicted relationship is obfuscated by the total, ritual logic that dominates the liminal space—bureau desk or office—where the bureaucrat and dependent single mother share encounters. Like the positive poles of two adjacent magnets, the bureaucrat and the single mother enter an encounter only to repel each other. Therefore, their pre-discursive reality cannot develop into discourse (Scott 1991, 794; see Ortner 1995, 188; see also Thrift 2008, 1–26).

Without discourse, there is no transformation of lived experience into "mimetic faculty"—the ability of the primitivized Other to produce and reproduce tactile experiences as stories of resistance against the U.S.-European colonizer (Taussig 1993). There is no catharsis, and therefore no time-space for agency.

The bureaucrat overseeing the single mother's case must assist her in achieving deliverance. Ostensibly, they share the same monothetic goals and belong to similar logical systems. With the application of bureaucratic logic, the ability of the bureaucrat to offer deliverance becomes indeterminate. The bureaucrat may not be able to give the single mother a welfare check—the very reason she was in the lines—because the system sent this check to the wrong bureau. Or the bureau's computer system requires the single mother to attend a job interview on what turns out to be a public holiday. For whatever reason, when the bureaucrat is unable to give or willfully denies the mother what she needs, the bureaucrat effectively becomes the administrator of torture. At the same time, the bureaucrat is convinced that all of her or his actions are in the service of the mother. Because the mother needs the deliverance that only the bureaucrat can offer, she has no choice but to enter this zone of repulsion again and again—and suffer the same torture again and again—just to accomplish basic goals related to daily survival.

Even if she obtains deliverance from the bureaucrat, a single mother is still subject to torture. Standing in multiple lines is physically exhausting and humiliating. When she finally has her encounter with the specific bureaucrat who might offer her deliverance, she must speak narrowly only about the issue at hand. Oftentimes, the mother, so traumatized by daily living, cannot help but gush out unsorted snapshots from her life to the bureaucrat in an effort to support her claims. The bureaucrat will not tolerate this lack of monothetic focus. She or he will send the mother away or ask the security guards to remove her, violently, if need be. In addition, a single mother must furnish original or notarized copies of all documents pertaining strictly to the narrow issue at stake. Without these, she may also get ejected from the bureaucrat's presence. The mother thus must dissociate herself from the pain of her daily life so that the bureaucrat tolerates her presence. Because the mother needs the deliverance only the bureaucrat can offer, she has no recourse but to brave this liminal repulsion zone again and again to accomplish basic goals related to daily survival.

The bureaucratic encounter is a self-perpetuating, ritual-like process where the bureaucrat unwittingly abuses the mother. This kind of ritual is not a once-in-a-lifetime rite of passage, such as an uncle making an incision on a neophyte to present the neophyte to the adult world (Bateson 1936). The rite repeats *ad infinitum*. The bureaucrat and mother lack awareness of their inflicting-inflicted relationship because the repulsion zone is a reification of the gap in linear bureaucratic logic. The gap occurs because bureaucratic logic continually makes changes in bureaucratic institutions, requiring the mother to continually adjust herself. By the time the mother adjusts, a new change happens, and she must adjust again. The finger of G-d proclaims that all "Ys" must be replaced by "Bs," with no advance notice. This endless cycle of adjustment can be seen as an implement of torture.

The single mother lives shrouded in a constant state of anxiety, but she cannot draw a direct line to the state as ultimate inflictor of this anxiety. The pain created is like an invisible knife making an invisible wound that sheds invisible blood. The mother cannot identify the cause of her torture, but the pain is palpable (see Krieger 2005). The state bureaucracy does violence to her organic relationships and communities by requiring her to expend all her time and energy in lines. Frustrations and anxieties build up and spill over into her familial and community relationships. Ultimately, the transposition of frustration amputates her ties to family, kin, neighbors, and friends (Handelman 2004, 36, 206). The lines rob her of time with loved ones and replace it with constant competition with the mothers of the lines for the state's scraps. Despite these traumas, she still allies herself with the state through mechanical solidarity (Durkheim 1961).

Documents as Implements of Torture

The torture of the bureaucratic encounter is not limited to the time-space where the mother interacts with the bureaucrat. The pain domino effect can as easily start when a single mother receives a mailed official document, such as the one that informed single mothers of their slashed NSB allowances. The pain inflicted from these official documents is in dialogue with the face-to-face torture the single mother experiences in the lines and in bureaucrat offices—both can occur in cycles, but can just as likely come unexpected. The document-inflicted torture, however, is even more elusive and more impossible to objectify because it involves the benign act of opening a letter.

The very act of reading official documents has a somatic effect of sending the body into shock. Upon opening the letter, it might not occur to the single mother that she has an emotional relationship with these documents, even though reading them may cause sharp stomach pains, heart palpitations, and increased anxiety. I tried to understand the connections between the document, the trauma it inflicts, and the mothers' dissociation from its pain by asking my fellow mothers in the lines to retrace their steps before, during, and after they opened one of these official letters. Many mothers told me that, after picking up their children from day care, they went home, found official letters, and opened them. Subsequent to that, they yelled at their children or burned the food they were cooking. Only after I questioned them did many realize the connection between the documents and their emotional states. The mother and the document suffer from the same logical gap as the mother and the bureaucrat. Thus, the document creates a zone of repulsion in the mother's own home, and even between her hands holding the document and the rest of her body. The origin of the repulsion is the origin of the letter — the same as the origin of the bureaucrat: the bureau that is supposed to aid the mother. Mother and document suffer the same logical gap as mother and bureaucrat, and exist in a repulsion zone extant in the mother's own home.

The documents often require a single mother to return to the lines and appear before a bureaucrat. Before going, she must sift through her own records to choose documents pertinent to her issue. If she chooses too widely, the clerk will lose patience. If she chooses too narrowly, she will be sent home for insufficient documentation. And that is when the mother takes pains to organize her documents. Many mothers leave their official documents unorganized on tables or in stacks near their beds because even handling them makes them physically sick. As when she first receives documents in the mail, going through her old documents causes her pain that cannot be objectified.

Bureaucracy's Essence: GendeRace

The underlying principle of the bureaucratic encounter is a phenomeno-logical essence. I term it "GendeRace." GendeRace is comprised of the Husserlian noesis-noema complementary binary that constructs the essence. Noesis is the conscious process of experiencing, perceiving, and directing attention, while noema is the essence experienced, directed to, and thought about (Husserl [1913] 1983). The Mizraḥi single mother is not aware of this essence even though she embodies it.[9]

The low-level bureaucrat, often Mizraḥi, is similarly unaware of this GendeRace essence. The bureaucrat is also unaware of the meaning imbued upon the essence through her or his actions on behalf of the mother. The meaning, however, is paradoxically dictated by this very GendeRace essence located at the foundation underneath the binary deep structure of Zionism—a paternalistic colonialist logic of androcentric Jewish, European superiority versus effeminate Muslim, Arab inferiority (Lavie 2007; Shohat 2001).

Democratic systems of governance, nonetheless, assume not only religious neutrality, but also gender and race neutrality. Gender and race, however, are actually the most important categorical principles sorting citizens (Gilroy 2000; Joseph 2000; Scott 2007). One becomes a citizen either through birth or through a process of naturalization—that is, having citizenship as one's nature, rather than culture. Race and gender hierarchize citizens through the fiction of equal rights propped up by corrective legislation. Not so in Israel. The Israeli regime assumes gender and race neutrality. Yet, any immigrant—whether Mizraḥi or Ashkenazi—can become an instant citizen of the "chosen land" by tracing a three-to-five-generation lineage of Jewish mothers, proving he or she belongs to the "chosen people." Thus the state will never admit its own intra-Jewish racial formation. Therefore, there is no affirmative action legislation that rectifies injustices against the Mizraḥim. In the Jewish state, all Jews are supposed to be equal.

The internal dynamics of the Israeli state are based on GendeRace as an essence. From early Zionism on, the chosen Jewish race was European. This was held as an axiom. Only secular European Jewish women were eugenically capable of (re)producing pure citizens (Stoler-Liss 1998;

chapter 1 of this book). The calcified amalgamation of gender and race, in Israel of the twenty-first century, is beyond construction. GendeRace is what makes the nation tick and stick. When asked about the racial formations of Israel, most disenfranchised Mizraḥim would say in one breath that Zionism is Ashkenazi racism, but that they also vehemently support the idea and practices of a Jewish state, and are therefore Zionists. For the sake of Zionism, they bracket the discrimination they suffer in favor of a phantom deracinated citizenship.

Jewish intra-gender relations are hierarchized according to the Ashkenazi-Mizraḥi racial formation. The public-sphere image of Mizraḥi men is hyper-masculine, yet warm and fuzzy, emotionally open, yet sexually violent. In contrast, the public-sphere image of Ashkenazi men is cold, logical, and calculated. It is the Ashkenazi minority that dictates Israeli heteronormativity. These norms become the default, and, thus, are transparent. Because of this transparency, the perfidies of Ashkenazi men are often dismissed (Shiran 1991).

The 2006 sexual harassment allegations against Israel's former deputy prime minister, Haim Ramon, an Ashkenazi, and former president Moshe Katsav, a Mizraḥi, illustrate the dynamics of this transparency. Both were known privately to demand sexual favors from female employees even though only one woman dared to complain against Ramon. He merely received community service. Subsequently, he returned to his ministerial position. Several women accused Katsav, however. Between December 2011 and December 2016, Katsav was imprisoned (BBC 2011).

Nevertheless, when I asked many Mizraḥi or Ashkenazi men about this typecasting, they denied it with vigor. Instead, they reminisced about their brotherhood formed during compulsory service in the IDF and annually renewed in reserve duty.

A similar dichotomy governs the public-sphere images of Ashkenazi and Mizraḥi women. Mizraḥi women are typecast on one hand as loud, traditionally garbed, "big mamas," birthing tribal families, and on the other as voluptuous and sexually loose items of exotica. In addition, before the Oslo Boomtime, Mizraḥi women mopped the floors and reared the children of Ashkenazi women. They still carry this cultural typecasting today, even though guest workers have taken over these jobs. The public-sphere image of Ashkenazi women is the analogue of the men: rational, cool, and calculated.

Most Israeli women dye their hair. Within this cultural decree is an embodied example of how gender and race constructions become essences. Spoken Hebrew differentiates between *blondinit* and *sh'hordinit*. A blondinit (singular) is a woman who is naturally blonde or who dyes her dark Semitic hair blonde. Sh'hordinit (singular) is a woman who dyes her hair blonde, but shows exposed dark roots. Nevertheless, nonnatural *blondiniyot* (plural) with exposed dark roots are not labeled *sh'hordiniyot* (plural). Perhaps this is because the sh'hordinit comes with olive-to-brown skin. To overcome this, she may invest in skin-bleaching ointment from the local drugstore. But then, the sh'hordinit may have an additional problem of her wide Semitic hips. She can resort to liposuction to tackle this issue. No matter what, however, an Arabic name deep in her family tree will always expose a sh'hordinit's lack of racial pedigree. Even if she does not exhibit guttural Arabic accent slippage in her Hebrew, the Arabic name will remain in her heritage. Blondinit and sh'hordinit are mutually exclusive to Ashkenazi and Mizrahi, respectively, and become primordial truisms. Vicky Knafo was a sh'hordinit.

Both Mizrahi men and women prefer Ashkenazi mates, who appear in personal ads as "European, cultured, and fair-skinned" (Blumenfeld 1997). Mizrahi women, in particular, prefer Ashkenazi men because they believe the marriage will free them from the Arab patriarchy of their fathers and brothers. They deny that their upgrade in capital and racial prestige comes at the price of the expectations of their Ashkenazi husbands and in-laws to be both exotic and subservient. Intermarriage, however, is not common, and when it happens, the Mizrahi often willingly goes through Ashkenazi-fication (Blumenfeld 1997; Shahar 1988). Ashkenazification in marriage includes the desertion of the Mizrahi extended family formation, embracing instead a compact nuclear family formation. Contact with the Mizrahi extended family tends to be limited to family visits on Shabbats and holidays. More frequent is contact with the Ashkenazi extended family, who can provide monetary aid to the young couple. Children of the married couple may grow up unaware of Mizrahi rules of propriety and extended family gender dynamics in favor of Ashkenazi chutzpah (a sense of uncritical enti-

9. Supermodel, actress, and television personality Miri Bohadana is a quintessential example of the *sh'hordinit*. She was born to Moroccan Jewish parents in the development town of Sderot, near the Gaza border. Another prominent female celebrity worth noting is Miki Haimovich, a highly respected former news anchor for Israel's Channel 2, and later Channel 10. Like Bohadana, Haimovich sports dyed blonde hair with dark roots. But as the daughter of a Turkish mother and a Romanian father, she is a quintessential *blondinit*, blessed with a last name ending with *-vich*, a perfect final syllable for an Ashkenazi surname. Haimovich and her agents refused to give permission for her image to be used in this text. Oded Karni.

tlement) and Ashkenazi gender dynamics (see Thorleifsson 2012). Thus, Mizraḥi women find themselves at the very bottom of Israel's Jewish gender pecking order. They are subject to two systems of patriarchal oppression — that of the Ashkenazi nation-state and that of their own Mizraḥi families. Nowadays, some Mizraḥi women admit to this. Many still do not.

Even enlightened Mizraḥi activists are not immune to GendeRace. Vardit Damri-Madar (2002) and Eli Bareket (2002) have wryly commented about what has become known informally in Mizraḥi feminist circles as the "Sexual Politics of the Mizraḥi Struggle" (Lavie 2006a) or even the "Erotics of the Mizraḥi Struggle." Among Mizraḥi post- and anti-Zionist activists who are men, the highly educated movers and shakers of Mizraḥi consciousness, the most common pattern of marriage is to wealthy Ashkenazi women, preferably with dual citizenship (and, more preferably, from North America), often to enable graduate studies abroad at a nonforeign tuition rate. These marriages also come with financial support in currencies more stable than NIS, courtesy of their wives' parents, as well as foreign passports just in case the state collapses.

A large percentage of Mizraḥi feminist activists are unmarried. They do not want to subject themselves to the scrutiny of prospective Ashkenazi in-laws. At any rate, the more desirable Mizraḥi men are largely taken by Ashkenazi women. Other Mizraḥi feminists are divorced. Very few are in long-term marriages to Mizraḥi men. The most financially successful, home-owning Mizraḥi feminists are married to Ashkenazi men.[10]

GendeRace assumptions are culturally learned constructions. Zionism's eugenic legacy (Falk 2006; Lavie 2007; Malka 1998; Stoler-Liss 1998), however, has calcified them into natural genetic decrees. Thus these decrees have cohered into a nonnegotiable essence — GendeRace (see Lavie and Swedenburg 1996a, 1996b). The GendeRace essence and the "chosen people–chosen land" divine decree work together with each other while simultaneously contradicting each other. "Chosen people–chosen land" demands a unilateral Jewish front against the goyim. At the core of this frail unity, however, is an essence of racial and gender difference. This is why "chosen people–chosen land" is evoked every time GendeRace surfaces in everyday life. "Chosen people–chosen land" pushes GendeRace back to its invisible, foundational modality that allows the state's bureaucratic logic to function as a mechanism of oppression.

Despite the feminist injunction against binary logic, let alone the calcified amalgamation of binary logic into an essence (Lavie 1983; Lavie and Swedenburg 1996a, 1996b), the mothers in the lines reify GendeRace. For disenfranchised Mizraḥi single mothers, GendeRace becomes the main principle for their bureaucratic classification—the source of their unarticulated torture.

Response to Bureaucracy: Bracketing

One way that the single mother might survive the reification of bureaucratic logic into torture is dissociation through phenomenological bracketing (Husserl [1900] 1970; see Lorde 1984, 58). She must limit her scope to the singular totality of the bureaucratic interaction itself. For instance, a single mother languishing in lines at a bureau will experience much more pain if she does not bracket away the discriminatory world outside the lines. Any agency enacted by the single mother to combat the GendeRace essence will be turned back on her, punishing her through further bureaucratic entanglement because she has dared to *le-hitbakhyen*. She is therefore incapable of Scarry's empowerment recipe—translating the objectification of her pain into mimetic discourse (Scarry 1985, 51). If she tries, she may have an audience for a short time. Her performance, nevertheless, will never lead to a systemic change.

A mother who brackets and gains deliverance from a bureaucrat manages only to receive "negative communitas" (Edie Turner, pers. comm.) from that deliverance. Each encounter contains suffering, and this suffering compounds—documents manufacture bureaucratic encounters manufacture time spent in lines manufacture new documents, ad infinitum. To withstand the increasing levels of suffering stored within her body, the mother must become numb by unconsciously disconnecting body from soul. The numbness may alleviate her suffering in the immediate term. It may even trick her into believing that through her compliance with procedure, she enacts docile agency (Mahmood 2001) to better her situation. Agency assumes a sovereign, autonomous individual or community. Enactments of agency are supposed to bring about change. But in the zone of repulsion, and with no resources, nothing changes.

The mother's soul, fatigued from the accumulation of pain, makes her procrastinate and slow down her fight for survival. Eventually, even bracketing fails. The wall the mother has erected between the encounter-numb self and the out-of-encounter, terrorized self collapses. When body and soul reconnect, she begins to comprehend how the vertical and horizontal systems of bureaucracy—each with its singular logic—cohere into a totality. She cracks up, falling prey to chronic panic attacks, depression, nervous breakdowns, ulcers, heart attacks, cancer, hypertension, aneurysms, autoimmune disorders, or the self-neglect of her body, leading to eventual death (see Krieger 2005). Furthermore, the ability of a mother's body to weather torture disintegrates because she uses herself as a human shield to shelter her children from forced boarding, homelessness, lack of medical treatment, and so on (Lavie 2011b).

The bureaucrat brackets as well. The mechanism that numbs the bureaucrat consists not only of following procedure for the sake of procedure, but also the fear that procedural failures may result in torture inflicted upon the bureaucrat by higher-ups. Feldman describes how Palestinian bureaucrats dissociate from the political agendas of the regimes colonizing Gaza, in order to "feel good about their own work" (2008, 220). In Israel, a bureaucrat enacting "Mizraḥi kapo syndrome" dissociates her- or himself from the mother's suffering. The bureaucrat feels good about the work because he or she embraces Zionism's political agendas. Furthermore, the bureaucrat is also convinced that following procedure actually helps the mother. Thus, the bureaucrat cannot draw a direct line between withholding deliverance and the single mother's physical decay. Repulsion-zone bracketing may not be articulated discursively, but is memorialized somatically (Krieger 2005).

Impossible Articulation, Impossible Agency

Agency in the zone of repulsion is futureless. It provides no way out. Scarry offers the human rights court as a possible way to enact agency. For Scarry, after a victim objectifies pain by articulating it, the human rights court can function as a mechanism for empowerment through legal mimesis (1985, 10). A wronged party may be able articulate pain through both testimonial and available legal language. But, though state and public cultures in Israel are highly litigious, GendeRace injuries the regime inflicts upon Mizraḥim cannot be articulated (Bitton 2011). There are three reasons why courts cannot offer justice that will heal single mothers' pain.

First, justice is a commodity. Only the power of the purse can procure adequate attorney services. There is free legal aid available for disenfranchised single mothers, but it is limited in scope. National Legal Aid to those with limited means, mainly Mizraḥim, is available through the Legal Aid Department of Israel's Ministry of Justice. National Legal Aid provides legal advice and court representation by government-appointed lawyers in criminal and civil court cases, at a rate based on income plus a participation fee. Even so, many applicants cannot afford the low rates and fees yet do not have enough documentation to show adequate need for a waiver. Most National Legal Aid attorneys are hired by the Ministry of Justice as independent contractors and tend to have low client loads in the private market. Once in the National Legal Aid system, these attorneys do not have enough time and monetary reward to treat each case properly. Plus, legal aid attorneys in the State of Israel are government-paid and are thus obliged to serve government interests over those of the client. The lone exception to this is in cases involving legal representation for Palestinian guerrillas or for relatives of guerrillas whose homes are to be demolished by the IDF. Some of Israel's top attorneys enlist themselves in National Legal Aid specifically to take these cases. These top attorneys, who are almost always members of the Ashkenazi elite, understand that such high-profile cases come with heavy North American and Western European mainstream media coverage.

Even if a single mother somehow manages to acquire the funds to pay a competent attorney's retainer fee, the attorney may reject her as a client. And, unlike Palestinian human and civil rights–focused NGOs, the poorly funded Mizraḥi NGOs cannot afford to employ human rights attorneys either as staff members or as private contractors. So attorneys usually consider Mizraḥi single mothers high risk. The mother's funding is never enough to see a case through multiple appeals, up to the Supreme Court. And appeals are almost always necessary. She is likely to initially lose in lower courts because the opposing counsel works for either the government bureaus or for her landlord. Both opponents far outstrip her in finances. Adding to those costs are court filing fees at every step. Moreover, to be granted permission to appeal, a single mother has to furnish half the estimated fees and costs of the opposing attorney in case she loses and becomes liable.

Second, a conscientious attorney will not accept a Mizraḥi single mother's case because justice is rarely attainable for her. The court will avoid deliberating over the specific facts of a Mizraḥi single mother's case. Rather, the court will focus on procedural minutia such as missing signatures on forms, proper stamps, or court fees. A judge may resort to backing and filling to delay any hearings and cross-examinations over the case's facts. At best, the court will refer the mother and her children again and again to be evaluated and reevaluated by social service welfare officials because of "changing circumstances." The judge can use the evaluation results to call for further evaluations, scheduled several months later. Such practices effectively postpone a court decision into a quasi-permanent stasis. After all, the court is yet another vertical system of the state's bureaucracy. A mother eventually surrenders her complaint. Backing and filling is done both to punish the Mizraḥi single mother for her deficient demureness in front of the regime's bureaucracy, and to avoid creating a record of rulings on intra-Jewish racism.

Oftentimes, different judges hold different fates for Mizraḥi single mothers. Ashkenazi women judges (Bogoch and Don-Yechiya 1999) and Mizraḥi men judges are the most likely to enact the kapo syndrome and deny them justice. Even worse are the rare Mizraḥi women judges. Their strain of kapo syndrome—enacted for survival and advancement—is the most severe.

Third, judges and attorneys in court levy upon any Mizraḥi single mother the socially constructed label of *mitbakhyenet*, the feminine noun form of the verb *le-hitbakhyen*. A mother daring to articulate her pain, even for a single time, brands herself a serial complainer to be marginalized by judges and bureaucrats. So the pain remains unspoken. For all these reasons, pain must be treated by the court and by the mother in the court as nonevidence. She always embodies her pain, but the people around her—including herself—rarely acknowledge it. With no alternative, the Mizraḥi single mother has no choice but to return back to the lines to repeat bureaucratic encounters and undergo more torture (see Krieger 2005, 353).

For disenfranchised Mizraḥim in the State of Israel—most of the Mizraḥim in Israel—bureaucracy casts its black magic spell by dictating and organizing biographies and personal experiences in accordance with its essence (Schutz 1962). This essence is divine. It requires the sacrifice of civil agency at the altar of security (Al-Haj and Ben-Eliezer 2006) to mount a united Ashkenazi-Mizrahi front against the non-Jewish Arab enemy by virtue of being the "chosen people in the chosen land."

Other than going to court, Scarry suggests that those in pain can heal themselves through creating works of the imagination, including painting, singing, and writing (Scarry 1985, 10–11, 161–65, 172, 314).[11] But for Mizraḥi single mothers who must engage in the constant and pervasive struggle for scraps, the concept of creating these works is far beyond reach. Creative pursuits require mental and physical time-space—luxuries these single mothers do not have. So not even through imagination can the mother obtain deliverance, for she is pitted against circumstances preventing her from mimeticizing the pain (see Krieger 2005).

The mother always arrives to return to her point of departure—GendeRace—a dark female form. A Mizraḥi woman.

An essence.

CHAPTER 4

Take 2

Ideology, Welfare, and Single Mothers

This chapter is a "thickly described" translation of an op-ed piece I wrote with Amir Paz-Fuchs, a law colleague. It appeared in Israel's daily *Globes: Israel Business News*, in the 16–17 July 2003 edition (Lavie and Paz-Fuchs 2003). *Globes* is the fourth-most-distributed Hebrew newspaper in Israel, and its readership is the business elite of the state. It is also the main media outlet for Israel's neocons. Just like London's *Financial Times*, *Globes* is printed on pink-colored pages. *Globes* publishes articles that other papers, with larger Mizraḥi readerships, refuse to publish, especially about the disenfranchised in Israel. The editors assume that its readers will skim these incendiary articles over morning coffee, then, unfazed, move on to the next story. For *Globes*, these articles serve as a bon ton to diversity.

In 2003, Amir, an upper-middle-class Ashkenazi, was a PhD student at Oxford Law School. I was a Mizraḥi feminist leader and welfare mom. We co-authored the op-ed using the dissociative language of social analysis—language stripped of emotion so that it might have a chance of passing as neutral and objective. This was our way to reach out to the readership of *Globes*—the elite policymakers and bureaucrats among them. *Globes* is so mainstream that it is not threatened by Mizraḥi feminism. So it welcomed the submission to its revered op-ed section and published it right away. An obviously Ashkenazi last name like Fuchs, Amir's Oxford cache, and my Berkeley PhD helped.

Amir and I titled this article "Ideology, Welfare, and the Ḥad Horit." So as not to agitate readers, we did not refer to Mizraḥim in the title. The mere mention of Mizraḥim in a major Israeli newspaper headline would be considered divisive. Still, the *Globes* editors saw fit to change the title to "But There Is Discrimination: The State Penetrates the Single Family's Bedroom." This unusually scandalous headline for *Globes* did not only allude to the alleged loose morals of single mothers. It also played up the Hebrew media's aura of peculiarity that surrounded any discussion of social justice not emanating from Ashkenazi Zionist Left.

Originally, our text conformed to the customary five-hundred-word length requirement. Luckily, Hebrew does not have many prepositions and has no vowels.

———

On 3 January 2003, the Knesset voted to change the criteria for disenfranchised single mothers who were entitled to income assurance and augmentation allowances. This is the latest amendment to Ḥok HaHesderim. On 29 June 2003, the National Security Bureau implemented the change. Under the rubric of such legislation hides a belligerent, patriarchal Ashkenazi ideology that has been with us since the days of the Yishuv.[1]

The law echoes the so-called welfare reforms that took place mainly in the United States and the United Kingdom in the early 1990s.[2] These neoclassical economic reforms focused on a forced rebirth of the traditional, deracinated, middle-class, nuclear family that had been waning since the feminism of the 1970s. To reinforce this familial dogma, legislators passed laws to provide economic incentives to white, Protestant, middle-class, married, heterosexual households. They called this "social engineering." The undeclared goal of these reforms in the United States was to eliminate the governmental costs of disenfranchised nonwhite single mothers and their families. About half of nonwhite households in the United States are single headed—90 percent of these headed by women. Historically, these single mothers have suffered through low-tracked education and racial discrimination in the workplace. Single mothers who attempted to form more traditional households with men or refused to take dangerous government-mandated birth control lost their welfare allowances.[3]

Unlike the prevailing image of the U.S. ghetto mother and the child born out of wedlock, most single mothers in Israel birth their children into a legal marriage or contractual partnership they hope to be long-term. In the Israeli state, normative personhood for a woman must entail marriage and motherhood. This decree cuts across race, ethnicity, class, nationality, and religion. Jewish babies and their mothers—whether Mizraḥi or Ashkenazi—are given preference because of Israel's existential anxiety over being a minority Jewish state in the middle of the Muslim, Arab World.[4]

Official language surrounding the terms "single mother" or "single-headed household" launders them of class, race, and historical and geographic location. Therefore, no official statistics, literature, or other data are available on the Israeli typology of single-headed households. In situ, however, I have discerned three types of single mothers. The first is the "hip alternative" single mother, usually an older professional Ashkenazi living in Israel before the post-Soviet immigration of the 1990s (otherwise known as AḤUSAL),[5] who either uses in vitro fertilization and raises the child by herself or enlists an Ashkenazi gay man, also a professional, to donate sperm and enter into a joint-custody arrangement. These mothers are largely supported by their families of origin, who are overjoyed at the new naḥat (contentment, Hebrew, slang for "grandchild"). The second is the post-Soviet immigrant single mother, who often had her children out of wedlock either prior to immigrating to Israel or after arriving. Her chief reason for immigrating is to take advantage of Israel's social welfare policies. Third is the postdivorce single mother, usually a younger woman. If child support is withheld by her ex-husband, she faces an impossible task of trying to collect it through the courts. Postdivorce Ashkenazi single mothers often can rely on their families of origin for financial support. Most Mizraḥi postdivorce single mothers lack intergenerational wealth, and thus are forced to become completely dependent on state welfare [see chapter 1 of this book for a more in-depth explanation of these single mother types].

Overall, the majority of single mothers in Israel are Mizraḥi. They and the post-Soviets survive mainly on NSB allowances and food donations. After the outbreak of the Al-Aqsa Intifada in 2000, followed closely by the global economic crisis of the dot-com collapse, hunger became widespread in Israel's impoverished communities. NGOs sprang up to gather expired, hand-me-down food from major supermarkets to distribute to an ever-growing number of welfare recipients. The largest of these NGOs was

10. High school students volunteer to hand out food donations at Pit'ḥon Lev to fulfill their school's community service requirement. Pit'ḥon Lev, 2011.

Pit'ḥon Lev (Open Heart, Hebrew). Almost all of these NGOs were Jewish, masorti, and right wing.

The 2003 amendment to Ḥok HaHesderim is at the center of the struggle led by Vicky Knafo. It comes at the peak of a decade marked by a backlash against the Rabin government's 1992 Knesset Law for Single-Headed Families—a law beneficial to single mothers. The Rabin law instructed the NSB to augment the incomes of all single-headed families up to half the poverty-level income. It was legislated at the height of post-Soviet immigration, and one year before the Oslo Peace Accords and the subsequent privatization of the Israeli economy.

Ten years of economic privatization immediately following the Law for Single-Headed Families eroded the law's benefits. The specific amounts paid by the NSB were to be adjusted for the cost of living index. But the cost of living increased at a rate much faster than the adjustments to the NSB payments. The 2003 amendment to Ḥok HaHesderim is merely an extension of this erosion—a drastic one.

After the amendment, a single head of a family making less than 487 NIS (about $112) a month continues to receive NSB income augmentation up to 3,200 NIS (about $736) for that month. But any single family head making 488 NIS (about $112.23) or more in a month gets income augmentation completely cut. The assumption of Bibi Netanyahu and the Finance Ministry professionals is that a single mother capable of earning more than 487 NIS in a month can earn the rest of the money by herself. They expect her to go and find more part-time jobs. Further, the latest amendment to Ḥok HaHesderim was officially put into law in January 2003, but its execution by the NSB was frozen until June 2003. At this time, single mothers earning more than 487 NIS monthly received notices from the NSB that they had accrued debt in the amount of income augmentation the NSB paid them from January to June 2003. Failure of a mother to pay this retroactive debt gave the NSB license to withhold all assistance until full remittance of her bill. The government immediately saved 760 million NIS a year because of the retroactive cut.[6]

Ḥok HaHesderim is based on the U.S.-UK neocon mind-set. The neocons' criticism of the welfare system reflects the traditional moral position of the socioeconomic right wing with regard to the normative family—a heterosexual, secular, middle-class married couple with two children. The neocons believe that welfare dissuades mothers from forming productive, normal families with men as providers and themselves as housewives and child-rearers. This, the neocons insist, reveals the welfare state to be rife with skewed incentives leading citizens into a "poverty trap" and "employment trap" when they rely on welfare. Abolishing allowances, neocons argue, will abolish their recipients' "entrapment" because they will simply go back to work, even if that entails cobbling together numerous part-time jobs to barely make ends meet. As a side benefit, citizens would not be able to organize and protest for lack of time and energy.

In Israel, the Zionist left wing has traditionally held this neocon economic view. The right wing simply followed in lockstep with the Left. Members of the Right voice their perpetual anxiety about the state's intrusion into the private sphere. But this anxiety exists only when it comes to their own dwellings, their own private sphere. They do not mind the state penetrating the bedrooms of single-headed families. The Left does not mind going into these families' homes, either. Under the guise of socialism, the Zionist Left routinely invaded the private spheres of impoverished Mizraḥi households. Thus, despite the discourse over the social rights of single-headed families, in practice, the rights of racialized, unemployed, or underemployed single mothers are regularly violated. A single-headed (read: female-headed) family has no right to exist because it is a societal disruption and does not suit the capitalism of the free market. Israeli leaders have decided that "social engineering" is necessary to eliminate these families.

Ḥok HaHesderim forces single mothers into a ruthless labor market characterized by late capitalism, deep recession, low wages, and high unemployment. And in this economic climate, the new 2003 amendment lowers income assistance instead of increasing it. The absurdity of Ḥok HaHesderim coupled with an astronomical cost of living highlights a fact that has been with us since the Zionist settlement of Palestine: there is a severe exploitation of women—married and single alike—because of a major gender-based income gap in the labor market. From the Yishuv on, even Ashkenazi women experienced high rates of unemployment and underemployment. Married women fortunate to find employment still must face high taxes on their second household incomes. Therefore, the most cost-effective way for them to contribute to the household economy is to become stay-at-home mothers. Ḥok HaHesderim imposes the rehabilitation of the heteronormative family cell by forcing mothers and prospective mothers to find suitable husbands on whom to depend for all their needs. The end result of the law is the hardening of the racial, gendered division of Israel's labor market.

The Mizraḥi single mother has no place in this racialized political economy. Without income assistance, and due to her age and children, a mother working to provide for her family faces low hourly pay and limited advancement options. Any young mother most probably will spend her income to pay for someone to mind her children while she is at work. Adding to that, the now allowanceless single mother (read: Mizraḥi single mother) must enter a labor market of low employer costs, almost nonexistent professional training, and a distinct lack of worker solidarity.

A tenured labor market exists parallel to this hourly labor market. The tenured market is characterized by positions that come with monthly pay, benefits, employment stability, and advancement possibilities—but only for those with professional training. Ashkenazi men with university educations and professional training control this market. Mizraḥi men who have climbed up into the middle class compete with happily wealthily married Ashkenazi women for whatever is left. Make no mistake—this market still suffers from layoffs. But Mizraḥi men and Ashkenazi women are always the first to be fired and rolled down to the hourly labor market as preferred candidates for hire.

Bibi and the Finance Ministry boys argue that the slashing of income assistance is a form of philanthropy that takes single mothers out of the poverty trap. Except now, in this two-tiered labor market, they are stuck in another trap—unemployment.

So, who is going to pay their bills?

Professor Smadar Lavie is an anthropologist and an unemployed single mother.[7]

Amir Fuchs is a law PhD candidate at Oxford University.

———

And that's the way it was on 16 July 2003.

CHAPTER 5

Take 3

Diary of a Welfare Mother

Take 2 was my "social-science-y" attempt to explicate pain without the feelings. Take 3 is both an embodiment and a reflection of my subaltern theorization of the GendeRace of bureaucratic torture and my dissociated analysis of the neocon ideology dictating welfare policies that impact single mothers. Take 3 repeats the same story as takes 1 and 2. Take 3 attempts to capture the magical realism of the mothers' confinement in bureaucratic webs woven together from their somatic, nondiscursive experiences. My hope is that the act of writing up the nonrepresentational somatic experiences of bureaucratic torture will validate them for readers. Even without my representation, these experiences are always already valid for the mothers.

Good. Now once more, with feeling.

12 August 2003

Shaheen and I entered the cafeteria of the Gilman Humanities Building at Tel Aviv University. We needed to kill an hour before Shaheen's cello lesson at the music academy. We opened the door, and the thick, perpetual cigarette haze hit us. So we headed straight for the area cordoned off for university professors. Willful trespassers, we were content to illicitly enjoy the smoke-free, air-conditioned zone.

Vicky and Ilana would never have sought relief from the sizzling summer in a faculty club. The privilege of my Berkeley PhD gave me the chutzpah to transgress into this space.

We sat at the table in the center of the section, surrendering ourselves to the dense cloud of L'Eau d'Issey Summer and Yves Saint Laurent's Opium.

The bouquet brought me back to the forbidden land of Ben Gurion Airport's duty-free shop. The room was strewn with bald, potbellied professors in Bermuda shorts, tight el-cheapo T-shirts, and Birkenstock-style sandals. The professors chatted with faculty wives and female professors with coiffed hair dyed and highlighted in copper shades, and with collagen-enhanced faces recommended by Dorit Landes, the celebrity, high-end cosmetic guru of yuppie *Haaretz*. The women sported chic garb with lace, zippers, and knotted fabric, often all in one piece. From my window-shopping in White City, Tel Aviv, I recognized the clothes as designer labels from Upper Dizengoff Boulevard boutiques.

In such a space, where no one tells Mizraḥim that they are not welcome (but they know it), almost everyone craned their necks and winced at our presence. All at once. Was it because they didn't expect darkies in their Ashkenazi space, let alone with a cello? Or did they identify Shaheen—and rightly so—as a scholarship kid from the barrio competing with their children? Like a pair of Pavlov's dogs, Shaheen and I switched to speaking English. The profs seemed to let down their territorial guard. Perhaps our carefree accents made us sound like hip Californians. But us? In the Bay Area, one sentence would suffice to peg us as native Hebrew speakers.

We had arrived at Gilman after five hours of standing in lines. That morning, we had gone to get my unemployment card stamped by a placement clerk at the employment bureau. The regime requires every disenfranchised single mother in Israel, myself included, to obtain a stamp as permission to receive a welfare check.

Once a month—every month—these single mothers from the slums pack themselves and their children into crowded buses to city centers. There is no affordable childcare. And the regime forbids welfare mothers from owning cars, even run-down jalopies. No exceptions.

At the employment bureau, mothers, clutching their children's hands tightly, dash inside and pounce upon ticket dispensers hung at European height. The higher the ticket number, the longer the wait. There are waiting areas, each with less than a dozen seats. But often, there are more than four dozen mothers waiting in front of each office. In the lines—amorphous throngs—mothers and children strain to hear placement clerks bark their numbers. Guards—handcuffs and batons dangling from their belts, pistols stowed in their holsters—stand ready to strike in case of a ruckus.

When a mother hears her number, she enters a placement clerk's office. About 50 percent of the time, the placement clerk hands the mother a print-out of a job opening, along with directions to the interview. These are jobs like changing diapers for the elderly in nursing homes or at-home cooking for disabled people. In Israel, these jobs require no special skills or degrees.

The mother then goes to her prospective employer. With her children. On the bus. She does the interview. G-d forbid if she misses it. If she does—no welfare. Never mind that the employer is certain to reject her for the position. Guest workers from Bulgaria, the Philippines, or Kerala have much lower employer costs.

Interview complete, the employer is supposed to report that the mother showed up and was rejected. At times, the employer, a man by default, may ask the mother to leave her children and follow him to the back of his office. She would know the offer he would make: his report back to the employment bureau in exchange for a blow job (Hertzog 1996, 2001).

After her interview, the mother returns to the employment bureau. With her children. On the bus. Upon arrival, she gets in line. Again. She takes a number. She waits to hear her number called. Only when in front of the placement clerk—for the second time—does she get her stamp. But even at this late stage, she cannot relax. So near to attaining her goal, the mother is more likely to succumb to a placement clerk's demands for sexual favors in exchange for the stamp. Finally, stamp in hand, she can travel to the NSB to obtain her welfare check.

And still one more hurdle. If she opens a bank account to deposit this lone check, she pays about 25 percent of the amount in fees and commissions. More likely, she cashes the check at the bank, pushes the wad of bills into her bra, goes straight home, wraps the money in plastic, and stuffs it into the gut of the lone chicken in the freezer.

This was the norm until 1 August 2003. Just as single mothers had gotten used to this routine, the Knesset ordered the Finance Ministry to halve the number of placement clerks. At the same time, the regime required that

11. Single mother at an appointment with an employment bureau placement clerk. His office is stocked with wines and spirits, as well as a parody of a prayer above the clerk's head in the same font as the Torah scroll: "All are governed by the creator of the universe. Thus, woe to you if you waste anyone's time." Meir Azulay, Beer Sheba, 2003.

mothers of children as young as two-and-a-half get the stamps from the employment bureaus. Previously, the law only applied to mothers of children aged five and up. So applicants more than doubled, and only half the clerks were available to service them.

Employment bureaus swelled with tangled strollers and crushed feet, the howls of toddlers, rattling toys, pungent diapers, Gerber's mashed pumpkin, and the mothers' sour sweat.

No participant observation for the anthropologist. I waited in those lines to hear my own number called. In my right pocket, my *tehillim*. And in my left, a small red granite stone from South Sinai's Naqb Shaheen — the majestic mountain pass where Shaheens, or royal falcons, once lived. The pass crosses the red, craggy cliffs that plummet into the blue depths of the ʿAqaba Gulf north of Dahab, my second home and long-term ethnographic field site. In my youth, when Naqb Shaheen was still pristine, before mass tourism descended upon it, I would retreat there to reflect and write my field notes. There, I dreamed of having a child as fierce and smart as the falcons.

The appointments with my placement clerk are always short and to the point. Lucky me, I had been assigned to a woman in 2001. Over the last two years, we had developed a good rapport.

"You are not eligible for The Wisconsin," she announced. "Too old."

For disenfranchised Israelis, *ha-Viskonsin* (The Wisconsin, Hebrew) does not refer to the name of the U.S. state of Wisconsin. It is a program. And a nightmare. This "Welfare-to-Work" initiative originated in the U.S. state of Wisconsin (Zilberg 2002). Dubbed *MeHaLev* (From the Heart, Hebrew) by the regime, it combines privatization of state-run programs with drastic cuts in welfare ('Eshet 2000). The elderly, physically disabled, and, yes, single mothers, are directly targeted. The regime requires welfare recipients to go to employment bureaus for thirty to forty hours a week to receive counseling, training, and job referrals. Individuals who still cannot find jobs are then conscripted into unpaid work painting schools or mowing public lawns. Only at the end of this process does a person receive welfare benefits (Adiv 2005).

"Overqualified," she declared in a Sabra-Hebrew accent, using the English word for lack of a Hebrew one. Her voice was somber. But I didn't have the energy to hypothesize if this was sympathy for my plight or disappointment that she wouldn't get her bonus for placing yet another single mother in The Wisconsin. Whatever. My heartbeat slowed down as my skin cooled in her air-conditioned office.

"Go to the *sotzialit*," she sighed. "Sotzialit" is Hebrew for "social worker case officer." "She'll TRY to slide you into the Committee for Exceptional Cases. Maybe they have a solution for a professor on cut welfare."

From March to June, I taught at the MA program at the Israeli branch of Lesley University and at Beit Berl Teacher's College. I worked six class hours a week and was paid by the hour. On average, I was making 1,200 New Israeli Shekels (about $276) a month. I was entitled to income augmentation of 447 NIS (about $103) from the NSB in order for me to reach half the minimum wage. The augmentation required that I go to the placement center, in vain, to seek additional jobs.

At the end of every semester, I was laid off. Hourly workers are not entitled to unemployment benefits. So I needed to go to the employment bureau to get the unemployment stamp for the NSB's full income assurance—once again, half the minimum wage.

Shaheen and I fried in the sun as we dragged ourselves from the employment bureau to the NSB. With his cello. On the bus. Before we even stepped inside, we waited in a line 78 people long to get through the security checkpoint. Once through the door, we joined another line of 213 people, all waiting to be sorted by a clerk into the right offices. After I was sorted, a clerk sent us to wait in one last line, some 155 people long. We stood the entire time.

Finally, I could speak to someone about my problem. I was to receive 447 NIS (about $103) income augmentation for June. This was apart from anything I was owed for July or August. My application for full income assurance had not kicked in yet. I wanted someone to explain why I received only 401 NIS (about $92) for my June income augmentation. The printout in my hands showed that I should have gotten 447.

How did the state expect a mother to provide for her son and herself on 401 NIS? Lucky for us, an anonymous donor saw "the unemployed single mother Berkeley professor" advocating Mizraḥi feminism on prime-time TV and paid our rent. For my middle-class American colleagues, a TV appearance is an act of agency. But for me? Divinity of Chance. For one month's rent. But what about my missing income augmentation? Would luck be on my side?

No. I found out that the missing money was because of a new amendment to Ḥok HaHesderim. This law cut the income augmentation for single mothers who dared to work. If a single mother didn't work, her income assurance was left intact and made her an excellent candidate for The Wisconsin.

Shaheen calculated our financial world in increments of milk bags. The weekly food donations from Operation Open Heart did not include milk. So we bought milk at the store. And 46 NIS meant nine bags, or about thirty-six cups of milk.

Every summer, I take my son to bear these lines. It is vital to me that he sees this process. A dark child with no trust fund and no one to pull strings for him to get ahead, he must understand the Mizraḥi struggle firsthand to survive.

Shaheen and I were trespassers across the Gilman border because of our skin. In the lines, we don't cross any race or gender border. Most of the humiliated mothers in these lines are Mizraḥi. The humiliators are also Mizraḥi—low-level welfare clerks and single mothers caught up in the state's welfare bureaucracy. No need for English. I can comfortably speak in Tel Aviv slang. An extra bonus is practicing our Arabic with the *muḥajja-bat* (veiled women, Arabic) from Jaffa in the next line.

21 July 2003

I must reply to the letter of Esther Rabinowitz[1]—what a classic Eastern European last name!—who heads the service for income assurance and augmentation at the NSB's Tel Aviv branch.

I must defer to her by using the official-style language that she herself uses—including the vestiges of Israel's socialist era, when comrades were addressed last name first. What follows is my letter to her. I use my Geertz translation machine to insert "thick descriptions" between the lines.

To the honorable
Rabinowitz Esther Claim Clerk
    [She used the masculine in Hebrew for clerk]
The National Security Bureau
The Service for Income Assurance and Augmentation
RE: Your 15 July 2003 Letter:

Dear Ms. Rabinowitz,

Your letter from 15 July, postmarked 16 July, arrived yesterday, 20 July. Enclosed is a copy of your letter, marked "Exhibit 1" for your convenience. I would like to call your attention to the following:

    1. Your letter states that I am entitled to receive income augmentation totaling 447 NIS. Yesterday I spent about half an hour with Ms. Davidi, the dedicated clerk at the post office branch on Ibn Gabirol Street. In a special gesture of goodwill, she spent nearly an hour on

the phone, traversing the hierarchy of Post Office Bank clerks to track down my missing income augmentation.

Why was I at the post office rather than the NSB?

Around the first of every month, the NSB paid out income assurances or augmentation in one of two ways: the first was by issuing a physical check that a welfare recipient would pick up at the NSB after getting the stamp from her placement clerk. In the second, the NSB deposited money directly into an account with Israel's Post Office Bank. A recipient would present a stamp to a claims clerk at the NSB, and then the clerk would clear her monthly allotment with the Post Office Bank. The recipient could then withdraw funds by showing her ID to a clerk at the post office.

Oftentimes, a single mother, with her children (on the bus), may have arrived to the post office to be told that there is no sum of money in her name, and that her check was probably at the NSB. And after the mother survived the lines at the NSB, the check-dispensing clerk would announce, "No check. Go back to the post office." This runaround could last up to three weeks. Since rent was always due on the first of the month, she would return home to find a seven-day eviction notice taped to her door.

And as no surprise:

She told me there was no sum of money in my name. Because of my repeated appeals to your office, I am urgently requesting you to personally investigate the disappearance of these funds.

2. As for the assertions raised in your letter, "Your phone appeal was full of ethnic—even racist—remarks bordering on insulting a public servant, and in the future, such an appeal will not be answered," please permit me to respond as follows: The way you addressed me was unconcerned, patronizing, and full of false accusations about me and all single mothers.

Rabinowitz's assertions, in the eternal present tense: single mothers spend tax money to bleach their hair blonde, get manicures and pedicures, and smoke imported cigarettes. Further, they eagerly open their legs to financially exploit men, but remain on the dole by failing to report any additional income to the NSB.

This is how the Israeli public views single mothers.

These have nothing to do with the limited scope of my specific request for you to track down my missing income augmentation.

3. Considering items 1 and 2 of this letter, and in light of our phone and written communications, non-orientals are also capable of exaggerating, being emotional, and telling tall tales. Perhaps the definition of *dimyon Mizraḥi* (oriental imagination, Hebrew) should be revised.

What the heck? She wasn't going to do anything, anyway.

BABAḤ,

Smadar Lavie

BABAḤ is an acronym for *BeBirkat Ḥaverim*, Hebrew for "With the Blessings of the Comrades." This is EXACTLY how she signed her letter.

Like many Israelis, I cc'd the ombudsman of the State Comptroller's Bureau, who was supposed to look out for the little guy. Just in case he would like to know. This was my modest, if futile, attempt to enact my subaltern agency designated for me by my radicals-of-the-keyboard colleagues. I went through the motions, even though I would have no effect at all on Rabinowitz. My only alternative, a competent attorney, would have cost me 1,200 cups of milk an hour.

7 May 2003

Here I am, clinging to life for Shaheen and me, and I get an email from a Fuchs at law-dot-Oxford-dot-ac-dot-uk. Ominous, and yet another reminder of my parallel lives as former University of California star professor, welfare

12. Armed guards man the outermost security checkpoint at the National Security Bureau in Jaffa. This guard, noticing the photographer, threatens to break the camera. Esti Tsal, 2013.

mother, and angry feminist advocating the Mizraḥi struggle in Israel's mainstream media. The email was from Amir Fuchs—I deciphered the privilege from his last name—an Israeli PhD student from Oxford Law School. In proper Oxbridge Hebrew, he asked for my commentary as a women's studies scholar on a draft of his case note about Ḥok HaHesderim.

I read it. I loved it. I shot back an email:

Dear Amir,

Thanks for sending me the draft of your case note regarding Ḥok HaHesderim. Your manuscript deals with my lived reality and provides a brilliant analysis of the ideologies and methodologies underlying the policies and implementations of Ḥok HaHesderim, whether historically, or through the prism of the economy of rational determinism. I appreciate your discussion of racialized social engineering throughout its history. In footnote 17, perhaps you should not only quote Kate Millett.[2] You need to consider the big dispute on issues of poverty, single motherhood, and the welfare state between the White radical feminists (Millett included), and the Black Civil Rights Movement. See also Toni Cade,[3] in *The Black Woman*, where she discusses the violence of the welfare state against non-White single mothers, and how White feminists, even radicals, conveniently ignore the racinated gendering of the welfare state, in the laissez-faire style of Rabbi Hillel, or blame dark women for their situations, like in the Halakhic school of Rabbi Shamai, who often blames victims for their sins.

Perhaps we ought to develop together an Israeli model outlining the interrelationalities between welfare legislation and the idiosyncratic patriarchy characterizing our (post)colonial settler state, where most of the immigrants are racinated dark, and the ruling minority has racinated itself White.

Cordially,

Smadar[4]

Diary—June 2003

How the fuck am I going to co-author a scholarly article when my brain is completely shut down from teaching and standing in lines?

I still manage to exchange a couple of co-authored drafts with Amir.

Email—10 July 2003

Amir—URGENT! No time for scholarlese! Vicky Knafo is already in Jerusalem! I wove the feminist theory portions and their relevance to Israel into your draft. We must cut, prep, and send it to a daily, ASAP! There's a media circus around Vicky, but no genuine discussion of policies or implementations. Tomorrow is Friday. I need to prepare for Shabbat. I won't be online. Please get back to me ASAP.

Smadar

6 August 2003

As a director on the board of Aḥoti — For Women in Israel, I have to apologize for an absence at a crucial event via email:

Good morning everybody,

Alas, but I won't be able to participate tomorrow in the Tishʿa B'Av march from the Knafoland encampment to the Western Wall.

Tishʿa B'Av. What a perfect day to hold a well-televised single mothers' "March of Dimes"!

Must take care of my granny. She is fasting, therefore grouchy. Only reciting the *Diwan*⁵ into her ear calms her fear of the divine.

As for thoughts on the future: on the one hand, there is the sectorial composition of Knafoland and the demonstrations around it — Mizraḥi and post-Soviet single mothers. How interesting that in Hebrew, "sector" is reserved as a descriptor for a disenfranchised group. Sectors constitute the Israeli majority. And how interesting it is that no one ever uses "sector" to describe the privileged junta who runs the country . . .

Remember, the mothers kicked out the Bedouin, and we chose not to interfere.

The history of such protests demonstrates that the regime can play sectors against each other, buying protesters one by one with seductive solutions, temporary as they may be.

On the other hand — in my modest opinion — the protest will expand if it includes other sectors, like middle-class single mothers on their way to becoming Knafos because the Supreme Court's 1997 appeal verdict 4445/96 makes collecting child support impossible.[6] Or families on the verge of financial bankruptcy who have lost their children to the forced boarding school system because they couldn't pay the bills[7] (this morning I must fill out an NSB form to consent to yet more surveillance — due to my poverty, the form suggests that I send my son to boarding school, a foster family, or wealthier relatives) . . .

How do we craft a platform to include all these sectors? How do we get it into the media? Like everything in Israel, it's not real until it shows up in the evening news.

> Let my spirit be with you,
>
> Smadar

29 June 2003

Ḥok HaHesderim goes into effect. No money for me at the Post Office Bank or the NSB. Rent is due the day after tomorrow.

Breathe. Stay calm. Count to five.

Nonetheless, I hear the Kabalic Angels of Wrath flapping.[8] I break free from the brackets. Here is my rage:

My Ashkenazi, white sisters to the scholarly struggle — I am your alien worker. I am your *schwartze* who does the black work[9] — the work you disdain. When you depart for your professorial sabbaticals to think and write, I teach your students. Not even an adjunct. No retirement. No access to research and development funds. No paid time to think, to write, not even to prepare for YOUR classes.

You throw me bones — a course here, a lecture there — one week of rent if I'm lucky. And despite the choke chain you put on me, I will not shut up.

I am your deformed mirror. You are afraid to look, scared that your enlightened racism will talk back at you:

Sisterhood? Who are your sisters — your white women colleagues at the university? Your elite-ivy-league American audiences, who buy the Israeli sisterhood you market in English? Who buys your enlightenment? We, the Mizraḥi majority, with our taxes, finance your lifestyle, so when you travel abroad, you can take the whole family as a research tax deduction.[10] Will your childhood friends, now on the bench, force you to vacate space for us around the faculty meeting table, even though we don't have parents or husbands who finance feminism as a hobby?

So you avoid me. You make valiant efforts to set yourselves apart from the regime as feminists and pacifists and humanists. How long can you keep your lies going?[11] There is a boycott going on. Academics and NGOs now document your compliance. Never mind that you have cultivated your handful of Mizraḥi and Palestinian academic pets.

The Education Ministry might surveil your syllabi. But the Propaganda Ministry sends you across the Atlantic to universities that dare let students have an Israel Apartheid Week. It pays your honoraria to entice their cash-strapped Mideast centers to place you on their speaker lists (Traubmann 2006).

You would never acknowledge that you actually are the willing participants in the Nicer Face of Israel's antiboycott campaign.

You prattle on in English about transnational feminist peace alliances. With whom? Your donors? At your conferences abroad, when you schmooze with academic journal editors to get your papers published? For whom? Not moms in the 'hoods. They graduate from the underfunded slum schools barely proficient in Standard Hebrew. Proper English isn't even on the menu.

From the podium, you quote Ruth Frankenberg,[12] but do you ever contemplate creating a support group, Frankenberg-style, to undo your own intra-Jewish apartheid?

1 August 2003

The fax machine clanks to life and spits out a fax. It is an article from Rafi Shubeli, a fellow activist—something he cut from the Law and Justice section of *Makor Rishon* (Primary Source, Hebrew). He sent it because we are both engaged in the consciousness-raising of the Mizraḥi public on their rights to due process in court.

It has been four years since the Israeli regime confiscated my Israeli passport and stranded me in this uppity puddle.[13] It is no longer startling to read the most probing critiques of the Israeli court's intra-Jewish affairs in the West Bank settlers' weekly paper.

Most settlers are Mizraḥim. Most *Makor Rishon* journalists are Ashkenazim. The intellectual elite consider these journalists pariah, however, because they publicly support the settlers. So, they don't have friends or relatives who spin around the revolving door between the bench, the faculties of Israel's law schools, and the legal desks of major dailies.

It's that time of year again. Every midsummer, the Committee for the Selection and Appointment of Judges announces the names of new judges.[14] What follows is the article I received in the fax. I once again charge up my Geertz translation machine to thickly describe the article.

Our Madam, the Judge
By Yair Shapira

If you are a Jerusalemite, an observant woman — but graduated from Tel Aviv's exclusive Alliance High School — moved on to major in law at the Hebrew University, and you are turning forty-three this year, you have a good chance at being appointed judge . . .[15]

Alliance High School is in Ramat Aviv, an exclusive Ashkenazi neighborhood and Tel Aviv's enclave of hypersecularism. Thus, it is quite impossible to be an observant woman AND an Alliance graduate. The author, in using available demographic data to create an oxymoronic composite, immediately elicits a smirk from the reader.

One ought not to disregard the ethnic profiling of the judges selected for the lower courts, because of the following:

First, they are in charge of solving most of society's conflicts — between one person and another, or between a person and state authorities.

Single mothers are at the complete mercy of these judges. A mother would need to secure an attorney to advocate for her—either pro bono through National Legal Aid or paid out of pocket[16]—to even have a chance against this lineup:

- Civil Court judges decide on evictions.
- Labor Court judges decide on cases with the NSB in disputes over the eligibility and sums of welfare.
- Collection Court judges decide how to collect and enforce debt.

   A mother might find herself in Collection Court to collect child support from a deadbeat dad. Though the Supreme Court verdict 4445/96 makes it almost impossible, a mother will always try.

   On the other hand, if a mother owes money to a creditor—the phone company, gas company, even a dry cleaner—a Collection Court judge can order the Collection Court Police Force to confiscate her refrigerator, stove, TV, and beds to be sold at government auctions to cover her debts, not to mention the creditor's legal costs.[17] The judge might even mail her a notice to show up to jail.

   A distraught mother might plead to a sotzialit for aid. But the sotzialit could very well submit, without the mother's consent, an expert opinion to Family Court against the mother—declaring her unable to provide her children with residential and nutritional stability.

- Family Court judges take in sotzialit recommendations to remove children from their families. Often, to quickly clear the clutter from their overloaded desks, they rubber-stamp the sotzialit's recommendations without a hearing.
- Youth Court judges decide if children are delinquent for skipping school to work, so the children's mother can afford an attorney, so that she can take the NSB to Labor Court, so the family makes rent, so they are not evicted, so the bills are paid, so that mom doesn't go to prison. Youth Court judges issue orders for children they deem delinquent to be removed from their homes and forcibly placed into boarding schools (Hertzog 1996, 2004a).[18]

Both the Collection Court Police and the Welfare Ministry Children's Van make sure to arrive at dawn to collect their quarry. It is the best time to find everybody at home.

It costs the Welfare Ministry seven times the amount to board a child than it does to provide a mother with direct financial assistance (Hertzog 1996, 2004a). But the boarding schools' staff are unionized and are therefore difficult to disband. Labor Court judges do not dare mess with powerful unions.

Sooner or later, attorneys for single mothers decide that these labyrinthine cases are practice killers. So they quit.

Back to *Makor Rishon*:

The second reason not to disregard the ethnic profiling of judges is that most district court judges are selected from the pool of lower court judges, and most Supreme Court judges are selected from the pool of district court judges . . .

In the present round of appointments, let us note that the majority of judges are women. One can applaud this triumph of affirmative action. Or one can perceive judgeship as the ideal working mother's job—regular working hours, short commutes, possibility to work from home, and, last, but not least, respectability.

All this political correctness from the Committee for the Selection and Appointment of Judges is nice and good . . .

Indeed, in the list of appointees, one can find a few male names attached to surnames like Itaḥ or Sharʿabi. [These are common Mizrahi last names.] But they drown in the ocean of Rotfeld, Wolfson, Greenfeld, and Abramowitz.[19]

Israel has no affirmative action. Mizrahi men compete directly for judgeships with Ashkenazi women. The committee sees both as "diversity candidates."[20] Ashkenazi women remind the committee members—men by default—of their mothers, aunties, sisters, and childhood sweethearts—Ashkenazi by default. Many of these women candidates are married to star attorneys in the private sector who are already networked into the legal system and thus pull strings for their wives.

———————————

There are only two Arabs. [Palestinians, that is—*Makor Rishon* wouldn't acknowledge them as such.] That is less than 7 percent of the appointees, far from the 20 percent that makes up their citizenry in Israel.

Only one of the appointees went to school in a development town.
In 'Arad.

———————————

'Arad is not your usual development town. Though it keeps up appearances with a well-bounded segment of slums—home to Ilana Azoulay—it boasts a large visible Ashkenazi community. Set in the biblical beauty of the desert plateau above the Dead Sea, it attracts *Anglo-Saxim* (Anglo-Saxons, Hebrew plural for Jewish immigrants from South Africa, Britain, Australia, and North America), the English-speaking crème de la crème of the Ashkenazi pecking order. They flock to 'Arad for its clean, dry air—good for asthmatics—and its manicured boulevards. Not to mention the tax breaks the Israeli regime gives to these pioneers who settle the frontier.[21] Even Israel's perennial candidate for the Nobel Prize in Literature, Amos Oz, makes his home in 'Arad.

The author of the article planned this denouement, envisioning his reader snickering behind the broadsheet.

22 July 2003

Late evening. Shaheen and I, back from Jerusalem, back in our rented apartment. Exhausted. Sunburned—not that anyone would notice the red hue of our olive skin. All afternoon we picketed, seared to succulence by the high summer sun.

Hooray! The coalition is growing! Two more sectors marched on Jerusalem: members of the NGOs, People Homeless and Hurt by Mortgages, and the Coalition of Homeless Single-Headed Families, along with Captive Infants, an NGO whose members fight against the shipment of children, without their parents' consent, to boarding schools, foster homes, and adoptions.[22]

Some good souls had brought *bristolim* (bristol boards, Hebrew plural) stapled to sticks and brightly colored Sharpies so protestors could make their own placards. These good souls also translated the protesters' slogans to English to catch the foreign press's eye. Shaheen and I came up with our own slogan in red and black letters, complete with postmodernist language games, parentheses and all:

Medinat (Tz)hok
Tugat HaʿOni

In Hebrew, *medinat hok* is a democratic state governed by a code of law. *Medinat tzhok*, literally, "a state of laughter," means a state that ridicules its own laws. We used parentheses to create a pun stating that Israeli laws make the state a parody of a democracy.

Below, we wrote *Tugat haʿoni*, meaning "the sorrow of poverty."

With the parentheses, this pair of passé structuralist binarisms disintegrated into Derridian traces deconstructing the Zionist simulacrum of the welfare state. What a killer line of gobbledygook for the former professor to plant in a cultural studies journal. Ripe for quotation . . .

"Mom, this doesn't translate to English," Shaheen wryly commented. "Only local media for us—if we're lucky." My son's second language was deconstruction. When he was a baby, and I a UC Davis junior professor, I schlepped him to class for lack of funds for a babysitter.[23]

One good soul in a khaki linen suit approached us. Who the heck wears a suit in July? An Anglo-Saxit (feminine singular for Anglo-Saxim) with a Dorit Landes face. She introduced herself in Hebrew—using her growling, English R—as a Jerusalem sotzialit on a late lunch break.

"Are you Yemeni or Ethiopian?" she cooed to Shaheen.

We glanced at each other, fear in our eyes. We shut up. Anything we said could be used against us. Instead, Shaheen clutched his sign, stuck it in front of her face. We kept marching.

No more field notes. The Kabalic Angels of Wrath, again, throbbing in my soul:

> You are our bosses
> You DSM us
> You judge us in court
> You primitivize us
> Write us up as your anthropology
> Uninvited, rob us of our PR
> Do our feminism for us
> It won't take off past philanthropy
> Occupational therapy
> Always sure you have your token
> A darn-good-looking little Yemeni
> What an exotic jewel
> Your CYA
> I refuse.

I hear mirages. Feminist theory of color. Classic lines rehearsed so many times in class:

Criticism by Black Women during this period [when the White Feminist movement established itself] was mixed with an undeniable tone of disdain. "There was no abiding admiration of White women as competent, complete people," [Toni] Morrison declared. Black women regarded them as "willful children, pretty children, mean children, ugly children, but never as real adults." That they were seen as children was because of their social situation in life—described by activist Eleanor Holmes Norton as one "sinking in a sea of close-quartered affluence where one's world is one's house, one's peers, one's children, and one's employer, one's husband." That this kind of woman was gaining power was what bothered many Black women—more than the goals of the women's movement or even NOW. (Giddings 1985, 307)

You show us not only the *Color of Privilege* (Hurtado 1996), but also that your fight against the patriarch is feigned. Instead, you seduce the patriarch for personal and professional profit. Oh so well-versed in the white-on-white postmodernist theoretical shoptalk, you use that veneer to hide your racist and classist politics.[24] Nothing has changed: "The avenues of advancement through marriage that are open to White women who conform to prescribed standards of middle-class femininity are not even a theoretical possibility for most women of color" (Ostrander, quoted in Hurtado 1996, 11).

Your feminism is not liberation. It is containment. The classic lines banging in my head:

> White women face the pitfall of being seduced into joining the oppressor under the pretense of sharing power. . . . The tokenism that is sometimes extended to us [Women of Color] is not an invitation to join power; our racial "otherness" is a visible reality. . . . For White women there is a wider range of pretended choices and rewards for identifying with patriarchal power and its tools. (Lorde 1984, 118–19)

The Angels of Wrath are gone. For now. The cheap yogurt I ladled onto my blistered arms has cooled their fire.

I open my laptop, gingerly trot my fingers across the keys to prevent the yogurt from dropping onto them. I send my U.S. friends the link to the *Los Angeles Times* piece on Vicky Knafo (see King 2003). My commentary reads: http://articles.latimes.com/2003/jul/18/world/fg-welfare18[25]

Please note that all foreign press articles but this one portray Knafo-land as a generic Israeli gender-focused social protest.

This LA *Times* piece puts the right color—dark—on Israel's Jewish poverty. Even if the author uses "Sephardim" rather than explain "Mizrahim" for her English-speaking readership. Likewise, this is the only article without quotes from Israeli university gender experts.

13. Ethiopians and Mizraḥim wait in a hunger line to receive food donations from NGO Pit'ḥon Lev (Open Heart, Hebrew). Pit'ḥon Lev operates out of an underground parking garage in Rishon LeZion, a city just outside of Tel Aviv. Pit'ḥon Lev, 2011.

A worker for SHATIL's English division of the NIF PR department—a fixture in Vicky's tent—was always ready to translate for foreign reporters interviewing Vicky. I too was in the tent but didn't want to make waves. So I said nothing. But I did note that the NIF translator always swapped in "poor Israelis" every time Vicky said "Mizraḥim."

Perhaps the translator did this because simple Israel-Palestine dualism makes the biggest news abroad. Or perhaps the translator was already calculating the donations to NIF from progressive diaspora Jews alarmed at the possibility of Jewish hunger and homelessness in the Jewish homeland.

Of course the translator couldn't afford to inform potential donors about the color of Israeli poverty. How would progressive diaspora

Jews—important contributors to civil rights and anti-apartheid movements—react to the revelation of Israeli intra-Jewish racism?

When the LA *Times* journalist showed up to interview Vicky, the NIF translator was not in the tent. She had gone to pee. I knew she would be gone for at least half an hour, because I had earlier heard her complain about the squat toilet port-a-potties the municipality had installed by the encampment. To use the Knesset's fancy public toilets, she had to cross the park, passing by the menorah plaza, and then go through security.

So I stepped in. But I refused to act as the academic gender expert for the journalist. Vicky is so eloquent that I simply translated her word for word.

29 July 2003

Late evening. Sitting in the cool garden of my granny in the Beit Israel 'hood. Before 1948, a fifteen-minute walk to the Western Wall. Between 1948 and 1967, a Mizraḥi slum bisected by the Jordanian border and cut off from the Wall. After 1967, Jordan was out. Granny could once again walk to the Wall on Shabbat. Along with the ultra-Orthodox Brooklyn Jews who bought out the Mizraḥim. Granny got a new next-door neighbor—the ultranationalist Rabbi Meir Kahane. I could walk our dog across the street to Palestinian Jerusalem and snoop out the next day's international headlines at the American Colony Hotel Bar. I just needed to convert some precious food coupons into enough NIS to buy a drink.[26]

I've just completed a gig for no less than WIZO, the Women's International Zionist Organization. I was a guest lecturer for the annual course of their School for Women's Political Leadership. The school organizers, as well as a handful of students, were Ashkenazim.

The Jerusalem WIZO center is in the superexclusive Talbiyya neighborhood. After 1948, the higher echelons of the government's professional elite took over Talbiyya's grandiose, hewn-stone mansions, built in the 1920s by the Palestinian elite. Talbiyya is the official residence of Israel's prime minister.

WIZO bussed most of its students to the weekly lectures in Talbiyya from the economically depressed Mizraḥi *moshavim* (farming co-ops) of the Jerusalem corridor.[27]

In the postlecture discussion, many women said that it was the first time in the course that they had felt present, and that the feminism I had lectured about was theirs.

With pauses and hesitations, they started to exchange their own stories about how they each wrestled with racism. They got it. A Eureka moment. Something beyond the individual cases of the lived experience they labeled "deprivation" or "discrimination."

But of course, this evening — like every time I give a lecture — an Ashkenazi stood up and addressed me with sugarcoated venom: "I really enjoyed your lecture. But all you've done is use haughty language and generalizations to talk about your own problems. We've all read about it in the press. We've seen you on TV. Is this really feminism?"

"And last week," piped up another Ashkenazi student, "when the gender studies professor taught us that in feminism the personal is political, I thought you'd come here and be our example. I disagree with her." She motioned toward the first student. "Smadar didn't exactly tell us her personal story. It was all theory talk."

Here we go. More "personalism" (Hurtado 1996, 33). Once again, I hold up the mirror so the white woman can see the reality she creates for me. And once again, she ignores the reflection. She trivializes my feminist paradigm into a festering wound she must watch me pick at. For her, my wound is for my psychotherapist, not a lecture (Hurtado 1996). Her wound can make the transition from the personal to the political in the name of sisterhood. My wound is divisive to the sisterhood. Therefore she won't let me expose it to the public. She refuses to understand that my wound is our wound.

When the student blames me for personalism, she "leaves us without a comprehensive theory for understanding the very real structural oppression that exists based on the simultaneity of gender, race, and class *group membership*" (Hurtado 1996, 33–34).

"Thanks for sharing." I slapped a smile on my face. "Can you please tell the group the ethnic backgrounds of your woman friends? Your best five, the ones you talk to on the phone or go to cafés with every Friday. Are they Ashkenazi? Mizraḥi? Secular? Religious? Maybe . . . Palestinians?"

No response. Only the hum of the air conditioner.

"I never a s k ." She fidgeted with her hands. "Actually, they are all Ashkenazi—Israeli, that is."

As I write this diary entry, I fish a book out of my bag—my brand-new copy of Orly Lubin's *Woman Reading Woman*, the last word in radical Hebrew poststructuralist feminist theory:

> The discussion of survival and modes of survival, subversion, and subversive activity, in formations of criticism or in the act of reading as a critical act, will take place, therefore, around creations of women and actions of criticism, subversion, and survival done mainly by women, but the discussion will relate to any act of criticism, subversion, and survival done by the margins, be these women, Mizraḥim, Palestinians, Homosexuals, Blacks, Hispanics, or the disabled. (Lubin 2003, 13)

Hallelujah. This is the penultimate sentence from the book's introduction, directly translated except for punctuation I add to make it easier to understand. How elegantly does Lubin transcend the specificities of oppressions' histories, national liberations, racial struggles, sexualities, cultures, even health. It is all about the Monochromatic Woman.

In the typical scholarly shortcut, I jump from the introduction to the bibliography and index in the back. Scrutinizing the bib—packed into twelve pages of itsy-bitsy font—I only spot two female theoreticians of color: Gayatri Spivak and bell hooks. Everyone quotes them. Where are the rest of the feminist-of-color classics? Feminists of color used poststructuralist, deconstructionist theory as a springboard for the critical analysis of the intersection of gender/sex, race, class, with citizenship and nation. Not in Lubin's subversive reads.

Aha! I'm so glad to meet the Mizraḥim in the index. Once again, we are the data to be ethnographed so the Ashkenazi professor can copyright our oppression for merit and promotion. Lubin only mentions Ella Shohat of NYU, and even then, only cites the sole work of Shohat that is not embedded in feminist theory of color. Where are the other Mizraḥi feminist voices? Where is Vicky Shiran, the founder of Mizraḥi feminism?

> Mizraḥi feminism is a school of critical thought shaped . . . by dialogue with . . . Black and Third World feminists. . . . This is how Mizraḥi feminism exposes the common practice of Ashkenazi feminism: how it advertises itself as a universalist platform that represents all Israeli women . . . as if Mizraḥi and Palestinian women are, indeed, equal partners in determining . . . the [Israeli feminist] discourse and struggles. . . .
> Mizraḥi feminists do not agree with how Ashkenazi feminists see Mizraḥi and Palestinian women—as decorative representation to their feminism. Mizraḥi feminists fight for genuine power sharing.
> Ashkenazi feminists are aware of Mizraḥi feminism's critique: that Ashkenazi feminists treat Mizraḥi and Palestinian women the same way men act toward women.
> So as their men deny gender-based discrimination, Ashkenazi feminists deny their discrimination against Mizraḥi and Palestinian women on grounds of class, ethnicity, and nation. This denial enables them to appear in a false show as if they represent . . . half of the state's citizens, when they are, in fact, sectorial representatives of their well-defined minority. . . .
> Facing our piercing critique, Ashkenazi feminists' tactics—like men's tactics—silence and denounce us. They say: "We all should fight the real oppression instead of fighting amongst ourselves."[28]
> Of course, it is easy for [Ashkenazi feminists] to achieve nods of agreement. In the prevalent hegemonic discourse in Israel, any kind of Mizraḥi criticism is always already condemned. (Shiran 2002)

Now I get the student's anxiety. Fragments of her sentences float in my mind:
When the gender studies professor taught us. . . . I thought you'd come here and be our example. . . . But you . . . all theory talk.

She wants me to be a piece of data indexed in the back of a feminist theory book (see Alarcón 1990).

Feminism of color redeemed white feminism from its ghettoization. But Ashkenazi feminists are afraid to recognize the jagged gulf of differences between us and them. They won't use their privilege to build bridges, to foster an economy that profits from diversity. Of course, even if they would, they would run the diversity industry like they run everything else in Israel. *Ya ḥaram!*[29] In "their America," people of color are called "minorities." But we ain't minorities. We are the 50 percent—with the Palestinian citizens of Israel, 70. They are afraid if they open that door, even just a crack, they'll eventually be kicked out.

But not to worry. The resistive power of our masses is kaput. As Shiran used to say, we birth our children not under a ceiling of glass, but one of cement.

18 August 2003

"Tomorrow, I'm going back home," rasped Ilana Azoulay last night. She was hoarse—maybe from screaming, maybe from smoking. Maybe from both. She and I huddled in her tent. Everyone else had gone up the hill to the park's vista point. Charlie Biton, cofounder of the Jerusalem Black Panthers and a retired Knesset member, was showing a film about the Panthers. Israeli Public TV was there to cover Biton with the single mothers and their fans. His PR agent probably texted the crew about the possible scoop: "The old Mizraḥi rebel educates the new."

Back in the tent, the air was cold and quiet. Ilana was quiet. Her hair was a newly styled, soft blonde, probably donated by a volunteer hairdresser— one of many who flocked to Jerusalem. In her tan, brawny arms, she cradled her old, three-legged Chihuahua. This was not the Ilana I had gotten to know, the pressed coil ready to spring.

I felt her resignation.

"I figured out Bibi's speech yesterday. A new work-placement plan. Same old stamps, same old lines." She snickered in staccato, her lips puckered inward over her gums. Dentists also flocked to volunteer for the mothers. Alas, philanthropy did not include dental implants.[30]

"Ethnic cleansing—this is what he is doing to us single moms. Ethnic cleansing."

My anthro-radar lit up. Ilana had said *tihur etni*, the literal Hebrew translation of "ethnic cleansing." During the identity-politics-happy 1990s, the term showed up in Hebrew op-eds and late-night TV *Apostrophe*-style roundtables as a descriptor for the Nakba.[31] The anti-Zionist Ashkenazi intelligentsia used *tihur etni* to quote the Palestinian diasporic intelligentsia's English-language Nakba scholarship. But Ilana? Using Nakba lingo? She was the one who initiated the move to kick Zeina, the Bedouin single mother, out of the encampment.

"These feminists came last week. They made us a weekend picnic. Yoga was cute. And what do they get from this? What? Were their kids taken away? Were their allowances cut? . . . So there were also Mizraḥi feminists there. So what? . . . If I'm destined to die, let it be in 'Arad. At least now they'll put me in subsidized housing, give me new teeth, and an electric wheelchair for my kid."

She referred to her deal with the encampment sotzialit—what she got in exchange for stopping her protest.

"And you? If you'd have come here from the start to live with your kid. . . . Damn them. May their names be erased. How they slashed you." She said this in a blasé tone, all the while her Chihuahua nuzzling her armpit. "At max, you would have gotten a buncha donation checks outta this. Not a university professorship outta this. Forget it. You—forbidden from going there. The university. There—no need for ethnic cleansing of Mizraḥim. There—Ashkenazim, all of 'em. No need."

"Why didn't you join everybody else to watch the film and get on TV?" I asked.

"Tell me," she said. "Have you hit your head? What will I get out of climbing to the top of the hill to see the film Charlie Biton brought about the Black Panthers?" She turned her head toward her dog, hugged it tight against the faded, stretched tattoo on her bicep. "So, buddy. What'd ya think? We've lost another photo-op on the nightly news."

CHAPTER 6

The Price of National Security

Knafoland—The End

The Knafo struggle ended the day after the conversation with Ilana about the Israeli regime's ethnic cleansing of Mizraḥi single mothers.

On the evening of 19 August 2003, a Palestinian suicide bomber dressed as an Orthodox Jew carried an explosive device aboard Bus #2 from the Western Wall into Jewish Jerusalem. The device detonated just past Peace Rd. #1 at the American Colony Hotel crossroad—the old 1967 border between Palestinian Jerusalem and Mizraḥi Jerusalem. Three hundred meters (around one thousand feet) away from my granny's house.

Twenty-three people died. Over 130 were injured. Most of the casualties were ultra-Orthodox Jews. One Filipina domestic worker also died.

This ended the hudna between Israel and Ḥamas.

Before the bombing, the national and international media whiled away the uneventful days of the hudna in their own encampment near Knafoland. When their beepers, cell phones, and two-way radios buzzed with news of the bombing, they all leapt up in unison. In a press corps caravan, they sped across town to cover the carnage at the border. Afterward, they went to the American Colony Hotel Bar to get drunk. So did I, with my converted food coupons to purchase a drink I would nurse for hours and my California English to gather information.

Forever the anthropologist, forever collecting data.

Without media coverage, the sotzialits took advantage. They offered mothers minimal incentives to leave and reminded them that if their children were not in school come 1 September, they'd be reported as delinquents to the Youth and Family Courts. The judges could then order the removal of

14. Paramedics, firefighters, police, and members of ZAKA, an emergency response team specializing in recovering Jewish bodies for proper burial, inspect the wreckage of Bus #2's suicide bombing. Lior Mizraḥi, 2003.

the children from their homes to be forcibly placed into boarding schools (Hertzog 1996, 2004b).

The plight of the single mothers was completely off the public agenda in favor of the Palestine-Israel conflict. Most mothers left the encampment within a few days of the bombing. Only Vicky and a few diehards stayed until 23 September 2003, when Vicky herself departed.

For Jewish New Year 2004, Vicky Knafo, strapped for cash, posed nude for an Israeli porn website. For this photo-op, she had written on her breasts: "The State Milks Single Mothers." Later, she sued the owners of the site because they didn't pay her what they promised.

On the eve of Jewish New Year 2005, Vicky's son committed suicide. Right after Jewish New Year 2006, Vicky joined the Meretz Party, the predominantly Ashkenazi, left-leaning, land-for-peace party, and started giving speeches about peace. Shortly thereafter, she completely disappeared from the public sphere.

From 2006 until January 2009, Bibi Netanyahu, head of Likud, led the Knesset's parliamentary opposition. Between 27 December 2008 and 18 January 2009, the IDF conducted Operation "Cast Lead." Its name was borrowed from a lyric about the miracle of Hanukkah written by Haim Nachman Bialik, Israel's national poet.[1] "My teacher gave me a dreidel cast from solid lead,"[2] Bialik wrote, to the tune of an Ashkenazi folk song. In Arabic, Operation "Cast Lead," is referred to as "The Gaza Carnage."[3] The operation involved a massive three-week bombing and invasion of the densely populated Gaza Strip. This was prime scheduling, as the United States would be deep in President George W. Bush's lame-duck period after the November 2008 elections and before the January 2009 inauguration of Barack H. Obama.

On 20 February 2009, after parliamentary elections, President Shimon Peres followed procedure and appointed Bibi prime minister to form a new government—on the Mizraḥi vote, yet again.

This Is Exactly What We Did

On 21 February 2005, I attended a convening of Israel's Women's Parliament. The day's topic was "Minimum Wage: A Woman's Perspective." One of the speakers was Dr. Linda ʿEfroni, a brilliant Iraqi economist and labor attorney. She is a prominent consultant for Israel's major labor unions on issues concerning income and work conditions and a member of the Israeli Council of Higher Education. At the time, she also had a weekly opinion column in *Globes: Israel Business News*. Yet, she has only been an adjunct at Tel Aviv University. In the discussion after the speeches, she told the following story:

Around 2001, I was invited by the Israeli College of National Security, where military officers are groomed to become generals, to give a lecture at Haifa University. Haifa University regularly hosts events of the college. The audience was made up of students in the special program, but also senior members of the SHABAK—Israel's secret police—military intelligence, the Israeli police force, and other senior officials in the national security apparatus. There were about forty people in all sitting around a large conference table.

This was around the time of the social unrest following the collapse of the Argentinian economy. They wanted to know if similar unrest was possible in Israel because of socioeconomic gaps, and how these gaps could be minimized. I offered my analysis: We have problems with security and with borders. These transcend socioeconomic protests. It would take nothing less than a miracle for any social protest to succeed.

If social unrest appeared in the news, I would not be surprised to hear about Ḥezbollah Katyusha rockets falling on Kiryat Shmona the next day. This would immediately shift public discourse back to security. I could not rule out that the Katyushas on Kiryat Shmona were a response to the IDF Air Force provocation of their fighter jets crossing the border deep into Lebanon. I told them that I didn't have the knowledge, but my intuition as an analyst told me that.

Everyone was quiet. Everyone was quiet. No one said a thing. And then we broke for a buffet lunch.

At the buffet, a corpulent man approached me. He said, "Shalom, my name is XY.[4] I used to be the media advisor for the Minister of Defense. And this is exactly what we did."

On 9 October 2010, I called Dr. ʿEfroni from Minneapolis to verify the quote. She said:

Yes, this is exactly what I said. And this is what he said. He didn't say that it was off the record. As for Vicky and the end of the hudna, I was in a meeting with Bibi in Jerusalem. She wanted me to join her. The man was very stressed. He sweated a lot. Very stressed. In hindsight, even in the Finance Ministry, they didn't believe it was going to be so easy. Ḥok HaHesderim nullifies the legislature. Israel is not a democracy. In the 2003 amendment, they saved 5 billion NIS.

They transferred the money to the upper echelons in the form of a tax refund. They could have done other things with this money. They were so surprised at how easy the transfer was. I think it is not impossible that they let the suicide bomber slip through.

15. Protesters in downtown Tel Aviv hold a banner that reads *Arḥal!* (Get out!, Arabic), the same cry shouted at Hosni Mubarak during the Arab Spring, 2011. Underneath, the sign also reads *Mitzrayim ze po* (Egypt is here, Hebrew). Oren Ziv, 2011.

Epilogue: Israel, Summer 2011

In summer 2011, tens of thousands of young Israelis, priced out of their rental leases or foreclosed on, protested the state's slashing of public services, echoing the Single Mothers' Protest of 2003, but on a larger scale. The protesters referred to this as "Tel Aviv's *Taḥrir*," after the Taḥrir Square demonstrations in Cairo, Egypt, that toppled Hosni Mubarak's neoliberal regime. Unlike in the Knafo protest, the leaders and spokespeople of summer 2011 were Zionist Left Ashkenazim, even though young Mizraḥim composed the majority of the protesters, reflecting Israel's demographics. The leaders were mostly single, from affluent families, and received preferential treatment from the authorities. Thus, the regime could not threaten them with the forced boarding of their children due to poverty.[5]

The '48 Arabs largely avoided participation, despite courting from the protest leadership using their common Israeli citizenship as grounds to join. Most criticized the protests for not clearly addressing the connections between Israel's economic troubles and the cost of the military occupation and civic Jewish settlements in the West Bank. The protest leadership's strategy was to avoid any mention of Palestine to reach consensus between all sectors of Israel's secular and religiously observant majority Jewish citizenry. Meanwhile, the Ministry for Hasbara and Jewish Diaspora went into action. It showcased the protest as an act of Jewish unity and Israeli democracy, even though the demonstrations went against the government. It was part of their "Nicer Face of Israel" campaign, aimed at Jewish communities and media outlets in Western Europe and North America.

Thanks to a lull in the Israel-Palestine conflict in summer 2011, the protest succeeded in getting international media attention. On 18 August 2011, Egyptian Bedouin guerillas from the South Sinai committed a suicide attack on an Israeli bus near Eilat. This prompted the IDF to bombard Palestinian civilian populations in Gaza, 260 kilometers (around 160 miles) north of where the bus attack took place. Ḥamas responded by bombarding civilian Jewish populations near Gaza. The Israeli regime used this attack to divert attention from the protest. Major mainstream Hebrew media outlets reported that SHABAK and the IDF had intelligence on the date, time, and place the bombing would occur. Netanyahu instructed them to keep quiet when the Knesset inquired about their lack of preventative measures (Azulay 2011; Melman 2011; Pepper 2011).

At the 27 January 2012 dinner for the World Economic Forum Annual Meeting in Davos, Switzerland, Israeli deputy prime minister and minister of defense Ehud Barak delivered a speech on the prospect of an Israeli attack on Iranian nuclear facilities. In the same speech, he referred to the social protest: "If the government will not respond to the protest, it will return with force and violence" (Rolnik 2012). The fact that these two subjects appeared side by side in Barak's speech went unnoticed by the international media (Elliott 2012).

The media also overlooked the prescience of Barak's statement. In summer 2012, the "Occupy"-style protesters from summer 2011 attempted to reinvigorate their movement against the ever-increasing rent, food, and gas prices coupled with the privatization of social services (see, for example, Davidovitch-Weisberg 2012). Following the model of Mohamed Bouazizi, the Tunisian vendor whose self-immolation sparked the Arab Spring of

16. During a demonstration on 14 July 2012, Moshe Silman, a middle-class Ashkenazi who lost his home and business to Israel's Collection Court, set himself on fire. His self-immolation followed the NSB's refusal to increase his inadequate disability allowance and provide him with public housing aid. Ben Kelmer, 2012.

2011 (Fahim 2011), Moshe Silman, a middle-class, middle-aged Ashkenazi, became distraught enough to light himself on fire in the middle of a public demonstration in Tel Aviv. On the verge of homelessness, he joined the protest movement after losing his business and home to Israel's Collection Court. He was refused public housing and could not provide for himself on a shoddy NSB disability allowance (Kaufman 2012; Rudoren 2012a). Others followed suit but did not get the international media attention that Silman got. They were Mizraḥim—isolated freak shows, at least in the eyes of the mainstream media (Cohen 2012).

Instead, the media concentrated on stories proclaiming increased Israel-Iran tensions (*New York Times* 2012). Both Barak and Netanyahu publicly pressed the importance of Israeli national unity against the Muslim goyim threat. Just like the Palestinian suicide bomber in 2003 that dissipated the Knafo movement.

In October 2012, Netanyahu called for a dismissal of the Knesset and for early elections closely following the inauguration of the new (or incumbent) U.S. president (Rudoren 2012b). The reason for the dismissal was the gridlock in the Knesset over Netanyahu's draconian national budget for 2013. But, conveniently for the regime, the call for elections also stole what little media attention the social protests of summer 2012 were receiving. In addition, the Labor Party actively recruited the young, upper-middle-class Zionist Left Ashkenazi protest leaders and enticed them with offers of high party standing, maximizing their Knesset chances. Two notable protest leaders did ascend to Knesset seats (Azulay 2012). After the 2003 Knafo protest, Vicky was recruited by the Meretz Party. But she was not offered a Knesset seat that comes with a generous monthly salary and guaranteed lifetime retirement.

Between 14 November 2012 and 21 November 2012, the IDF conducted Operation 'Amud 'Anan (Hebrew), or "Pillar of Cloud," taken from the divine cloud that guided the Israelites out of Egypt. "And the Lord went before them by day in a pillar of a cloud, to lead them the way; and by night in a pillar of fire, to give them light," as written in Exodus 13:21 in the King James Bible.[6] The operation involved a massive series of airstrikes in the densely populated Gaza Strip (Lendman 2012; Mekelberg 2012). This was prime scheduling, as the United States would be deep in President Barack H. Obama's lame-duck period after his November 2012 election, and before the January 2013 inauguration.

After the Israeli parliamentary elections on 22 January 2013, President Shimon Peres followed procedure and on 2 February 2013 appointed Bibi prime minister to form a new government (BBC 2013) — on the Mizrahi vote, yet again.

The young leftist Ashkenazi protest leaders of summer 2011, as well as right-wing Ashkenazi political leaders, used the Mizrahim for their own benefit. For the Zionist Left, the Mizrahim provided bodies in the mass demonstrations of 2011. For the Right, the Mizrahim provided votes cast in reaction to the protest leaders' machinations with the Labor Party. In both cases, the Mizrahim were on the front lines, marching in the streets or casting votes at the polls, but on the bottom of the list to benefit from their efforts (Ha'Okets 2013).

17. In October 2003, Benjamin Netanyahu, as finance minister, attended an official reception in Mitzpe Ramon to celebrate the Single Mothers' March that ended in September 2003. Bibi's public relations team arranged for Vicky Knafo to attend as guest of honor. Since Mitzpe does not have a flower shop, Bibi brought a bouquet from Jerusalem to present to Vicky. Meir Azulay, 2003.

Yes they hate us because we vote Likud. Of course we vote for the Right. They didn't do these crimes to us. It was the Labor Party and the rest of 'em Left.

Likud screwed with us too. But we must support them. They're not wishy-washy with peace mumbo-jumbo. Look here: when the Left is in power, there are wars with the 'Aravim—'48, '56, '67,'73 ... even now, with Flora's brother. He's Labor. With Likud and the Right, there's quiet. The 'Aravim are afraid to come out of their cubbyholes. The Right doesn't talk peace. They're honest. When in war, act like it's war.

The words of Mitzpe's single mothers return like a steady drumbeat. An eternal return.

The present-day U.S.-based scholar in me wishes to step back and consider alternative interpretations to Dr. 'Efroni's analysis. But in light of the 2003 Knafo protest, and its echoes in the Israeli protests in 2011, 2012, and into 2013, it is difficult to disagree with her assessment. The alternative to her

analysis is a simple fallback to the Israel-Palestine binary: the Jewish homeland must defend itself against non-Jews who threaten its nationhood. Some
scholars may take issue with Dr. 'Efroni's analysis and respond that intra-
Jewish race relations most likely do not exist and that the ingathering of the
Jewish diasporas in the State of Israel is a fait accompli—"ethnic groups and
boundaries" (Barth 1969) have morphed into Mizrahi-Ashkenazi hybridities
(Shenhav 2005; see also Bhabha 1994). The phenomenological analysis this
book offers looks deeper into the ways bureaucracy undermines scholarly
assumptions. My research and fieldwork align themselves with Dr. 'Efroni's
assessments. In Israel, bureaucracy denies the agency of identity politics
through a gendered and racial essence that lies in wait for unsuspecting
subjects to draw near. Forever spinning their lethal bureaucratic webs, the
Israeli regime makes Mizrahim pay the price of Israeli national security.

How long can the regime depend on Mizrahi docile loyalty to the
Jewish state?

Afterword(s)

Gaza 2014 and the Mizraḥi Predicament

I submitted the full book manuscript of *Wrapped in the Flag of Israel* in February 2013, and it came out on 15 April 2014. I had finished the first complete draft in 2011 as the events of the Arab Spring unfolded. My original publisher did not have high hopes for the book. As the authoritarian regimes of the Arab World disintegrated into bedlam, U.S.-European media presented the State of Israel as a shining island of democratic stability. What insights could scholars and activists interested in the Israel-Palestine conflict gain from the life of Mizraḥi single mothers?[1] Why examine intra-Jewish racial and gendered dynamics in the State of Israel while postcolonial Arab and Muslim states were decolonizing into religious sectarianism? How do bureaucratic structures preempt feminist resistance?

But I expected otherwise. The release of my first ethnography, *The Poetics of Military Occupation: Mzeina Allegories of Bedouin Identity Under Israeli and Egyptian Rule* (Lavie 1990), coincided with the early 1990s American invasions of Iraq and the Oslo Peace Process. Conflict begets interest. Since *Poetics* came out, some policy makers, academics, and activists have started to question the binary thinking that has dominated since 1948: Jew-Arab; Israel-Palestine; Israel-the Arab World; the Jewish People-Islam. These binaries have not and cannot yield lasting, positive results. Throughout my life as an activist and scholar, I have tried to transcend the simplistic binary. Indeed, *Wrapped in the Flag of Israel* has done well. As I toured academic departments, activist groups, and bookstores, I was humbled by the congenial response and deep engagement with my work. Three prints sold out in eighteen months. And here we are, releasing a revised edition in paperback. My heartfelt thanks to University of Nebraska Press for their hospitality to Mizraḥi single mothers.

In *Wrapped in the Flag of Israel* I have argued that equating bureaucratic entanglements with pain — or what, arguably, can be seen as torture — might seem strange. But for single Mizraḥi welfare mothers, somatization of bureaucratic logic as physical pain precludes the agency of identity politics. I elaborated on Don Handelman's scholarship on bureaucratic logic as divine cosmology (Handelman 1990) and posited that Israel's bureaucracy is based on a theological essence that amalgamates gender and race. I termed this amalgamation GendeRace. The book employs a World Anthropologies' theoretical toolkit (Ribeiro and Escobar 2006) to represent bureaucratic torture in multiple narrative modes, including anger, irony, and humor, as a counterexample to dominant U.S.-UK formulae for writing and theorizing culture.

Wrapped in the Flag of Israel describes and analyzes Mizraḥi single mothers' daily vagaries and the historical context that accounts for their suffering. They organized and marched on Jerusalem, but their movement eventually failed. During my years in Israel as a welfare mother and Mizraḥi feminist leader (1999–2007), I experienced firsthand the propensity for Mizraḥi social protests to crumble. One factor that allowed the protests to grow was international media coverage. Sometimes, these protests made it into the headlines, but only when there was a lull in the usual reporting on the binary Israel-Palestine conflict. A breaking event such as violence in Gaza, military conflicts with Lebanon's Ḥezbollah, or a soon-to-happen Israeli bombardment of Iran's nuclear facilities would blanket news outlets just as a protest gained momentum. Once the Israel-Palestine front exploded, it would effectively crush the movements. Mizraḥi protesters would quickly bracket their causes and unite with Ashkenazim to defend the Jewish fortress against threatening *goyim* (non-Jews, Hebrew; enemies, colloquial Hebrew). This book is about the relationship between bureaucracy, resistance, and warfare. It demonstrates that the most efficient tool to squelch Mizraḥi protest is a pincer-like sequential strategy: entangle protest leaders in a lethal web of bureaucracy and create a national crisis through military spectacle.

Thus, *Wrapped in the Flag of Israel* illustrates that even though Mizraḥim form the majority of the Israeli Jewish population, they do not control the policies of the Israeli state. Policy is still driven by the ruling Ashkenazi minority. In striving to prove themselves to be just as Israeli as the Ashkenazi elite, many Mizraḥim have been the staunchest supporters of Israeli ultranationalism and, by extension, all of Israel's wars against its neighboring Arab states and Palestinians—from the 1948 Nakba to Gaza 2014.

Bureaucratic Torture: When Agency Becomes Impossible

This Afterword(s) is in the plural. It consists of two parts: first, it grapples with some of the questions that scholarly audiences have raised around the book's analysis of the moment when enacting feminist agency becomes impossible. It interrogates whether bureaucratic entanglements can be conceptualized as torture. Second, it tells the story of the 2014 War on Gaza. The second part grounds the interplay between Mizraḥi social protest, neoliberal economics, and military violence in Gaza 2014 in the larger narrative of truncated Mizraḥi agency since the publication of *Wrapped in the Flag of Israel* in April 2014. The crux of these protests was the confluence of GendeRace with ethnoreligious nationalism and citizenship. Their failure demonstrated that resistance to intra-Jewish racism cannot be separated from the "Question of Palestine" (Said 1979). Because Mizraḥi feminist activism against intra-Jewish racism has chosen to strategically disassociate itself from the Question of Palestine, issues raised by particular protests, such as the 2003 Mizraḥi Single Mothers' March on Jerusalem, eventually dissipated. The national conflict between the State of Israel and Palestine, ever present, resumed its place at the center of the public sphere.

The Translation Block

In *Wrapped in the Flag of Israel* I wrote about how grassroots Mizraḥi scholarship is stymied in its journey from Hebrew to English. This translation block is not isolated to academia. Even in mainstream and alternative media, the simplistic binary Israel-Palestine dominates news aimed at international consumption as well as U.S.-European foreign policy decisions regarding the State of Israel. Mizraḥi single mothers transcend this binary.

English editions of Hebrew outlets such as *Haaretz* or *Y-Net*, and alternative media outlets like +972, have only recently started publishing stories on Mizraḥim. These stories are written for an international audience, depicting the internal decay of a Jewish state that was once celebrated by the progressive Ashkenazi diaspora in North America and Western Europe as a "project of compassion," or affirmative action on a national scale (Feldman 2015, 145, 197). This coverage is never connected to the larger Question of Palestine.

These English-language outlets cater to U.S.-European interest in Palestine and vehemently deny their white, Ashkenazi privilege and participation in an intra-Jewish racial order. The interconnectedness between the Israel-Palestine conflict and intra-Jewish racism is lost. The reasons for this lacuna are clear: exposure of Israel's intra-Jewish racism would alarm the financial machine of the pro-Israel lobby. Whereas progressive diaspora Jews, who are Israel's broadest base of support, are mostly Ashkenazim, and identify with the ruling minority in the State of Israel, they have also been deeply involved in anti-apartheid movements in South Africa, civil rights movements in the United States, and anti-colonial movements in Latin America. It is unlikely that they would continue to support colonialist and racist ideologies and practices directed at Jews of Color in the Homeland of the Jews, where all Jews are supposedly equal.

Agency

The main point of contention for some of the book's critics has been my critique of identity politics and the agency immanent in its enactment. The impossibility to enact agency on the part of Mizraḥi women was a radical departure from my previous work on the poetic resistance of the Sinai Bedouin in Egypt against Israeli occupation (Lavie 1990). I went on to theorize the authorial poetic agency in the Israel-Arab borderzone through the lives and words of Mizraḥi and Palestinian authors whose mother tongue is Arabic but chose to write their poetry and prose in Hebrew (Lavie 1992, 1995, 1996).

Much of North American and Western European social anthropology and feminist theory insists that agency is intrinsic—that all oppressed people have it no matter their situation. It is little wonder that scholars and activists who engaged with the book struggled with my figurations of agency. They insisted that the activists I have written about—both single mothers

and community leaders like myself—were exercising their agency by protesting. As my previous work demonstrated, I believed the same.

To analyze this steadfast Mizraḥi activism that did not generate hoped-
for social change, my data led me to engage with ancient, foundational theories, such as Durkheim's concepts of organic and mechanic solidarities
and anthropology's theories of classifications (Durkheim 1961; Durkheim
and Mauss 1963, 65). Likewise, in the writing process, I found myself defy-
ing the feminist injunction against binary logic when I analyzed the intersection of gender-race-class with religion as a space of primordial divinity
that forms the basis of citizenship (see Crenshaw 1991; Joseph 2000). Integral to my discussion of Mizraḥi single mothers was their distinct lack of
personal and communal agency when dealing with the state bureaucracies
they depended on to survive.

By delving into how citizenship is made into a transcendental essence,
I found that the sanctity of the state on its bureaucratic apparatus short-
circuited agency and its capacities to resist oppression. This deep love of
the very state that hurt Mizraḥi women has explained the repeated failures
of Mizraḥi feminist social protests advocating for real change. Agency has
often been superimposed on the subaltern by scholars who can regroup and
replenish in the safety of their tenured academic positions, rather than in
shantytowns (Spivak 1988). But the ruling concept for the Mizraḥi public
has been "be complacent, survive."

A number of my critics deeply immersed in Palestinian nationalism have
suggested that these single mothers still exercised ample agency, simply by
"hating Arabs." This criticism has done more to prove my point than refute
it. Hating Arabs does not improve the situation of single mothers struggling
to care for themselves and their families. The welfare system remains unfair
and byzantine. The sanctity of the state remains unsullied. The bureaucratic
apparatus becomes even more resilient to change.

While I addressed the themes of agency and torture in the context of social
movements and state bureaucracy analytically, the book also examined the
heavy personal and professional price activists pay. Unlike single mothers,
other Mizraḥi activists in the social movements described in *Wrapped in the
Flag of Israel* were able to enact a modicum of agency on behalf of the com-

munities they dedicated themselves to. The price for this agency was high, however. They were robbed of gainful employment, homes, and health. And eventually, when these activists died—far too young—they left very few traces, if any, after departing from the tangible world.

Torture

The lens of analysis employed in *Wrapped in the Flag of Israel* depicts secular government bureaus as sites of sacred, religious pilgrimage. Welfare aid depended not on civil rights, but on serendipity. People in all parts of the world, of all classes and races, have run-ins with bureaucracy. Those with means can either ignore or sidestep bureaucracy's ill effects by hiring specialist professionals, that is, lawyers and accountants, to navigate labyrinthine systems for them. But disenfranchised populations, in the Middle East and elsewhere, often do not have the ability to voice their concerns to those who would listen. Bureaucracy's lethal webs cannot be easily brushed aside.

Mizraḥi families are not the only ones afflicted by bureaucratic entanglements. Yet activists and scholars of the Middle East neglect the centrality of bureaucratic transformation to any viable social change. Feminists who write and organize around intersectionality overlook the interplay between gender-race-class, religion, and bureaucracy. Bureaucratic structures themselves do not provide a clear target to coalesce against. One of the failures of the Arab Spring stemmed from the absence of an alternative to the labyrinthine bureaucracies that control almost all aspects of citizens' lives.

This book offers a case study to demonstrate how the State of Israel used bureaucracy as the main tool for the state to create a docile body of citizens and eliminate resistance. At bureaus, single mothers on welfare often had to wait in long lines with no promises that their problems would be resolved. Many times, they reached a bureaucrat, only to be sent to another bureau. Bureaucratic encounters created a zone where pre-discursive reality could not undergo transformation into discourse.[2] Anthropologists conceive of discourse as a point of departure for cultural analysis. Without discourse, the three-step process of healing through talking about torture and transforming it into mimetic representation became impossible to enact (Scarry

1985, 101). Bureaucratic torture is unspeakable. It is one of the state's gross crimes, even though it might not fit the narrow legal definition of "torture."

If the well-being of a child, payment of rent, and access to low-income housing depended on a single mother giving a blow job to a clerk, the clerk became an executioner of state torture, and the mother, the tortured. This existence—bouncing from bureau to bureau and back—forced single mothers to live in a constant state of anxiety that was almost impossible to escape. Moreover, the psychic and somatic effects of single mothers' bureaucratic encounters—whether standing in line or in their own homes—gradually destroyed their bodies and souls.

———

In what follows, I examine the events leading up to the 2014 War on Gaza. The IDF attack on Gaza was known in Hebrew as Operation Tzuk Eitan. This translates as "mighty cliff,"[3] showing yet again the phallic imagery typical of IDF operations. Hamas called it al-'Asf al-Ma'akul, or "the Consuming Storm." In English, it was referred to as Operation Protective Edge. Palestinians simply termed it "the War on Gaza."

Wrapped in the Flag of Israel tracked sequences that began with Mizrahi protest and ended with elections that bolstered the power of the political Right. In between was another bloodletting cycle between the IDF, the Palestinian Authority (PA), and Israel's neighboring Arab states. My analysis of Gaza 2014 will focus on the possible links between Mizrahi protest, the globalization of the Israeli economy, and the sanctity of the Jewish state. I will examine the relationship between intra-Jewish racism and the ways that the state uses war to divert attention, both national and international, away from domestic issues of racial and gender justice and onto the security of a Jewish colonial-settler state in the midst of the Arab World.

Since the publication of *Wrapped in the Flag of Israel*, I have continued to systematically examine the relationship between Mizrahi feminism and the Question of Palestine. My data, culled from extensive interviews, conversations, Hebrew print and electronic media analysis, and investigation of social media, will illustrate the perspectives of some Israeli Jews and almost all Mizrahi activists. Mainstream and alternative printed and electronic materials supported my conversations with activists. Since the book's 2014 publication, Facebook has become a major platform for Mizraḥi political and cultural discussions and calls for action. One of the major assumptions expressed in the data is that Gaza 2014 was launched to preempt Mizraḥi protests, to preclude resistance to the further privatization and deregulation of the Israeli economy. In addition, Gaza 2014 was to break the Ḥamas-PLO coalition. Furthermore, many Israeli Jews across the board exercise the idiom *yod'im ve-shotkim* (knowing and keeping silent, Hebrew). This is particularly the case around issues pertaining to the security of the state during episodes of military conflict (Herzog and Lahad 2006). Due to the translation block, it has not been easy for English-language readers to access information about the ways that Mizraḥi protest might be connected to Gaza 2014. The analysis that follows is an attempt to fill this lacuna.

This Afterword(s) includes many dates, but these are not simply extraneous details. Rather, the progression of dates points to two separate but parallel tracks, or timelines. The first timeline indicates events unfolding on the political and national track—the Israel-Palestine binary. This is the timeline that the non-Hebrew-speaking world can follow in the news. It reflects the dominant narrative produced by Israel and the PA and adopted by international media in which victimhood rarely departs from the category of the nation. It delineates conflicts between Israel and Palestine and between Israel and the Arab World. The other, less familiar to non-Hebrew-speaking consumers of news, tracks the timeline of internal social affairs—intra-Jewish racism. To trace these two parallel tracks is to examine the interplay between Mizraḥi protest and Israel's wars. A particular sequence of events becomes apparent: first there is Mizraḥi protest, then Israel chooses war, elections follow, and finally, the government moves further to the Right.

One People One Heart: The War on Gaza 2014

All Israel in pledge to each other
All Israel in pledge to each other
All Israel in pledge to each other
All Israel brethren

One people, one heart
One people, one name
One people — one man
Hear, O Israel, One people
(Almagor 1972)

The New Black Panthers, or HaLo Neḥmadim

In May 2013, I was nominated by Aḥoti (Sistah) for the Heart at East Honorary Award for lifetime achievement from the Coalition for Equal Distribution of Cultural Funds in Israel in recognition of my scholarship on and activism in the Mizraḥi community. Since the publication of *Wrapped in the Flag of Israel*, Aḥoti has become one of the largest and most visible feminist organizations in Israel. "Heart at East," initiated by Aḥoti, is a coalition of twenty NGOs dedicated to promoting community consciousness as it exposes and defies Israel's folkloric marginalization of Mizraḥi cultures. It was launched as a result of a 2009 study and 2012 follow-up report by Aḥoti (2011, 2012).[4] The report found that the Israeli regime has always distributed the overwhelming majority of public funds and other resources, more than 90 percent, to Ashkenazi cultural institutions and initiatives.

I was somewhat surprised to be chosen for the award. The Heart at East NGO coalition has strong Zionist associations.[5]

Just as I returned to San Francisco, a photograph appeared in my Facebook feed. On the night of 9 June 2013, Carmen Elmakiyes led a group of activists from Aḥoti and other NGOs of Heart at East, among them, HaLo Neḥmadim (the not-nice, Hebrew), to glue the names of Mizraḥi artists, authors, and historical figures over Tel Aviv's almost entirely Ashkenazi street signs.[6] This "direct action" (Graeber 2009) protested the exclusion of Mizraḥi history from Tel Aviv's public sphere. The event was important enough for *Haaretz* to sum up in its English edition. The translation block, yet again. The story appeared in English, but skipped over the larger historical context of Mizraḥi discrimination. It remained well within the realm of internal social affairs — the timeline of intra-Jewish racism.

18. HaLo Neḥmadim activists in Tel Aviv replace the sign for Allenby Street, named after British general Edmund Allenby, with Vicki Shiran, founder of Mizraḥi feminism. Allenby was not Ashkenazi. He led the British army when it took control of Palestine from the Ottomans. Allenby Street is an exception among Tel Aviv's largely Ashkenazi street names. Daniel Bar-On/*Haaretz*, 2014.

HaLo Neḥmadim was the most militant among the NGOs in the Heart at East Coalition. They trace their Hebrew name to a stormy meeting between the Jerusalem Black Panthers and Golda Meir on 13 April 1971. She was outraged by their use of violent means of protest such as launching Molotov cocktails at Jewish police officers. Meir summed up their resistance with the trivializing phrase: "they're not nice." Rather than dealing with their plight, she established a committee for youth delinquency and crime in Mizraḥi 'hoods (Mann 1998, 84–85). Their English name, "the New Black Panthers," asserts this lineage. HaLo Neḥmadim is a nonpartisan group of 'hood activists who organized after the failure of the 2011 protest when the concerns of denizens of the 'hoods were overshadowed by Ashkenazi youth leadership. Its key actors are also leaders of Aḥoti. The group explicitly challenged Israel's racist policies against Mizraḥim and socioeconomic discrimination.

Their advocacy focused on the fight against gentrification evictions, home-lessness, poverty, and all other issues of race-related neglect in Black City, Tel Aviv, and Israel's largely Mizraḥi development towns. For the summer of 2014, HaLo Neḥmadim planned to follow up their nonviolent street-sign protest with violent demonstrations against further neoliberal economic reforms (Levy 2016; see Misgav 2015, 150).

Summer is an auspicious time for street protest because landlords who often price families out of their apartments, or banks enacting foreclosures, aim to coincide these efforts with the end of the school year. This is because they are less likely to be served with anti-eviction lawsuits. Evicted fami-lies, in theory, can use the summer break to look for housing or to protest. Warm weather allows for demonstrations and tent living in urban parks or on shaded boulevards. School is out, and volunteers who sympathize with the protesters keep their children occupied with games and activities. Protesters hope that the presence of families will reduce police violence. Thus, summer 2014 was ripe with possibility for HaLo Neḥmadim to rouse Israeli streets.

Ḥok HaHesderim 2014

On 10 February 2014, the Knesset's Finance and Economics Committee presented an irregular interim amendment to Ḥok HaHesderim: the same biannual deregulatory budget-cut legislation that sparked the 2003 pro-tests. While the law was amended the previous year and was not sched-uled for amendment until 2015, the Knesset planned to vote on it in late spring 2014. After reading a first draft on 17 February, the Knesset returned the amendment to the Finance and Economics Committee for revisions (Knesset 2014a). "The only way it's going to pass is under the smokescreen of a war," an old-timer Mizraḥi rasped to me over Skype one winter Shab-bat. The first group to be further harmed would be Mizraḥi single mothers.

On 26 May 2014, the Knesset Finance and Economics Committee met and prepared for a vote on the amendment to Ḥok HaHesderim (Knesset Finance Committee 2014). It proposed the privatization of state-owned utilities com-panies and ports and their possible sale to conglomerates based in the Neth-erlands, the Philippines, Germany, or China. Furthermore, the amendment detailed the cancellation of a 1 billion NIS low-income housing project. It is probable that these funds were reallocated to partially cover the 3.14 billion NIS debt of Israeli Military Industries (IMI). The regime planned to sell 49 percent of the IMI to outside investors who were wary of the IMI's deep debt. The funds to pay the IMI's debt did not come from taxation or foreign aid. In fact, they may have belonged to Mizraḥim. In the late 1990s, the Mizraḥi Democratic Rainbow had led a successful campaign for the sale of low-income housing units to their tenants, so that they might bequeath them to their children instead of continuing to pay subsidized rent. This resulted in 2001 legislation that transferred housing ownership rights from the Housing Ministry to low-income Mizraḥim and generated about 1 billion NIS. It is likely that these were the funds headed to the IMI.[7] The regime's choice of date for this irregular amendment was puzzling; it conjoined financial policies directed at Israeli citizens with foreign affairs—the two seemingly disparate time tracks of the state.

The government's neoliberal reforms were not consistent with similar budgetary cuts and privatization policies around the world in response to the global financial crisis of 2008. Indeed, the crisis did not affect the State of Israel (Klein 2007 485–590; Rozenhak and Shalev 2011, 47). The 2006 Lebanon War bolstered the Israeli economy. The regime funneled vast sums of money to the IMI to restock weapons, rebuild the Galilee after the Hezbollah bombardments, and fund post-trauma social services. Just as international media applauded Israel's financial stability, the Israeli government enacted more austerity measures toward disenfranchised populations (Davidoff 2014).

Labor Hill B-Jamusin

The catalyst for HaLo Neḥmadim's major mobilization was a plan to evict, demolish, and gentrify the Mizraḥi neighborhood Givʿat ʿAmal Bet (Labor Hill B, Hebrew), a vestige of Israel's socialist era. Before the 1948 Nakba, Labor Hill B was the Palestinian village Jamusin.[8]

Labor Hill sits in the middle of White City, Tel Aviv, stuck between elegant apartment buildings and skyscrapers on one side and the IDF Central Command on the other. As Labor Hill's population grew, housing regulations for refugees, inherited from the British Mandate, transformed it into a heap of temporary structures, since the rules prohibited permanent foundations and roofs. Well-heeled White City Ashkenazim would visit for authentic Mizraḥi food (or drugs) and often shake their heads: "This is just like the Untouchable shantytowns we saw in India on our big South-Asian tour." Gazan and West Bank Palestinians who would visit their blue-collar bosses would often rub their eyes in disbelief: "This is just like a refugee camp." But unlike other Mizraḥi ghettos in Black City, Tel Aviv, Labor Hill occupied prime real estate in Ashkenazi Tel Aviv.

From 1954 on, Labor Hill fell under *Pinuy-Binuy* (Evacuate and Build, Hebrew) of Tel Aviv's municipal master plan.[9] *Pinuy-Binuy* is the term city planners adopted for Mizraḥi barrios during gentrification. For residents, the reality has been dispossession-destruction-exile. Standard practice is that any belongings residents cannot salvage are to be bulldozed. Palestinian homes are simply demolished. For sixty years, the people of Labor Hill suffered through a labyrinth of court orders and bureaucratic procedures while the Israel Land Administration Authority sold Labor Hill's Palestinian land to private contractors, who sold it to other private contractors because residents remained steadfast. They could not afford even below-market-rate buy-ins in the new development. The era of postponement came to an end in March 2014. The regime approved the deployment of YASAM (the anti-terror Israel Police Special Patrol Unit) to forcibly evict two families from their homes. YASAM is the same riot-control, counterterrorist unit that uses live fire to squelch Palestinian demonstrations inside pre-1967 Israel.

Young activists started trickling into Labor Hill. Most were Mizraḥim, many Aḥoti activists, many from HaLo Neḥmadim. Some were Ashkenazi-Israeli anarchists, Jewish members of Israel's Communist Party, and North American and Western European internationals from the International Solidarity Movement (ISM) who had a history of demonstrating against the Separation Wall and demolitions of Palestinian homes.[10]

Were these outside protesters and residents of Labor Hill strange bedfellows?[11] *Wrapped in the Flag of Israel* explains the historical reasons why Mizraḥim have always supported the Zionist political Right. It was the Socialist Zionist Left that advanced the ideologies and policies of intra-Jewish racism. In addition, like all Mizraḥim, the people of Labor Hill have relatives whose only way to escape the slums was to move to affordable housing in larger West Bank settlements. This is exactly what anarchists, communists, and ISM activists oppose. But unlike most Ashkenazim on the Israeli Left, these anti-Zionist, direct-action activists have begun to realize the significance of the relationship between Mizraḥi and Palestinian precarities. Five more expulsion-demolitions for Labor Hill were scheduled for summer 2014. Encouraged by international support in the spring, HaLo Neḥmadim started to make Molotov cocktails and amass gas tanks. Together with residents, they planned to resist the YASAM by blowing themselves up in front of the five families' homes.

In spring 2014, the world's major media was busy reporting on the Ebola outbreak and the disappearance of Malaysian Airlines Flight 17. No blowups in the Israel-Palestine borderzone. HaLo Neḥmadim hoped the lull would continue into the summer and thus grant their spectacular resistance international media coverage.

Lethal bureaucratic entanglements soon followed, just as they had in the summers of 2011 and 2003. Like every Mizraḥi social movement, this one also had its paid SHABAK (Israel's secret police) informers, and they did their jobs well. Activists' old parking tickets, ancient water bills, and long-forgotten bounced checks, including interest and late fees, suddenly resurfaced. These were the same tactics that preempted the long-term social change that was the hoped-for result of the Single Mothers' March on Jerusalem in 2003. Some men among protest leaders were called up with "Order Eight" (Tzav Shmone, Hebrew), the IDF's immediate extra-active reserve-duty summons, enlisting them into the War on Gaza 2014.

The Ḥamas Salary Fiasco

In spring 2014, the PLO and Ḥamas shifted their attention from Israel to the task of forming a coalition. After the Oslo Peace Accords of 1993, the PA, whose main political party was the PLO, had become the largest employer in the West Bank and Gaza. When the Ḥamas opposition won elections in January 2006, thereby turning the PLO into the opposition, the PA had about 200,000 employees. As a result of the 2006 election victory, Ḥamas and the PLO formed a unity government for both Gaza and the West Bank until 2007. The PA prohibited its employees from working for Ḥamas. Ḥamas was forced to establish a whole new bureaucratic apparatus that gradually grew to include 45,000 people. Their salaries were paid out primarily from heavy taxes Ḥamas placed on goods smuggled through tunnels connecting Egypt to the Gaza Strip.[12] After a 2006–7 series of violent clashes, Ḥamas ended up in control of the Gaza Strip, and the PLO in control over the West Bank (Levitt and Zilber 2015; Mor-Ḥaim 2014).

In July 2013, Abdul Fataḥ al-Sisi led a military coup in Egypt and suspended the Egyptian constitution (Kirkpatrick 2013). In early March 2014, an Egyptian court declared all Ḥamas activity in Egypt illegal (*Al Jazeera* 2014). The Egyptian military proceeded to close half of the tunnels. Revenues from smuggling diminished. This meant no salaries for Ḥamas bureaucrats. The Ḥamas financial crisis resuscitated the attempt to form a unity government with the PLO and resulted in a May 2014 reconciliation agreement (BBC 2014b). The agreement's crux was an arrangement whereby the emir of Qatar would transfer funds generated from natural gas exports to the PA. The PA, in turn, would then transfer part of this sum to Ḥamas, who would, in turn, pay its employees (Levitt and Zilber 2015; AFP 2014).[13]

The Israeli government responded by threatening banks involved with sanctions for "financing terrorism," should they affect the transfer of Qatari funds to Ḥamas. Robert H. Serry, the UN secretary-general's personal representative to the PLO and PA, warned the world of a rapidly approaching boiling point—Ḥamas missile attacks on Israel if Qatar was indeed prevented from transferring the money (Akram and Rudoren 2014).

End of the lull.

Israel, the United States, and the PA refused to listen. The international time track took precedence yet again. Avigdor Lieberman, Israel's ultranationalist foreign minister, even threatened to declare Serry a Ḥamas collaborator, a persona non grata in Israel (*Al-Akhbar* 2014; Keinon 2014).

Operation Brother's Keeper

The media focus on HaLo Neḥmadim came to an abrupt end on 12 June 2014. An extremist splinter of Ḥamas kidnapped three Israeli teenagers, Naftali Frankel, Gilad Shaʿer, and Eyal Yifraḥ, while they hitchhiked in the West Bank. This was in response to a series of IDF atrocities in Gaza that followed the Ḥamas-PLO reconciliation agreement.

Right after the Ḥamas-PLO signing ceremony, the IDF air force launched two missiles at a motorbike driving through Gaza. Israeli intelligence assumed that the driver was a high-up Ḥamas leader. The effort failed. Instead, the missiles severely injured seven passersby. In early June, the IDF continued these attempts to target Palestinian guerrillas with heavy-duty bombs, but managed only to kill a seven-year-old Gazan boy. In addition, Israel tightened the Gaza blockade in its efforts to break the Ḥamas-PLO coalition (Landau 2014b).

How did the Ḥamas splinter cell choose its targets? The decision might have heeded the recommendations of the 2010 Ḥamas "Kidnapper's Guidebook" (Channel 2 News 2010).[14] The guidebook's author explains that the preferred target bears an Ashkenazi, nonmuscular phenotype because the Israeli regime has historically proven more amenable to releasing prisoners in exchange for Ashkenazi, rather than Mizraḥi, hostages. A long-time grassroots Mizrahi feminist leader put it to me over Skype:

> Yifraḥ, a classic Yemeni, he just looked it, and his last name. Make no mistakes about Frankel—it's the last name and color. No wonder his mom was all over the press. Shaʿer looked white. I guess they asked him his last name. It's Arabic. Surprise, surprise. With two Mizraḥim and one Ashkenazi you can't negotiate much.[15]

GendeRace yet again—that calcified amalgamation of gender and race that happens in the blink of an eye. This instant typecasting has been one of the main arguments of *Wrapped in the Flag of Israel*. In the case of Israel, a foundational classification. GendeRace is a primordial truism. It petrifies the amalgamation of "the intersection." Rather than moving through it, people are stuck. They are therefore unable to construct racialized and gendered identities that lend themselves to enact political agency.[16] Even the "Kidnapper's Guidebook" stays faithful to the racial formations of Zionism. They seem to work. Ḥamas resumed its place at center stage.

Operation Brother's Keeper began on 15 June 2014 in response to the kidnappings. What was ostensibly a search effort to find the boys and their captors in the West Bank included massive air strikes against Gaza. The IDF killed nine Palestinians and raided 1,300 properties, including commercial and residential buildings in the West Bank. More than 500 Palestinians were arrested without charge or trial. The IDF enforced a curfew across the Hebron area (*Times of Israel* 2014).

The national mood in Israel turned somber. Sad songs with lyrics of bravery and loss poured out of radios and TVs.

One people, one heart.

On 15 June, 25,000 people attended mass prayers at Jerusalem's Western Wall for the safe return of the boys (*Haaretz* 2014).

On 28 June at Tel Aviv's Rabin Square, the Western Wall's antithesis, the starting point for LGBTQ pride parades and lefty antigovernment mass demonstrations (Misgav 2015, 163),[17] tens of thousands rallied in solidarity with the boys' families (Hartman 2014).

Between the two demonstrations, and twelve days after the kidnapping, Bibi sent the boys' mothers to the UN Human Rights Council in Geneva to plead for the safe return of their sons (UN Watch 2015).

An entire nation united behind the hopes of the three families at any cost—even the exchange of Palestinian guerillas with "blood on their hands."

All Israel in pledge to each other.

Fortification of Labor Hill against the planned expulsions-demolitions stopped.

I followed these events in my pajamas. I was in San Francisco, cuddling with my laptop in bed. The academic year was over. Outside, the city was jubilant with pride flags and revelers. But I felt the loneliness of exile. My laptop, my umbilical cord to home. Skyping with friends. In the background, shrieks of Qassam missiles and roars of the Iron Dome Air Defense System.

Bibi and the regime knew the boys were already dead. On the evening of the kidnapping, 12 June, at 10:25 p.m., Gilad Sha'er had called the emergency hotline (Edmiston 2014).

A cry of pain.

Close-range gunfire.

On 26 June, the IDF identified the kidnappers (Erdman 2014). Civilian volunteers, not the IDF, found the three boys' bodies in a field outside Hebron four days later.

Why did the regime withhold knowledge of the boys' fates? Why wait eighteen days to tell the public that the boys were dead? Was it a tactic to foster national unity?

As the mothers made futile pleas for the return of their sons, HaLo Neḥmadim went home. The entire July-August summer break lay ahead of them. They hoped to revive their momentum when the national mood recovered following the funerals of the boys. But instead, Order Eight (Jerbi 2014; *Jerusalem Post* 2014).[18]

The War on Gaza — Protective Edge

Between 8 July and 27 August 2014, the IDF launched Operation Protective Edge, the War on Gaza. The operation involved a forty-nine-day massive aerial and ground artillery bombardment followed by a deployment of IDF soldiers who fought in the streets and homes of Gazans.

In this round, Ḥamas missiles struck White City, Tel Aviv. The Palestinian death toll was approximately 2,200 and consisted mostly of civilians (BBC 2014a). More than 11,000 were wounded (Defense for Children International 2015). According to a UN Development Programme report (2014), one in four people in Gaza was forced to flee their home during the seven-week Israeli operation. IDF air force, ground artillery, and infantry destroyed almost all Gazan infrastructure. Hospitals, schools, and mosques were reduced to rubble. Gazans suffered an Israeli-made disaster that was unparalleled since the 1948 Nakba. During that same period, sixty-six Israeli soldiers and seven civilians were killed. One thousand six hundred and twenty soldiers and 837 civilians were wounded (BBC 2014a). The War on Gaza destroyed what Oslo Boomtime foreign capital had built. It hammered the last nail in the coffin of the two-state solution peace plan. While the Nakba exiled Palestinians from their homeland, the Zionist regime had left infrastructure intact, at least temporarily, to accommodate a forthcoming mass migration that was mostly Mizraḥi. Soon thereafter, the Israeli regime detonated most of it. Gaza 2014 was even more destructive. It hardly left anything intact.

The escalation roused me from bed. I shuffled in my pajamas to my Palestinian neighbors next door. They have satellite, *al-dish*. Other diasporic Arabs from our 'hood came for the extra-large TV and brought potluck. These

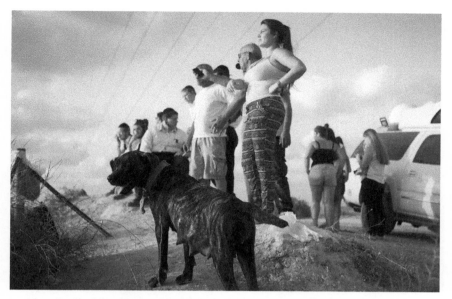

19. Sderot's Mizraḥi residents gather at dusk to watch July 2014 bombings of the Gaza Strip. Oren Ziv/ActiveStills, 2014.

were Ramadan nights. We were to feast. But shrouded in the San Francisco fog, we huddled in front of the screen. No one ate a thing.

I had to shake it off. So I headed to the Mendocino Middle Eastern Music and Dance Summer Camp. It is nestled in towering, ancient redwoods. What a blast! Each summer, it attracts some of the best Middle Eastern musicians and performers in North America for weeklong master classes, jam sessions, and classical dance. There was neither Internet access nor cell-phone reception. We tried to embrace the California mantra and live in the moment. But yet again, that umbilical cord. Folks carpooled to town to log on for Gaza updates. When they returned, I timidly asked for the latest from Ashdod and Tel Aviv. No one is smiling in my photos.

Scanning my Facebook feed, I glimpsed a photo showing a scene at dusk outside Sderot, a small, largely Mizraḥi desert town about five kilometers from the Israeli border with the Gaza Strip. It has also been a constant target for Ḥamas rockets for the past fifteen years. PTSD is endemic. The town is a stronghold of Mizraḥi culture (Saada-Ophir 2006). With high unem-

20. A Palestinian family celebrates the feast of ʿId al-Fiṭr during the Gaza 2014 ceasefire. Their home lies in ruins following the IDF bombardment. ʿAli Ḥassan/ Anadolu, 2014.

ployment rates, an ever-increasing cost of living, and shrinking social services, Sderotis were to join forces with HaLo Neḥmadim. In the Facebook photo, Sderotis were instead taking in the military spectacle of IDF bombardments on Gaza. As the Mediterranean breeze wafted east from the Gaza shores, they left the cool comfort of their air-conditioned homes to spend the summer outside watching the war while picnicking, drinking espresso, and eating popcorn (Mackey 2014).

"One people, one heart," is a popular bumper sticker.

Halfway through the Gaza War, Israel granted the Palestinians a respite. Ever resilient, Palestinian families used the cease-fire to celebrate the end of Ramadan, ʿId al-Fiṭr, to enjoy a holiday meal amid the rubble of their homes and mosques.

Responding to the extent of the civilian carnage, six months later, in December, the European High Court decided it would remove Ḥamas from their list of terrorist organizations (Withnall 2014).[19]

As Ḥamas bombarded Tel Aviv, Mizraḥi feminist activist Naʿamit Mor-Ḥaim published a captivating analysis of Gaza 2014 on *HaʿOkets*, the leading Mizraḥi blog. It bore a magical realist title: "The Stunning Story of How I Got Entangled in a Ḥamas Bookkeeping Quarrel."

> Did we engage in war mongering over twenty million dollars of salaries just as Ḥamas was trying to unite ranks with the PLO? Was it worth it? That is, I get the timing—this week [the government] okayed the wiping out of three billion of IMI debt a moment before its sale [to private investors] . . . and that every round of Gaza boosts IMI sales five to ten billion dollars. This bonanza is soaring over my head as the interceptors are roaring to meet nozzle-rockets that don't even arrive in one piece. It all feels to me a bit Kafkaesque from [the improvised shelter of] my staircase, to think that I got entangled with Ḥamas' accountants. This all could have been avoided by [Israel's] facilitating the Ḥamas salary payments and by loosening the Gaza blockade for the people of Gaza to regain a bit of normalcy. . . .

> We can play with terrorism as a language game, but this [military operation] is about electricity, ports, and basic goods for . . . families, hundreds of thousands of people and children, even though we've chopped their numbers in recent days. All to create more nests of resistance and more people with good reasons for wanting revenge, so that we are able to yell: "Hate! hate!" and continue to control the city of lab rats to test our weapons. Until the next round. (Mor-Ḥaim 2014)[20]

Under the Smokescreen of War

As Mor-Ḥaim and other residents of central Israel spent the summer sweating in crowded, make-do shelters, the Knesset continued with its regular legislative schedule. The irregular amendment to Ḥok HaHesderim was scheduled for a second reading before the Knesset plenum on 14 July, only two days into Protective Edge. Expectedly, both Hebrew and international media outlets were focused on the carnage.

The streets of Tel Aviv were empty. To Tel Aviv natives, the ultimate indicator of panic was easily available parking in the normally bustling White City. No tent cities of protesters were set up along tree-lined boulevards. Those who could afford it had flown to Europe or North America for vacation. Ben Gurion Airport was packed. Some sought solace in the dry, cool evening breeze of Mitzpe Ramon. Since the 2003 Knafo march and the 2006 Lebanon War, Mitzpe's marketing as an eco-friendly, remote artists' retreat bore fruit. It now counted over a dozen hotels, ranging from a hostel to high-end hotel-spas. All beyond the means of HaLo Neḥmadim activists and their constituents.

As early as winter 2014, Mizraḥi activists predicted that if the HaLo Neḥmadim protests gathered momentum, an international crisis would follow. Public attention would shift.

By June 2014, "Not to worry, a war is coming—one people, one heart," was appearing in my Facebook newsfeed.

The 14 July Knesset session to discuss the amendment to Ḥok HaHesderim started at 16:01 with a welcome from the chairman, post-Soviet emigré MK Yuli-Yoel Edelstein of Likud (Knesset 2014b):

"Knesset members . . . Today, is the Seventeenth of Tammuz."[21]

The Seventeenth of Tammuz is a fast day and the first holiday of the *Beyn HaMetzarim* (between the straits, Hebrew), three weeks in the Jewish calendar for memorializing the process of the Temple's destruction. The period culminates in Tisha B'Av.

"[Today] marks the eighth anniversary of the eruption of the Lebanon 2 War. In these hours, not only the people of the south, but all of us, together, confront the present security crisis. Lest we forget, this is a day for hundreds of families to visit military cemeteries and mourn loved ones."

It is a Jewish custom to visit the graves of family and friends on minor fast days. Cemeteries have special areas for fallen soldiers.

"These days, we can clearly see the lessons learned from the Lebanon 2 War by the political ranks as well as the IDF. . . . The present battle demonstrates that we have put those lessons into operation."

Much of the Israeli public interpreted Lebanon 2 as a loss to Ḥezbollah.

"We ought to separate criticism levied at decision-makers . . . from our support of IDF troops. They are all our sons . . . some in the regular service, others on Order Eight, protecting our people and state, so that here in the Knesset, we can continue our parliamentary deliberations in peace. . . . [I] send blessings and well wishes to the soldiers now on duty who continue down the path of the fallen, in the hope that they bring peace to us all."

Palestinian MK *Moḥammad Barakeh (*ḤADASH, *then the only non-Zionist left-wing political party) received permission to address the Speaker first.*

"Mr. Chairman and Knesset members, these days we are told: 'Quiet, We're Shooting'" (*sheket, yorim,* Hebrew).

"Quiet, We're Shooting" is a shortened 1970s song lyric that has become a cultural reference. The full line, "Dear Father, Quiet, We're Shooting," is taken from Ḥanoch Levin's play *Queen of the Bathtub.* It was performed during the War of Attrition with Egypt in the Suez Canal and the PLO in the northern Jordan Valley (1969–70).[22] The play, highly critical of Israel's military death cult, was censored by the Council for the Oversight of Plays and Cinema.[23]

Since then, "Quiet, We're Shooting" has become a colloquialism in Hebrew. From the 1982 Lebanon War on, the phrase lost its gallows' humor and became a call for unity in wartime. MK Barakeh was purposefully evoking an expression that spans many registers of Hebrew language and Israeli culture.

He continued:

My heart goes out to entire families that IDF bombardments extinguished. . . . What is the aim of Netanyahu and his government? Do they still cling to the delusion that the more dead Palestinians, the safer Israelis are? . . . Netanyahu's agenda is cynical. . . . He advances a political agenda against his opposition from inside and outside the coalitional government by means of war [against the Palestinians]. . . . Has Israel gone to this war, really, to protect its citizens? . . . The death of six-year-old Bassam ʿabd al-Raḥman Ḥatab is a war on terror? The killing of four-year-old Yasmin Muḥammad Mutawak is a war on terror? . . . The death of eighteen-month-old Ghanem Juda ʿabd al-Ghafur is a war on terror? . . . Eighty-year-old Ḥjjaziyya Ḥamed al-Ḥilu? . . . This is a crime against humanity.[24]

Mr. Chairman, I'm being heckled!

Israel defends the occupation and endangers its citizens' lives as it commits war crimes. . . . I'm calling on those Israelis who broke the silence by marching in an antiwar demonstration with Palestinians in Tel Aviv. . . . The protesters were attacked by fascists and the police. . . . The mark of Cain on the forehead of Israeli democracy. If the streets are going to be filled with fascist gangs attacking people for their opinions, I'm telling you, fascism is not at our doorstep, it's already here.

The chairman, Yuli Edelstein, interjected: "Please end up."

MK Barakeh referred to a demonstration held on 12 July in Tel Aviv. At its core, "the 250," or "the Regulars," as they are dubbed by Mizraḥi activists.

These same well-heeled Ashkenazim attend every demonstration against Israel's military atrocities directed at Palestinians. Yet they are rarely seen at Mizraḥi demonstrations protesting hunger, homelessness, and insufficient health care in Mizraḥi communities. This time, a few thousand Zionist leftists, mainly Ashkenazim, joined "the Regulars."

From my bed in San Francisco, my laptop's screen filled with photographs and videos of young, muscular brown men. Wrapped in Israeli flags. Waving Israeli flags. Between them and the predominantly middle-aged, paler antiwar demonstrators—Mizraḥi and Ethiopian-looking policemen, some mounted on horseback.

Underneath these violent demonstrations lay a deep racial wound with a long past—"before a scab is formed, it hemorrhages again" (Anzaldúa 1987, 2–3). First blood. The 1882 importation of Yemeni "natural workers" to labor for the first wave of Ashkenazi-Zionist settlers in Palestine. The genesis of Zionism's racial formations and the Ashkenazi Left's white privilege.[25]

Back to the Knesset session. Shortly after the obligatory statements of solidarity with soldiers and silencing of MK Barakeh, MK Gila Gamliel (Likud) took up the role of chairperson. The discussion turned to the crux of this unusual session.

Prof. Avishay Braverman, a key Labor Party MK and head of the Knesset Finance Committee, took the floor. A Stanford alum, he is a renowned economist and former president of Ben Gurion University.

"Her honor, the chairwoman . . . Knesset members . . . We are to continue with the everyday work of governance. Our heart is with all those who fight and those who withstand, as they all unite in pledge for each other. . . .

"It is my honor to present to you for a second and third read, Amendment no. 14, 2014 to Ḥok HaHesderim . . ."

When Prof. Braverman was done introducing the law, and Gaza 2014 continued to roar, the Knesset proceeded to consider the sale of surveillance equipment to Singapore. Then, they turned to national funding for marine research. The penultimate item had to do with forced boarding schools and children who ran away from them. The proposed law was to make harboring these children illegal. It is well known to Mizraḥi single mothers that boarding schools do not screen for pedophiles in their staff-hiring process. The proposed law required anyone with information about a runaway to make a report to the police—in the child's best interest, or as not to hurt the boarding school's business.

Despite sparse attendance, Amendment 14 to Ḥok HaHesderim was voted into law.

As Chairwoman MK Gamliel was ending the session, she addressed the visitors' gallery. She began in Hebrew, "I want to welcome our guests, tourists from the United States." Then she shifted to English: "Welcome to Jerusalem! Welcome to the Parliament! The Knesset! The parliament of Israel!"

The Knesset adjourned at 19:26.

The Israeli public only learned about the amendment's ratification as law on 24 July, when it was published in the Israeli Statutes at Large.[26] The session had aired live on the Knesset television channel, but public attention was focused on Gaza, rather than the "everyday business of governance."

Hebrew media finally covered the amendment three days later. Channel 2 reported that the IMI had already received bids from Dutch, German, Chinese, and Philippine investors, and the 49 percent of state-owned utilities companies and ports that were newly listed for exchange on the stock market received bids as well (Channel 2 News 2014). Finance Minister Yair Lapid used the spectacle of war to torpedo a billion NIS plan to remodel dilapidated low-income housing projects and build new ones (Busso 2016). It is possible that the funds originated in sales of low-income apartments to their long-term tenants as a result of 2001 legislation initiated by the Mizraḥi Democratic Rainbow. Lapid may have reallocated this earmarked billion NIS to cover part of the IMI's debt, investigative journalists in the mainstream media contended. New military contracts to restock the IDF with weapons were expected to further bolster the industry.

Knesset members also succeeded in securing a pay raise for themselves. Every summer, MKs receive an annual cost-of-living salary increase. But during Operation Brother's Keeper, 21,000 citizens signed a petition and then presented it to the Knesset on 11 July. The petition demanded an immediate discussion of an MK salary freeze. Many public-sector employees were already subject to salary freezes and furloughs, and thus underemployment. Some lost their jobs to downsizing. Order Eight reservists' monthly incomes were cut. The petition argued that an MK salary increase in such times of war was not only frivolous, but irresponsible (Movement for Quality of Government in Israel 2014). The petition was ignored.

Operation Protective Edge ended on 27 August 2014. That day I flew to Cork to begin the book tour for *Wrapped in the Flag of Israel* as a guest of the Irish-Palestine Solidarity Campaign (IPSC). After eight centuries of British colonialism, Irish activists are the most sophisticated audience that a scholar of the Ashkenazi-Mizraḥi racial divide can expect. They get the relevance of intra-Jewish racism to the Zionist colonization of Palestine.

It so happens that my visits to Cork have often coincided with major IDF atrocities in Gaza. What could Mizraḥi feminism teach this seasoned audience about the current crisis in Gaza? Aḥoti members were indeed among the leaders of HaLo Neḥmadim. How would I explain the relationships between HaLo Neḥmadim, Ḥok HaHesderim, the Ḥamas salary dispute, and Gaza 2014? The interplay examined in *Wrapped in the Flag of Israel* between intra-Jewish racism, neoliberalism, and divine bureaucracy as these relate to the struggle for a free and independent Palestine? That oddly familiar sequence? I had stage jitters. While almost every Mizraḥi activist gets it, would my Irish audience?

From Dublin I traveled to Tel Aviv for the Aḥoti book launch party and the Jewish High Holidays. My friends and sisters in the Mizraḥi struggle, the effort to end the Occupation, and the coalition to recognize children as the inalienable property of their mothers all came to celebrate with me.[27] To my relief, everyone got along—right-wingers and left-wingers, Ashkenazi peace activists and Mizraḥi feminists, traditionalists in long sleeves and kerchiefed heads and secularists, scantily dressed to alleviate the late summer's humid heat. None of my Arab '48 friends showed up, however. After Gaza 2014, they would not dare venture to Aḥoti Home in Black City, they apologized. Much of South Tel Aviv is a right-wing bastion. Knowing of my ethnographer's compulsion to chat, my friends repeatedly told me to shut my big mouth about Gaza 2014. Fascist gangs roaming Black City with chains and knives will simply break your bones, they warned. But I was home. No stage jitters. When I compared the ends of the 2003 Knafo march and Occupy 2011 with the truncated protests against the expulsion-demolition of Labor Hill, the packed room made the connection to Gaza 2014 before I could even spell it out.[28]

Two days later, on Rosh Hashanah Eve, the urban din of Tel Aviv quieted. At dusk, groups of fathers and children wearing white shirts walked to synagogue. On my Facebook feed: a photograph of a family eating their holiday meal in front of the ruins of their home. That morning, the YASAM had arrived with the developers' bulldozers to destroy five more Labor Hill houses. They had chosen the date carefully. The public, exhausted by Gaza 2014, was preparing for the second-most sacred Jewish holiday. At dusk on Rosh Hashanah Eve, the entire country shuts down. That morning, Labor Hill residents had posted a call to arms on Facebook. A few die-hard Aḥoti and HaLo Neḥmadim activists came to protest the expulsions-demolitions, only to be treated with extreme violence by the YASAM. The next day, the developers and police assumed, and rightly so, that not many activists would disrupt the first day of the new Jewish year 5775 to hold mass protests in solidarity. Instead, concerned citizens brought potluck to share with families whose homes were demolished. Together, they prayed and ate the holiday meals in front of the rubble.

One people, one heart.

Elections 2015: The Center Moves Further to the Right

Having been directly in the line of fire in 2014, many voters for the "land-for-peace" parties, well-off Ashkenazim and base voters for Labor or Meretz, became disillusioned with the peace process. For the first time in their lives, they considered voting for ultranationalist parties, despite the courtship and

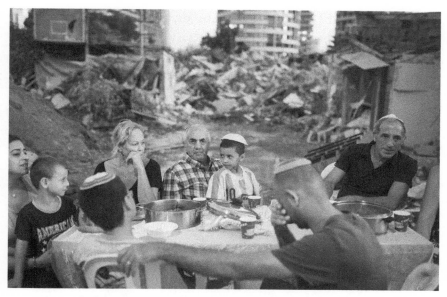

21. Residents of Labor Hill eat their Rosh Hashanah meal in front of their demolished homes. Shiraz Grinbaum/ActiveStills, 2014.

perks promised by the Labor-Meretz block. Elections were scheduled three years later. But the Knesset voted to disband in December 2014. The dissolution followed a series of cabinet ministers' resignations and parliamentary gridlock over Bibi's draconian budget proposal for the upcoming year.

Here they go again. Just as the Tel Aviv–Taḥrir 2011 protests had preceded the IDF Operation Pillar of Cloud in Gaza, that preceded an early October 2012 call for elections after parliamentary gridlock over a draconian budget proposal for the upcoming year.[29]

Israelis went to the polls for parliamentary elections on 17 March 2015. The political Center moved even further Right, yet again.

Out of 120 Knesset seats, Likud won thirty and the Zionist Union twenty-four. The '48 Arab party, having united several smaller parties into the "Joint Arab List," won thirteen seats, becoming the third-largest party. This shocked many Israeli Jews. Another new party, Kulanu (all of us, Hebrew), also right wing on Palestine, won ten. Their diverse list even brandished a Druze. Led by Moshe Kaḥlon, whose parents immigrated to Israel from Libya, Kulanu's

platforms focused on income inequality, cost of living, and other socioeconomic issues. It had Mizraḥim on its advisory board and list of candidates.
Kaḥlon, however, distanced himself from anything ethnic. His platforms
therefore lured some of the disappearing middle class, both Ashkenazi and
Mizraḥi. Many seasoned activists' Facebook posts accused Kaḥlon of run-
ning on a false social ticket.

President Reuven Rivlin followed procedure and on 25 March 2015
appointed Bibi prime minister to form the thirty-fourth government of
the State of Israel—on the Mizraḥi majority vote, yet again (Hoffman 2015).

Here they go again.

A day before Israeli elections, the United States and Iran began historic,
direct negotiations for a nuclear treaty. Bibi invited himself to the U.S. Congress in an attempt to sabotage any possible U.S.-Iranian agreement (Rudoren
2015). This foreign-policy grandstanding deflected the media's attention
from the spike in the cost of living and the rapid deterioration of nutritional
stability and public health care for Israel's disenfranchised.

Meanwhile, the Ashkenazi real estate bubble in central Israel continues to
expand. Buying homes in pre-1967 Israel has become completely unaffordable for most young Mizraḥim. As the political "Center" has been moving
to the extreme Right, the West Bank settlements present one of the few
options for newlyweds to become homeowners. The accelerating housing
crisis has intensified the unchecked growth of the large, urban West Bank
settlements near the 1948 armistice line.

In addition, more middle-aged, middle-class Mizraḥim, who gained
equity in the real estate bubble of pre-1967 central Israel, are selling their
homes to Ashkenazim. Many parents of young Ashkenazi couples can no
longer afford to help their children make a down payment for housing
in upper-middle-class enclaves in Israel's center. So they are buying out
the homes of the Mizraḥi middle and lower-middle classes. Mizraḥi parents are dividing the cash from the sales of their pre-1967 central Israel
homes among their children. This cash is facilitating down payments
for affordable housing in the settlements. The "apartheid road system"
(B'Tselem 2004; McGreal 2005) grants settlers a quick commute to pre-
1967 Israel, where most of their jobs are located. Whole Mizraḥi neigh-

borhoods and towns in the center of Israel are thus being gentrified and ethnically reconstituted.

The difficulties of rebuilding Gaza under a stricter Israeli blockade and stringent regulations were relegated to the back pages, if featured in the press at all.

Right after the 2015 elections, Bibi relented on Iran to prevent further damage to his relationship with the Obama White House. He focused his energies on the Boycott, Divestment, and Sanctions movement (BDS) as Israel's most acute crisis of the moment.

Since September 2015, the Israel-Palestine conflict has yet again escalated into what international media has dubbed "the Intifada of the Knives." As of statistics posted in May 2016, 34 Israelis have died and 380 have been injured as a result of car rammings, stabbings, and shootings (Magen David Adom 2016). Two hundred and eight Palestinians have lost their lives, and an estimated more than 1,400 have been injured (*Middle East Monitor* 2016; UNOCHA n.d.).[30]

Jamusin, or Labor Hill, is no longer on the public's radar. The Israel-Palestine conflict persists.

The Mizraḥi Cultural Renaissance

For those who have the right skin color
and the right eye color
For those born in the right city
in the right neighborhood
and went to the right school
and the right university.
For those who speak the right language
with the proper accent.
For those who were born to the right sex
the right religion
the right nationality
with the right passport.
For those who were born at the right time
and have the right future.

One day
when they come
to knock on the door
they won't ask for a cup of sugar.
They will ask to rip the door from its frame
and tear down the house.
(Keissar 2014)

Since the publication of *Wrapped in the Flag of Israel*, Mizraḥi art, theater, music, and poetry have burst into the Ashkenazi-dominated cultural mainstream. Aḥoti and Heart at East issued their landmark studies (Aḥoti 2011, 2012) about racism in the distribution of public funds for Mizraḥi culture.[31] Who are the major players in this cultural renaissance? They sardonically refer to themselves as "the new elites" (Caḥlili 2014).[32] Most recent Mizraḥi calls for action have focused on collective cultural rights. In 2002, when I brought this concept of cultural rights before a quorum of the Mizraḥi Democratic Rainbow, fellow activists wondered, are you out of your mind? How will culture bring nutritional stability to our communities? Years later, the Mizraḥi struggle for cultural rights seems to have eclipsed the burning political and economic needs of Mizraḥi communities. The renaissance that has brought the creative arts to the forefront of Mizraḥi discourse includes ʿArs Poetica,[33] a collective of young militant poets; the philharmonic Andalusian Orchestra; filmmakers; theater groups; visual artists; authors; singers; and bands (Misgav 2015, 149). The renaissance culture workers turn their creativity inward to explore intra-Jewish racism.

Misgav writes: "Aḥoti has started focusing more on cultural issues of Mizraḥi identity, unlike the activism that supported the Vicky Knafo protest." He quotes an older activist, critical of this cultural renaissance:

These days the cultural agenda is leading . . . [Aḥoti] is invested in exhibits, book publications, and various coalitions that advance Mizraḥi culture. Aḥoti Home has become a gallery of sorts. The Mizraḥi artists, men and women alike, benefit from this. They get networked into the [Ashkenazi] art scene [as diversity assets]. Meanwhile, the women who advanced the feminist, economic . . . working-class agenda around labor and gainful income have gradually disappeared from the NGO. Focusing on culture is not bad, but we always need to ask, do we still have space for vibrant dialogue whereby Mizraḥi feminist worldviews meet the reality of racialized women and generate activism relevant to their dire daily lives? (Misgav 2015, 131)

Addressing this cultural renaissance is Meir Amor, a gifted sociologist at Concordia University in Montreal. While tenured in Canada, he could not even secure an adjunct position at an Israeli university. Since the 1980s, Amor has questioned the cultural focus of the Mizraḥi struggle (Amor 2002). Amor argues that intra-Jewish racism should be explicated in more than cultural terms. The possibility to have a civil society that clearly defines the rights and duties of its citizens—Jews and '48 Arabs—he maintains, depends on its "Mizraḥization," that is, politicizing Mizraḥi reality so that the Mizraḥi majority assumes citizenship rights (Amor 2016). Civil rights should be extended not only to the well-funded Ashkenazi minority mainstream, but also to the Mizraḥi majority and Palestinian minority. Amor's method for realizing this has been advocating a nonviolent refusal to participate in Ashkenazi-run civic life—almost all of Israel's civic life. To achieve full equality, Amor demands that the Ashkenazi ruling elite make room for Israel's majority in state and society. Otherwise, he advises civil disobedience: Mizraḥim should disengage from paying taxes, voting, and other civic engagements. Recently, Amor has even dared to call for refusing to serve in the military.[34] But the sanctity of military service in Israeli state and society, and the recent role of the military in Mizraḥi upward mobility into the Ashkenazi elite, make it difficult—if not impossible—for Mizraḥim to heed Amor's advice (see Misgav 2015, 124). Neither Amor nor the renaissance culture workers, however, question how the divinity of a chosen people in a chosen land translates into the racial formations of Zionism in the context of Palestine-Israel. Amor's main arena of activism is social media, where his ideas and calls for action are gaining a growing audience. His activism is completely voluntary.

But the Mizraḥi cultural renaissance has garnered financial backing. As this Afterword(s) is being written, in spring 2016, Israel's right-wing regime is becoming the official sponsor of this renaissance. Since the 1980s, whenever Likud was in power, its cultural and education ministers invested time and effort to push the dons of Ashkenazi high culture to loosen their grip over public funds. Alongside these cultural overtures to cater to right-wing voters, the Likud regime has turned West Bank settlements into project renewals for those wishing to leave the crowded ghettos in central pre-1967 Israel. Funds flowed to Mizraḥi culture workers as long as they limited their Arabness to conjuring the imagined world their parents and grandparents left behind. Their version of Palestinian culture is largely depoliticized. No land or water issues (Abargel and Lavie 2009). This reallocation of funds was an uphill struggle.

In 2015, Bibi appointed brigadier general and Likud MK Miri Regev to be Israel's minister of culture and sport (Erlanger 2016). She joined the Likud after an impressive military career that included roles as army press and media censor and IDF spokesperson. She is of Moroccan origin. Regev is wresting funds from Ashkenazi cultural elites to the movers and shakers of the Mizraḥi cultural renaissance by any means necessary. Meanwhile, her Likud Party is accelerating neoliberal restructuring and West Bank settlement expansion. The culture workers of the Mizraḥi renaissance, therefore, have their tongues tied by their reliance on Regev, who has become their new financial patron. Just like Mizraḥi feminists, the renaissance culture workers are factionalized along the same lines as the Ashkenazi Left cultural elite: Socialist Zionists, Post-Zionists, and Anti-Zionists. Just like the strategy of Mizraḥi feminists, rarely do these culture workers dare expose these factions, or their position on the Question of Palestine. They do not encroach on this well-funded Ashkenazi elite turf. This is not only because Regev's culture ministry would not fund them. They must have constituencies and audiences. The Mizraḥi public continues to move even further to the political Right of greater Eretz Israel.

Under the right-wing reign, the renaissance culture workers are the new ambassadors of Israel's Ministry of Internal Security, Strategic Affairs, and Hasbara. They are emissaries of *hasbara* (explanation and outreach, Hebrew). The ministry sends Moroccan and Iraqi musicians, Yemeni singers and poets, and Egyptian playwrights to North America and Europe. Outside Palestine-

Israel, they are to display the diversity and cultural tolerance of Israeli Jewish society. The message: Israel belongs to the cultural fabric of the Arab World and it calls for peace through artistic performance. These emissaries are allowed to express their doubts on the military occupation and settlement project, even Gaza 2014, under the thin veneer of Zionist humanism and universality.[35] But on one state for Israel-Palestine, the right of return for Palestinian refugees, or BDS as a civil disobedience tactic—the three cornerstones of any genuine dialogue with Palestinians—they must shut up.

Back in the early 1990s, I focused on the Mizraḥi-Palestinian cultural borderzone. I recognized the agency immanent in Mizraḥi poetic articulations. But I was cautious. I noted that Zionist frontier ideology and practices tended to "strategically cannibalize" (Hurtado 1996, 42; see also Alarcón 1990) the creativity of borderzones while the Ashkenazi mainstream annexes them as tokens of diversity (Lavie 1992, 1995, n.d.; Lavie and Swedenburg 1996a, 1996b). While the agency of cultural renaissance workers is a powerful, generative shift, it is also delimited, this time, by the Mizraḥi ultranationalist mainstream of the early twenty-first century.[36]

Another voice to speak out against the implications of the Mizraḥi cultural renaissance is Orly Noy, the Iranian-born writer, translator, and activist. She has pointed to the ways that this emphasis on Mizraḥi culture dehistoricizes and anesthetizes the Mizraḥi struggle (Noy 2015a, 2015b). She writes: "Identity politics is very powerful. . . . But when it becomes disconnected from the larger political context . . . it is morally defective" (2015b).[37] For Noy, the political context is the Israel-Palestine conflict and its embeddedness in regional politics. Like Amor, she questions the recent cultural focus of the Mizraḥi struggle. She goes further, however, and engages with volatile issues such as the Palestinian right of return and one-state Israel-Palestine. Many Mizraḥi culture workers, writes Noy, take it as an axiom that Israel's current welfare state is to be found in large West Bank settlements. They do not problematize the military occupation with their communities' predicament. The cultural turn of the Mizraḥi struggle, says Noy, idealizes old times, when Mizraḥim and Arabs lived together (2015a, 2015b).

Noy argues that Mizraḥi renaissance culture workers, like the Mizraḥi public, articulate hatred of the Ashkenazi Left. *Wrapped in the Flag of Israel* points to the hypocrisy of the Ashkenazi Left, whose white privilege allows it to advocate for Israeli-Palestinian peace—a successful tool to fund both its NGOs and cosmopolitan lifestyle. "Hatred of the Ashkenazi Left cannot be a basis for a Mizraḥi-Palestinian coalition," writes Noy (2015a). "If the Ashkenazi Left has become an obsession with . . . the new Mizraḥi discourse, the Palestinians are in an even more problematic place. . . . First, they've disappeared. And now," as Mizraḥi communities turn further into ultranationalism, "the Palestinians come back as the catapult with which to shoot the Ashkenazim" (2015b).

Amor and Noy are not the only ones pondering the figurations of agency in this lyrical move. Can one examine this cultural renaissance as a poetic counternarrative that grew out of the 2011 Occupy movement? Martin Stokes, analyzing the 2013 Gezi Park protests against neoliberal urbanization, has shown how Istanbul, like London, Shanghai, and other globalized cities, even Tel Aviv, has become a space for counterreading through poetics (Stokes 2013).[38] A historical imagination is revived by new poetic forms that are anchored in the present and future. From Tel Aviv, 'Ars Poetica would argue that this is exactly what they are doing. Stokes further asks: Does this poetic counternarrative—with its reorganization of mimetic emotion—bring social and economic justice to the subaltern?

For Stokes, mono-ethnic nationalisms do away with minorities and diasporic populations. Nations have to manufacture national sentiment, and for that, says Stokes, they need to find a negative object to juxtapose the nation against. Mononationalism relegates minorities, diasporics, and exiles to folklore that serves only to spice up the nationalist machine. In the Gezi Park protests, Turkish demonstrators resisted such folklorization. *Wrapped in the Flag of Israel* illuminates the State of Israel's mononationalism. Despite the diversity discourse celebrated by the Mizraḥi cultural renaissance, Judaism defines citizenship. Ashkenazim and Mizraḥim continue to rally together against the goyim threat—Stoke's negative object to juxtapose the nation against—like in the War on Gaza 2014.

In the global city, minorities, diasporics, and exiles evoke nostalgia and sentimentalize the narrative of imagined origins through art, music, theater, and poetry. This discourse supplants the romance of indigeneity. Stokes argues that eventually, the poetic cultural turn improves the daily lives of subjects under neoliberal austerity. Cultural struggles will lead to political, social, and economic change. Like many academics, Stokes theorizes the agency of resistance. He is hopeful.

In Israel, the perpetual shift toward ultranationalism is not only Mizraḥi. After Gaza 2014, many Ashkenazim are souring on the peace process. The occupation is completely normalized. The Mizraḥi cultural renaissance, romantic and nostalgic, is now in the mainstream media. Does it replace the role of the atavistic and indigenous Palestinian for the Ashkenazi Left? How can this historical imagination of Jewish coexistence in the Arab World undo the present and future of Israeli imperialism?

The cultural renaissance has not changed much for the Mizraḥi single mother. Is this renaissance yet another way to valorize the cultural arts of people of color? Does it also serve to exacerbate the power structures immanent in citizenship's racial formation? But alas. The relationship between (neo)liberal mononationalism and its diversity assets does not change the bureaucratic structure of gendered citizenship (see Melamed 2006). The torture of standing in long lines under the blazing sun, and the sexual favors the single mother might have to offer clerks to redeem her welfare benefits, make mimetic redemption impossible. She can mistily watch on TV the Andalusian Philharmonic performing songs she learned at their mother's knee. Her painful efforts to make ends meet, however, remain the same (see also Leibner 2015).

Furthermore, as spectators to this cultural renaissance and consumers of the news, Mizraḥi single mothers have more reasons to cast their votes for the Right. The plight of the Palestinians is far removed from their daily efforts to survive. The connections between their dire financial circumstances and Israel's insatiable military spending are lost. Moreover, after Gaza 2014, they are willing to sacrifice even more of this meager existence to fortify the last Jewish stronghold in the midst of the Arab World—"a villa in the jungle."[39]

The Steady Drumbeat of Eternal Return

The aim of this Afterword(s) is to reflect on how the arguments in the first edition of *Wrapped in the Flag of Israel* are related to the events leading to the 2014 Gaza War. How do the gender and race of bureaucratic torture fit in the larger landscape of the Israel-Palestine conflict and the Arab World? And what is the relevance of Mizraḥi single mothers to regional politics?

International media and much of the world's public opinion conceived of Gaza 2014 as a watershed moment: the most destructive attack by Israel on the Palestinians since the Nakba. Journalists covered Gaza 2014 and the events leading up to it, but it is the Israel-Palestine binary that dominated the print and electronic media. Yet again, they failed to connect Israel-Palestine to the Mizraḥim, who are perceived as an internal problem for Israel. The media like clear-cut victims. After Gaza 2014, Palestine has been moving into the mainstream. It is taking center stage in the larger conversation about race, class, and neoliberal restructuring. These days, communities of color are connecting Ferguson to Palestine (Feldman 2015). Mizraḥi 'hoods are seldom, if ever, included.[40]

This Afterword(s) engages with broader issues related to the book's reception. I have addressed my critics on the themes of agency and torture that run throughout the book. The case of the War on Gaza 2014 illustrates that the parallel tracks of Israel's intra-Jewish racism and the Israel-Palestine conflict cannot be separated.

Some critics charged that the book's main arguments read more like conspiracy theory than ethnography. The usual lens for examining the gender-race-class intersectionality model is secular. It overlooks the divine. But my book is about miracles. The State of Israel is a miracle—the ingathering of Jewish diasporas in mandated Palestine. When Mizraḥi single mothers obtain welfare benefits—it is also a miracle.

The notion of a conspiracy theory connotes shadowy meetings in secret rooms between members of a cabal. This is not happening in Israel-Palestine. Gaza 2014, like the 2011 Tel Aviv "Taḥrir Is Here" Occupy protests, or the suicide bombing that ended Vicky Knafo's 2003 Single Mothers' protest, all happened out in the open. Regime officials publicly talk about Ḥok HaHesderim cuts in parliament. And military leaders freely admit: "This is exactly what we did."[41]

Not a conspiracy, but a steady drumbeat: state Judaism, divinely decreed and therefore nonnegotiable, versus the ever-present onslaught of the goyim.

One beat, then two. The State of Israel plays with the binary. It uses war as a unifying force to divert attention from domestic issues of racial and gender justice through the sanctity of the chosen people in their chosen land. And Israeli Jews—Ashkenazim and Mizraḥim alike—are completely in thrall to the binary.

Not to worry, a war is coming—one people, one heart.

Since submitting the manuscript for *Wrapped in the Flag of Israel* to its initial publisher, new full-length ethnographies on bureaucracy under neoliberalism have appeared. The book's analysis of bureaucratic torture has resonances with these accounts (Bear 2015; Gupta 2012; Hull 2012; Mathur 2015). But the majority of these studies, like Feldman's (2008), rely on a Weberian-Foucauldian perspective. Others, like David Graeber (2015), employ Marxist approaches of historical materialism. *Wrapped in the Flag of Israel* does neither. Instead, it draws on religion, ritual, and the phenomenology of transcendental essences to examine neoliberal bureaucracy in times of austerity. It does so by conjoining intersectionality with divinity. Furthermore, the transcendental essence of bureaucratic suffering is nondiscursive and thus nonrepresentational. *Wrapped in the Flag of Israel* dares conjure the unspeakable.

This Afterword(s) might not satisfy those who seek responses to their particular engagements with *Wrapped in the Flag of Israel*. Why should scholars and activists move beyond their comfort zone for a compassionate examination of feminists of color who do not challenge their communities' ultranationalism? To ignore the significance of Mizraḥi feminism is to ignore the role of women in most Mizraḥi protest movements, like HaLo Neḥmadim, and their majoritarian centrality to the Israel-Palestine conflict, even as they strategically avoid advocating for Palestine.

This book is a departure from the usual political perspective—the Israel-Palestine binary. It presents a new analytical toolbox. It challenges assumptions that the domestic politics of welfare distribution and the international relations of the Middle East are two distinct domains of political life, each supposedly sequestered in its internal or external domain. The plight of Israel's Mizraḥim and the plight of Palestinians are complementary conditions, even if among Palestinian and Mizraḥi feminists there is a sense of competition for the attention of progressives around the world. In the long lines, Mizrahi and Arab '48 women terrorize each other. Lives within the welfare system micromanaged by lower-level Mizrahi bureaucrats.

Rather than offering neat, happy, scholarly solutions, *Wrapped in the Flag of Israel* only offers jagged edges.

Although I am the author of *Wrapped in the Flag of Israel*, the book is a Mizrahi feminist co-creation. Like a mother, I have watched it grow and develop a life of its own. I no longer have sovereignty over the conversations and questions that germinate from it.

As of the writing of this Afterword(s), the beat slowly grows louder once again. Shades of Bush 2008 and Operation Cast Lead, Obama 2012 and Operation Pillar of Cloud. Now, a new U.S. president in 2016: Donald Trump. Prime scheduling.

The eternal return of the question:

How long can the regime depend on Mizrahi docile loyalty to the Jewish state?

It's a racial wound inflicted by the Left. So deep, yet invisible. Caught in the relentless bureaucracy, everyone knows their place. Mizrahi mothers, sleepwalking, entranced by the drumbeat of the miraculous ingathering of the diasporas.

And more questions follow: Will Mizrahim continue at the bottom of the benefits list for their efforts on the killing fields, on the streets, and at the polls in support of the same right-wing parties that implement the neo-liberal policies that work against them? How many poems, concerts, paintings, and films can fix this?

The government has abandoned us not only on the battlefield but also in their bomb shelters.

They're corrupt—all of 'em. What can we do? Nothing.

ACKNOWLEDGMENTS

It is fitting that even the acknowledgments to this book's first edition are fraught with difficulty. Singling out individuals and entities to offer gratitude to comes at the risk of implying that some deserve more thanks than others. I have endeavored to attribute thanks where it is deserved, but the list of people I owe for this book spans three continents and over twenty years.

The time spent writing this book has not been the typical scholarly writing experience. No sabbaticals, no salary or benefits, no tenured position, and no residential stability. This is in stark contrast to the period when I conducted preliminary anthropological fieldwork and archival research for the "Hebrew as Step-Mother Tongue" project between 1990 and 1994, funded by the Wenner-Gren Foundation, the University of California Humanities Research Institute at Irvine, and the University of California, Davis Junior Faculty Research Grant. The bulk of anthropological fieldwork and archival research for this book was conducted between 1999 and 2007, supported by inadequate single-mother welfare allowances provided to me by Israel's National Security Bureau and sporadic, low-paying adjunct jobs at Beit Berl Teachers College. Moreover, the composition of this book has been fraught with all manner of relentless campaigns by those elements in academia that would rather have me and my research disappear.

Only thanks to the love, friendship, and collegiality of the institutes, organizations, and individuals named below is this book able to exist. To denote a person who has passed away, I use the traditional z"l acronym for *zikhrono/a leBrakha* (may his or her memory be blessed, Hebrew) after the name.

I would like to thank the institutes and organizations that lent their support to me during the writing of this book. First, I wish to extend a bouquet of thanks to my sister activists in Aḥoti—for Women in Israel and my fellow activists in the Mizraḥi Democratic Rainbow. As well, I thank my anthropology and women's studies colleagues, staff, and librarians at Beit

Berl Teacher's College. I express my gratitude toward Nissim Tziyoni and the volunteers at the Pit'hon Lev NGO who helped keep food on our table. In the same vein, the Israel Free Loan Association (IFLA) assisted with paying our monthly rent.

I also cannot neglect the entities that provided my son, Shaheen, with merit scholarships. Without these organizations and programs, I could not have raised him to be a responsible, good person. Thanks go out to Thelma Yellin High School, the staff at the Mishkenot Sha'ananim classical music program, the staff at the Dr. Bessie F. Lawrence International Summer Science Institute at the Weizmann Institute of Science, the staff at Tel Aviv University's Unit for Science-oriented Youth, the staff at the Israel Conservatory of Music in Tel Aviv, and the staff of the America-Israel Cultural Foundation's classical music program. I am deeply indebted to the parents and staff, especially Ya'el Ha'elyon (z"l), of the Tel Aviv School for the Arts. Collectively, they took care of us like family.

Time and space to write this book was made possible by affiliations with the Institute of Advanced Studies and Department of Anthropology at the University of Minnesota, the Institute for Social Science in the 21st Century at University College Cork, and the Beatrice Bain Research Group and the Center for Middle Eastern Studies, both at the University of California, Berkeley. I wish to express my profound gratefulness to the Centro Incontri Umani Ascona, Switzerland (CIU). During my 2011 residency at CIU, the beauty, quietude, and equanimity provided the opportunity for my creativity to flower.

There are so many people who have contributed so much to my ability to complete this project. In an effort to show my gratitude in the fairest way possible, I simply list individuals' names in alphabetical order, separated by location. This in no way downplays my gratitude for their contributions.

A bouquet of thanks to all those in Israel-Palestine who stood alongside me in protests and who helped coordinate consciousness-raising events for Mizrahi causes. And also to those who came to my aid when I had to rely on welfare for survival: Reuven Abargel, Larry Abelson, Fadhia Abu-Leil, Yardena 'Alon (z"l), Meir 'Amor, Rachel 'Amram, Yael 'Arami, Kokhi 'Arava, Fabienne Attal, Irit Averbuch, Moty Avital, Ilana Bakal, Rabbi Daniel Bar-Muha, Natalie

Baruch, Hanna Beit Halachmi, Rivka Ben-Bassat, Doli Ben-Habib, Smadar Ben Natan, Sari and Micha Berkovich, Meir Shoef, and our buddies at the Ort Food Forum, Shaul Bibi, Shlomit Bitan, Yifʿat Bitton, Ron Cahlili, Avi and Bracha Chalfon, Esther Chalfon, Hanna Cohen-Langer, Alona Dahan, Ilanit Dahan, Irit Daloumi, Vardit Damri-Madar, Erella Eckstein, Marcelle Edery, Kuba (David) Elkobi, ʿEdna El-Rom, Tania Forte (z"l), Israel Zvi Gilat, ʿIra Givʿol, Itzik Goʾel, Zehava Goldstein, Lev Grodin, Rutie Gur, Galit Hadad, Avinoʿam Halevi, Talma Handler and Judd Neeman, Claris Harbon, Hagit Harel, Yali Hashash, Snir Hassin, Marion Hefer, Esther Hertzog, Yaakov (z"l) and Erika Hetzroni, Yifʿat Hillel, Inas Jabali, Shmuel Jellineck, Hagar Kadima, Noam Kaminer and Smadar Nehab, Reuven Kaminsky, Miri Katz, Yussuf and Hussam Kawasmeh, Hila Kobo, Hagar Kot, ʿAdi Kuntsman, Talia Levi, Michael Longo, Gabi and Janush Lukacs, Salwa and Zuheir Majadleh, Yonit Mansour, ʿEran Marinberg, Emanuel Marx, Nisreen Mazzawi and her late mother, Shamai Mentch, Zeʾevik Meraro, Tali Meyron-Shatz, Nina Mizrahi, Rahella Mizrahi, Jerri Musallam, David Nashtir, Hala Natur, Dorit Nesher, Shabtai Noy (z"l), Shira Ohayon, Mimi and Dana Peleg, Yossef Puri, Yaffa Puzailov, Ruth Resnick, Zmira Ron, Yaʿir Ronnen, Tsafi Saʿar, Christian Sabatier, Anat Saragusti, Yishai Sarid, Rhona Schuz, Dudu Selaʿ, Bracha Serri (z"l), Erella Shadmi, Ilana Shamai, Michal Shamai, Assaf Sharʿabi, Ahuva Shimʿoni, Haim Shiran, Vicki Shiran (z"l), Rafi Shubeli, Flora Shoushan, Ilana Sugavker (Shazor), Shimʿon Tajouri, Lisa Taraki, Ronit Tmisit-Dagan, Tamara Traubmann, Toine van Teeffelen, Mazal Veres, Aviva and Avner Weis-gal, Sarit Yitzhak, Aharon Yitzhaki, Beni Zaken, Orna Zaken, Iris Zarini, Nirit Zarum, Shoshi Zeid, and Hillel Zori.

I am deeply indebted to my colleagues and dear friends in the Greater Bay Area, California, for solidarity, support, and friendship: Norma Alarcón, Nezar AlSayyad, Anna Babka, Paola Bacchetta, Claudia Bernardi, Carol Bruch, John Cho, Keith Feldman, Terry Fletcher, Susan Galleymore, Emily Gottreich, Sora Han, Jack Hirschman, Lynn Joachim, Suad Joseph, Helena Knox, Sarah Lamble, Libby Lewis, Laurie Lippin, Andrea McHenry, Janet MacLeod, Larry Michalak and Karen Trocki, Mirit Mizrahi, Hilton Oben-zinger and Estella Habal, Cinda and Dan Pearlman, Csaba Polony (z"l), Andrew Reiner, Annie Robbins, Kim Robinson, Lisa Rofel and Graciela Trevisan, Will Rosco, Tony Ryan, David Salk, Bracha Serri (z"l), Buthaina Taha, Tony Tanke, Joy Totah-Hilden and Bob Hilden, Dongmei Wang, Mary Lou Weprin, Greg Youmans, and Mei Yuan.

I wish to extend thanks to my colleagues and friends in the Twin Cities, to whom I am grateful for emotional and scholarly support, and for their hospitality: Hend Al-Mansour, Lisa Albrecht, Bill Beeman, Afifa Benwahoud, Jerry Burg, Melissa Cathcart, Rabbi Reuven and Bat Sheva Drori, Pamela Feldman-Savelsberg, Itai Himelboim and Jonathan Eoloff, Karen Ho, Judy Hornbacher and Steve Benson, Patricia James, Amy Jonson, Diyah Lara-sati, David Lipset, Todd Lurie, Stuart McLean, Margareth Miller and the OTB writing group, Scott Morgensen, Richa Nagar, Esther Ouray, William Prottengeier and my yoga classmates, Peter Rachleff, Flo Razowsky, Karen Redleaf, Arun Saldanha, Sylvia Schwarz, Rizwan Shaikh, Lindsay Taylor, David Valentine, and Dmitry Volovik.

In Boston, I express my gratitude to Libby Bouvier and Andrea DeVine, Steve Caton, Shoshi Madmoni-Gerber, Alice Rothchild and Dan Klein, and Donna Spiegelman.

Though my stay in Charlottesville was relatively short, I treasure the time I spent with Amy Lee Baik, Majida Bargash, Patricia Cancro, George Mentore, Farzaneh Milani, Justin Schaffner, Edie Turner, Kath Weston and Gita Patel, and the faculty of the University of Virginia Department of Anthropology and the Women, Gender & Sexuality interdisciplinary program.

A great amount of credit and thanks go to those in Switzerland and northern Italy who offered friendship and hospitality while I resided at the Centro Incontri Umani Ascona: Gabriel Ash, Gabriella Bernieri, Verna Burckhalter, Angela Hobart, Caroline Ifeka, Tom Kennedy, Christos Lynteris, Rania Madi, Milli De Monticelli, Laura Simona, Susanna Sinigaglia, Eduard and Evelyn Wahl, and Tanya Zivkovic.

I wish to thank my colleagues in Britain for their collegiality and professional solidarity: Haim Bresheeth, John Gledhill, Stephan Feuchtwang, Hilary Gilbert, Toby Kelly, 'Adi Kuntsman and Yehudit Keshet, Radhika Mohanram, Martha Mundy, Nicola Pratt, Madeleine Reeves, Hilary and Steven Rose, Chris Weddon and Glen Jordan, Dick and Pnina Werbner, and Nira Yuval-Davis and Alain Hertzmann.

Many thanks to Kathy Glavanis, Caitriona Ni Laoire, and the members of the Ireland-Palestine Solidarity Campaign in Cork, Ireland, for their generosity and hospitality. To Jim and Penny Bowen, in particular, I extend my gratitude.

I thank Alejandro Castillejo Cuéllar, Heidi Grunebaum, and the organizers and participants of the Berlin Workshop on Ethnographic Approaches to Transitional Scenarios: Perspectives from the Global South for their comparative insights into my work.

Very special thanks to those who have come to my aid at many different times and in many different places, those who have helped me think through ideas and get them into print, and those who have guided me in assessing the logistic matters of life: Mustafah ʿAbdallah, Ammiel Alcalay, Rachelle Choukroun, Ilise Cohen-Ben-Shousan and Dan Rice, Dina Dahbany-Miraglia, Faye Harrison, Heidi Jane Isakoff, Naʿeem Jeenah, Eric Lassiter, Rachel Levi, Marcy Newman, Gustavo Lins Ribeiro, Joan Scott, Joyanna Silberg, Richard Silverstein, Becky Torstrick, Fotini Tsibiridou, and Joyce Zonana.

I could not have completed this book without the love and support of my adopting Mzeini family in Dahab, Egypt. Their understanding was vital as I groped for calmer words to write up our years of separation while I was stranded in Israel.

This book underwent dramatic changes as it grew from a chapter in another book to a book in its own right. Reinhardt Suarez worked with me side by side, either in person or across continents and time zones via Skype, to assemble this book from fragments of scholarship, diaries, archival materials, and print and electronic media. We worked together under surreal conditions. I vividly recall one nighttime session when I sat in a remote gas station in the hills below Jerusalem, using its weak Internet access to connect to Reinhardt in Minneapolis. From the nearby Israeli air force base, we could both hear squadrons of jet fighters screaming through the thick summer air. From the newsfeed in my browser window, I read that Gaza was being bombed at that same moment. I applaud Reinhardt for his commitment, professional flexibility, and open heart.

As for *The Poetics of Military Occupation*, Don Handelman continued to contribute his insightfulness, brilliance, and wisdom to my work. It was

Don who inspired me to study the fields of symbolism, phenomenology, ritual, and play that have been with me since my undergraduate days at the Hebrew University of Jerusalem. He offered me his invaluable and fastidious commentary on every chapter, and directed me toward applicable scholarship that could bolster the book's theoretical aspects. This book would not have attained its high quality without him.

This book is dedicated to my son, Shaheen. As a young child, he spent countless hours in my Berkeley office or with babysitters, and joined me in my home-fieldwork in Israel-Palestine as I researched the book project that was to be "Hebrew as Step-Mother Tongue." In exchange for that time, I promised him that I would dedicate the book to him. Over the years, he would periodically ask me about "his book." It was a rhetorical question meant to highlight the tragic absurdity of our lives in Israel. He knew that in the welfare lines there was neither space nor time for a project like that. Only later did he become aware that some colleagues took advantage of my diverted attention and appropriated my published and unpublished work as their own with no citation.

I am profoundly grateful to have him in my life. As we bore our dire life circumstances in Israel together, his patience and resilience were my inspiration. I will never forget how, after I apologized for our impoverishment and homelessness, he comforted me: "My real home is my relationship with you."

Now that this book is complete, I humbly offer it to him.

GLOSSARY OF HEBREW, ARABIC, AND YIDDISH TERMS

AHUSAL (sing.), AHUSALIM (pl.) A Hebrew acronym, used in social science, for Ashkenazi, *hiloni* (secular, Hebrew), *vatik* (old timer, Hebrew), socialist, and liberal. It denotes a privileged Ashkenazi Jew. In colloquial Hebrew, Israelis say "Ashkenazi" to mean AHUSAL.

Anglo-Saxi (sing. masculine), Anglo-Saxit (sing. feminine), Anglo-Saxim (pl.) (Anglo-Saxons, Hebrew) Jewish immigrants of Ashkenazi, Yiddish-speaking descent, from English-speaking countries such as South Africa, Britain, Australia, and from North America.

'Aravi (sing.), 'Aravim (pl.) (Arabs, Hebrew) Hebrew shorthand for all Arab non-Jews, primarily Israel's Palestinian citizens.

Ashkenazi (sing.), Ashkenazim (pl.) Jews with origins in Central and Eastern Europe and who have Yiddish-speaking origins. They are 30 percent of the citizenry in the State of Israel.

badal (exchange, Arabic) A kind of marriage, common among Yemeni immigrants to Palestine, that involved a brother and sister from one family marrying a brother and sister from another family. The swap saved on bridewealth and dowry.

behemat bayit ktana (little domestic beast, Hebrew) Yemeni young girl laborer who worked on *moshavot* during the Yishuv. Her salary was meager, and she received almost no food from employers.

Beit ha-'Am (people's home, Hebrew) A community center that provides low-cost lectures, concerts, and theater performances that the entire community can afford to attend.

blondinit (sing.), blondiniyot (pl.) (blonde, Hebrew) A woman who is naturally blonde or who dyes her dark Semitic hair blonde.

Bor (pit, Hebrew) A slang term referring to the IDF war room in central Tel Aviv.

brara (pl.) (imperfects, Hebrew) A slang term meaning "riffraff."

dimyon Mizraḥi (oriental imagination, Hebrew) A quality of reporting reality in exaggerated terms attributed to Mizraḥim.

Diwan (Judeo-Arabic) The collection of poems written in Judeo-Arabic during the seventeenth century by Rabbi Shalom Shabazi. When recited individually, outside of communal rituals, Diwan is supposed to calm down the soul.

du raglit (two-legged, Hebrew feminine) Shorthand for *ḥayot du ragliyot*, a zoological term denoting bipedal animals in the plural.

Eʿeleh ba-Tamar (ascendance via palm trees, Hebrew) The first wave of Arab-Jewish labor migration from Yemen to Palestine in 1882. The name is taken from a phrase in Song of Songs 7:9.

Em Zara (alien mother, Hebrew) The term given to Mizraḥi mothers by Ashkenazi Zionist family experts.

etsbaʿ Elokim (the finger of G-d, Hebrew) Divine providence.

goyim (pl.) (non-Jews, Hebrew and Yiddish) One of the Hebrew slangisms for "enemies."

Gruzinim (pl.) (Hebrew plural masculine) Jews who immigrated to Israel from Georgia.

gvarot (pl.) (ladies, Hebrew) Upper-class Ashkenazi women who, during the Yishuv, pursued charitable activities, including the establishment of charities and other volunteer organizations.

Ha-Em ha-ʿIvriya (Hebrew Mother, Hebrew) The term given to secular Ashkenazi mothers by family experts.

ḥad horit (sing.), Ḥad horiyot (pl.) (single parent, Hebrew feminine adjective) The Hebrew term used to refer to a single mother. It is shorthand for *em ḥad horit*, or "single parent mother."

halakha (Hebrew) The collective body of Jewish religious laws.

ḥalutzot (pl.) (pioneers, Hebrew) Ashkenazi women who lived on agricultural cooperatives during the early 1900s and worked as daily unskilled laborers.

Ḥaredi (sing.), Ḥaredim (pl.) (Hebrew) Ultra-Orthodox Jews.

havdala (Hebrew) The ritual ending the Sabbath and demarcating the beginning of another week.

hishtaknezut (Ashkenazification, Hebrew), **le-hishtaknez** (to become an Ashkenazi, Hebrew verb) A process by which Mizraḥim shed their ethnic markers, such as dress style, extended family commitments, accent, surnames, political views, and musical tastes as they attempt to move upward in socioeconomic class.

Ḥok HaHesderim (Arrangements Law, Hebrew) The 2003 law passed by the Israeli Knesset meant to deregulate and downsize government, reduce spending, decrease taxes for the upper classes, and ease inflation through monetary control.

Hudna (calmness, Arabic) The ceasefire between the Israeli government and Ḥamas during the Al-Aqsa Intifada. It originates from the 628 CE truce between Prophet Muḥammad and the Quraysh tribe of Southern Arabia.

Indiyanim (pl.) (Indians or Native Americans, Hebrew) A Hebrew slangism for "primitives."

Intifada (uprising, Arabic) The sustained Palestinian uprising against the Israeli state's occupation of the Gaza Strip and West Bank. The first Intifada occurred between 1987 and 1993. The second Intifada—called the Al-Aqsa Intifada—occurred between 2000 and 2005.

Kabala (acceptance by transmission, Hebrew) A school of thought focused around Judaism as mysticism.

Kavkazi (sing.), Kavkazim (pl.), Kavkaziyot (pl. feminine) Immigrants who arrived in Israel from the Asian republics of the former USSR, and who do not have Yiddish-speaking origins. Kavkazim constitute about 2 to 4 percent of Israel's citizenry. AḤUSALIM and Russim count Kavkazim with the Mizraḥim.

Kehilot Ashkenaz (Ashkenazi communities, Hebrew) Official terminology for the population of Ashkenazim living inside the State of Israel.

kibbutz (sing.), kibbutzim (pl.) (gathering, Hebrew) Collective agricultural communities.

kushi sambo (sambo nigger, Hebrew) Slang term for a dark-skinned Mizrahi.

le-hitbakhyen (whining and being a crybaby, Hebrew) A term that refers to excessive complaining. The feminine noun form of le-hitbakhyen is *mitbakhyenet*.

Likudnik (sing.), Likudnikim (pl.) Supporters of Israel's right-wing Likud Party.

masorti (traditional, Hebrew) A traditional Jew, neither an Orthodox observant, nor a reform or conservative.

mezuzah (Hebrew) A sacred parchment stored in a protective casing and mounted on the doorposts of Jewish homes. The parchment is a handwritten version of Numbers 6:4–9 and 11:13–21 from the Torah.

mitzpe (sing.), mitzpim (pl.) (observation points, Hebrew) In the plural, Mitzpim are highly exclusive, gated, mainly Ashkenazi communities towering above Galilean Palestinian villages.

Mizraḥi (sing.), Mizraḥim (pl.) (Easterners or Orientals, Hebrew) Jews with origins in the Arab and Muslim World and the margins of Ottoman Europe. The Mizraḥim make up 50 percent of the Israeli state's citizenry. *Sephardim* (Spaniards, Hebrew) is another term used to denote Mizraḥim.

mohel (circumciser, Hebrew) A sacramentally trained, but not medically educated, Jewish ritual circumciser.

moshav (sing.), moshavim (pl.) A town or settlement composed of small individual farms of similar size, established as part of the Zionist statebuilding program from the Yishuv onward. Farmers cooperated, pooling labor and resources to provide for themselves.

moshava (sing.), moshavot (pl.) (farming colonies or plantations, Hebrew) Farming colonies or plantations that mainly sat on lands Baron Edmund de Rothschild bought for a pittance from Palestinian land owners or from Bedouin sheikhs in the late 1880s.

muḥajjabat (pl.) (Arabic) Veiled women.

naḥat (sing.) (contentment, Hebrew) Slang term for "grandchild."

Nakba (catastrophe, Arabic) The 1948 expulsion of most Palestinians from their homes, villages, and towns in order to carve out the State of Israel.

nesikhim (pl.) (princes, Hebrew) A nickname for Ashkenazi politicians with a longstanding family lineage in the Likud Party.

nosaḥ (sing.) The set of liturgical melodies for chanting the Torah, the layout of text in Jewish prayer books, and a set of traditions and customs associated with both holidays and everyday life.

ʿozrot bayit (domestic laborers, Hebrew) Women employed in households by *gvarot*. Prior to the foundation of the State of Israel, these
women were usually Palestinian Jewish women, or immigrants to Palestine's Yishuv from Muslim countries. After 1948, these were mainly
Mizraḥi women.

Pravoslavim (pl.) (Russian Orthodox Christians, Hebrew) Immigrants
from the former Soviet Union who use fake documents to show their
Jewish heritage.

pulḥan ha-imahut (motherhood rite of passage, Hebrew) Secular Ashkenazi motherhood as conceived by Zionist family experts.

Russi (sing. masculine), Russim (pl. masculine), Russiyot (pl. feminine) Post-Soviet Ashkenazim who immigrated from the European
parts of the former Soviet Union to Israel in the early 1990s. Russim
constitute about 10 to 12 percent of Israel's citizenry and are the visible
and vocal post-Soviet immigrants to Israel.

SHABAK An acronym for Sherut Bitahon Klali, or General Security Service, Hebrew. This is Israel's internal security service and secret police,
known for its physical and emotional methods of interrogation.

schwartze (black, Yiddish) Short for the Yiddish expression *schwartze
ḥayye* (black animal, Yiddish). This is a derogatory term that some Ashkenazim call Mizraḥim, or a term that bigoted American Jews call African Americans.

Sephardi (sing.), Sephardim (pl.) Descendants of the non-Yiddish-
speaking Jews who were expelled from Spain and southern Europe in
1492. Though Sephardim constitute only one group of Mizraḥim, the
name is often used as a blanket label for all Mizraḥim.

sheinale schwartzale (nice little Black, feminine, Yiddish) An Ashkenazi
appellation used to describe a young, good-looking Mizraḥi woman.

sh'ḥordinit (sing.) (Hebrew) A woman who dyes her hair blonde but
shows exposed dark roots.

Shiknaz (Palestinian and Yemeni-Jewish Arabic) Ashkenazim.

Shoah (catastrophe, Hebrew) The term used to refer to the Holocaust, the
Nazi extermination of Jews during World War II.

shomrei masoret (pl.) (Hebrew) Keepers of the tradition.

sotzialit (sing.) (Hebrew) Social worker case officer.

tehillim (Hebrew) The name for the scriptural Book of Psalms. It is also the name of the physical book of psalms many carry with them as a prayer book.

teimonichka (sing.) (little Yemeni woman, Yiddish) A name *gvarot* gave to Yemeni women who worked for them as domestic laborers.

Tish'a B'Av (Hebrew) The annual fast day on the ninth day of the Jewish month Av, commemorating the destruction of both the First and Second Temples in Jerusalem.

Tnu'at ha-Po'elet (Women's Labor Movement, Hebrew) The movement started in 1911 by Ashkenazi women who aspired to be like pioneer men.

tihur etni (Hebrew) Ethnic cleansing.

walad 'am (Arabic) Paternal, parallel cousins.

ya ḥaram (it is legally forbidden by Islamic law, Arabic) An expression that means "What a pity!" or "Hands off!" The term has become Mizraḥi slang.

Yahud (pl.) (Jews, Arabic) A term pre-1948 Palestinians used to refer to Mizraḥi immigrants who were not from Yemen. It is now used in Arabic slang to refer to both Israeli Jews and diaspora Jews.

Yamaniyun (pl.) (Yemenis, Arabic) A term pre-1948 Palestinians used to refer to Yemeni Jewish immigrants.

yelidei ha-Aretz (born in Israel, Hebrew) The Israeli state's official demographic category denoting Israeli Jews who were born in the State of Israel.

Yiddishkeit (sing.) (Eastern European shtetl Jewish way of life, Yiddish) A term that refers to the way of life lived by Jews in nineteenth-century Eastern European ghettos.

Yishuv (settlement, Hebrew) The term, first used in the 1880s, to refer to the period of the Ashkenazi settlement of Palestine between 1882 and 1948.

zayin (Hebrew) The seventh letter of the Hebrew alphabet. In everyday Hebrew, it also means "weapon" or "penis."

NOTES

Introduction

1. Mitzpe Ramon is the full name of Vicky Knafo's hometown. The literal meaning of *mitzpe* (Hebrew) is "observation point." Ramon is the Hebraization of the Arabic *Raman*, meaning "Romans." Wadi Raman is a dry riverbed descending from the top of the Negev Desert plateau into the cirque, and then leading to the 'Arava, until the head of the 'Aqaba Gulf. Wadi Raman was part of the Perfume Road, one of the most important ancient trade routes from the times of the Pharaohs until the collapse of the Ottoman Empire. It stretched from the southern Arab peninsula to the Mediterranean coast. It was used by the Nabateans, and then the Romans who conquered them. In Israel, possessive town names, such as the Mitzpe of Ramon, often get shortened in colloquial speech. Mitzpe Ramon is known as "Mitzpe." While the full name is pronounced mitz-PEH ra-MON, the shortened version is pronounced MITZ-pe. In Hebrew slang, a migration of a word's emphasis from the last syllable to the first denotes the Yiddishization of the term.

2. Vicky got her last name, Knafo, through her ex-husband, who was of Moroccan descent. She kept this last name after the divorce. Her precise ethnic background remains a mystery. According to the Mitzpe Ramon rabbi, Vicky had conducted a Sephardic funeral for her mother. In the past, a few activists who have run afoul of her have spread rumors that she is actually of Romanian descent. Romanian Jews sit at the bottom of the Ashkenazi pecking order and are sometimes thought of as the "Mizraḥim" among Ashkenazim. Nevertheless, Vicky identifies as a Mizraḥi and is treated accordingly.

3. In the broadest definition of *Mizraḥim*, that is, Jews with Israeli citizenship whose genealogical origins lie in non-Yiddish-speaking countries, Ethiopians are counted as Mizraḥim and constitute between 6 to 8 percent of that demographic. Certain circumstances often lead Ethiopians to be set apart from other Mizraḥim, however. They immigrated much later than other Mizraḥim—two waves immigrated to Israel from the mid-1970s to the mid-1990s. They also did not come from a Muslim country, and they have an African phenotype rather than an Arab one. Most prominently, Ethiopian Jews receive a disproportionate amount of funding from American Jewish donors,

who heavily influence many institutions in Israeli civil society, including NGOs. Some Mizraḥi activists speculate that wealthy American Jews fund Ethiopian NGOs as a way to make up for strained black-Jewish relations in the United States. This book does not address the specificities of Ethiopian Jewish communities or their funding, nor does it explore the field of Ethiopian Jewish studies that has become popular in Israeli anthropology.

4. Clare Louise Ducker's (2005) findings on Israel's demographics are the most recent. Ducker accounts for the large-scale post-Soviet immigration to Israel in the 1990s, yet she is careful to distinguish between the Asian and European post-Soviet Jewish and non-Jewish immigrants. The Central Asian post-Soviet immigrants to Israel are counted as Mizraḥim. The more visible and vocal post-Soviet immigrants to Israel, however, are Ashkenazim.

5. Ashkenazim also have an ultra-Orthodox fundamentalist Jewish minority, some of whom do not identify with Zionism. Nevertheless, this minority, as well, is very careful to separate itself from Mizraḥim.

6. In my two decades of ethnographic fieldwork, I have observed many more Ashkenazi men marrying Mizraḥi women than the opposite. I was not able to find quantitative data or research that offer fixed percentages of these marriages. Perhaps this is because the topic is embarrassing to census officials. As Barbara S. Okun and Orna Khait-Marelly (2006) report, "Thus, we expect that the children of an Ashkenazi father and Mizraḥi mother will have better socioeconomic outcomes than children of a Mizraḥi father and an Ashkenazi mother. Abraham Yogev and Haia Jamshy (1983) found this to be true, but mostly because, in their sample, couples composed of Mizraḥi women and Ashkenazi men were characterized by higher socioeconomic status than were couples with Ashkenazi wives and Mizraḥi men." They do not provide a detailed rundown of percentages, however. For more in-depth explanation of Ashkenazi-Mizraḥi mixed marriages, see chapters 1 and 3 of this book.

7. Throughout this book, all the Hebrew-English translations are mine. Much of the quoted dialogue was stated in fluent Hebrew slang. Other Hebrew translations include official lingo and shorthand. As I translated the Hebrew to English, I did my best to retain the meaning of the words and the Semitic, urban rhythm of the original. To avoid stripping the colloquial embeddedness, natural flow, and raw emotion from the original Hebrew, I did not provide a pedantic, annotated literal translation (see Apter 2006, 6; Budick and Iser 1996, 207).

8. For an English translation of the Declaration of the Establishment of the State of Israel, see Israel Ministry of Foreign Affairs (2008).

9. In colloquial Hebrew, the suffix -stan has grown in popularity to replace land in the last half decade or so. This has coincided with the rise of deeply involved

U.S. military operations in countries that have *stan* at the end. The shift happened with the growing Israeli fears of radical Islam from locales such as Afghanistan and Pakistan. For example, the Ḥamas-run Palestinian refugee camps in the West Bank and Gaza Strip are referred to in colloquial Hebrew as Ḥamastan. Ultra-Orthodox Ḥaredi neighborhoods are referred to as Ḥaredistan.

10. The Israeli NSB and the U.S. Social Security Administration (SSA) have a few differences. The SSA currently handles many services online. In Israel, you must go in person to the NSB. SSA allowances more closely reflect the U.S. median cost of living than NSB allowances do the Israeli median cost. Since many Israeli social welfare scholars were academically trained in the United States, the philosophy of NSB stems directly from the U.S. logic of the 1950s.

11. As this book is being brought to print, the November 2012 recommendations of the Shifman Committee are up for review by the Knesset. Headed by Pinkhas Shifman of the Hebrew University School of Law and appointed by Israel's Justice Ministry, the committee proposes to completely do away with the concept of child and spousal support in divorce cases. The Shifman Committee recommendation is based on the 2008 recommendation by the Schnitt Committee, headed by Daniel Schnitt of Tel Aviv University's School of Social Work, and again, appointed by Israel's Justice Ministry. The Schnitt Committee recommended that joint custody from birth onward should be mandated in all divorce cases involving child custody. Each parent is responsible for creating a safe and stable household for their children, solely funded by their own income. This ignores the gender-based income disparity among Israeli citizens and the usual role division of the mother and father up until divorce, where the woman must reduce or eliminate her workload to take on house and child-rearing duties. The Schnitt Committee recommendation also assumes that the children are goods to be divided equally among the parents. The Schnitt Committee recommendation was not voted into law by the Knesset, not because of Israel's active feminist lobby opposition, but because of the opposition of the Orthodox and ultra-Orthodox coalition parties. The Jewish family law segment of halakha, the collective body of Jewish religious laws, advocates the Tender Age Doctrine that states that postdivorce children until the age of six ought to stay in the sole custody of the mother, with regular fatherly visitations. Still, Israeli family court judges adopted the Schnitt Committee recommendation into their rulings, creating a legal precedent that continues to be followed today.

12. Because of fluctuating exchange rates of the U.S. dollar versus the NIS, it is impossible to assign an exact value over a year's duration. This amount was calculated per Bank of Israel exchange rate on 31 December 2010. The amount could be higher.

13. Rent was calculated in U.S. dollars using figures provided by the Bank of Israel at http://www.bankisrael.gov.il/firsteng.htm (accessed on 14 February 2013).

14. In his first visit to Israel in 1977 as an official economic consultant, Friedman met with Israel's finance minister, respected academics, and financial movers and shakers. He preached a doctrine of economic deregulation that included relinquishing governmental controls over foreign currency trade (*Y-Net* 2006).

15. While the "Beilin-'Abed Rabbo Flying Circus" was the term the media used, the public dubbed the clique the "Beilin-Abu Mazen Flying Circus." Abu Mazen is also known as Mahmoud Abbas. It is ironic, because after 'Arafat's death, it was Abu Mazen who removed 'Abed Rabbo from the PA cabinet.

16. As a frame of reference, the purchase price of a run-down 80-square-meter (around 260 square feet) flat in mainly Mizrahi south-side Tel Aviv as of April 2011 was around $350,000. This would have bought a well-maintained 250-square-meter (around 2,500 square feet) single-family house (not including full basement) in an upscale neighborhood in Minneapolis, Minnesota.

17. Until the Al-Aqsa Intifada (2000–2005) Palestinians and Israelis were generally able to use many of the same roads in the West Bank. Once the Intifada began, Palestinian guerrillas started carrying out sniper attacks on Israeli Jewish drivers going to and from the West Bank and pre-1967 Israel. The government responded by investing a tremendous amount of funds to create a whole new system of roads "for Israeli citizens only." Palestinian traffic was relegated to narrow, poorly maintained roads, or even dirt roads, even though Palestinians are the majority of West Bank residents (see Atzmon 2011). It is interesting to note that while the high-quality, Jews-only apartheid roads have been featured in major media and studied by mainstream human rights organizations such as B'Tselem, as of 2013 I could not find an academic book published by top-tier university presses on the subject. Neither could I find academic journal articles published with first-tier journals that address the topic.

18. It is noteworthy to point out that in appropriating *hudna* for use by Israel's colonial apparatus in the West Bank and Gaza, Ginat effectively warped its original meaning. The hudna between Mecca and Medina involved two equal "sister groups" within a larger "mother group." But Ginat's hunda was not an agreement of equals.

19. The primary financier of the New Israel Fund (NIF) is no longer Levi's Jeans. From the mid-2000s, the Ford Foundation took over (New Israel Fund 2007). According to James Petras (2002), the Ford Foundation works very closely with the United States and its client states. For further discussion on how the NIF controls and contains the division of Israeli protest labor, see Lavie (2010; 2011a).

20. On 29 June 2003, the NIS was worth approximately $0.23. Exchange rates are calculated using figures provided by the Bank of Israel. See note 13.

21. I lost custody over my son to his father due to the court's determination of Parental Alienation Syndrome (PAS). PAS was a charge often used in divorce proceedings in the 1990s. PAS is a controversial theory based on the assumption that a child's estrangement from a violent father most likely precipitates from the mother causing alienation between the father and child. Child psychiatrist and pedophilia advocate Richard A. Gardner coined in the term in 1985, and it quickly gained popularity with attorneys representing fathers in child custody cases, despite its lack of scientific foundation. The PAS defense became so successful that many courts awarded fathers alleging PAS sole custody of their children. PAS allowed the courts to discount the credibility of the children's abuse charges, even with physical evidence. In 2003, faced with criminal charges, Gardner committed suicide when his malpractice insurance could no longer cover legal costs from defending lawsuits by now-grown children who were affected by PAS accusations in court. Among the accusations levied against him was faking empirical data, given most of his workload consisted of collecting court testimonies on behalf of deadbeat dads, many of whom were pedophiles. He admitted in court that only 2 percent of his time was devoted to clinical research (Bruch 2002; Dallam 1999; Heim et al. 2002; see also Silberg 2012). In my own case, a California court-appointed child custody evaluator determined that PAS was relevant to the case. He said that if I were to be given additional custody of Shaheen, there would be a higher probability that I could potentially alienate him from his father. I therefore lost custody of him. Israel's family courts, its family court services run by the Welfare Ministry to assist the courts in custody cases, and many private practitioners in Israel's psychotherapeutic and psychiatric establishment have adopted PAS as the official policy of family courts (Tzur 2001). Before he died, Gardner was invited by Israel's Welfare Ministry to educate licensed social workers on PAS policy and treatments. At the same time, he was disinvited from many professional functions in Western Europe.

22. As part of her master's thesis, "Mizraḥi Women Professors in Israel's Academe" (2011), Iris Zarini surveyed the estimated five thousand professors, associate and up, in Israel's government service and institutions of higher learning. Even more marked than the lack of Mizraḥi women in Israeli academe is the present state of Israel's Palestinian academics. Of Israel's five thousand total professors, a mere sixty-nine are Palestinian. There was only one woman among them, in the Tel Aviv University School of Education.

23. In spring of 1992, I was a member of the "Dependency and Autonomy: The Relation of Minority Discourse to Dominant Culture" research group at the University of California Humanities Center, Irvine. While there, I wrote a paper titled "Silenced from All Directions: Third World Israeli Women Writing in the Race/Gender Borderzone." I intended to include it in "Hebrew as Step-Mother Tongue." Still a relatively young scholar, I naïvely shared it with colleagues also working on Mizraḥi topics. They went on to use the analysis in their own work. In 2004, I again foolishly shared it, and my raw data, with another colleague in Israel. That colleague went on to establish a prominent place in the field of Mizraḥi studies in Hebrew. On the whole, my published and unpublished articles from the "Hebrew as Step-Mother Tongue" project continue to be used uncited by many scholars in Mizraḥi studies.

24. Vicky's family was settled into the South of Israel. Emanuel Marx's analysis identifies similar processes of bureaucratic entanglement when 1950s Mizraḥi immigrants were settled by the Israeli regime into former Palestinian villages on the Lebanese border.

25. See *Merriam-Webster Online Dictionary*, s.v. "torture," http://www.m-w.com (accessed 14 February 2013).

26. Israel does not have internationally recognized borders. Between 1949 and 1967, it held to armistice lines outlined in the 1949 Armistice Agreements between Israel and neighboring Egypt, Lebanon, Jordan, and Syria. After the 1967 war, Israel technically had no borders, as the war had broken the armistice. Israel occupied the Hashemite Jordanian Kingdom's West Bank of the Jordan River (of which it annexed the formerly Jordanian part of Jerusalem), the Syrian Golan Heights (which it annexed), the Egyptian-controlled Gaza Strip, and the Egyptian Sinai Desert. Between 1979 and 1982, as a result of the Camp David Accords, Israel returned the Sinai Desert to Egypt. Between 1978 and 2000, Israel occupied the southern part of Lebanon. In 2005, Israel pulled out of the Gaza Strip. Such pullouts never deter the IDF from conducting war operations in those locales, or anywhere in the Arab World. Abba Eban, Israel's most notorious foreign minister, diplomat, and politician, exemplified the thinking behind Israel's treatment of borders. According to him, Israel's pre-1967 armistice lines had a "memory of Auschwitz" (Burston 2007).

27. I wish to express my thanks to Don Handelman for suggesting the phrase "Divinity of Chance" to describe the serendipitous magic required for a lower-class mother to accomplish goals within a bureaucratic system.

28. "Finger of G-d" is a biblical expression that describes an event that takes place with the interference of a supreme or transcendent power. The origin of the expression is in Exod. 8:18–19 of the King James Bible: "And the magicians did

so with their enchantments to bring forth lice, but they could not: so there were lice upon man, and upon beast. Then the magicians said unto Pharaoh, This is the finger of God: and Pharaoh's heart was hardened, and he hearkened not unto them; as the LORD had said."

29. Abner Cohen, an Iraqi Jew who immigrated to Israel in the early 1950s, was funded by a British Council scholarship to study anthropology at Manchester University's Anthropology Department. He was to work on a PhD with the legendary Max Gluckman and Emrys Peters. Cohen studied there around the same time that Ashkenazi anthropologists were funded by the Bernstein Research Project. All anthropology PhD graduates out of the Bernstein Project obtained academic jobs in Israel. But Cohen did not enjoy the same initial success. Despite being shut out from academic employment in Israel, he was endowed with a chair at the School of Oriental and African Studies (SOAS), University of London (see Lavie 2003; Parkin 2001).

30. In March 2004, a coalition of NGOs composed of Aḥoti—For Women in Israel, the Mizraḥi Democratic Rainbow, and Mossawa—The Advocacy Center for Arab Citizens in Israel, formed into the Mizraḥi-Palestinian Coalition Against Apartheid in Israeli Anthropology (CAAIA). Together, CAAIA sent Israel's State Comptroller an official grievance, asking for clarification as to the almost total absence of Mizraḥi and Palestinian anthropologists in full-time equivalent positions in Israeli universities, inquiring about the systematic violations of Mizraḥi and Palestinian communal intellectual and cultural rights, and calling attention to the absence of any code of ethics to guide Israel's anthropological research and writing (see also Lavie 2003, 2005; Lavie and Shubeli 2006; Blachman 2005; Bar Shalom, Daas, and Bekerman 2008; Madmoni-Gerber 2009). As of 2004, 67 percent of anthropological studies in Israel's universities focused on Mizraḥim and Palestinians (Lavie 2003, 2005; Lavie and Shubeli 2006).

31. According to Don Handelman, Israeli ethnographies produced by Gluckman's students as part of the Bernstein Research Project did indeed conflate Peace in the Feud-type conflict resolution with the Manchester Extended-Case Study. These ethnographies used the case study in very conservative ways and worked toward the happy end of Zionism. This was implicit, rather than outwardly stated (pers. comm.).

32. I use the term "racial formation" here and throughout the book following the path-breaking tome of Omi and Winant (1986).

33. These numbers are based on cross-referencing data from the Israel Central Bureau of Statistics (Romanov et al. 2011), the MiMizraḥ Shemesh NGO (http://mizrach.org.il/, accessed 12 February 2013), and my own research.

1. Left Is Right, Right Is Left

1. See endnote 21 in the Introduction.
2. Since 2005, this law has been changed. The Israeli parliament voted that single mothers are allowed to travel outside Israel four times a year before they lose NSB income allowances and augmentations. The vote was put into law as of 24 January 2012. This change was initiated by post-Soviet Knesset members to facilitate visits by post-Soviet single mothers to their families in the former USSR.
3. Hebrew intelligentsia slang borrows "BCBG" to mean *bon chance, bon genre* (good luck, good class, French). It describes a well-heeled class.
4. Like all Jewish citizens of Israel, Mizraḥim must serve in the army. The military is still an avenue for upward mobility for Israeli Jews. Since the 1982 Lebanon War, however, actual combat has gradually become less attractive to Ashkenazim, who are eligible to be assigned to the high-tech behind-the-lines units, thanks to their superior schools in affluent neighborhoods. Young Mizraḥim do not enjoy the same mobility. When the State of Israeli goes to war, the Hebrew media emphasizes the Ashkenazi contribution to the defense of the nation. This honor is not extended to the fallen Mizraḥi, Druze, Bedouin, or Ethiopian soldiers, even though they are largely responsible for the "ongoing security"—and thus higher casualties—in Gaza and the West Bank (Abargel and Lavie 2006, 2009; see also Levy 2003, 2013).
5. As of January 2013, there were twelve hotels—providing a range of accommodations from a clean traveler's hostel to very high-end hotel-spas—in Mitzpe Ramon and the immediate vicinity. While still forlorn, Mitzpe's marketing as an artist's retreat bore fruit.
6. For further details, see the news report at http://www.ynet.co.il/articles/0 ,7340,1-2034254,00.html (accessed on 14 February 2013). See also Dahan-Kalev (2006).
7. Architect Sharon Rotbard (2005) provides an eloquent analysis of the division of Tel Aviv into a "White City" and a "Black City."
8. For further details, see Gurevitch (2011).
9. When the media asked Vicky Knafo about the mayoral transition from Sami to Flora, she weighed in: "Passing the throne of the kingdom from husband to wife? Where are we—Morocco?" See Hebrew article at: http://www.ynet.co.il /articles/0,7340,L-3315780,00.html (accessed on 23 February 2013). The passing of the throne from Sami to Flora is an example of Mizraḥi power through kin connections. A complementary set of data is offered by Michael Inbar and Chaim Adler (1977). Adler's work has been criticized as eugenic determinism by many Mizraḥi activists.

10. The mitzpim fall under the rubric of Israel's Acceptance to Communities Bill that anchors discrimination and separatism into law. This bill calls for the creation of "acceptance committees" in small satellite suburbs of spacious single-family residences in the Negev and Galilee. According to the bill, the acceptance criteria for residence in these communities include "fitting with the life of the community" and "fitting with the social fabric." According to Gil Gan-Mor, attorney for the Association for Civil Rights in Israel (ACRI), this allows committees to "reject 'unwanted' communities that wish to live in the village—such as Arabs, single parents, disabled persons, same-sex couples, Mizrachi Jews, religious people, and so on" (ACRI 2011). Gan-Mor's full legal opinion is available at http://www.acri.org.il/en/wp-content/uploads/2011/03 /Acceptance-to-Communities-Bill-ACRI-position-211210.doc (accessed on 14 February 2013).

11. The term *Yishuv* comes from Zionist historiography. The word itself is short for *ha-Yishuv* (the settlement, Hebrew). Historiographers originally used two terms: *ha-Yishuv ha-Hadash* (the new settlement, Hebrew, i.e., the Ashkenazi colonization of Palestine) and *ha-Yishuv ha-Yashan* (the old Yishuv, Hebrew, i.e., the Jews who lived in Palestine before Zionism's 1880s onset). Creating two types of Yishuv, flowing from "old" to "new," assumes a continuity between Jews indigenous to Palestine and Jews who came to colonize Palestine, glossing over the colonialism immanent in the new Yishuv project. Over time, the distinction between old and new Yishuv disappeared, making all Jews in pre-1948 Palestine into colonizers in the eyes of Palestinians, or pioneers in the eyes of the Zionists.

12. Every Israeli town and city used to have a *Beit Ha'am* (people's home, Hebrew for community center), established in the 1930s by the Labor Party, who also controlled Israeli labor unions, to provide low-cost lectures, concerts, and theater performances that the entire community could afford to attend. The concept was later brought to mainly Mizraḥi development towns in the hinterlands. Most of the performers were Ashkenazim from the Tel Aviv area.

13. The original audio transcript of this talk includes audience interjections. These interjections, while important to the experience, are not part of this chapter's function as historical overview. The women's comments tended to be redundant, and could be classified into two categories: protests against a point I raised, or comments providing examples to support a point I raised. For the sake of space and focus, I have omitted them.

14. The following section is the work I read on 3 August 2006, at Luna's apartment. I wrote it using the Brill house style author's guide provided to me by the encyclopedia's editors. This style does not include parenthetical references in the

main text and only includes major works that contribute to the article. I used many more references than appear in the short bibliography accompanying the entry. I have included the major EWIC references in the overall reference list for this book as a separate bibliography. I wish to thank Hila Kobo and Shaheen Lavie Rouse for their diligent work gathering, copying, and summarizing hundreds of reference sources for me to review. I also wish to thank the librarians at the Beit Berl Library and Beit Ariella, Tel Aviv's main library, for their tireless efforts to assist Shaheen, Hila, and myself find what we needed in their stacks, archives, and interlibrary loan.

15. Among almost all Israeli Jews, it is shocking not to have a son circumcised. Even more shocking to these women was that Herzl, the number one icon of Zionism and the Jewish state, blocked his own son's circumcision (Stewart 1974, 202).

16. See Blumenfeld (1997); Thorleifsson (2012); Okun and Khait-Marelly (2006; 2010, 384); and Shahar (1988). These references were added to the text after the publication of the encyclopedia entry.

17. According to Don Handelman, one of the major weaknesses of the anthropology of Israel is the relative absence of kinship studies (pers. comm.). I might add here that as more women entered the anthropology faculty and gave up motherhood in favor of publications for merit and promotion, kinship studies—one of the pillars of the discipline—faded away. One laudable exception is Suad Joseph, whose work on Arab family dynamics is of vital importance beyond the specialized field of Middle East anthropology (Joseph 1994, 2000).

18. Redcliffe Nathan Salaman (1874–1955) was a prominent figure in Zionist eugenics. Many of his writings feature the anti-Mizraḥi bias popular among Ashkenazim in the early twentieth century: "The real Jew is the European Ashkenazi, and I back him against all-comers" (Salaman 1920, 28); and "In point of view of the purity, that is to say the absence of mixture with outside blood, during the last 1800 years, there is no doubt that the Ashkenazim can show a far clearer bill than the Sephardim who are known to have absorbed in no small quantity both Moorish and Iberian blood" (Salaman 1911).

19. This emphasis on eugenics is meticulously documented in Sahlav Stoler-Liss's master's thesis, written in Hebrew for Tel Aviv University (see Stoler-Liss 1998). It is interesting to note that when publishing her findings in English, she uses the less potent and more accepted trope of "building the new Jew's body."

20. The information I presented in 2006 on Mizraḥi women professors in Israeli universities was based on Zarini 2004. This research has since been superseded by Zarini 2011.

21. The women listening to my lecture were familiar with incidences of Mizrahi babies sold for adoptions without parental consent. And most of these
women had relatives affected by unconsented medical experimentation on
Mizrahim. The most notable affair involving children sold for adoption is
known as "The Yemenite Babies Affair" (Madmoni-Gerber 2009; Zeid 2001).
Between 1935 and 1965, but primarily between 1948 and 1954, thousands of
Yemeni and other Mizrahi babies were sent to hospitals and later reported
missing or dead. The babies' parents were never given straightforward
answers about their children's deaths. Years later, however, many of these
parents received IDF draft notices for their children. Upon this revelation,
parents started to investigate, bringing the entire affair to light. When a
few of the parents were reunited with their grown children, they found out
that their children were illicitly given or sold to childless Ashkenazi parents
in Israel, North America, and Australia. The "Ringworm Affair" (1948–60) is
the name given to Israel's most famous case of unconsented medical experimentation. Told they were receiving treatment for ringworm, subjects
were exposed to highly dangerous doses of ionizing X-rays. Around 150,000
people in Israel were affected by these treatments, most of them children
of newly arrived Mizrahi immigrants from North Africa and the Middle
East. These experiments were funded by the United States, who could no
longer conduct them on racialized U.S. populations (Belhassan and Hemias
2004; Malka 1998).
22. Lapid shrewdly took on a semblance of "diversity" by including a handful of
Mizrahim as Yesh ʿAtid-affiliated representatives. This included two Ethiopian Jews, one of whom was the first-ever Ethiopian woman to win a Knesset
seat. No other party on the Left or Right could boast such an achievement. His
affluent Ashkenazi voters, however, perceived the gesture as little more than
a nod toward diversity that did not endanger their own race-class privileges.
Very few votes for these diversity candidates came from Ethiopian ghettos or
Mizrahi barrios. It was very transparent to those populations that Yesh ʿAtid
was using racial tokenism to cater to the young, sensitive Ashkenazim who
took to the streets in summer 2011. I discuss the almost exclusively Ashkenazi
social protests of summer 2011 in chapter 6 of this book.
23. Michael Selzer is an Ashkenazi Jew whose parents emigrated from Europe to
the part of colonial India that later became Pakistan.
24. Until 1968, MAPAI (Hebrew acronym for Workers' Party of the Land of Israel)
had been the most dominant political party in Israeli politics. In 1968, it
cemented its power by merging with other Socialist Zionist parties and
changed its name to the Israeli Labor Party.

25. These quotes have been reproduced on the HaZatetet Blog (http://hazatetet
.wordpress.com/), dedicated to quotes about Mizraḥim by leading Zionist figures in the Yishuv and early years of the Israeli State.

26. According to a January 2009 interview with Reuven Abargel, one of the Jerusalem Black Panthers co-founders, Black Panther ʿOvadia Harari was executed by
Israeli police death squads from short range during a chase in May 1971. Black
Panther Daniel Saʾil fled from Israel in 1975. He first went to France, and then
Spain. Abargel states that rumors were that he broadcasted anti-Israeli propaganda in Arabic from Iraqi radio and then returned to Spain. He then entered
the Israeli consulate there and was never seen again (Fischer 1996). Another
panther, Koko (Yaʿakov) Derʿi, was violently beaten during the 1977 demonstrations. In the 1980s, when many Black Panthers were criminalized for their
resistance activity and imprisoned at the Beer Sheba Jail, they organized a
revolt, of which Derʿi was a key organizer. For the first time in Israel's history,
prison guards shot tear gas and smoke grenades into the small cells of Jewish prisoners. In doing so, they targeted Derʿi. Yeḥezkel Cohen, another Black
Panther, was arrested for being a part of a mainly Ashkenazi group, Shining
Path, who was blamed by the Israeli regime for collaboration against the state.
The most celebrated prisoner from this group was an Ashkenazi kibbutznik,
Udi Adiv. He was given special comfortable conditions in the prison. Cohen,
the only Mizraḥi in the group, was the one most exposed to torture, emerging
from his long jail term with untreated broken bones. In addition, he lost his
vision almost completely due to prison torture. See http://www.planetnana.co
.il/r_aberjel10/O_a.r_dvar_hapanterim.htm (accessed on 14 February 2013).

27. The inflated prices of real estate in central Israel, where most employment
is to be found, rose sharply in the early 1990s due to the large wave of immigration to Israel by former Soviet Union Ashkenazim, which the Labor Party
leadership referred to as the white ʿaliya (literally, "ascendance," Hebrew; also
the term for Jewish immigration to Israel) that was to redeem Israel from Mizraḥization. The European former Soviet Jewish immigrants—as opposed to
those from Central Asia—were given large governmental subsidies for rent or
purchase of housing. They preferred to live in the central cities' slums so that
they would be closer to employment and better education for their children
rather than in Israel's hinterlands, where housing is better but schools and
unemployment worse (Lavie 1991).

28. Pisgat Zeʾev literally translates to "the Wolf's Peak"—a name that romanticizes
the imperialist endeavor, given that the neighborhood overlooks the majestic
desert wilderness dropping sharply from the Ramallah mountain range into
the below-sea-level oasis of Jericho. However, it is also possible that the neigh-

borhood is named after Ze'ev Jabotinsky, one of the founders of the right-wing Ḥerut Party, precursor to the present-day Likud Party.

29. Examples of Ashkenazi feminists who benefited from their Ashkenazi kinship ties are Shulamit Aloni, wife of Reuven Aloni, a longtime member of the Labor Party establishment; Yael Dayan, Moshe Dayan's daughter; and the much younger Meirav Michaeli, niece of Mordechai Namir, one of the Labor Party's leaders.

30. Women-to-Women USA-Israel's mission statement is "To provide economic empowerment and support to Israeli women" (http://www.guidestar.org /organizations/13-3085199/u-s-israel-women-women.aspx#mission [accessed 29 January 2013]). It is one of the chief donors to gender and women's studies programs in Israeli universities. In 2005, Women-to-Women USA-Israel became part of the National Council of Jewish Women.

31. While NIF funds activities showcasing the humanitarian and enlightened nature of the Israeli Ashkenazi minority mainstream, it has limits. In 2006, Palestinian NGOs based in Israel issued a joint document titled "The Future Vision for Palestinian Arabs in Israel." The document can be found at http:// www.knesset.gov.il/committees/heb/material/data/H26-12-2006_10-30-37 _heb.pdf (accessed on 14 February 2013). It recommends that Israel become a state for all of its citizens, without privileging Jews over non-Jews. Some of the NGOs participating in this document were funded by the New Israel Fund. According to some of the signatories, whom I interviewed and who wish to remain anonymous, they received threats that the NIF would cut their funding and, therefore, their salaries, if they continue to initiate and participate in events that the NIF interprets as doing away with what the NIF defines as Israel's Jewish democratic character.

Such issues resurfaced again in a reported meeting on 8 July 2010, between NIF's CEO and Ashkenazi-run NGOs on the pro-Palestinian side of the Israeli nonprofit map. Among them were Physicians for Human Rights, Bimkom — Planners for Planning Rights, Rabbis for Human Rights, the Public Committee against Torture, and MachsomWatch. In this meeting the NIF CEO provided criteria that may endanger the disbursement of their funds held with NIF. These criteria targeted NGOs supporting the international campaign of Boycott, Divestment, and Sanctions (BDS) Against Israel, and those NGOs that sought universal jurisdiction over Israel's violations in the West Bank and Gaza. NIF insisted that the Israeli justice system was sound and that there was no need to circumvent it in favor of international courts. Most prominently, NIF would refuse to channel money to NGOs engaged in activities that created by-products challenging the Israeli state as the sovereign expression of world Jewry's right to territorial self-determination.

The NGOs balked, stating that NIF's guidelines would discourage donors from the United States and Western Europe from donating to Israeli NGOs. NIF backed off, but the impression of its stance remained with the NGOs. Remarkable in their absence were the Palestinian NGOs that NIF threatened in 2006 but continued to fund. I learned of this meeting from a well-connected source who wishes to remain anonymous. This source also noted that, unlike NIF's normally lavishly catered meetings, this meeting only had fruits and nuts for the attendees.

32. It is interesting to note that, unlike many feminist movements in both the First and Third Worlds, neither Ashkenazi nor Mizraḥi feminists challenge the primacy of kinship, marriage, family, and childbirth. Many feminists justify the lack of critique against such patriarchal institutions by citing the traumatic history of the Jewish people. Family focus, according to these feminists, is the sole possession that survivors of persecution and anti-Semitism have. Even after the Jews had found a homeland in Mandatory Palestine, Israeli citizens are still taught to feel that they have no European or Arab lands to return to. Thus, all their efforts are placed into intergenerational continuity through women's wombs, marriage contracts, and extended family pressure to keep them. Some feminists may joke that in an environment of extreme gender discrimination in the labor market, the safest mode of subsistence for a woman in a society that enshrines motherhood, yet provides minimal financial or social support to mothers, is to marry and become reliant on a husband to earn a living wage.

33. International Volunteer Day is a holiday started by the United Nations to "recognize the dedication of volunteers, their admirable spirit of service, and their wide-ranging efforts to promote the goals of the United Nations" (Ki-Moon 2011). On this day, Israel's Education Ministry instructs schoolteachers to conduct class discussions on community volunteerism (Education Ministry of the State of Israel 2006).

2. Protesting and Belonging

1. In her research about Palestinians in the IDF, Rhoda Kanaaneh (2009) interviewed former Bedouin soldiers. One went on to become an Israeli diplomat. He told her: "I'm of the third generation of Bedouins whose fate is tied to the community who came to establish Israel." Kanaaneh then described how this man's grandmother learned Yiddish from the early Ashkenazi colonists of Palestine. The diplomat referred to Bedouin dying during IDF service as making "the ultimate sacrifice." He was proud of "his efforts to be even more loyal to the state than many Jews" (Kanaaneh 2009, 61).

2. Marcelle Edery, leader of the tent movement of the 1990s, responding to landlords hiking up rents in favor of well-funded post-Soviet Jews, left the encampment soon after. She was disgusted by the infighting. She went on to establish a nomadic tent city that hopped from town to town, settling usually in the central public garden. She kept this up until the movement died from loss of public interest.

3. Women in Black is a worldwide women's antiwar movement. Initially started in 1988 by Ashkenazi feminists in Jerusalem, it has grown to boast an estimated membership of 10,000 activists worldwide. Women in Black is one of the founding organizations of the Coalition of Women for Peace (CWP), established in 2000 after the outbreak of the Second Intifada. CWP states that it seeks to end the occupation of Palestine and to create a more just society while enhancing women's inclusion and participation in public discourse. While Women in Black and CWP were "largely invisible to the Israeli public" (Swirsky 2002, 238), they have generated an abundance of English-language academic publications generally inaccessible to most Israelis (see, for example, Cockburn 1998, Emmett 2003, Shadmi 2004b, Sharoni 1995, Stasiulis and Yuval-Davis 1995).

4. Other examples of ethnoreligious states can be found in Northern Ireland (Donnan 2005) Pakistan (Verkaaik 2004), and Cyprus (Cockburn 2004). In 1947, India was partitioned to create West Pakistan and East Pakistan (Bangladesh), the State of Israel was carved out of Palestine, and the Republic of Ireland Act was passed. Partition has been resorted to as a colonial intervention method to regulate or eliminate ethnoreligious national conflicts in the (post) colony. Some argue it has instead increased such conflicts (Cockburn 2004; Donnan 2005; McBride 2001; Verkaaik 2004).

5. While this chapter discusses right-wing, religious nationalism, it does not engage Bruce Kapferer's comparison on Sri Lankan and Australian nationalisms as religious systems (Kapferer 1988). Unlike Israel, Australia separates church and state. Kapferer's Sri Lankan research points to the politicization of violence in Sinhalese Buddhism. But he does not discuss the embodied bureaucratization of political violence. My book focuses on the bureaucratization of violence into a sacred regime.

6. To circumvent public transport laws, private taxi and minivan companies do operate on Shabbat for an extra charge.

7. Jewish immigrants from the former Soviet Union, many of whom still consumed pork and seafood, insisted on having public stores that sold nonkosher foods. Many of these immigrants went to court for it. Municipal rabbis, not wanting to risk setting a legal precedent in the immigrants' favor, settled many

238 | NOTES TO PAGES 82–86

of these disputes outside of the courtroom. Nowadays, chain supermarkets in areas heavily populated by former Soviet immigrants sell nonkosher foods out in the open. One notable nonkosher chain, Tiv Taʿam, decided to become kosher only outside of Tel Aviv. They were losing too much money as they expanded outside the post-Soviet enclaves, to locations where the majority of customers made purchases along kosher regulations. Like food stores, restaurants and cafes also mostly observe kosher dietary laws. Outside Tel Aviv, only a few high-end eateries in the budding gourmet scene of Israel's urban centers serve nonkosher foods.

8. Many male former Soviet immigrants arrived in Israel in the 1990s uncircumcised. They felt obliged to put themselves and their sons through surgical or mohel circumcision. This was one of the few ways they could redeem their benefits package for being a Jewish immigrant to Israel.

9. In fact, as much as the Umma al Islamiya, or the Nation of Islam, is transnational and includes all Muslims in the world, so is "the Jewish Nation." A Jew that can prove a lineage of Jewish mothers five generations back is automatically a member of this nation. Eighty-five percent of this nation's members are Ashkenazim, most of whom live outside of Israel in North America, Western Europe, Australia, and South Africa.

10. Compare, for example, major English-language media outlets covering the ultra-Orthodox "exotics" (*Globe and Mail* 2013; Kershner 2011; Mitnick 2012; Sherwood 2011) with posts on the highly regarded Mizraḥi news portal *HaʿOkets* (Behar 2011; Noy 2012; Shriki 2012). *HaʿOkets* exposes how this skirmish between the ultra-Orthodox minority and the secular Ashkenazi minority serves the Ashkenazi elite by obscuring the Mizraḥi-Ashkenazi rift. It is also interesting to note the proximity in time between the positive international publicity given to the Mizraḥi-Palestinian Coalition Against Apartheid in Israeli Anthropology (CAAIA) in the American Anthropological Association's highly circulated *Anthropology News* (Lavie 2003, 2005; Lavie and Shubeli 2006) and the shift by Israeli university-based anthropologists from studying the "exotic" Mizraḥim and '48 Arab to the "exotic" ultra-Orthodox.

11. See this resource list http://mizrach.org.il/category/socio-sight/ (accessed 2 February 2013) at the MeMizraḥ Shemesh website for up-to-date essays on the population breakdown of Israeli Jews and on the population category of masortim.

12. There is an extensive body of scholarly literature that presents case studies concluding Israel is an apartheid state. See Adam and Moodley 2005; Ben-Yair 2002; Carter 2006; Davis 2003, 86–87; Gazit 2011; and Massad (2006). For the discussion of Israel's Mizraḥi-Ashkenazi "Color Line" (DuBois [1903] 1989) as

a system of intra-Jewish apartheid, see Lavie and Shubeli 2006, Malka 1998, Shenhav and Yonah 2008, Shohat 1988, and Yitzhaki 2003.

13. See, for example, endnote 16 below on Muzika Mizrahit.

14. While there are a multitude of references on minority agency and resistance, I cite here the first few that are prominent in my mind.

15. Kuntsman (2009) analyzes another kind of chauvinistic ethno-religious nationhood—that of the post-Soviet immigrants to Israel.

16. Many Mizrahi scholars and activists have posited *Muzika Mizrahit* (Mizrahi Music, Hebrew) as a form of cultural resistance that catalyzed the politically and economically focused Mizrahi identity politics of the 1990s, or during the Oslo boomtime. These scholars and activists argue that, post-Oslo, Muzika Mizrahit has become the main mode of Mizrahi identity politics as a performative way of enacting resistive agency (Saada-Ophir 2006, 2007). Recent literature in Mizrahi studies tends to present Muzika Mizrahit without attachment to the Question of Palestine. Thorleifsson (2012) aptly demonstrates how the Zionist regime currently employs Muzika Mizrahit and other forms of popular culture to maintain its status quo regarding the perception of Palestine in popular culture.

17. A good example of the regime showcasing such movements can be seen in the way the Israeli Ministry for Hasbara (explanation and outreach, Hebrew) and Jewish Diaspora attachés in Western European and North American embassies portrayed the Israeli mass protest of summer 2011. This protest, led by young Ashkenazi professionals, included almost all sectors of Israeli Jewish society, not only Mizrahi single mothers. See chapter 6 of this book.

18. This book focuses on how regimes preempt PRE-discursive subalternity and deny the subaltern her agency. Thus, it does not fully engage these authors or their classic texts about the actual discourse of subaltern resistance and agency. The subaltern is not a category that can speak. It is a place from which one can speak when one overcomes discursive blockages (see Morris 2011). Subaltern resistance studies, with agency as a main focus, is a highly respected field within intersectionality studies—exploring zones between and among race, ethnicity, gender, colony, and the nation-state (see Gilroy 1987; Hall and Jefferson 1993; Rhodes 2007; San Juan 1992). Similarly astute are ethnographies of resistance, with agency as a main focus, from Latin America, sub-Saharan Africa, and South-Southeast Asia (see Kearney 1996; Scott 1985; Wolf 1969). I chose to cite Mahmood and Abu-Lughod because of their well-deserved canonization beyond the field of Middle East anthropology. Until 9/11, academic circles considered Middle East anthropology a specialized field, requiring literacy in Arabic, Farsi, or other languages spoken in the Muslim

World, and a great command of the Arab World's history. Therefore anthropology of the Arab World was considered arcane (see Rodinson 1988). It is all the more remarkable that the works of Abu-Lughod and Mahmood, both in Egypt, not only overcame all these considerations, but lent themselves to cross-cultural comparisons and became "traveling theory" (Said 1983). Abu-Lughod's and Mahmood's works appeared in leading scientific journals. But it is arguable that other scholars not seated at elite Ivy League institutions of the Western metropolitan and not publishing in English also deserve to be cited in resistance studies (for Israel, in Hebrew, see Gamlieli 1965; Lavie 2006b; Yitzhaki 2003). World Anthropologies caution against unidirectional "traveling theory" from North American–Western European institutions to form the sole analytical basis of the subaltern (Ribeiro and Escobar 2006; see Gledhill 2004, 2005).

19. The cosmology of this chosenness is discussed in Handelman (1990, 194).

20. "GendeRace" is my own neologism combining "gender" and "race." It is much less unwieldy to use than the phrase "a calcified amalgamation of gender and race," especially when I repeat the concept throughout the book. As a theoretician, I have the liberty of coining new shorthand terms. In 1986, Kirin Narayan, Renato Rosaldo, and I submitted a panel to the American Anthropological Association (AAA) meeting titled "'Othering': Representations and Realities," based on the groundbreaking work of Mary Louise Pratt, later published in Pratt 1992. The panel faced difficulties in getting accepted into the program because the neologism *Othering* was not a recognized English word or theoretical concept. The panel was eventually accepted but relegated to a very small room. Nonetheless, it drew a crowd bigger than the room could hold. So we asked everyone to take their chairs and move to the lobby. It is interesting to note the vocal protests by Israeli Anthropological Association members during the three paper presentations about the Palestine-Israel conflict. Since then, *Othering* has become a commonly used term in cultural analysis (see Lavie 1986).

21. Harrison (1997) was among the first to interpret intersectional theory for cross-cultural anthropological analysis outside North America and Western Europe.

22. West Germany and the State of Israel signed an agreement on 10 September 1952 for West Germany to pay compensatory funds for slave labor and persecution to Jews who survived the Nazi Holocaust. The only Israeli political opposition to this agreement came from the Ḥerut Party, precursor of Likud, headed by Menachem Begin. Ḥerut believed that it was unfathomable to quantify the suffering of Holocaust survivors, in German marks, no less. Ḥerut was also concerned about the large income and power gap such an imbalanced influx of funds would create between Ashkenazim and Mizraḥim. On 5 October 1952, Dov Shilansky, a member of Ḥerut and Holocaust survivor, was

arrested for attempting to bomb the Israeli Foreign Ministry in Tel Aviv. He had walked into the basement of the ministry building carrying a suitcase containing twenty-five sticks of TNT. His aim was to halt the reparation agreement process. After a two-year prison sentence, Shilansky went onto a career in law and politics, rising to the position of Knesset chairman between 1988 and 1992. He was a fierce advocate for Mizraḥi equality and is admired by Mizraḥi communities throughout Israel (see also Segev 2003).

23. *Ḥai* is a combination of the letters *ḥeit* and *yod*. *Ḥeit* and *yod* have numerological values of eight and ten, respectively. *Ḥai* in Hebrew also translates to "alive." Many Israeli Jews wear *ḥai* pendants around their necks.

24. In the analysis of bureaucratic webs, this book does not engage with Louis Althusser (1971). While Althusser's "citizen-subject" showcases institutional structure, his model is monochromatic and leaves no room for real people in real time. Sandoval (2000) offers a racialized and gendered rendition to remedy Althusser's monochromatism. Her rendition, however, still focuses on institutional structures themselves. My main concern is exactly what Althusser leaves out—the everyday lives of dark women scrambling through institutional structures for their survival.

25. It is interesting to note Ruth Behar's success with monographs at major scholarly presses. Scholarly presses, unlike academic journals, value a book's sales potential as much as its scholarly contributions. Because Behar is a quality writer, and her name alone can boost sales, the presses are eager to publish her work.

26. See the Zora Neale Hurston bibliography at https://www.cliffsnotes.com/literature/t/their-eyes-were-watching-god/zora-neale-hurston-biography (accessed 9 October 2017).

27. An interesting commentary on the politics of research, writing, and publishing ethnography can be found in Anne Meneley and Donna Young 2005. The contributors to the Meneley and Young collection, however, are working from within the U.S.-UK paradigm of knowledge, with most being tenured at major U.S. universities. Tenure affords these scholars with enough financial stability that they are able to research and write about topics seemingly controversial to the liberal agenda of U.S. academe. Gloria Anzaldúa and Zora Neale Hurston wrote and researched in exactly the opposite situation, without the security of tenure. Thus, the scholars contributing to Meneley and Young's book can afford to taut the "radical" label without fear of negative financial ramifications. It is still telling that a major university press did not publish the collection.

28. Faye Harrison courageously critiques North American and Western European anthropology: "The transformed anthropology I envision . . . would recognize that although the profession's institutional centers have been dominated by

British, American, and French axes of authority, the intellectual life of the discipline has extended well beyond the North's major metropolitan centers to a variety of sites, typically devalued as peripheral zones of theory around the world" (2008, 11; 2012).

29. See also endnote 18, this chapter.

30. Geertz's point of departure for the methodology of "thick description" is Kenneth Burke's (1968) and Susanne Langer's (1956) school of "New Criticism," a major school of U.S. literary criticism between 1930 and 1960. It is interesting to note that in the dark days of the beginning of the Cold War, the "New Literary Critics" dealt with the literary text as an aesthetic object, culturally embedded in symbols, yet decontextualized from the political economy of its production and consumption.

3. Take 1

1. Avi Shoshana (2006) discusses Handelman through the optics of Mizraḥi experience. His analysis, however, overlooks gender and fails to challenge the basic tenets of Zionism. Likewise, I do not include Michael Herzfeld's analysis of Greek bureaucracy (1992). Herzfeld conceptualizes bureaucracy as a language game reproduced and altered through linguistic usage. He favors language over somatic experience. Like Handelman and Feldman, Herzfeld discusses neither bureaucracy as a racialized formation, nor the nation-state as a racialized construct. Unlike them, according to Susana Narotzky (2006, 136), "Herzfeld unforgivingly disavows southern European anthropologists as colleagues who might share polemic anthropological ground" as "epistemological nativists" to be ethnographed in his dispassionate U.S.-UK-style monograph.

2. Either because of a "translation block" (see Lavie 2006b) or because they are stymied in English-language journal review processes, World Anthropologies references on the topic, in English—the language of transnational quotation—are rare. Thus, this chapter offers my own subaltern read of Peter Berger and Thomas Luckman (1967, 30–34, 43, 54–58, 174), Mary Douglas (1970, 50–51), Susanne Langer (1956, 44–45, 72), and Alfred Schutz (1962, 36–39, 67–96, 128, 136, 227, 247–49, 283–85, 347–52; 1966, 117–25). Elaborations of Schutz's theory of social relevance and typification are presented in Richard Grathoff (1970, 19–28) and Don Handelman and Bruce Kapferer (1980).

3. The panopticon was originally invented by British philosopher Jeremy Bentham ([1787] 1995), but this text deals with Michel Foucault's scholarship on the concept (1977). Even though the scholarly community associates Bentham's model with divinity, the panopticon originally was a practical construct of prison design.

4. According to Turner's ritual theory (Turner 1969; Turner and Turner 1978), the *limen* (Latin) is the threshold through which one departs from the everyday to transcend to the liminality of the sacred.

5. I spent academic year 2009–10 at the University of Virginia-Charlottesville. It was an honor to be a colleague of Professor Edie Turner, the driving force behind "Notes on Processual Symbolic Analysis," the most concise glossary and design schematic for the ritual process (Turner and Turner 1978, 143–55). Every other Sunday, we would get together to discuss communitas typologies. She helped me think through "negative catharsis." Edie suggested "negative communitas" for the phenomena I described to her.

6. The initiation to nationalism through pain-inflicting rituals is discussed in Einat Bar-On Cohen (2009) and Adi Kuntsman (2009, 221–22). The work of Arthur and Joan Kleinman (1985, 1994) may seem to be relevant to my analysis of the repulsion zone. It discusses the reductions employed in the representation of violence, including the reduction of the violated to passivity in order for them to receive the help they need. The Kleinmans themselves, however, do not get involved politically, professionally, or economically with the plight of the people they study. I do. Additionally, their work is foregrounded in psychological anthropology. Colvin (2004) focuses on the problematics of Western psychological/psychoanalytical models of trauma superimposed on other cultures to fit the Western healing model. Feldman (2008, 33–37) thoroughly analyzes how bureaucracy produces and categorizes files that legitimize the production of (post-)colonial authority. She juxtaposes these archives with elderly bureaucrats' lives and words (63–120). My book, by contrast, addresses the immediacy of crises that beset bureaucracy's clients.

7. Claudia Bernardi, a survivor of Argentina's Dirty Wars, started an art school called Walls of Hope in Perkin, El Salvador. Trauma survivors—mainly Native Americans—go there to paint the events of their traumas. Bernardi believes that the idea of healing from trauma, such as in the model presented by Scarry, is a U.S.-Eurocentric model imposed on survivors elsewhere. She compares trauma to an amputation and thinks that one has to learn to live with an absence that never heals (Claudia Bernardi, pers. comm.; see Colvin 2004).

8. SHABAK is an acronym for Sherut Bitahon Klali, or General Security Service, Hebrew. This is Israel's internal security service and secret police, known for its physical and emotional methods of interrogation.

9. I resort to essentialism to discuss the cultural construction of the primordial Mizraḥi woman's body. Stuart McLean, through the language of deconstruction, evokes similar essentialism, arguing that the body is "the recalcitrant matter that both enables and perennially thwarts cultural and historical

understanding" (2004, 161). Even though Lévi-Strauss explicitly distanced his structuralism from the experiential philosophy of Husserl (Lévi-Strauss 1961), the noesis-noema relation at the crux of essence is that of a Claude Lévi-Straussian binary opposition (Lavie 1983).

10. *Nisu'ei nadlan* (real estate marriages, Hebrew) is slang describing a marriage between a Mizraḥi whose family does not possess intergenerational wealth, and an Ashkenazi whose family does have intergenerational wealth. The source of this wealth may be from Holocaust reparation payments, real estate obtained cheaply during the Yishuv, or from business dealings. It is usually this money from the Ashkenazi side of the marriage that facilitates the purchase of the young couple's first home in the better neighborhoods of Israel's center.

11. While Mizraḥi single mothers do not have access to healing creative arts, Palestinians do benefit from NGOs that help them in creative pursuits.

4. Take 2

1. For a more in-depth discussion of the Yishuv, see chapter 1 of this book.
2. Rather than overburdening the reader with ample references discussing the neocon reforms of the welfare system in the United Kingdom and the United States, I have relied on the excellent surveys and analysis by Amir Paz-Fuchs (2004, 2008).
3. A discussion of the United States forcing welfare mothers to undergo sterilization and use carcinogenic birth control can be found in Beale (1970) and Cade (1970).
4. This point is eloquently supported by Kanaaneh (2002).
5. See the introduction of this book for more information on AḤUSALIM.
6. See Paz-Fuchs (2004, 357 n11).
7. Unlike the U.S. academic ranking of professorial typology (assistant, associate, and full), all tied to academic employment, in Israel the appellation "professor" connotes a rank one level above a senior lecturer. Once attained, the professor may use the title, even without a university affiliation.

5. Take 3

1. I have given the claim clerk a pseudonym that is an onomatopoeia of her real name.
2. Kate Millett is the author of the classic *Sexual Politics* (1970). She is one of the main thinkers in separatist feminism, a form of radical feminism that espouses complete separation of women away from men in order to combat the dynamics of patriarchy inherent in any male-inclusive society.
3. Toni Cade was an African American novelist, poet, and scholar who stood against radical feminist separatism. Her groundbreaking anthology, *The Black Woman*, was one of the first works that formed the base of the Feminist Theory of Color.

4. Emails were edited as part of updating the manuscript.

5. *Diwan* here refers to the collection of poems written in Judeo-Arabic during the seventeenth century by Yemeni rabbi Shalom Shabazi. When recited individually, outside of communal rituals, they are supposed to calm down the soul, mantra-style—at least for my granny and her circle of friends.

6. For a more details on the Supreme Court's 1997 appeal verdict 4445/96 (Bar-Noy verdict), see the introduction of this book.

7. See Esther Hertzog 2004a, 2009.

8. The Kabala (acceptance by transmission, Hebrew) is a school of thought focused around Judaism as mysticism. The Kabala discerns between several types of angels, each grouped into its own choir. The ones who seem to be the most wrathful, *mal'akhei 'evra va-za'am* (Hebrew), rank closest to the worldly power of rulers.

9. *Schwartze* means "black" in Yiddish. In the context of Mizrahi-Ashkenazi relations, it is shorthand for the colloquial Yiddish expression *schwartze hayye* (black animal, Yiddish). To "have a schwartze" or to have a *teimonichka* (a little Yemeni woman, Yiddish) means to have a housemaid. Aside from Ethiopians, Yemenis are the darkest of the Mizrahim. *Schwartze* is also a term that bigoted American Jews call African Americans.

10. The nonacademic Israeli public, mainly Mizrahim, term Israeli university professors the "Ashkenazi Academic Junta," or "the Academic Junta." This term indicates the public's estrangement from the impenetrable networks of Israel's Ashkenazi academic elite (Blachman 2005; Zarini 2004).

11. See Bruno Latour 2004.

12. Ruth Frankenberg (1993) discusses the obliviousness to race among first-wave white feminists. During second-wave feminism, many white feminists organized support groups to discuss how to unlearn their white privilege.

13. The full expression referred to here is "uppity piss puddle." It is used by globetrotting Anglo-Jewish immigrants as a sardonic, yet affectionate, nickname for Israel.

14. The Israeli courts are an autonomous entity that appoints its judges with little or no resistance from the legislative or executive arms of the regime. This de facto autonomy places them beyond the democratic principle of governmental oversight.

15. Original article was printed in Hebrew (Shapira 2003).

16. For more on National Legal Aid, see chapter 3 of this volume, page 122.

17. The law recommends that the Collection Court Police not take appliances and furniture that are the bare necessities of life. But, in many cases, there is nothing else to take.

18. Anthropologist and feminist activist Esther Hertzog has dedicated her life to exposing the atrocities committed by Israel's welfare bureaucracy against

mothers and children. She has published many op-ed public anthropology columns in Israel's high-circulation dailies (Hertzog 2004b). Some can be found at http://www.alia.co.il/herzogsefer/ (accessed 14 February 2013). In her role as convener of Israel's Women's Parliament, she organized several sessions about the misappropriation of public funds used to further hurt Israel's disenfranchised (see Hertzog 2009).

19. Several examples of surname discrimination; see Moshe Ronen and Amos Nevo 2000.

20. These diversity appointments work unlike in Western Europe or North America, where men of color, particularly Latinos, blacks, and natives, are conceived as a threat, and thus the preferable diversity candidate is a woman of color. Mizraḥi men serve with Ashkenazi men in the IDF and therefore are less threatening to them than Mizraḥi women, whose public image hovers between temptress and housewife-cum-baby factory.

21. The Mizraḥim living in in the other desert development towns usually don't qualify for these tax breaks because they don't make enough money.

22. Ha'amuta le-nifga'ei mashkanta'ot ve-ḥasrei diyur is Hebrew for "People Homeless and Hurt by Mortgages." Ha-koalitzya shel mishpa'ḥot ḥad horiyot meḥusarot diyur is Hebrew for "The Coalition of Homeless Single-Headed Families."

23. This was mainly done when my son was sick and could not attend a day care center.

24. It is interesting to note that among the women who constitute Israel's professors, judges, and other positions requiring postgraduate education, almost none of them have asymmetrical features, are overweight, or are visibly disabled. Some of my Israeli male colleagues jokingly refer to some female colleagues as "centerfold girls." When these women advance, the gossip often says that "they popped Vitamin Z." The Hebrew expression pronounces the "zee" as in English, short for zayin, the seventh letter of the Hebrew alphabet. In everyday Hebrew, it also means "weapon" or "penis."

25. The URL is for the article written by Laura King (2003).

26. On each of my visits to the sotzialit in charge of single mothers in my South Tel Aviv 'hood, she gave me coupons redeemable at kosher supermarket chains. She also gave me a referral to be able to stand in the lines of the Pit'ḥon Lev NGO to collect expired food donations from those same supermarkets. She suggested that, like most single mothers and their children, Shaheen and I should go to the affluent branches of these supermarket chains in North Tel Aviv, where affluent Ashkenazim shopped. Because we could get free food through Pit'ḥon Lev, eating it at our peril, we could exchange the food coupons for much-needed cash. So on early Thursday evenings, either Shaheen or I would stand next to a cashier when people were doing their weekly shopping

before Shabbat. We would ask shoppers if they intended to pay with cash or credit card. If a shopper was paying with cash, we would say that we were from poverty-stricken South Tel Aviv, and that we needed to exchange our coupons for cash, as per our sotzialit's instructions. This process was humiliating. The most embarrassing occasions occurred when affluent parents of Shaheen's classmates would identify me or Shaheen. Most of this cash obtained in this way was used to pay for expenses like transportation and school supplies, as well as monthly utilities. I treated this infrequent foray to the American Colony Hotel Bar as a necessary professional expense for my scholarly future.

27. The Jerusalem corridor sits on the pre-1967 border with Jordan. Before 1948, the corridor was made up of Palestinian villages and fields. After the Nakba expulsions, the regime ordered newly arrived Mizrahi immigrants to take over the Palestinian homes and fields. Until 1967, the corridor was a remote, dangerous, and therefore economically depressed, place. Palestinians who wished to visit their old homes would sneak across the border. Some were armed commandos.

28. In the context of Israel, the Jewish state, the real oppression is by the goyim against the Jews.

29. *Ya ḥaram* comes from Arabic, but is also Mizrahi slang. Literally, it means "it is legally forbidden by Islamic law." It is used to mean "What a pity!" or "Hands off!"

30. In Israel, the national health care plan does not cover the private market of dentistry. Therefore, dental work is expensive.

31. *Apostrophe* was a French TV show based in France that aired on the station Antenne 2 between 1975 and 1990. The intellectual interview/debate format of the show became popular on Israeli TV, but only for very late-night shows.

6. The Price of National Security

1. The miracle of Hanukkah involved the inexplicable refilling of a single container of ritual oil used to light the Temple of Jerusalem. Invading Greeks around the second century BCE desecrated the temple. When the Temple was liberated by the Maccabees, they found that all but one container of ritual oil had been defiled. Though the container should have lasted only a single day, the Maccabees were able to use it to light the temple for eight days straight, enough time to press a new supply of oil. Thus, the overt allusion in Operation "Cast Lead" to the Hanukkah miracle, and the struggle of a small group against a marauding force, was not lost on Israeli Jews.

2. Bialik was notorious for his racism for anything non-European. In a press conference at the Hebrew University on 11 May 1933, just as the Nazis gained power in Germany, he said, "Like Hitler, I believe in the power of the idea

of the purity of blood" (quote taken from HaZatetet Blog at http://hazatetet
.wordpress.com/). For the full text of Bialik's speech, see http://benyehuda.org
/bialik/dvarim_shebeal_peh38.html (accessed 14 February 2012). When Bialik's Hanukkah miracle poem became popular, it was shortened. In the shortened version, the father, and not the teacher, gives the child a cast lead dreidel.
For more information on the history of Bialik's dreidel poem, see http://www
.zemereshet.co.il/song.asp?id=3 (accessed 14 February 2012).

3. See Lavie and Abargel 2008, United Nations Human Rights Council 2009.

4. While 'Efroni mentioned the individual's full name, this author fears potential
   retribution for publishing it.

5. As of this writing, the protests stemming from summer 2011 have not completely died down, and events continue to unfold. In-depth analysis of it
   would be premature.

6. For more references to the biblical pillar of cloud, see Exodus 13:21–22, 14:19,
   40:38; Numbers 14:14; and Nehemiah 9:19 in the King James Bible.

Afterword(s)

1. Please note that *Mizrahi* is conventionally spelled—online and in the media—
   without the dot under the *h* that renders it the Hebrew letter *ḥeit*. In accordance with IJMES transliteration standards, for the Hebrew *ḥeit* I have used
   the dot under the *h*. This applies to several terms in this text: *Aḥoti*, *ḤADASH*,
   HaLo Neḥmadim, *Ḥamas*, *Ḥok HaHesderim*, and *Ḥezbollah*. In transliterating the
   Hebrew *ḥeit*, Yiddish transliteration conventions are sometimes followed in
   published texts so that the *ḥ* appears as *ch*—as in *Mizrachi* or *Achoti*.

2. See p. 101 of this book.

3. The +972 author Idan Landau (2014b) translates *eitan* as "solid," but I think the
   proper translation is "mighty."

4. Most of the research for the original report (Aḥoti 2011) was done by Shira
   Oḥayon, the pedagogical director of the Andalusian Philharmonic, who is a
   longtime co-founder of Mizraḥi feminism. Oḥayon brought the orchestra
   to the mainstream media and often appears on prime-time TV to speak on
   Mizraḥi culture.

5. Many of the NGOs that make up Heart at East use the term *Arab Jew* instead of
   Mizrahi in English. *Arab Jew* is familiar to the diasporic populations on whom
   the NGOs depend for funding. It is constituted of two familiar words in the
   English language. Most Israeli Mizraḥim vehemently reject the term (see p. 2
   in this book). Before the 2013 prize ceremony, Oḥayon told me: "I insisted that
   you get it, even though there were so many opposed to giving it to you because
   you're anti-Zionist. But you are one of the few Arab Jews among us, and not

because Arab Jews are the latest fad. You spent almost four decades studying the Sinai Bedouin. It's way beyond research, it's family."

Dr. Erella Shadmi presented me with the award. Since the mid-1990s, she has called on Ashkenazi peace feminists to inspect their white privilege (Shadmi 2004b).

6. The image featuring Carmen Elmakiyes is no longer available. The woman in the image is another member of HaLo Neḥmadim.

7. According to my sources, the government "took a haircut" of about 2.5 billion NIS from the IMI debt. This datum can be corroborated by media reports (Azulay 2014; Ḥasson 2014; Channel 2 News 2014).

8. The village's full name was Jamusin al-Gharbi, meaning "the west side where the water buffalo live." Near marshlands, it belonged to a belt of Palestinian villages surrounding Jewish Tel Aviv and Palestinian Jaffa. After the Nakba, the Zionist regime renamed many Palestinian villages to reflect Socialist Zionist imagery— therefore Givʿat ʿAmal Beit, or "Labor Hill B." There was also "Labor Hill A." Until recently, Israeli Hebrew speakers often referred to pre-1948 Palestinian place names in everyday speech, so they used Jamusin. To create a broad coalition, HaLo Neḥmadim strategically began using the Hebrew name, Labor Hill, omitting the B. This was probably done to avoid the Arabic name. Arabic has gradually been erased from public spaces in Israel (see Suleiman 2004). Throughout this Afterword(s), I use "Labor Hill" when referring to the neighborhood.

9. *Pinuy-Binuy* is the status for dilapidated one- or two-story residential homes slotted for demolition to make room for multistory residential complexes in the name of space efficiency. The Ministry of Housing can declare a Pinuy-Binuy zone using an order that lasts six years and is renewable. Although Pinuy-Binuy became official Housing Ministry policy in 1998, it has been an integral part of gentrification and urban development in major Israeli cities since the 1950s. The process began in the 1950s and would later borrow from similar American initiatives in the 1970s.

10. The ISM is a Palestinian-led civilian social movement founded in 2001 that is committed to nonviolent protest to support Palestinians in the Israel-Palestine conflict.

11. Such a coalition between right-wing Mizraḥim, Jewish members of Israel's Communist Party, anti-Zionist anarchists, and ISM members happened for the first time in 2007 during the expulsions-demolitions in Salameh-Kfar Shalem. See Lavie 2007a.

12. Since the 1980s, there has been a system of tunnels connecting the Gaza Strip to Rafaḥ (Egypt), the main town at the west end of the Gaza Strip, with its eastern part controlled by Ḥamas, and its western part returned to Egyptian sovereignty since 1982. The tunnels were dug to smuggle goods that cannot be brought into

Gaza from the Israeli port of Ashdod because of the Israeli blockade. They are also used to smuggle people and weapons between Egypt and Gaza.

13. The emir of Qatar has been hospitable to Ḥamas leaders exiled by Israel from Gaza and the West Bank.

14. The author of the guidebook is Moḥammed Ḥassan Aḥmed ʿArman from Kharbata in the West Bank. He is one of the leaders of the ʿIzz al-Din al-Qassam Brigades. He was arrested in 2002, tortured, and received thirty-six life sentences. In 2014, he was elected to the committee that represents Ḥamas prisoners. See *Middle East Monitor* 2014 and Issacharoff 2010.

15. Shaʿer's Arabic last name revealed his Mizraḥi origins. About halfway through Operation Brother's Keeper, the media Hebraized Shaʿer's last name (meaning "poet," Arabic) to Shaʿar (gate, Hebrew).

16. For an explanation of GendeRace, see pp. 90–93 of this book.

17. Misgav's brilliant dissertation examines the spatial and urban contexts of activism, gender, and sexuality in Tel Aviv. Social and political change can take different forms and address different publics with different identities, Misgav demonstrates, and is not necessarily a conventional expression of resistance and protest, even if it appears in this form.

18. The IDF killed the abductors of the three boys in a shootout that took place in the basement of a Hebron carpentry workshop on 23 September 2015. IDF chief of staff Lieutenant General Benny Gantz declared the end of Operation Brother's Keeper that same day (Ben Yishai and Levi 2014).

19. The decision to remove Ḥamas from the list of terrorist organizations had two major implications. First, it recognized the political sovereignty of Ḥamas over the PA, and second, it recognized Ḥamas as the PA's official defense. EU foreign ministers appealed the decision in 2015 (AFP 2015).

20. Amir Oren, an acclaimed military analyst with access to reputable sources inside Israel's security forces, examined how Netanyahu was pressured to escalate Gaza 2014 into a ground campaign (Oren 2016). Oren discovered that the escalation was initiated by Naftali Bennett, leader of the extreme right-wing modern Orthodox party, "the Jewish Home" (HaBayit HaYehudi, Hebrew), and Avigdor Lieberman, leader of the right-wing secular party "Israel Is Our Home" (Israel Beiteinu, Hebrew). Both Bennett and Netanyahu are veterans of the same elite commando unit that conducted Operation Entebbe in 1976. Lieberman's military service was lackluster, however. The Hebrew media emphasized that it was Bennett and Lieberman who issued orders to the IDF top brass. They often provided Netanyahu with details of IDF maneuvers only after the fact. Bibi ostensibly continued to cooperate with Bennett and Lieberman to maintain his coalition.

Oren went on to explain that when IDF infantry fought inside Hamas tunnels, both sides suffered high casualties. The IDF destroyed tunnels with Israeli soldiers still inside, even resorting to the Hannibal Directive—a protocol that allows IDF infantry to be sacrificed to prevent prisoner exchanges. Most infantry were Mizrahim (see Levy 2013). Bennett's party is almost solely Ashkenazi. Oren described how Israel's Emergency Cabinet discovered Bibi's short-circuiting of Bennett and Lieberman's plans to bring all of the Gaza Strip under Israeli occupation. On 5 August 2014, Justice Minister Tzipi Livni left a top-secret Emergency Cabinet meeting for just a few minutes. When she stepped away from the meeting, she discovered that Channel 2 was airing a story on a top-secret military presentation for conquering all of the Gaza Strip. This highly classified presentation had just taken place at the last meeting of the Emergency Cabinet ministers. Right after the meeting, Bibi leaked the plan to the press. The broadcast triggered a public outcry over forecasted casualty rates. This outcry was exactly what Bibi had intended. According to Oren's sources, Hamas leaders also benefited from the leak. They too were worried about the possible occupation of the entire Gaza Strip and civilian bloodshed that a total takeover by the IDF would bring. The broadcast signaled an end to the carnage. As of 26 January 2016, Oren notes that Bibi has not been charged for what can only be legally interpreted as high treason.

21. These excerpts come from Session 157 of the Nineteenth Knesset. The translations are the author's.

22. The War of Attrition (Milhemet HaHatasha, Hebrew; Harb al-Istinzaf, Arabic) between Israel and Egypt occurred between 8 March 1969 and 7 August 1970. Egyptian strategy focused on bombarding Israeli bunkers and conducting attacks along the Suez Canal (occupied by Israel from Egypt since the 1967 War). Also, the PLO bombarded Israeli settlements in the northern part of the Jordan Valley, south of the Sea of Galilee, from inside the Hashemite Kingdom of Jordan. Bombardments stopped after Black September 1970, when King Hussein banished the PLO from his kingdom.

23. The Council for the Oversight of Plays and Cinema is the same government body that had banned the Beatles from performing in Israel. The council determined that the Beatles would be a negative influence on the pioneer spirit of Israeli youth.

24. Arabic names are transliterated from the Knesset Hebrew minutes. It is possible that the transcriber erred in recording the correct names. I have matched them with Arabic last names I know. I apologize if these names are impossible to trace.

25. On the history of Zionism and Mizrahi labor from 1882 onward, see chapter 1 in this book.

26. The text of the 27 July 2014 ratification to the irregular amendment to Ḥok HaHesderim does not spell out the issues appearing in the Knesset transcript of 14 July 2014. Rather than reflecting the contents of the Knesset sessions, this one-page document contains procedural legalese. See Knesset of the State of Israel 2014a and b.

27. There were no books for the launch event, however. The first print sold out halfway through the Ireland tour.

28. See pp. 161–68 in this book.

29. The fall 2014 Knesset dissolution stemmed from two other points of contention that took a backseat to the budget: disagreement over negotiations with the Palestinians and the drafting of ultra-Orthodox men into the military.

30. Unlike the readily available numbers for Israel's dead and wounded, there are no easily obtainable figures for Palestinian casualties. The UN Office for the Coordination of Human Affairs, Occupied Palestinian Territory (UNOCHA) provides an estimate as of December 2015.

31. See endnote 4 above.

32. Caḥlili's new elites constitute ʿarsim and freḥot. In Arabic, ʿars (singular, ʿarsim plural) means "pimp." Until the recent Mizraḥi renaissance, ʿars was a derogatory term for the stereotypical Mizraḥi male aesthetic. This parallels with black America's "pimp" culture and rap or cholo aesthetics. In Hebrew slang, freḥa (singular, freḥot plural) is a woman who looks ditzy, uneducated, delinquent, and vulgar. The Arabic translation of freḥa is "happy one" or "gay one," the equivalent of the English Joy or Joyce. But in the 1950s, it became Hebrew slang for women who emigrated from the Arabic-speaking world, mostly Morocco and Iraq. It has become a derogatory term, one of the Ashkenazi stereotypes for a Mizraḥi woman. The poetic renaissance brought about the reappropriation of these terms, the same way dyke, fag, and queer have been used by the LGBTQ community.

33. "Ars Poetica," or "The Art of Poetry," by Horace c. 19 BCE, advises poets on the art of writing poetry and drama. In Hebrew, ars poetica exists as a literary term. The Mizraḥi cultural guerrilla group ʿArs Poetica borrows its name from "Ars Poetica." They pronounce the ars with an ʿayin, however. Rather than ars (Latin), this ʿars means "pimp" in Arabic. They explicitly targeted an audience of ʿarsim (plural of ʿars) and freḥot (plural of freḥa). See endnote 32. The group began with poetry slams held about once a month that grew to fill industrial hangers in ghettos and barrios. Its key members include Israel Dadon (2013), Tehila Ḥakimi (2014), Roy Ḥasan (2014), Shlomi Ḥatuka (2015), and ʿAdi Keissar (2014).

34. Amor was a captain of a combat unit. In the aftermath of the Sabra and Shatila massacres in Lebanon in 1982, he was one of the few Mizraḥim who publicly refused to fulfill his IDF reserve duty.

35. See the discussion in this book on Israel's Propaganda Ministry and universities abroad, p. 146.

36. Feldman, pers. comm., 12 May 2016.

37. It is interesting to note that +972 translated Orly Noy's essays on Palestine into English, but not her work on Mizraḥim. Noy has suffered hateful online attacks for both her Hebrew and English essays.

38. The 2013 Gezi Park Protests began after city officials in Istanbul introduced an urban development plan for Istanbul's Taksim Gezi Park. The protests spread across Turkey and grew into a movement against neoliberal restructuring. An estimated 3.5 million of Turkey's 80 million citizens took part in an estimated 5,000 demonstrations across Turkey that were connected to the original protest.

39. See p. 62 of this book.

40. Israeli and international media sought to compare the spring 2015 upheavals in Baltimore to Ethiopian demonstrations against police brutality in Tel Aviv and Jerusalem. Like Mizraḥim, more than 90 percent of Israeli Ethiopians vote for ultranationalist right-wing parties. Like Mizraḥim, Ethiopians are overrepresented in the IDF infantry and suffer high casualty rates. During the protests, Ethiopians accused the regime of ignoring their contributions to Israel's security (see, for example, Activestills 2015).

41. See p. 164 of this book.

REFERENCES

Abargel, Reuven, and Smadar Lavie. 2006. "Another Act in the Mizrahi-Palestinian Tragedy." *Electronic Intifada*, 24 July. http://electronicintifada.net/content /another-act-mizrahi-palestinian-tragedy/6182. Accessed 14 February 2013.
————. 2009. "A Year into the Lebanon 2 War: NGO-ing Mizrahi-Arab Paradoxes, and a One State Vision for Palestine/Israel." *Left Curve* 33:29–36.
Abu-Lughod, Lila. 1990. "The Romance of Resistance: Tracing Transformation of Power through Bedouin Women." *American Ethnologist* 17 (1): 41–55.
Activestills. 2015. "Ethiopian-Israeli Protest against Police Brutality Is Met with Violence." *+972*, 1 May. http://972mag.com/mass-ethiopian-israeli-demo-turns -violent/106161/. Accessed 11 May 2016.
Adam, Heribert, and Kogila Moodley. 2005. *Seeking Mandela: Peacemaking between Israelis and Palestinians*. Philadelphia: Temple University Press.
Adiv, Assaf. 2005. "Wisconsin in Israel: Punishing the Poor." *Challenge: A Magazine Covering the Israeli-Palestinian Conflict* 93 (September/October). http://www .challenge-mag.com/en/article__88. Accessed 14 February 2013.
Agence France-Presse (AFP). 2014. "Qatar to Pay Former Hamas Civil Servant Salaries." *al-Ahram Online*, 13 June. http://english.ahram.org.eg/NewsContent/3/12 /103598/Business/Economy/Qatar-to-pay-former-Hamas-civil-servant-salaries .aspx. Accessed 3 May 2016.
————. 2015. "EU Keeps Hamas on 'Terror' List Despite Court Ruling." *al-Bawaba*, 27 March. http://www.albawaba.com/news/eu-keeps-hamas-%E2%80 %98terror%E2%80%99-list-despite-court-ruling-674672. Accessed 5 May 2016.
Agrama, Hussein Ali. 2010. "Secularism, Sovereignty, Indeterminacy: Is Egypt a Secular or a Religious State?" *Comparative Studies in Society and History* 52 (3): 495–523.
————. 2012. *Questioning Secularism: Islam, Sovereignty, and the Rule of Law in Modern Egypt*. Chicago: University of Chicago Press.
Aḥoti. 2011. *Bureaucracy of Inequality: Discrimination in the Allocation of Cultural Resources in Israel. Case Study of Mizrahi Culture in 2009 Presented to Israel Culture Ministry*. [In Hebrew.] 3 May. http://www.achoti.org.il/?p=509. Accessed 5 May 2016.
————. 2012. *Cultural Resources in Israel, 2008–11: A Call for Allocating Resources on the Basis of Equality, Pluralism, and Distributive Justice. 2012 Report Presented to the Cultural Ministry by Heart at East, the Coalition for Equal Distribution of Cul-*

tural Resources in Israel. [In Hebrew.] 7 June. http://www.achoti.org.il/?p=1188. Accessed 5 May 2016.

Akram, Fares, and Jodi Rudoren. 2014. "Issue of Pay for 2 Sets of Workers Tugs at Palestinian Pact." *New York Times,* 26 June. http://www.nytimes.com/2014/06 /27/world/middleeast/hamas-fatah-palestinian-salary.html?_r=0.

Al-Akhbar. 2014. "Israel Threatens UN over Qatari Funds to Gaza." 22 June. http:// english.al-akhbar.com/node/20274. Accessed 3 May 2016.

Alarcón, Norma. 1990. "The Theoretical Subjects of This Bridge Called My Back and Anglo-American Feminism." In *Making Face, Making Soul (Haciendo Caras),* edited by Gloria Anzaldúa, 356–69. San Francisco: Aunt Lute Books.

Al-Haj, Majid, and Uri Ben-Eliezer. 2006. *In the Name of Security: The Sociology of Peace and War in Israel in Changing Times.* [In Hebrew.] Haifa: Pardes and Haifa University Press.

Al Jazeera. 2014. "Egypt Court Bans Palestinian Hamas Group." 5 March. http:// www.aljazeera.com/news/middleeast/2014/03/egypt-court-bans-palestinian -hamas-group-201434835810990.html.

Almagor, Dan. 1972. "One People One Heart." [In Hebrew.] *YouTube* video, 3:40. Posted 25 March 2013. http://v.mzemer.com/%D7%90%D7%99%d7%9c%d7 %9f-%d7%95%d7%90%d7%99%d7%9c%d7%a0%d7%99%d7%aa-%d7%a2%d7 %9d-%d7%90%d7%97%d7%93-%d7%9c%d7%91-%d7%90%d7%97%d7%93-1972 -video_b674bb126.html.

Althusser, Louis. 1971. "Ideology and the Ideological Apparatuses." In *Lenin and Philosophy and Other Essays,* 127–86. New York: Monthly Review Press.

Amor, Meir. 2002. "Israeli Citizenship: From Multi-Culturalism to Inter-Culturalism." [In Hebrew.] In *Mizraḥim in Israel: A Critical Observation into Israel's Ethnicity,* edited by H. Hever, Y. Shenhav and P. Motzafi-Haller, 244–71. Jerusalem and Tel Aviv: Van Leer Jerusalem Institute and HaKibbutz HaMeu'had.

———. 2016. "There Is No Room to Repair Society or the Left without a Mizrahi Revolution." [In Hebrew.] *Siḥa Mekomit* (Local Conversation). 12 April. http:// mekomit.co.il/%D7%aa%D7%a9%D7%95%D7%91%D7%94-%D7%9c%D7%92 %D7%a8%D7%9c%D7%99%D7%a5/. Accessed 17 May 2016.

Anzaldúa, Gloria. 1987. *Borderlands/La Frontera: The New Mestiza.* San Francisco: Aunt Lute Books.

Apter, Emily. 2006. *The Translation Zone.* Princeton NJ: Princeton University Press.

Association for Civil Rights in Israel (ACRI). 2011. "Final Vote Today on Nakba Law and Acceptance to Communities Bill." http://www.acri.org.il/en/2011/03/22 /final-vote-on-nakba-law-and-acceptance-to-communities-bill/. Accessed 14 February 2013.

Atzmon, Gilad. 2011. *The Wandering Who?: A Study of Jewish Identity Politics*. Hampshire UK: Zero Books.

Avidov, Racheli. 2004. "'Postmodern' Feminism in Israel: Mizrahi Feminism." [In Hebrew.] Master's thesis, Haifa University.

Aviv, Yoni. 2007. "The Pure against the Polluted: Menachem Begin's Holocaust Consciousness and Its Impact on His Political Path." [In Hebrew.] *Once Upon a Time: A Stage for Young Historians* 6:63–96.

Azulay, Moran. 2011. "Netanyahu Instructed the Head of SHABAK to Shut up in the Knesset." [In Hebrew.] *Y-Net*, 8 September. http://www.ynet.co.il/articles/0,7340,l-4119695,00.html. Accessed 14 February 2013.

———. 2012. "Herzog Wins Labor Primaries; Merav Michaeli 5th on Party List." [In Hebrew.] *Y-Net*, 30 November. http://www.ynetnews.com/articles/0,7340,l-4313786,00.html. Accessed 14 February 2013.

Azulay, Yuval. 2014. "Tomorrow, Knesset's Finance Committee Expected to Confirm Privatization of IMI." [In Hebrew.] *Globes*, 23 April. http://www.globes.co.il/news/article.aspx?did=1000933034. Accessed 3 May 2016.

Bacchetta, Paola, and Margaret Power. 2002. *Right-Wing Women: From Conservatives to Extremists around the World*. New York: Routledge.

Bakhtin, Mikhail. 1981. "Discourse in the Novel." In *The Dialogic Imagination*, edited by Michael Holquist, 259–442. Austin: University of Texas Press.

Barʿam, Nir. 2003. "Exposing the Face of the 'Left.'" [In Hebrew.] *Maʿariv*, 27 June. Op-Ed.

Bareket, Eli. 2002. "Why Do They Marry Ashkenazi Women?" [In Hebrew.] In *ʿAzut Mezah: Mizrahi Feminism*, 58–60. Jerusalem: ZAH, Students for Social Justice.

Barneʿa, Nahum, and Shimʿon Shiffer. 1999. "The State of Israel Is Not a Kindergarten, and I Am Not a Kindergartener." [In Hebrew.] *Yediʿot Aharonot*. 26 November, Saturday Supplement, 2–3.

Bar-On Cohen, Einat. 2009. "Kibadachi—Pain and Crossing Boundaries within the Lived-in-Body and within Sociality." *Journal of the Royal Anthropological Institute (Incorporating Man)* 15 (3): 610–29.

Bar Shalom, Yehuda, Ruba Daas, and Zvi Bekerman. 2008. "Where Have All the Palestinians Gone?" *International Journal of Critical Pedagogy* 1 (2): 172–85.

Barth, Fredrik. 1969. *Ethnic Groups and Boundaries: The Social Organization of Culture Difference*. Oslo, Norway: Universitetsforlaget.

Bartsidis, Michalis. 2011. "The Waves of the Arab Revolution: Exodus from Internal Exclusion toward Cosmopolitics." Paper presented for the conference "*Karama* and Tradition in the Middle East and North Africa: Negotiating Subjectivity and Civic Virtue Through Social Revolts," University of Macedonia, 9 December.

Bar Zohar, Ofir. 2011. "Like Iran and Afghanistan—The Mark of Israel on the International Index on Freedom of Religion—Zero." [In Hebrew.] *Haaretz*, 13 December. http://www.haaretz.co.il/news/education/1.1590530.

Bateson, Gregory. 1936. *Naven: A Survey of the Problems Suggested by a Composite Picture of the Culture of a New Guinea Tribe Drawn from Three Points of View.* Stanford CA: Stanford University Press.

Beale, Francis. 1970. "Double Jeopardy: To Be Black and Female." In *The Black Woman: An Anthology*, edited by Toni Cade, 95–98. New York: New American Library.

Bear, Laura. 2015. *Navigating Austerity: Currents of Debt along a South Asian River.* Stanford CA: Stanford University Press.

Behar, Almog. 2011. "Before We Bring Out Rosa Parks." [In Hebrew.] *Ha'Okets*, 19 December. http://www.haokets.org/2011/12/19/%D7%9C%D7%A4%D7%A0%D7 %99-%D7%A9%D7%A9%D7%95%D7%9C%D7%A4%D7%99%D7%9D-%D7&90 %D7%AA-%D7%A8%D7%95%D7%96%D7%94-%D7%A4%D7%90%D7%A8%D7 %A7%D7%A1/. Accessed 14 February 2013.

Behar, Ruth. 1993. *Translated Woman: Crossing the Border with Esperanza's Story.* Boston: Beacon Press.

Belhassan, David, and Asher Hemias. 2004. *The Ringworm Children.* DVD. Directed by David Belhassen and Asher Hemias. Israel: Casque D'or Films.

Bentham, Jeremy. [1787] 1995. *The Panopticon Writings.* Edited, and with introduction by Miran Božovič. London: Verso Books.

Ben-Yair, Michael. 2002. "The War's Seventh Day." [In Hebrew.] *Haaretz.* 3 March. http://www.haaretz.com/print-edition/opinion/the-war-s-seventh-day-1.51513.

Ben Yefet, Ya'el, and Aharon Maduel. 2011. "Housing for the Elderly Across the Board." [In Hebrew.] *Ha'Okets*, 30 March. http://www.haokets.org/2011/03/30 /%D7%93%D7%99%D7%95%D7%A8-%D7%9C%D7%A7%D7%A9%D7%99%D7 %A9%D7%99%D7%9D-%D7%9E%D7%9B%D7%9C-%D7%94%D7%A1%D7%95 %D7%92%D7%99%D7%9D/. Accessed 14 February 2013.

Ben Yishai, Ron, and Elior Levi. 2014. "End of Story: Israel Kills the Boys' Murderers." [In Hebrew.] *Y-Net*, 23 September. http://www.ynet.co.il/articles/0,7340,L -4574136,00.html. Accessed 3 May 2016.

Berger, Joseph. 1996. "Israeli Executives Urge Moderation on Netanyahu." *New York Times*, 8 June, A3.

Berger, Peter L., and Thomas Luckman. 1967. *The Social Construction of Reality (A Treatise in the Sociology of Knowledge).* Garden City NY: Anchor Books.

Bergman, Ronen, and David Ratner. 1997. "The Man Who Swallowed Gaza." *Haaretz*, 4 April, Weekend Supplement. http://www.mfa.gov.il/MFA/Archive /Articles/1997/THE%20MAN%20WHO%20SWALLOWED%20GAZA%20- %2004-Apr-97.

Bevington, Douglas, and Chris Dixon. 2005. "Movement-Relevant Theory: Rethinking Social Movement Scholarship and Activism." *Social Movement Studies* 4 (3): 185–208.

Bhabha, Homi. 1994. *The Location of Culture.* New York: Routledge.

Bichler, Shimson, and Jonathan Nitzan. 2001. *From War Profits to Peace Dividends: The Global Political Economy of Israel.* [In Hebrew.] Jerusalem: Carmel.

Bitton, Yifʿat. 2011. "Mizrahim in Court: Nothingness as Being." [In Hebrew.] *Mishpatim* 41:315–77.

Blachman, Israel. 2005. "Mizrahim in the Faculty of Israeli Research Universities." [In Hebrew.] Master's thesis, Tel Aviv University.

Blumenfeld, Miri. 1997. "A Single, Handsome European Man Searches for Same." [In Hebrew.] *LaIsha* 2595:88–92.

Bogoch, Bryna, and Rachelle Don-Yechiya. 1999. *The Gender of Justice Bias against Women in Israeli Courts.* [In Hebrew.] Jerusalem: Jerusalem Institute for Israel Studies.

Bogopa, David L. 2010. "Challenges Facing Young Researchers in South Africa: The Case of Funding, Publication and Intellectual Property Rights." Walter Sisulu University Research Conference Proceedings, East London, South Africa, 25–27 August 2009, 201–7.

Boskovic, Aleksandar, ed. 2008. *Other People's Anthropologies: Practice on the Margins.* New York: Berghahn Books.

Boyarin, Daniel, and Jonathan Boyarin. 1993. "Diaspora: Generation and the Ground of Jewish Identity." *Critical Inquiry* 19 (4): 693–725.

British Broadcasting Corporation (BBC). 2011. "Israel Ex-President Katsav Begins Jail Term for Rape." BBC News, 7 December. http://www.bbc.co.uk/news/world-middle-east-16064840.

———. 2013. "Benjamin Netanyahu Asked to Form Israeli Government." BBC News, 2 February. http://www.bbc.co.uk/news/world-middle-east-21309820.

———. 2014a. "Gaza Crisis: Toll of Operations in Gaza." BBC News, 1 September. http://www.bbc.com/news/world-middle-east-28439404.

———. 2014b. "Hamas and Fatah Unveil Palestinian Reconciliation Deal." BBC News, 23 April. http://www.bbc.com/news/world-middle-east-27128902.

Bruch, Carol. 1998–1999. "The Hague Child Abduction Convention: Past Accomplishments, Future Challenges." *European Journal of Law Reform* 1 (1–2): 97–118.

———. 2000a. "Religious Law, Secular Practices, and Children's Human Rights in Child Abduction Cases under the Hague Child Abduction Convention." *New York University Journal of International Law and Policy* 33:49.

———. 2000b. "Temporary or Contingent Changes in Location under the Hague Child Abduction Convention." In *Gedächtnisschrift Alexander Lüderitz*, edited by Haimo Schack, 43–62. Munich, Germany: Beck.

———. 2002. "Parental Alienation Syndrome and Alienated Children: Getting It Wrong in Child Custody Cases." *Child and Family Law Quarterly* 14 (4): 381–400.

———. 2003. "An Expert Opinion Concerning the Effective International Implementation of the November 17, 2003, Israeli Custody Decision, which was Entered Following the Conclusion of Hague Proceedings that Denied the Return of Shaheen Lavie Rouse to California." 5 December.

B'Tselem—The Israeli Information Center for Human Rights in the Occupied Territories. 2004. "Forbidden Roads: The Discriminatory West Bank Road Regime, August 2004." http://www.btselem.org/publications/summaries/200408 _forbidden_roads. Accessed 14 February 2013.

Buck-Morss, Susan. 1989. *The Dialectics of Seeing: Walter Benjamin and the Arcades Project*. Cambridge MA: MIT Press.

Budick, Sanford, and Wolfgang Iser. 1996. *The Translatability of Cultures*. Stanford CA: Stanford University Press.

Burke, Kenneth. 1968. *Language as a Symbolic Action: Essays on Life, Literature and Method*. Berkeley: University of California Press.

Burston, Bradley. 2007. "Here's to the '67 Borders, the New Middle of the Road." *Haaretz*, 31 December. http://www.haaretz.com/news/here-s-to-the-67-borders -the-new-middle-of-the-road-1.236269.

Bushinsky, Jay. 2005. "New Rules for Jews Immigrating to Germany." *San Francisco Chronicle*. 31 July. http://www.sfgate.com/cgi-bin/article.cgi?file=/c/a/2005/07 /31/MNGKVEONEO1.DTL&type=printable.

Busso, Nimrod. 2014. "MKs Fold: Lapid's Planning Body Will Not Be Required to Provide Public Housing." [In Hebrew.] *The Marker*, 23 July. http://www .themarker.com/realestate/1.2385945. Accessed 5 May 2016.

Cade, Toni. 1970. "The Pill: Genocide or Liberation." In *The Black Woman: An Anthology*, edited by Toni Cade, 163–64. New York: New American Library.

Caḥlili, Ron. 2014. *'Arsim and Freḥot: The New Elites*. [In Hebrew.] Documentary film series. Directed by Ron Cahlili. Israel: Channel 8 TV.

Carey, James W. 1993. "The Ethnographic Context of Illness among Single-Women-Headed Households in Rural Peru." *Health Care for Women International* 14 (3): 261–70.

Carmeli, Daphna Birenbaum, and Yoram S. Carmeli. 2010. *Kin, Gene, Community: Reproductive Technologies among Jewish Israelis*. New York: Berghahn Books.

Carter, Jimmy. 2006. *Palestine: Peace Not Apartheid*. New York: Simon and Schuster.

Chachage, Chachage Seithy L. 2004. "The World Social Forum: Lessons from Mumbai." Published in six installments in *The African* (English daily, Dar Es Salaam). 23–28 February.

Channel 2 News. 2010. "The Official Hamas Guide to Kidnapping Soldiers." [In Hebrew.] 3 June. http://www.mako.co.il/news-military/security/Article -45c7f03696bf821004.htm. Accessed on 1 May 2016.

———. 2014. "Finance Minister Lapid Hijacking the Economy to Detriment of the Public during the War." [In Hebrew.] YouTube video, 3:49. Posted 27 July 2014. https://www.youtube.com/watch?v=yi-vVp9c44s&feature=youtu.be&app= desktop. Accessed 4 May 2016.

Chetrit, Sami Shalom. 2004. The Mizrahi Struggle 1948–2003: Between Oppression and Emancipation. [In Hebrew.] Tel Aviv: 'Am 'Oved.

Cho, Grace. 2007. "Voices from the Teum: Synesthetic Trauma and the Ghosts of the Korean Diaspora." In The Affective Turn: Theorizing the Social, edited by Patricia Ticineto Clough and Jean Halley, 151–69. Durham NC: Duke University Press.

Chomsky, Noam. 1978. Language and Mind. [Translation into Hebrew of 1968 English-language edition.] Tel Aviv: Sifriyat Poalim.

Clifford, James, and George E. Marcus, eds. 1986. Writing Culture: The Poetics and Politics of Ethnography. Berkeley: University of California Press.

Coalition against Apartheid in Israeli Anthropology (CAAIA). 2004. "Formal Grievance Issued to Israel's State Comptroller about the Various Violations of Cultural Rights Performed by Israeli Anthropologists." http://www.ha-keshet.org.il /english/complaint.htm. Accessed on 14 February 2013.

Cockburn, Cynthia. 1998. The Space between Us: Negotiating Gender and National Identities in Conflict. London: Zed Books.

———. 2004. The Line: Women, Partition and the Gender Order in Cyprus. London: Zed Books.

Cohen, Gili. 2012. "Elderly Woman Lights Herself on Fire, Becoming Fourth Israeli Self-Immolator in a Month." Haaretz, 8 August. http://www.haaretz.com/news /national/elderly-woman-lights-herself-on-fire-becoming-fourth-israeli-self -immolator-in-a-month-1.456875?block=true.

Collins, Patricia Hill. 1990. Black Feminist Thought: Knowledge, Consciousness and the Politics of Empowerment. New York: Routledge.

Colvin, Christopher J. 2004. "Ambivalent Narrations: Pursuing the Political through Traumatic Storytelling." PoLar 27 (1): 72–89.

Combahee River Collective. 1983. "A Black Feminist Statement." In This Bridge Called My Back: Writings by Radical Women of Color, edited by Cherríe Moraga and Gloria Anzaldúa, 210–18. New York: Kitchen Table/Women of Color Press.

Crenshaw, Kimberle. 1991. "Mapping the Margins: Intersectionality, Identity Politics, and Violence Against Women of Color." Stanford Law Review 43 (6): 1241–99.

Curtiss, Richard H. 1994. "Call to Divert Russian Jews from U.S. to Israel Draws Angry Criticism." *Washington Report on Middle East Affairs* (February/March): 36.

Dadon, Israel. 2013. "'Ars Poetica Slam #3." [In Hebrew.] *YouTube* video, 2:24. Posted 17 March 2013. https://www.youtube.com/watch?v=czdgB8TJJLM. Accessed 4 May 2016.

Dahan-Kalev, Henriette. 2006. "A Laborer's Narrative: Havatzelet Ingber, a Leader in the Independence Sewing Workshop, Mitzpe Ramon 2000." [In Hebrew.] *Academic Summaries Are Us.* http://socialscience.fav.co.il/index.php?dir=app_sites&page=article&op=item&id=14645. Accessed March 22, 2012.

Daily Telegraph. 2007. Obituary of Maurice Wohl. 16 July. http://www.telegraph.co.uk/news/obituaries/1557539/Maurice-Wohl.html.

Dallam, Stephanie J. 1999. "Parental Alienation Syndrome: Is It Scientific?" In *Expose: The Failure of Family Courts to Protect Children from Abuse in Custody Disputes,* edited by E. St. Charles and L. Crook. Los Gatos CA: Our Children Our Future Charitable Foundation. http://www.leadershipcouncil.org/1/res/dallam/3.html. Accessed 14 February 2013.

Damri-Madar, Vardit. 2002. "My Brothers, the Mizrahim." [In Hebrew.] In *'Azut Mezah: Mizrahi Feminism,* 54–57. Jerusalem: ZAH, Students for Social Justice.

Danet, Brenda. 1989. *Pulling Strings: Biculturalism in Israeli Bureaucracy.* Albany: SUNY Press.

Davidoff, Steven. 2014. "Overhaul of Israel's Economy Offers Lessons for United States." *New York Times,* 7 January. http://dealbook.nytimes.com/2014/01/07/overhaul-of-israels-economy-offers-lessons-for-united-states/?_r=1.

Davidovitch-Weisberg, Gavriela. 2012. "The Producers Increased Prices 5 Percent, the Chains Have Hiked Up the Prices Much More." [In Hebrew.] *Haaretz— The Marker,* 12 December. http://www.themarker.com/consumer/1.1884334. Accessed 14 February 2013.

Davis, Uri. 2003. *Apartheid Israel: Possibilities for the Struggle Within.* London: Zed Books.

Defense for Children International Palestine. 2015. *Operation Protective Edge: A War Waged on Gaza's Children.* 16 April. http://www.dci-palestine.org/operation_protective_edge_a_war_waged_on_gaza_s_children_resource. Accessed 3 May 2016.

Donnan, Hastings. 2005. "Material Identities: Fixing Ethnicity in the Irish Borderlands." *Identities: Global Studies in Culture and Power* 12 (1): 69–105.

Douglas, Mary. 1970. *Natural Symbols.* New York: Pantheon Books.

Ducker, Clare Louise. 2005. "Jews, Arabs, and Arab Jews: The Politics of Identity and Reproduction in Israel." Research Paper, Institute of Social Studies, The Hague, Netherlands.

Du Bois, W.E.B. [1903] 1989. *The Souls of Black Folk.* New York: Penguin.

Durkheim, Émile. [1893] 1984. *Division of Labour in Society.* New York: Free Press.

———. 1961. "On Mechanic and Organic Solidarity." In *Theories of Society: Foundations of Modern Sociological Theory*, edited by Talcott Parsons, 208–13. New York: Free Press.

Durkheim, Émile, and Marcel Mauss. 1963. *Primitive Classification.* Translated, edited, and introduced by Rodney Needham. Chicago: University of Chicago Press.

Edleson, Jeffrey L., Taryn Lindhorst, Gita Mehrotra, William Vesneski, Luz Lopez, and Sudha Shetty. 2010. "Multiple Perspectives on Battered Mothers and Their Children Fleeing to the United States for Safety: A Study of Hague Convention Cases." A research report submitted to the National Institute of Justice, Office of Justice Programs, U.S. Department of Justice. Final Report, NIJ #2006-WG-BX-0006. [This report has not been officially published by the department.]

Edmiston, James. 2014. "Chilling New Recording of Israel Teen's Emergency Call to Police May Have Captured the Boys' Last Minutes Alive." *National Post*, 2 July. http://news.nationalpost.com/news/world/israel-middle-east/investigator -played-israeli-teens-panicked-police-call-for-his-mother-told-her-not-to-be -alarmed-by-sound-of-gunfire-interview.

Education Ministry of the State of Israel. 2006. "International Volunteer Day." [In Hebrew.] http://cms.education.gov.il/Educationcms/Units/Noar/Miscell /mitnadvim.htm. Accessed 14 February 2013.

Eliade, Mircea. 1971. *The Myth of the Eternal Return, or Cosmos and History.* Translated by Willard R. Trask. Princeton NJ: Princeton University Press.

Elliott, Larry. 2012. "Israel Calls for Tougher Iran Sanctions." *Guardian*, 27 January. http://www.guardian.co.uk/world/2012/jan/27/israel-tougher-iran-sanctions -barak-nuclear.

Emmett, Ayala H. 2003. *Our Sisters' Promised Land: Women, Politics, and Israeli-Palestinian Coexistence.* Ann Arbor: University of Michigan Press.

Epstein, Barbara. 1991. *Political Protest and Cultural Revolution: Nonviolent Direct Action in the 1970s and 1980s.* Berkeley: University of California Press.

Erdman, Shelby Lin. 2014. "Israeli Authorities Identify the Suspects in Teens' Kidnapping." *Cable News Network* (CNN), 26 June. http://www.cnn.com/2014/06/26 /world/meast/israel-kidnapped-teenagers-hamas/.

Erlanger, Steven. 2016. "Israel, Mired in Ideological Battles, Fights on Cultural Fronts." *New York Times*, 29 January. http://www.nytimes.com/2016/01/30 /world/middleeast/israel-mired-in-ideological-battles-fights-on-cultural -fronts.html&gt.

Erlich, Eyal. 2005. *Hudna: A Political Adventure.* [In Hebrew.] Ramot Hashavim, Israel: Aryeh Nir.

ʿEshet, Gidʿon. 2000. "How Do You Establish a Risk-Free Company?" [In Hebrew.] *Yediʿot Aharonot*, 7 March, Financial Supplement.

Evens, Terence M. S. 2006. "Some Ontological Implications of Situational Analysis." In *The Manchester School: Practice and Ethnographic Praxis in Anthropology*, edited by T. M. S. Evens and Don Handelman, 49–63. New York: Berghahn Books.

Evens, Terence M. S., and Don Handelman. 2006. "Introduction: The Ethnographic Praxis of the Theory of Practice." In *The Manchester School: Practice and Ethnographic Praxis in Anthropology*, edited by Terence M. S. Evens and Don Handelman, 1–12. New York: Berghahn Books.

Fabian, Johannes. 1983. *Time and the Other: How Anthropology Makes Its Object*. New York: Columbia University Press.

Fahim, Kareem. 2011. "Slap to a Man's Pride Set Off Tumult in Tunisia." *New York Times*, 21 January. http://www.nytimes.com/2011/01/22/world/africa/22sidi .html?pagewanted=all&_r=0.

Falk, Raphael. 2006. *Zionism and the Biology of the Jews*. [In Hebrew.] Tel Aviv: Resling.

Feldman, Ilana. 2008. *Governing Gaza: Bureaucracy, Authority, and the Work of Rule, 1917–1967*. Durham NC: Duke University Press.

Feldman, Keith. 2015. *A Shadow over Palestine: The Imperial Life of Race in America*. Minneapolis: University of Minnesota Press.

Firth, Raymond. 1961. *Elements of Social Organization*. London: C. A. Watts.

———. 1972. *Symbols: Public and Private*. Ithaca NY: Cornell University Press.

Fischer, David. 1996. *They Buried Him Alive*. Film. Directed by David Fischer. Israeli TV, Channel 1, 70 min.

Foucault, Michel. 1977. *Discipline and Punish: The Birth of the Prison*. Translated by Alan Sheridan. New York: Random House.

Fox, Richard G. 1991. *Recapturing Anthropology: Working in the Present*. Santa Fe NM: School of American Research Press.

Frank, Daniel H., ed. 1993. *A People Apart: Chosenness and Ritual in Jewish Philosophical Thought*. Albany: SUNY Press.

Frankenberg, Ruth. 1993. *White Women, Race Matters: The Social Construction of Whiteness*. Minneapolis: University of Minnesota Press.

Fuss, Diana. 1989. *Essentially Speaking: Feminism, Nature, and Difference*. New York: Routledge.

Gamlieli, Nissim Binyamin. 1965. *Yemen and the "Salvation" Camp: the History of Jews in Yemen, on the Road, in Adan, and in the Refugee Camps*. [In Hebrew.]. Ramleh, Israel: Dadon.

Gazit, Shlomo. 2011. "Yes Mr. Lieberman, I'm a Proud Jewish Terrorist." *Haaretz*. 19 July. http://www.haaretz.com/print-edition/opinion/yes-mr-lieberman-i-m-a -proud-jewish-terrorist-1.373979.

Geertz, Clifford. 1973. *The Interpretation of Cultures*. New York: Basic Books.

Giddens, Anthony. 1985. *The Nation-State and Violence*. Cambridge: Polity Press.

Giddings, Paula. 1985. *Where and When I Enter: The Impact of Black Women on Race and Sex in America*. New York: Bantam.

Giladi, G. Naim. 1990. *Discord in Zion*. London: Scorpion.

Gilroy, Paul. 1987. *"There Ain't No Black in the Union Jack": The Cultural Politics of Race and Nation*. London: Hutchinson.

———. 2000. *Against Race: Imagining Political Culture beyond the Color Line*. Cambridge MA: Belknap Press of Harvard University Press.

Ginat, Joseph. 2006. "Hudna: Origins of the Concept and Its Relevance to the Arab-Israeli Conflict." In *Arab-Jewish Relations: From Conflict to Resolution?*, edited by Elie Podeh and Asher Kaufman, 251–76. Portland OR: Sussex Academic Press.

Gledhill, John. 2004. "Beyond Speaking Truth to Power: Anthropological Entanglements with Multicultural and Indigenous Rights Politics." Manchester Anthropology Working Papers. http://www.socialsciences.manchester.ac.uk /disciplines/socialanthropology/research/workingpapers/documents/Beyond _Speaking_Truth_to_Power.pdf. Accessed 14 February 2013.

———. 2005. "Reinventing Anthropology, Anew." *Anthropology News* (October): 6–7.

Globe and Mail. 2013. "In Beit Shemesh, a Cauldron of Conflict." 17 January. http:// www.theglobeandmail.com/news/world/in-beit-shemesh-a-cauldron-of -conflict/article7509036/.

Gluckman, Max. 1955. "The Peace in the Feud." *Past and Present* 8 (1): 1–14.

———. 1968. "The Utility of the Equilibrium Model in the Study of Social Change." *American Anthropologist* 70 (2): 219–37.

Gómez-Peña, Guillermo. 1996. *The New World Border: Prophecies, Poems, & Loqueras for the End of the Century*. San Francisco: City Lights.

Graeber, David. 2009. *Direct Action: An Ethnography*. Oakland CA: AK Press.

———. 2015. *The Utopia of Rules: On Technology, Stupidity and the Secret Joys of Bureaucracy*. Brooklyn NY: Melville House.

Grathoff, Richard. 1970. *The Structure of Social Inconsistencies: A Contribution to a Unified Theory of Play, Game, and Social Action*. The Hague: Martinus Nijhoff.

Greenbaum, Li'or. 2003. "The Arab Single Mothers Demonstrated in Front of the Finance Ministry: Our Situation Is More Difficult than Knafo's." [In Hebrew.] *Globes: Israel Business News*, 23–24 July, 4.

Greenstein, Yossi. 2000. "Unemployment Reaches Its Biggest Peak in History: 220,000 Unemployed in Early October." [In Hebrew.] *Ma'ariv*, 24 November, Economics Supplement, 3.

Gupta, Akhil. 2012. *Red Tape: Bureaucracy, Structural Violence, and Red Tape in India*. Durham NC: Duke University Press.

Gurevitch, Yossi. 2011. "Stormy Hora on the Blood." [In Hebrew]. *Friends of George* (blog). http://www.hahem.co.il/friendsofgeorge/?p=2278. Accessed 14 February 2013.

Haaretz. 2014. "25,000 Pray for Kidnapped Teens at Western Wall." 16 June. http://www.haaretz.com/israel-news/.premium-1.598975.

Ḥakimi, Tehila. 2014. *Tomorrow We'll Work.* [In Hebrew.] Tel Aviv: Tangier Books.

Hall, Stuart. 1988. "New Ethnicities." *ICA Documents* 7:27–44.

Hall, Stuart, and Tony Jefferson, eds. 1993. *Resistance through Rituals: Youth Subcultures in Post-War Britain.* London: Routledge.

Ha'Okets. 2013. "Afterparty: All Sorts of Good and Bad Thoughts Marking the Election Campaign and Launching of the Israeli Parliament, Take 19." *Ha'Okets,* 6 February. http://www.haokets.org/2013/02/06/%D7%90%D7%A4%D7%98%D7%A8-%D7%A4%D7%90%D7%A8%D7%98%D7%99/. Accessed 14 February 2013.

Handelman, Don. 1990. *Models and Mirrors: Towards an Anthropology of Public Events.* Cambridge: Cambridge University Press.

———. 1994. "Contradictions between Citizenship and Nationality: Their Consequences for Ethnicity and Inequality in Israel." *International Journal of Politics, Culture, and Society* 7 (3): 441–59.

———. 2004. *Nationalism and the Israeli State: Bureaucratic Logic in Public Events.* Oxford: Berg.

———. 2005. "Introduction." In *Ritual in Its Own Right,* edited by Don Handelman and Galina Lindquist, 1–32. New York: Berghahn Books.

———. 2006. "The Extended Case: Interactional Foundations and Prospective Dimensions." In *The Manchester School: Practice and Ethnographic Praxis in Anthropology,* edited by Terence M. S. Evens and Don Handelman, 94–117. New York: Berghahn Books.

———. 2016. "The Ethic of Being Wrong." In *Reflecting on Reflexivity,* edited by Terence M. S. Evens, Don Handelman, and Christopher Roberts. New York: Berghahn Books.

Handelman, Don, and Bruce Kapferer. 1980. "Symbolic Types, Meditation, and the Transformation of Ritual Context: Sinhalese Demons and Tewa Clowns." *Semiotica* 30 (1/2): 41–71.

Harrison, Faye V. 1997. "The Gendered Politics and Violence of Structural Adjustment: A View from Jamaica." In *Situated Lives: Gender and Culture in Everyday Life,* edited by Louise Lamphere, Helena Ragoné, and Patricia Zavella, 451–68. New York: Routledge.

———. 2008. *Outsider Within: Reworking Anthropology in the Global Age.* Champaign: University of Illinois Press.

———. 2012. "Racism in the Academy: Toward a Multi-Methodological Agenda for Anthropological Engagement." In *Racism in the Academy: The New Millennium,* edited by Audrey Smedley and Janis F. Hutchinson, 13–32. Arlington VA: American Anthropological Association.

Hartman, Ben. 2014. "Tens of Thousands Rally in Solidarity with the Kidnapped Teens' Families." *Jerusalem Post*, 29 June. http://www.jpost.com/National-News /Mothers-of-kidnapped-teens-set-to-speak-at-massive-rally-in-Tel-Avivs -Rabin-Square-360926.

Harvey, David. 1990. *The Condition of Post-Modernity: An Enquiry into the Origins of Cultural Change*. Oxford: Blackwell.

Ḥasan, Roy. 2014. *The Dogs that Barked in Our Childhood Were Muzzled*. [In Hebrew.] Tel Aviv: Tangier Books.

Hashai, Niron. 2002. "The Morning After: Implications for the Business and Economic Environment in Israel." [In Hebrew.] In *The Morning After, the Era of Peace—No Utopia*, edited by M. Benvenisti, 169–202. Jerusalem: Harry S. Truman Research Institute for the Advancement of Peace, Hebrew University.

Ḥasson, Nir. 2014. "Legal Advisor to Cabinet: Profits from Public Housing Sales Should Not Be Used to Purchase New Public Housing Apartments." [In Hebrew.] *Haaretz*, 23 September. http://www.haaretz.co.il/news/education/.premium-1.2442558.

Ḥatuka, Shlomi. 2015. *Eastern Moon*. [In Hebrew.] Tel Aviv: Tangier Books.

Heim, Sheila, Helen Grieco, Sue Di Paola, and Rachel Allen. 2002. *California National Organization for Women Family Court Report 2002*. Sacramento CA: California Now.

Helpman, Elhannan, and Manuel Trachtenberg. 2000. "A Question of Sixty-One Percent." [In Hebrew.] *Haaretz*, 16 June, Friday Supplement.

Herzog, Hanna, and Kinneret Lahad, eds. 2006. *Knowledge and Silence: On Mechanisms of Denial and Repression in Israeli Society*. [In Hebrew.] Jerusalem and Tel Aviv: Van Leer Institute and HaKibbutz HaMeu'had.

Hertzog, Esther. 1996. "Who Benefits from the Welfare State?" [In Hebrew.] *Teoria uBikoret* 9:81–101.

———. 1999. *Immigrants and Bureaucrats: Ethiopians in an Israeli Absorption Center*. [In Hebrew.] New York: Berghahn Books.

———. 2001. "The Industry of Parasites." [In Hebrew.] *Maʿariv*, 11 September.

———. 2004a. "Bureaucratic Violence and the Best Interest of the Child." [In Hebrew.] In *Justice Crusaders: Studies in Crime and Law Enforcement in Israel*, edited by L. ʿEden, E. Shadmi, and Y. Kim, 257–94. Tel Aviv: Cherikover.

———. 2004b. *Op-Eds: Feminism and Social Justice in Israel*. [In Hebrew.] Tel Aviv: Cherikover.

———. 2009. "Does the Social Welfare Apparatus Assist the Poor, or Does It Make Poverty Permanent and Hurt the Lower Classes?" [In Hebrew.] *HaMerhav HaTziburi* 3:157–66.

Herzfeld, Michael. 1992. *The Social Production of Indifference: Exploring the Symbolic Roots of Western Bureaucracy*. London: Berg.

Hoffman, Gil. 2015. "Netanyahu to Receive Mandate on Wednesday to Form Government." *Jerusalem Post*, 25 March. http://www.jpost.com/Israel-News/Politics-and-Diplomacy/Netanyahu-to-receive-mandate-on-Wednesday-to-form-government-395019.

Horev, Shai. 2007. *We . . . and All the Others*. [In Hebrew.] Haifa: Dukhifat.

Hull, Matthew S. 2012. *Government of Paper: The Materiality of Bureaucracy in Urban Pakistan*. Berkeley: University of California Press.

Hurston, Zora Neale. 1937. *Their Eyes Were Watching God*. Philadelphia: J. B. Lippincott.

Hurtado, Aida, ed. 1996. *The Color of Privilege: Three Blasphemies on Race and Feminism*. Ann Arbor: University of Michigan Press.

Husserl, Edmund. [1900] 1970. *Logical Investigations*. 2 vols. Translated by G. N. Gindlay. London: Routledge and Kegan Paul.

———. [1913] 1983. *Ideas Pertaining to a Pure Phenomenology and to a Phenomenological Philosophy, First Book: General Introduction to a Pure Phenomenology*. Translated by Fred Kersten. The Hague: Martinus Nijhoff.

Inbar, Michael, and Chaim Adler. 1977. *Ethnic Integration in Israel: A Comparative Case Study of Moroccan Brothers Who Settled in France and Israel*. New Brunswick NJ: Transaction Books at Rutgers University.

Israel Ministry of Foreign Affairs. 2008. English Translation of the Declaration of the Establishment of the State of Israel. http://www.mfa.gov.il/MFA/Peace+Process/Guide+to+the+Peace+Process/Declaration+of+Establishment+of+State+of+Israel.htm. Accessed 14 February 2013.

Issacharoff, Avi. 2010. "Israel's Spy in Ḥamas Part II." *Haaretz*, 25 February. http://www.haaretz.com/blogs/mess-report/israel-s-spy-in-hamas-part-ii-1.263752.

ʿIton Aḥer [An Other Paper, Hebrew]. 1988–94. 32 issues. [In Hebrew.] Kiryat Ata, Israel: Yated NGO.

Jameson, Frederic. 1991. *Postmodernism, or the Culture of Late Capitalism*. Durham NC: Duke University Press.

Jerbi, Rafi. 2014. "Dozens Order Eight Reservists Drafted for Operation Brother's Keeper." *Maʿariv*, 18 June (in Hebrew). http://www.maariv.co.il/news/new.aspx?pn6Vq=E&Or9VQ=FJHJG.

Jerusalem Post. 2014. "Gantz: Operation Brother's Keeper Has Come to an End." 23 September. http://www.jpost.com/Breaking-News/Gantz-Operation-Brothers-Keeper-has-come-to-an-end-376127.

Joseph, Suad. 1994. "Brother/Sister Relationships: Connectivity, Love and Power in the Reproduction of Arab Patriarchy." *American Ethnologist* 21 (1): 50–73.

———. 2000. "Gendering Citizenship in the Middle East." In *Gender and Citizenship in the Middle East*, edited by Suad Joseph, 3–32. Syracuse NY: Syracuse University Press.

Kanaaneh, Rhoda Ann. 2002. *Birthing the Nation*. Los Angeles: University of California Press.

———. 2009. *Surrounded: Palestinian Soldiers in the Israeli Military*. Stanford CA: Stanford University Press.

Kapferer, Bruce. 1988. *Legends of People, Myths of State: Violence, Intolerance, and Political Culture in Sri Lanka and Australia*. Washington DC: Smithsonian Institution Scholarly Press.

———. 2006. "Situations, Crisis, and the Anthropology of the Concrete: The Contribution of Max Gluckman." In *The Manchester School: Practice and Ethnographic Praxis in Anthropology*, edited by Terence M. S. Evens and Don Handelman, 118–58. New York: Berghahn Books.

Kaufman, Ami. 2012. "Moshe Silman's Self-Immolation Is a National, Not Just a Personal, Tragedy." *Guardian*, 18 July. http://www.guardian.co.uk/commentisfree/2012/jul/18/moshe-silman-self-immolation.

Kearney, Michael. 1996. *Reconceptualizing the Peasantry: Anthropology in Global Perspective*. Boulder CO: Westview Press.

Keissar, ʿAdi. 2014. *Black on Black*. [In Hebrew.] Tel Aviv: Cultural Guerrilla.

Keinon, Herb. 2014. "Lieberman Seeks to Expel UN Envoy Robert Serry for Trying to Give Aid to Hamas." *Jerusalem Post*, 22 June. http://www.jpost.com/Diplomacy-and-Politics/Report-Liberman-seeks-to-expel-UN-envoy-for-trying-to-give-aid-to-Hamas-360109.

Kempney, Marian. 2006. "History of the Manchester 'School' and the Extended-Case Method." In *The Manchester School: Practice and Ethnographic Praxis in Anthropology*, edited by Terence M. S. Evens and Don Handelman, 180–202. New York: Berghahn Books.

Kershner, Isabel. 2011. "Israeli Girl, 8, at Center of Tension over Religious Extremism." *New York Times*, 27 December. http://www.nytimes.com/2011/12/28/world/middleeast/israeli-girl-at-center-of-tension-over-religious-extremism.html?pagewanted=all&_r=0.

Keshet, Yehudit Kirstein. 2006. *Checkpoint Watch: Testimonies from Occupied Palestine*. London: Zed Books.

Ki-Moon, Ban. 2011. "Secretary-General's Message for International Volunteer Day." United Nations Secretary-General. http://www.un.org/en/events/volunteerday/sgmessages.shtml. Accessed 22 March 2012.

Kim, Hanna. 2002. "The Tragic Alliance." [In Hebrew.] *Haaretz*, 12 November, B1.

Kimmerling, Baruch. 2001. *The End of Ashkenazi Hegemony*. [In Hebrew.] Jerusalem: Keter.

King, Laura. 2003. "Single Moms' Beef Draws Israel's Focus Home." *LA Times*, 18 July. http://articles.latimes.com/2003/jul/18/world/fg-welfare18.

Kingfisher, Catherine, and Michael Goldsmith. 2001. "Reforming Women in the United States and Aotearoa/New Zealand: A Comparative Ethnography of Welfare Reform in Global Context." *American Anthropologist* 103 (3): 714–32.

Kirkpatrick, David D. 2013. "Army Ousts Egypt's President; Morsi Is Taken into Military Custody." *New York Times*, 3 July. http://www.nytimes.com/2013/07/04 /world/middleeast/egypt.html?_r=0.

Klein, Naomi. 2007. *The Shock Doctrine: The Rise of Disaster Capitalism*. New York: Metropolitan Books.

Kleinman, Arthur, and Joan Kleinman. 1985. "Somatization: The Interconnections in Chinese Society among Culture, Depressive Experiences, and the Meanings of Pain." In *Culture and Depression*, edited by Arthur Kleinman and Byron Good, 429–90. Berkeley: University of California Press.

———. 1994. "How Bodies Remember: Social Memory and Bodily Experience of Criticism, Resistance, and Delegitimation Following China's 'Cultural Revolution.'" *New Literary History* 25 (3): 707–23.

Knesset of the State of Israel. 2009. "The Arrangements Law." http://www.knesset .gov.il/lexicon/eng/hesderim_eng.htm. Accessed 14 February 2013.

———. 2014a. Session 116 of the Nineteenth Knesset. [In Hebrew.] [17 February.] *The Knesset Annals* 19:101–6. http://main.knesset.gov.il/Activity/Legislation /Laws/Pages/LawSecondary.aspx?lawitemid=548662.

———. 2014b. Ratification of Amendment to Ḥok HaHesderim on 27 July. *The Book of Laws* 2461:638. Full text available at: http://fs.knesset.gov.il//19/law/19 _lsr_303825.PDF.

Knesset of the State of Israel Finance Committee. 2014. Meeting Minutes No. 271 on Legislative Amendment no. 14 to Ḥok HaHesderim. Nineteenth Knesset. [In Hebrew.] 26 May. http://main.knesset.gov.il/Activity/Legislation/Laws/Pages /LawSecondary.aspx?lawitemid=548662. Accessed 4 May 2016.

Koizumi, Junji. 2005. "Pluralizing Anthropology." *Anthropology News* (October): 9.

Koptiuch, Kristin. 1991. "Third-Worlding at Home." *Social Text* 28:87–99.

Korin-Leber, Stella. 2002. "The Palestinian Name Roulette." [In Hebrew.] *Globes: Israel Business News*, 19–20 August, B1.

Krieger, Nancy. 2005. "Embodiment: A Conceptual Glossary for Epidemiology." *Journal of Epidemiology & Community Health* 59:350–55.

Krimsky, Joseph. [1919] 1977. *Pilgrimage and Service*. Reprinted from a copy in the Jewish Historical Society Library. New York: Arno Press.

Kuntsman, Adi. 2009. *Figurations of Violence and Belonging: Queerness, Migranthood and Nationalism in Cyberspace and Beyond*. Bern, Switzerland: Peter Lang, AG International Academic.

Landau, Idan. 2014a. "The Unfolding Lie of Mighty Cliff." [In Hebrew.] *Idan Landau* (blog). 9 July. https://idanlandau.com/2014/07/09/unfolding-lie-of -protective-edge/. Accessed 3 May 2016.

———. 2014b. "The Unfolding Lie of Operation Protective Edge." +972 (blog). 15 July. http://972mag.com/the-unfolding-lie-of-operation-protective-edge /93605/. Accessed 3 May 2016.

Langer, Susanne K. 1956. *Philosophy in a New Key: A Study in the Symbolism of Reason, Rite, and Art.* Cambridge MA: Harvard University Press.

Latour, Bruno. 2004. "Why Has Critique Run out of Steam? From Matters of Fact to Matters of Concern." *Critical Inquiry* 30 (2): 225–48.

Lavie, Smadar. 1983. "Symbols—Structure and Construction: Anthropological Experiment in Mediating Positivism and Hermeneutics." Presentation toward PhD requirements. University of California, Berkeley.

———. 1986. "Silence, or 'Why Won't You Write My Genealogy?': Inscriptions of Tribal Identity." Paper presented at Annual Meeting of the American Anthro-pological Association, in the panel "'Othering': Representations and Realities," organized by Kirin Narayan, and Renato Rosaldo, and Smadar Lavie, Philadel-phia, 4 December.

———. 1990. *The Poetics of Military Occupation: Mzeina Allegories of Bedouin Identity under Israeli and Egyptian Rule.* Berkeley: University of California Press.

———. 1991. "Arrival of the New Cultured Tenants: Soviet Immigration to Israel and the Displacing of the Sephardi Jews." *Times Literary Supplement* 4602, 14 June, 11.

———. 1992. "Blow-ups in the Borderzones: Third World Israeli Authors' Grop-ings for Home." *New Formations* 18:84–106.

———. 1995. "Border Poets: Translating by Dialogue." In *Women Writing Cul-ture*, edited by R. Behar and D. Gordon, 412–27. Berkeley: University of Cali-fornia Press.

———. 1996. "Blowups in the Borderzones: Third World Israeli Authors' Gropings for Home." In *Displacement, Diaspora, and Geographies of Identity*, edited by Sma-dar Lavie and Ted Swedenburg, 55–96. Durham NC: Duke University Press.

———. 2003. "Lilly White Feminism and Academic Apartheid in Israel." *Anthro-pology News* (October): 10–11.

———. 2005. "Israeli Anthropology and American Anthropology." *Anthropology News* (January): 8–9.

———. 2006a. "Sexual Politics of the Mizrahi Struggle: Preliminary Thoughts." Presented at the conference "Out of Place: Interrogating Silences in Queer-ness/Raciality," Lancaster University, Lancashire UK, 24–25 March.

———. 2006b. "Transnational English Tyranny." *Anthropology News* (April): 9–10.

————. 2006c. "When the Noble Savage Invades the Home." Review of the Hebrew translation of *Works and Lives: The Anthropologist as Author*, by Clifford Geertz. [In Hebrew.] *Haaretz*, 14 March, Literary Supplement 681, 14.

————. 2007a. "Dry Twigs." *Electronic Intifada*. 2 August. https://electronicintifada.net/content/dry-twigs/7079. Accessed 1 May 2016.

————. 2007b. "Imperialism and Colonialism: Zionism." In *Encyclopedia of Women in Islamic Cultures*, 6:9–15. Leiden: Brill.

————. 2010. "De/Racinated Transcendental Conversations: Witchcraft, Oracle and Magic among the Israeli Feminist Left Peace Camp." *Journal of Holy Land Studies* 9 (1): 71–80.

————. 2011a. "Mizrahi Feminism and the Question of Palestine." *Journal of Middle Eastern Women's Studies* 7 (2): 56–88.

————. 2011b. "Staying Put: Crossing the Israel–Palestine Border with Gloria Anzaldúa." *Anthropology and Humanism Quarterly* 36 (1): 101–21.

————. n.d. "Silenced from All Directions: Third World Israeli Women Writing in the Race/Gender Borderzone." Unpublished research paper written in 1992 as part of the Dependency and Autonomy: The Relation of Minority Discourse to Dominant Culture research group at the University of California Humanities Center, Irvine.

Lavie, Smadar, and Reuven Abargel. 2008. "A Year into the Lebanon-Gaza War: A Mizrahi Guide to the Perplexed, and the One State Vision." [In Hebrew.] *Sedek: A Hebrew Nakba Periodical* 1 (2): 71–79.

Lavie, Smadar, A. Hajj, and Forest Rouse. 1993. "Notes on the Fantastic Journey of the Hajj, His Anthropologist, and Her American Passport." *American Ethnologist* 20 (2): 363–84.

Lavie, Smadar, and Amir Paz-Fuchs. 2003. "But There Is Discrimination: The State Penetrates the Single Family's Bedroom." [In Hebrew.] *Globes: Israel Business News*, 16–17 July, 3.

Lavie, Smadar, and Rafi Shubeli. 2006. "On the Progress of Affirmative Action and Cultural Rights for Marginalized Communities in Israel." *Anthropology News* (November): 6–7.

Lavie, Smadar, and Ted Swedenburg. 1996a. "Between and among the Boundaries of Culture: Bridging Text and Lived Experience in the Third Timespace." *Cultural Studies* 10 (1): 154–79.

————. 1996b. "Displacement, Diaspora, and Geographies of Identity." In *Displacement, Diaspora, and Geographies of Identity*, edited by Smadar Lavie and Ted Swedenburg, 1–26. Durham NC: Duke University Press.

Lavie, Zvi. 2003. "The Top Tenth Hold Two Thirds of Israel's Financial Capital." [In Hebrew.] *Globes: Israel Business News*, 2–3 December, 8.

Leibman, Charles S., and Elihu Katz, eds. 1997. *The Jewishness of Israelis: Responses to the Guttman Report*. Albany: SUNY Press.

Leibner, Gerardo. 2015. HaTikva Encampment, 2011. "The Ambiguous Agency of the Marginalized." *Current Anthropology*. 56 (11): 159–68.

Leibovitz-Dar, Sarah. 2002. "Oslo Is Still Far Removed from Ofakim." [In Hebrew.] *Haaretz*, 1 February, Weekly Supplement, 8.

Lendman, Stephen. 2012. "Israel's Operation Pillar of Cloud." *Centre for Research on Globalization*, 15 November. http://www.globalresearch.ca/israels-operation -pillar-of-cloud/5311929. Accessed 14 February 2013.

Lévi-Strauss, Claude. 1961. *Tristes Tropiques*. Translated by John Russell. New York: Criterion Books.

———. 1967. *Structural Anthropology*. Garden City NY: Anchor Books.

Levitt, Steven, and Neri Zilber. 2015. "The EU Still Has Issues with Hamas." *Washington Institute Policy Analysis*, 2 April. http://www.washingtoninstitute.org /policy-analysis/view/the-eu-still-has-issues-with-hamas. Accessed 4 May 2016.

Levy, Gal. 2016. "Shaking the Tree or Rocking the Boat: Lo Neḥmadim-Lo Neḥmadot—Protest and Radical Democracy in Israel." [In Hebrew.] *Israeli Sociology* 17 (2): 29–51.

Levy, Rachel. 2007. "Post-Divorce Mobility: Israeli Travel Bans on Dual-Citizen Mothers." Paper presented at the Conference on Child Abduction and Relocation, Shaʿarei Mishpat College, 1 January.

Levy, Yagil. 2003. *An Army of Others for Israel: Materialistic Militarism in Israel*. [In Hebrew.] Tel Aviv: Yediʿot Aharonot.

———. 2013. *Casualty Aversion in a Militarized Democracy*. New York: NYU Press.

Levy, Ze'ev. 1976. *Structuralism: Method and Theory*. [In Hebrew.] Tel Aviv: Sifriyat Poalim.

Lockhart, Chris. 2008. "The Life and Death of a Street Boy in East Africa: Everyday Violence in the Time of AIDS." *Medical Anthropology Quarterly* 22 (1): 94–115.

Lorde, Audre. 1984. *Sister Outsider*. Berkeley CA: Crossing Press.

Lubin, Orly. 2003. *Woman Reading Woman*. [In Hebrew.] Haifa and Or Yehuda, Israel: Haifa University and Zmora Bitan.

Lustick, Ian. 1988. *For the Land and the Lord: Jewish Fundamentalism in Israel*. New York: Council on Foreign Relations Books.

Mackey, Robert. 2014. "Israelis Watch Bombs Drop on Gaza From Front-Row Seats." *New York Times*, 14 July. http://www.nytimes.com/2014/07/15/world/middleeast /israelis-watch-bombs-drop-on-gaza-from-front-row-seats.html?_r=0.

Madmoni-Gerber, Shoshana. 2009. *Israeli Media and the Framing of Internal Conflict: The Yemenite Babies Affair*. New York: Palgrave MacMillan.

Magen David Adom [Red Cross of Israel]. 2016. "Wave of Terror Throughout Country Continues: A Summary of Casualties from the Beginning of Events During the Wave of Terror." 2 May. https://www.mdais.org/news/3704-%D7 %92%D7%9c-%D7%98%D7%A8%D7%95%D7%A8-%D7%91%D7%A8%D7%97

%D7%91%D7%99-%D7%94%D7%90%D7%A8%D7%A5-%D7%A0%D7%9e%D7
%A9%D7%9a-%D7%A1%D7%99%D7%9b%D7%95%D7%9d-%D7%A0%D7%A4
%D7%92%D7%A2%D7%99%D7%9d-%D7%9e%D7%Aa%D7%97%D7%99%D7%9c
%D7%Aa-%D7%94%D7%90%D7%99%D7%A8%D7%95%D7%A2%D7%99%D7
%9d-%D7%91%D7%92%D7%9c-%D7%94%D7%98%D7%A8%D7%95%D7%A8.
Accessed 5 May 2016.

Mahmood, Sabah. 2001. "Feminist Theory, Embodiment, and the Docile Agent: Some Reflections on the Egyptian Islamic Revival." *Cultural Anthropology* 6 (2): 202–36.

———. 2010. "Can Secularism Be Other-wise?" In *Varieties of Secularism in a Secular Age*, edited by Michael Warner, Jonathan VanAntwerpen, and Craig Calhoun, 282–99. Cambridge MA: Harvard University Press.

Malka, Haim. 1998. *The Selection: The Selection and Discrimination in the Immigration and Absorption of the Jewry of Morocco and North Africa 1948-1956.* [In Hebrew.] Israel: Adi Tal Print House (privately printed).

Mann, R. 1998. *It's Inconceivable.* [In Hebrew.] Or Yehuda, Israel: Hed Artzi.

Marcus, George E., and Michael M. J. Fischer. 1986. *Anthropology as Cultural Critique: An Experimental Moment in the Human Sciences.* Chicago: University of Chicago Press.

Marx, Emanuel. 1976. *The Social Context of Violent Behavior.* London: Routledge and Kegan Paul.

Masalha, Nur. 2001. "The Historical Roots of the Palestinian Refugee Question." In *Palestinian Refugees: The Right of Return*, edited by Naseer Aruri, 36–67. London: Pluto Press.

Massad, Joseph Andoni. 2006. *The Persistence of the Palestinian Question: Essays on Zionism and the Palestinians.* Oxford: Routledge.

Mathur, Nayanika. 2015. *Paper Tiger: Law, Bureaucracy and the Developmental State in Himalayan India.* Delhi, India: Cambridge University Press.

McBride, Ian, ed. 2001. *History and Memory in Modern Ireland.* Cambridge: Cambridge University Press.

McClaurin, Irma. 1998. "Making Ends Meet: How Single Mothers Survive Welfare and Low-Wage Work." *American Anthropologist* 100 (1): 231–32.

———. 2001. "Theorizing a Black Feminist Self in Anthropology: Toward an Autoethnographic Approach." In *Black Feminist Anthropology: Theory, Politics, Praxis, and Poetics*, edited by Irma McClaurin, 49–76. Piscataway NJ: Rutgers University Press.

McGreal, Chris. 2005. "Israel Accused of 'Road Apartheid' in West Bank." *Guardian*, 20 October. http://www.commondreams.org/headlines05/1020-04.htm.

McLean, Stuart. 2004. *The Event and Its Terrors: Ireland, Famine, Modernity.* Stanford CA: Stanford University Press.

Mearsheimer, John J., and Stephen M. Walt. 2007. *The Israel Lobby and U.S. Foreign Policy*. New York: Farrar, Strauss, and Giroux.

Mekelberg, Yossi. 2012. "'Pillar of Cloud' Spreads Dust of War across Middle East." CNN *Opinion*, 16 November. http://www.cnn.com/2012/11/16/opinion/mekelberg-israel-gaza-conflict/index.html. Accessed 14 February 2013.

Melamed, Jodi. 2006. "The Spirit of Neoliberalism: From Racial Liberalism to Neoliberal Multiculturalism." *Social Text* 24 (4): 1–24.

Melman, Yossi. 2011. "Will Netanyahu Initiate Military Operation to Divert Public Opinion from the Social Protest?" [In Hebrew.] *Haaretz*, 5 August. http://www.haaretz.co.il/misc/1.1371642.

Meneley, Anne, and Donna J. Young. 2005. *Auto-Ethnographies: The Anthropology of Academic Practices*. Calgary, Alberta, Canada: Broadview Press.

Middle East Monitor. 2014. "Hamas Chooses Its Leadership inside Israeli Jails." 17 February. https://www.middleeastmonitor.com/20140217-hamas-chooses-its-leadership-inside-israeli-jails/. Accessed 5 May 2016.

———. 2016. "Deaths and the Jerusalem Intifada." Online resource updated daily at https://www.middleeastmonitor.com/specials/intifada/. Accessed 12 May 2016.

Mihesuah, Devon Abbott, and Angela Cavender Wilson. 2004. *Indigenizing the Academy: Transforming Scholarship and Empowering Communities*. Lincoln: University of Nebraska Press.

Millett, Kate. 1970. *Sexual Politics*. New York: Doubleday.

Misgav, Chen. 2015. "Spatial Activism in the City: Perspectives of Body, Identity and Memory." PhD diss., University of Tel Aviv.

Mitchell, J. Clyde. 2006. "Case and Situation Analysis." In *The Manchester School: Practice and Ethnographic Praxis in Anthropology*, edited by Terence M. S. Evens and Don Handelman, 23–44. New York: Berghahn Books.

Mitnick, Joshua. 2012. "From Back of the Bus, Israeli Women Fight Segregation." *Wall Street Journal*, 5 January. http://online.wsj.com/article/SB10001424052970204368104577136253309226604.html.

Mor-Ḥaim, Naʿamit. 2014. "The Stunning Story of How I Got Entangled in a Hamas Bookkeeping Quarrel." [In Hebrew.] *HaʿOkets*, 20 July. http://www.haokets.org/2014/07/20/. Accessed 11 May 2016.

Morris, Benny. 1987. *The Birth of the Palestinian Refugee Problem, 1947–1949*. Cambridge: Cambridge University Press.

Morris, Rosalind. 2011. "A Violent Affinity: Anthropology, Kinship, War." Keynote address at LOVA International Conference 2011, "Ethnographies of Gender and Conflict," University of Amsterdam, 6–8 July.

Movement for Quality of Government in Israel. 2014. "Movement for Quality of Government Contacted MK Yariv Levin to Request Update on Status of Knesset Discussions of Levi Committee Recommendations Determining MK Salaries" [In Hebrew.] Press release, 11 July. http://www.mqg.org.il/%D7%9E%D7%90%D7%92%D7%A8%D7%9E%D7%99%D7%93%D7%A2/%D7%94%D7%95%D7%93%D7%A2%D7%95%D7%AA%D7%95%D7%A4%D7%99%D7%A8%D7%A1%D7%95%D7%9E%D7%99%D7%9D%D7%91%D7%AA%D7%A7%D7%A9%D7%95%D7%A8%D7%AA/tabid/93/ctl/Detail/mid/656/ItemID/13635/Default.aspx?SkinSrc=%5BG%5DSkins%2Fmqg%2FAnnouncment+Skin+-+Full+Width. Accessed 5 May 2016.

Nahman, M. 2013. *Extractions: An Ethnography of Reproductive Tourism.* New York: Palgrave Macmillan.

Narotzky, Susana. 2006. "The Production of Knowledge and the Production of Hegemony: Anthropological Theory and Political Struggles in Spain." In *World Anthropologies: Disciplinary Transformations Within Systems of Power,* edited by Gustavo Ribeiro and Arturo Escobar, 133–66. Oxford: Berg Publishers.

Navaro-Yashin, Yael. 2009. "Affective Spaces, Melancholic Objects: Ruination and the Production of Anthropological Knowledge." *Journal of the Royal Anthropological Institute* 15 (1): 1–18.

New Israel Fund. 2007. "Ford Foundation and New Israel Fund Announce $20 Million Fund for Grant Making in Israel." http://www.nif.org/media-center/press-releases/ford-foundation-and-new.html. Accessed March 22, 2012.

New York Times. 2012. "Israel and Iran." *New York Times,* 14 August, A18.

Novak, David. 1995. *The Election of Israel: The Idea of the Chosen People.* Cambridge: Cambridge University Press.

Noy, Orly. 2012. "Tough Love." [In Hebrew.] *Ha'Okets,* 5 December. http://www.haokets.org/2012/12/05/%D7%90%D7%94%D7%91%D7%94-%D7%A7%D7%A9%D7%95%D7%97%D7%94/. Accessed 14 February 2013.

———. 2015a. "Hatred of the Ashkenazi Left Cannot Be a Basis for a Mizraḥi-Palestinian Coalition." [In Hebrew.] *Siḥa Mekomit* [Local Conversation], 9 September. http://mekomit.co.il/%D7%94%D7%90%D7%95%D7%94%D7%93%D7%99%D7%9d-%D7%94%D7%97%D7%93%D7%A9%D7%99%D7%9d-%D7%A9%D7%9c-%D7%96%D7%97%D7%90%D7%9c%D7%A7%D7%94/. Accessed 17 May 2016.

———. 2015b. "When Identity Politics Loses Its Historical and Political Context." [In Hebrew.] *Siḥa Mekomit* [Local Conversation], 4 September. http://mekomit.co.il/%D7%A1%D7%93%D7%A8%D7%Aa-%D7%A0%D7%91%D7%99%D7%90%D7%99%D7%9d-%D7%9b%D7%A9%D7%A4%D7%95%D7%9c%D7%99%D7%98%D7%99%D7%A7%D7%Aa-%D7%94%D7%96%D7%94%D7%95%D7%99%D7%95%D7%Aa-%D7%9e%D7%90%D7%91%D7%93%D7%Aa/. Accessed 17 May 2016.

Ohayon, Shira. 2015. "Feminists. Mizrahi. In SHAS. You've Heard It." [In Hebrew.] *Ha'Okets*, 15 March. http://www.haokets.org/2015/03/15/%D7%A4%D7%9e%D7 %99%D7%A0%D7%99%D7%A1%D7%98%D7%99%D7%95%D7%Aa-%D7%9e %D7%96%D7%A8%D7%97%D7%99%D7%95%D7%Aa-%D7%91%D7%A9%D7 %A1-%D7%9b%D7%9c-%D7%94%D7%Aa%D7%A9%D7%95%D7%91%D7%95 %D7%Aa/. Accessed 1 May 2016.

Okun, Barbara S., and Orna Khait-Marelly. 2006. "Socioeconomic Status and Demographic Behavior of Adult Multiethnics: Jews in Israel." Working Paper No. 2006-01, Department of Sociology and Anthropology, Faculty of Social Sciences, Hebrew University of Jerusalem. http://sociology.huji.ac.il/docs/Okun -paper-2006-01.pdf. Accessed 14 February 2013.

———. 2010. "The Impact of Intermarriage on Ethnic Stratification: Jews in Israel." *Research in Social Stratification and Mobility* 28:375–94.

Omi, Michael, and Howard Winant. 1986. *Racial Formation in the United States: From the 1960s to the 1980s.* New York: Routledge.

Oren, Amir. 2016. "A Very Senior Suspect." [In Hebrew.] *Haaretz*, 11 January. http:// www.haaretz.co.il/opinions/.premium-1.2818873.

Ortner, Sherry B. 1995. "Resistance and the Problem of Ethnographic Refusal." *Comparative Studies in Society and History* 37 (1): 173–93.

Pappe, Ilan. 2006. *The Ethnic Cleansing of Palestine.* London: Oneworld.

Parkin, David. 2001. "Abner Cohen: Master Anthropologist Weighing Old Arguments and New Fashions." *Guardian*, 25 May. http://www.guardian.co.uk/news /2001/may/25/guardianobituaries.socialsciences.

Parmar, Paraminder, and Ronald P. Rohner. 2005. "Relations among Perceived Intimate Partner Acceptance, Remembered Parental Acceptance, and Psychological Adjustment among Young Adults in India." *Ethos* 33 (3): 402–13.

Paz-Fuchs, Amir. 2004. "The Welfare Reform: Between Capitalism and Patriarchy—On Arrangements Law, 2003, and the Slashing of Income Augmentation and Assurance Allowances for Single Mothers and the Young Unemployed." [In Hebrew.] *Hevra, 'Avoda veMishpat* 10:339–61.

———. 2008. *Welfare to Work: Conditional Rights in Social Policy.* Oxford: Oxford University Press.

Pepper, Anshel. 2011. "SHABAK Argues: IDF Had an Exact Prediction." [In Hebrew.] *Haaretz*, 18 August. http://www.haaretz.co.il/news/politics/1.1559211.

Petras, James. 2002. "The Ford Foundation and the CIA." *Centre for Research on Globalization*, September. http://globalresearch.ca/articles/PET209A.html. Accessed 14 February 2013.

Plotzker, Sever. 2001. "Lautmann and the Seamstresses." [In Hebrew.] *Yedi'ot Aharonot*, 3 August, Financial Section.

Pratt, Mary Louise. 1992. *Imperial Eyes: Travel Writing and Transculturation*. London: Routledge.

Pratt, Nicola. 2007. *Democracy and Authoritarianism in the Arab World*. Boulder CO: Lynne Rienner.

Puar, Jasbir. 2005. "Queer Times, Queer Assemblages." *Social Text* 23 (3–4): 84–85.

Rappaport, 'Amir. 2003. "Who Gets Attacked More? Palestinian Terror Hurts Us All, but Some Populations Are Much More Exposed to Murderous Attacks." [In Hebrew.] *Ma'ariv*, 14 September, B2–3.

Reger, Tikvah. 2011. "Deadbeat Dads—It's the Public Who Pays. GRANIT-Association for Aid to Women before, during, and after Divorce Proceedings." [In Hebrew.] http://www.granitwomen.org/37203/pr. Accessed 14 February 2013. Abbreviated version reprinted in *Haaretz*, 14 November, in Letters to the Editor section.

Regev, David. 2006. "Employer Cost of Senior Managers—Twenty Times More Than the Median Salary." [In Hebrew.] *Yedi'ot Aharonot*, 17 December, A9.

Reider, Vera. 2006. "The Right, for One, Does Not Lie." [In Hebrew.] *Mizad Sheni* 14–15:32–37.

Reuter, Thomas. 2005. "Towards a Global Anthropology." *Anthropology News* (October): 7–8.

Rhodes, Jane. 2007. *Framing the Black Panthers: The Spectacular Rise of a Black Power Icon*. New York: New Press.

Ribeiro, Gustavo Lins. 2005. "A Different Global Scenario in Anthropology." *Anthropology News* (October): 5–6.

———. 2006. "World Anthropologies: Cosmopolitics for a New Global Scenario in Anthropology." *Critique of Anthropology* 26 (4): 363–86.

Ribeiro, Gustavo Lins, and Arturo Escobar, eds. 2006. *World Anthropologies: Disciplinary Transformations within Systems of Power*. Oxford: Berg Publishers.

Robinson, Geoffrey. 1995. *The Dark Side of Paradise: Political Violence in Bali*. Ithaca NY: Cornell University Press.

Rodinson, Maxime. 1988. *Europe and the Mystique of Islam*. Translated by Roger Veinus. London: I. B. Tauris.

Rolef, Susan Hattis. 2006. "The Arrangements Law: Issues and International Comparisons." Translated by Susan Hattis Rolef. Jerusalem: Knesset Research and Information Center. http://www.knesset.gov.il/mmm/eng/papers_eng.asp. Accessed 14 February 2013.

Rolnik, Guy. 2012. "Ehud Barak: If the Government Will Not Respond, the Protest Will Come with Force and Violence. The Defense Minister Surprised at the Annual Dinner at Davos with an Atypical Message and Devoted a Large Part of his Speech to the Social Protest." [In Hebrew.] *Haaretz—The Marker*, 27 January. http://www.themarker.com/wallstreet/davos2012/1.1627746. Accessed 14 February 2013.

Romanov, Dmitri, and Mark Feldman, Nir Fogel, Haim Portnoy, Israela Fridman, Nava Shau-Mena, Dan Amedey, Ruth Sehayek, and Gustavo Schifris. 2011. "Measurement and Estimates of the Population of Ultra-Orthodox Jews." [In Hebrew.] Working Paper on the Subject of Population, Israel Central Bureau of Statistics. http://www.cbs.gov.il/reader/paper_work/pwt_e.html. Accessed 14 February 2013.

Ronen, Moshe, and Amos Nevo. 2000. "When They Invited Yossi Kasirrer for an Interview—I Wept." [In Hebrew.] Yedi'ot Aharonot, 10 April, 24 Hours Section, 2–3.

Rosaldo, Renato. 1989. Culture and Truth: The Remaking of Social Analysis. Boston: Beacon.

Rotbard, Sharon. 2005. White City, Black City. Tel Aviv: Babel Publishing.

Rozenhak, Ze'ev, and Michael Shalev. 2011. "The Political Economy of the 2011 Protests: A Class and Generational Analysis." [In Hebrew.] Teoria uBikoret 41:45–68.

Rudoren, Jodi. 2012a. "Israeli Protester Dies after Self-Immolation." New York Times, 20 July. http://www.nytimes.com/2012/07/21/world/middleeast/israeli -protester-moshe-silman-dies-after-self-immolation.html.

———. 2012b. "Netanyahu Calls for Early Elections in Israel." New York Times, 9 October. http://www.nytimes.com/2012/10/10/world/middleeast/netanyahu -calls-for-early-elections-in-israel.html?_r=0.

———. 2015. "Netanyahu Says Speech to Congress Is His Duty." New York Times, 10 February. http://www.nytimes.com/2015/02/11/world/middleeast /netanyahu-says-speech-to-congress-is-his-duty.html.

Saada-Ophir, Galit. 2006. "Borderland Pop: Arab Jewish Musicians and the Politics of Performance." Cultural Anthropology 21 (2): 205–33.

———. 2007. "Mizrahi Subaltern Counterpoints: Sderot's Alternative Bands." Anthropological Quarterly 80 (3): 711–36.

Said, Edward. 1979. The Question of Palestine. New York: Random House.

———. 1983. The World, the Text, and the Critic. Cambridge MA: Harvard University Press.

Salaman, Redcliffe N. 1911. "Heredity and the Jew." Journal of Genetics 1 (3): 273–92.

———. 1920. "Palestine Reclaimed: Letters from a Jewish Officer in Palestine." London: G. Routledge & Sons.

Sal'i, Uri. 2003. "Upper Ashdod." [In Hebrew.] Yedi'ot Aharonot Weekly Magazine, 8 August, 48–56, 100.

San Juan, Epifanio, Jr. 1992. Racial Formations/Critical Transformations: Articulations of Power in Ethnic and Racial Studies in the United States. Atlantic Highlands NJ: Humanities Press.

———. 2002. *Racism and Cultural Studies: Critiques of Multiculturalist Ideology and the Politics of Difference.* Durham NC: Duke University Press.

Sandoval, Chela. 2000. *Methodology of the Oppressed.* Minneapolis: University of Minnesota Press.

Sangtin Writers and Richa Nagar. 2006. *Playing with Fire: Feminist Thought and Activism through Seven Lives in India.* Minneapolis: University of Minnesota Press.

de Saussure, Ferdinand. 1959. *Course in General Linguistics.* Edited by C. Bally and A. Sechehtrans with A. Riedlinger. Translated by W. Baskin. New York: Philosophical Library.

Scarry, Elaine. 1985. *The Body in Pain: The Making and Unmaking of the World.* Oxford: Oxford University Press.

Schutz, Alfred. 1962. *Collected Papers.* Vol. 1, *The Problem of Social Reality.* Edited by Maurice Natanson. The Hague: Martinus Nijhoff.

———. 1966. *Collected Papers.* Vol. 3, *Studies in Phenomenological Philosophy.* Edited by Ilse Schutz. The Hague: Martinus Nijhoff.

Schuz, Rhona. 2001. "Policy Considerations in Determining the Habitual Residence of a Child and the Relevance of Context." *Journal of Transnational Law and Policy* 11 (1): 2–61.

———. 2002. "The Hague Child Abduction Convention and the United Nations Convention on the Rights of the Child." *Transnational Law and Contemporary Problems* 12 (2): 393.

———. 2004. "The Rights of Abducted Children: Is the Hague Convention (Return of Children) 1991 Consistent with the Doctrine of the Rights of the Child?" [In Hebrew.] *Bar-Ilan Law Studies* 20:421–91.

———. 2008. "In Search of a Settled Interpretation of Article 12(2) of the Hague Child Abduction Convention." *Child and Family Law Quarterly* 20 (1): 64–80.

Schwartz, Michal. 1997. "A Secret Account in Tel Aviv Funds Arafat's Oppression." *Challenge: A Magazine Covering the Israeli-Palestinian Conflict* 43. http://www .challenge-mag.com/43/article.html. Accessed 14 February 2013.

Schweid, Eliezer. 1985. *The Land of Israel: National Home or Land of Destiny.* Translated by Deborah Greniman. Cranbury NJ: Associated University Presses.

Scott, James C. 1985. *Weapons of the Weak: Everyday Forms of Peasant Resistance.* New Haven CT: Yale University Press.

Scott, Joan W. 1991. "The Evidence of Experience." *Critical Inquiry* 17 (4): 773–97.

———. 2007. *The Politics of the Veil.* Princeton NJ: Princeton University Press.

Segev, Tom. 2003. *The Seventh Million: The Israelis and the Holocaust.* Translated by Haim Watzman. New York: Hill and Wang.

Segev, Tom, and Arlen Neal Weinstein. 1986. *1949: The First Israelis.* New York: Free Press.

Selzer, Michael. 1967. *The Aryanization of the Jewish State*. New York: Black Star.

Shadmi, Erella. 2004a. "The Police: Servant of the Hegemony." [In Hebrew.] Paper delivered at Ashkenazim Conference, Beit Berl College, Israel. 3 June.

———. 2004b. "The Israeli Woman and the Feminist Commitment." In *Who's "Left" in Israel? Radical Political Alternatives for the Future of Israel*, edited by Dan Leon, 151–60. Brighton UK: Sussex Academic Press.

———. 2012. *Secure Land: Police, Policing and the Politics of Personal Security in Israel*. [In Hebrew.] Tel Aviv: HaKibbutz HaMeu'had.

Shadmi, Haim. 2003. "Solidarity Visit of Taʿayush at the Rose Garden." [In Hebrew.] *Haaretz*, 10 August.

Shahar, Rina. 1988. "Choosing a Mate among the Youth." [In Hebrew.] PhD diss., Bar Ilan University, Israel.

Shapira, Yair. 2003. "Our Madam, the Judge." [In Hebrew.] *Makor Rishon*, 1 August, 8–9.

Shapiro, Yonathan. 1993. "The Historical Origins of Israeli Democracy." In *Israeli Democracy Under Stress*, edited by Ehud Sprinzak and Larry Diamond, 65–82. Boulder CO: Lynne Rienner.

Sharoni, Simona. 1995. *Gender and the Israeli-Palestinian Conflict: The Politics of Women's Resistance*. Syracuse NY: Syracuse University Press.

Shelah, ʿOfer. 2002. "Beilin Beardless." [In Hebrew.] *Yediʿot Aharonot*, 22 November, Saturday Supplement.

Shenhav, Yehuda. 2005. "On Hybridity and Purification: Orientalism as a Wide Marginal Discourse." [In Hebrew.] *Teoria uBikoret* 26:5–11.

Shenhav, Yehuda, and Yossi Yonah, eds. 2008. *Racism in Israel*. [In Hebrew.] Jerusalem and Tel Aviv: Van Leer Institute and HaKibbutz HaMeu'had.

Sherwood, Harriet. 2011. "The Battle of Bet Shemesh." *Guardian*, 31 October. http://www.guardian.co.uk/commentisfree/2011/oct/31/bet-shemesh-haredi-jews-school.

Shiran, Vicky. 1991. "Political Corruption: The Power of the Game." PhD diss., John Jay College of Criminal Justice.

———. 1996. "Mizrahiyot and Others." [In Hebrew.] *Metzad Sheni* 5–6:26–29.

———. 2002. "Deciphering Power, Creating a New World." [In Hebrew.] *Panim* 22. http://www.itu.org.il/Index.asp?ArticleID=1415&CategoryID=521&Page=1. Accessed 14 February 2013.

Shmueli, Smadar. 2001. "Ariel Sharon's Housemates." [In Hebrew.] *Y-Net*, 29 January. http://www.ynet.co.il/articles/0,7340,L-477788,00.html. Accessed 14 February 2013.

Shohat, Ella. 1988. "Sephardim in Israel: Zionism from the Point of View of Its Jewish Victims." *Social Text* 19–20:1–35.

———. 2001. *Taboo Memories: Toward a Multicultural Thought.* [In Hebrew.] Tel Aviv: Bimat Kedem.

Shoshana, Avi. 2006. "The Invention of a New Social Category: The Deprived Gifted." [In Hebrew.] *Teoria uBikoret* 29:125–47.

Shriki, Moshe. 2012. "Haredim for the Common Good." [In Hebrew.] *HaʿOkets*, 14 May. http://www.haokets.org/2012/05/14/%D7%97%D7%A8%D7%93%D7%99 %D7%9d-%D7%9c%D7%98%D7%95%D7%91-%D7%94%D7%9b%D7%9c%D7%9c %D7%99/. Accessed 14 February 2013.

Shubeli, Rafi. 2006. "It Is Not the Occupation That Corrupts." [In Hebrew.] *Mizad Sheni* 14–15:38–41.

Silberg, Joyanna L. 2012. *The Child Survivor: Healing Developmental Trauma and Dissociation.* London: Routledge.

Sinai, Rutie. 2002. "81 percent of Capital Is in the Hands of 10 Percent of the Households." [In Hebrew.] *Haaretz*, 3 December, A5.

———. 2003. "The Ministers Fought about How to Treat the Single Mothers." [In Hebrew.] *Haaretz*, 23 July.

Smith, Linda Tuhiwai. 1999. *Decolonizing Methodologies: Research and Indigenous Peoples.* London and Dunedin, New Zealand: Zed Books and University of Otago Press.

Smith, Sidonie, and Julia Watson. 2011. "Witnessing, False Witnessing and the Metrics of Authenticity." Paper presented at conference "Life Writing and Human Rights: Genres of Testimony," Kingston University, London, 11–13 July.

Sobel, Zvi, and Benjamin Beit-Hallahmi, eds. 1991. *Tradition, Innovation, Conflict: Jewishness and Judaism in Contemporary Israel.* Albany: SUNY Press.

Spivak, Gayatri. 1988. "Can the Subaltern Speak?" In *Marxism and the Interpretation of Culture*, edited by Cary Nelson and Larry Grossberg, 271–313. Urbana: University of Illinois Press.

Stasiulis, Daiva, and Nira Yuval-Davis, eds. 1995. *Unsettling Settler Societies: Articulations of Gender, Race, Ethnicity and Class.* London: Sage.

Sternhell, Zeev. 1999. *The Founding Myths of Israel: Nationalism, Socialism, and the Making of the Jewish State.* Translated by David Maisel. Princeton NJ: Princeton University Press.

Stewart, Desmond. 1974. *Theodor Herzl: Artist and Politician.* Garden City NY: Doubleday.

Stokes, Martin. 2013. "Love and Justice in Music." Bloch Lectures, University of California Berkeley, Department of Ethnomusicology, Fall Semester.

Stoler-Liss, Sahlav. 1998. "Raising a Zionist Baby: An Anthropological Analysis of Parents' Guidebooks." [In Hebrew.] Master's thesis, Tel Aviv University.

Strathern, Marilyn. 1987. "Out of Context: The Persuasive Fictions of Anthropology." *Current Anthropology* 28 (3): 251–81.

Suleiman, Yasir. 2004. *A War of Words: Language and Conflict in the Middle East.* Cambridge: Cambridge University Press.

Swirski, Shlomo. 1989. *Israel: The Oriental Majority.* London: Zed Books.

Swirsky, Gila. 2002. "Feminist Peace Activism during the al-Aqsa Intifada." In *Women and the Politics of Military Confrontation: Palestinian and Israeli Gendered Narratives of Dislocation,* edited by Nahla Abdo and Ronit Lentin, 234–39. New York: Berghahn Books.

Taussig, Michael. 1986. *Shamanism, Colonialism, and the Wild Man: A Study in Terror and Healing.* Chicago: University of Chicago Press.

———. 1993. *Mimesis and Alterity.* New York: Routledge.

Tedlock, Denis. 1983. *The Spoken Word and the Work of Interpretation.* Philadelphia: University of Pennsylvania Press.

Thorleifsson, Cathrine. 2012. "Peripheral Nationhood: Being Israeli in Kiryat Shmona." PhD diss., London School of Economics.

Thrift, Nigel. 2008. *Non-Representational Theory: Space, Politics, Affect.* New York: Routledge.

Tilly, Charles. 2004. *Social Movements, 1768–2004.* Boulder CO: Paradigm.

Times of Israel. 2014. "Israel Rounds up Senior Hamas Men in West Bank Sweep." 15 June. http://www.timesofisrael.com/israel-rounds-up-senior-hamas-men-in -the-west-bank/.

Topol, Yaʿel. 2005. *Ringworm Girl: Lessons in Yemeni Pottery.* Rehovot, Israel: Self-published.

Torstrick, Rebecca L. 2000. *The Limits of Co-Existence: Identity Politics in Israel.* Ann Arbor: University of Michigan Press.

Traubmann, Tamara. 2006. "A Different Way to Fight Academic Boycotts." *Haaretz,* 6 May. http://www.haaretz.com/print-edition/news/a-different-way-to-fight -academic-boycotts-1.188502.

Tsur, Yaron. 1997. "Carnival Fears: Moroccan Immigrants and the Problem of the Young State of Israel." *Journal of Israeli History* 18 (1): 73–103.

Turner, Victor W. 1957. *Schism and Continuity in an African Society: A Study of Ndembu Village Life.* Manchester: Manchester University Press.

———. 1969. *The Ritual Process.* Chicago: Aldine.

———. 1973. "The Center Out There: Pilgrim's Goal." *History of Religions* 12:191–230.

Turner, Victor W., and Edith L. B. Turner. 1978. *Image and Pilgrimage in Christian Culture: Anthropological Perspectives.* New York: Columbia University Press.

Tyler, Steven A. 1987. *The Unspeakable: Discourse, Dialogue, and Rhetoric in the Post-modern World.* Madison: University of Wisconsin Press.

Tzimuki, Tova. 1999. "The State of Discrimination." [In Hebrew.] *Yediʿot Aharonot,* 6 December, 15.

Tzur, Ronit, ed. 2001. *Reader for Licensed Social Workers of the Family Court Services: Articles, Professional Literature, Laws and Regulations.* Tel Aviv: State of Israel, The Work and Welfare Ministry—Family Services.

UN (United Nations) Development Programme. 2014. *Detailed Infrastructure Damage Assessment Gaza 2014.* http://www.ps.undp.org/content/dam/papp/docs /Publications/undp-papp-research-dammageassessment2014.pdf. Accessed 3 May 2016.

UN Human Rights Council. 2009. "United Nations Fact-Finding Mission on the Gaza Conflict" (Goldstone Report). http://www2.ohchr.org/english/bodies /hrcouncil/docs/12session/A-HRC-12-48.pdf. Accessed 14 February 2013.

UN Office for the Coordination of Humanitarian Affairs, Occupied Palestinian Territory. n.d. http://www.ochaopt.org/content.aspx?id=1010057. Accessed 12 May 2016.

UN Watch. 2014. "Mother of Kidnapped Israeli Teenager Neftali Frankel Addresses UN." 24 June. http://blog.unwatch.org/index.php/2014/06/24/mother-of -kidnapped-israeli-teenager-neftali-frankel-addresses-un/. Accessed 3 May 2016.

Van Der Veer, Peter, ed. 1996. *Conversion to Modernities: The Globalization of Christianity.* New York: Routledge.

van Teeffelen, Toine. 1977. *Anthropologists on Israel: A Case Study in the Sociology of Knowledge.* Amsterdam: Antropologisch-Sociologisch Centrum, Universiteit van Amsterdam.

Verkaaik, Oskar. 2004. *Migrants and Militants: Fun and Urban Violence in Pakistan.* Princeton NJ: Princeton University Press.

Viswanathan, Gauri. 1996. "Religious Conversion and the Politics of Dissent." In *Conversion to Modernities: The Globalization of Christianity*, edited by Peter Van Der Veer, 89–114. New York: Routledge.

WAN (World Anthropologies Network) Collective. 2003. "A Conversation about a World Anthropologies Network." *Social Anthropology* 11 (2): 265–69.

———. 2005. "Establishing Dialogue among International Anthropological Communities." *Anthropology News* (November): 8–9.

Weber, Max. [1948] 1991. "Bureaucracy." In *From Max Weber: Essays in Sociology*, edited by Hans Heinrich Gerth and C. Wright Mills, 196–244. Oxford: Routledge.

Weiner, Merle H. 2008. "Intolerable Situations and Counsel for Children: Following Switzerland's Example in Hague Abduction Cases." *American University Law Review* 58 (2): 335–403.

Willner, Dorothy. 1969. *Community and Nation-Building in Israel.* Princeton NJ: Princeton University Press.

Withnall, Adam. 2014. "Hamas Removed from List of Terror Organisations by EU Court." *Independent*, 17 December. http://www.independent.co.uk/news/world

/middle-east/hamas-removed-from-list-of-terrorist-organisations-by-eu-court
-9930124.html.

Wolf, Eric R. 1969. *Peasant Wars of the Twentieth Century.* Norman: University of
Oklahoma Press.

Yadgar, Yaacov. 2010. "Masortim in Israel: Modernity Without Secularity." [In
Hebrew.] Jerusalem: Keter and the Shalom Hartman Institute.

———. 2011. *Secularism and Religion in Jewish-Israeli Politics: Traditionalists and
Modernity.* Oxford: Routledge.

Yitzhaki, Aharon. 2003. *The Mask: Introduction to the Ethnic Strategy in the State of
Israel—Comparative Research.* [In Hebrew.] Israel: Kotarot Publishing.

Yogev, Abraham, and Haia Jamshy. 1983. "Children of Ethnic Intermarriage in Israeli
Schools: Are They Marginal?" *Journal of Marriage and Family* 45 (4): 965–74.

Y-Net. 2006. "The Economist Milton Friedman has died." [In Hebrew.] Obituary.
Y-Net, 16 November. http://www.ynet.co.il/articles/0,7340,l-3329187,00.html.
Accessed 14 February 2013.

Zeid, Shoshi. 2001. *The Child Is Gone: The Yemeni Children Affair.* [In Hebrew.] Jerusalem: Geffen Publishers.

Zarini, Iris. 2004. "Capital and Networking: Socialization Processes of Mizrahi
Women Professors in Israeli Academe." [In Hebrew.] Seminar Paper Submitted
to the Open University, Israel.

———. 2011. "Mizrahi Women Professors in Israel's Academe." [In Hebrew.] Master's thesis, Be'er Sheva University.

Zilberg, Tami. 2002. "Back to Work." [In Hebrew.] *Globes: Israeli Business News,* 26–
27 November, 12.

Zomer, Navit. 2001. "Delta Textile Closes Its Textile Plant in Khurfeish: Two Hundred Women Workers Will Be Laid Off." [In Hebrew.] *Yediʿot Aharonot,* 30 July,
Economics Section, 1.

Reference List For "On Zionism" In Chapter 1

Alcalay, Ammiel. 1993. *After Jews and Arabs: Remaking Levantine Culture.* Minneapolis: University of Minnesota Press.

Atran, Scott. 1989. "The Surrogate Colonization of Palestine, 1917–1939." *American
Ethnologist* 16 (4): 719–44.

Bamaʿaraha [In struggle, Hebrew]. 1961–84. 13 volumes. [In Hebrew.] Jerusalem:
Vaʿad ʿAdat HaSfaradim.

Berlovitz, Yaffa, ed. 2001. *Women's Stories from the First ʿAliya.* [In Hebrew.] Hod
HaSharon, Israel: Astrolog.

Bernshtein, Deborah. 1987. *A Woman in Israel.* [In Hebrew.] Tel Aviv: HaKibbutz
HaMeu'had.

Chetrit, Sami Shalom. 2004 . *The Mizrahi Struggle 1948–2003: Between Oppression and Emancipation*. [In Hebrew.] Tel Aviv: ʿAm ʿOved.

Cohen, Tovah, ed. 2001. *"Her Hand Work": A Woman Between Work and Family*. [In Hebrew.] Ramat Gan, Israel: Bar Ilan University Press.

Damri-Madar, Vardit. 2002. "My Brothers, the Mizrahim." [In Hebrew.] In *ʿAzut Mezah: Mizrahi Feminism*, 54–57. Jerusalem: ZAH, Students for Social Justice.

Droyan, Nitzah. 1982. *Without a Magic Carpet*. [In Hebrew.] Jerusalem: Ben Zvi Institute for the Study of Eastern Jewry.

Ducker, Clare Louise. 2005. "Jews, Arabs, and Arab Jews: The Politics of Identity and Reproduction in Israel." Research Paper, Institute of Social Studies, The Hague, Netherlands.

Eliachar, Eliyahu. 1975. *Living with Palestinians*. [In Hebrew.] Jerusalem: Misgav.

———. 1980. *Living with Jews*. [In Hebrew.] Jerusalem: Marcus.

Foyerstein, Emil Menahem. 1989. *Women who Made History*. [In Hebrew.] Tel Aviv: Israel's Defense Ministry Press.

Gamlieli, Nissim Binyamin. 1965. *Yemen and the "Salvation" Camp: The History of Jews in Yemen, on the Road, in Adan, and in the Refugee Camps*. [In Hebrew]. Ramla, Israel: Dadon.

HaLevi, Ilan. 1987. *A History of the Jews: Ancient and Modern*. Translated by A. M. Berrett. London: Zed Books.

Hashash-Daniel, Yali. 2004. "Sex/Gender, Class and Ethnicity in the Policy of Birth in Israel 1962–1974." [In Hebrew.] Master's thesis, Haifa University.

Israeli, Daphna. 1984. "'Hapoʿalot' Movement in Israel from its Beginning until 1927." [In Hebrew.] *Katedra*, 109–40.

ʿIton Aher (An Other Paper, Hebrew). 1988–94. 32 issues. [In Hebrew.] Kiryat Ata, Israel: Yated NGO.

Kapara, Pinhas. 1978 . *From Yemen to Shaʿarayim*. [In Hebrew.] Rehovot, Israel: Self-published.

Orlan, H., trans. 1947. *The Protocol of the First Zionist Congress in Basel, 29–31st August 1897*. [In Hebrew.] Jerusalem: Reuven Mass.

Pirkey Hapoʿel Hazaʿir (Chapters of the Young Laborer, Hebrew). 1935–39. 13 issues. [In Hebrew.] Tel Aviv: Tverski.

Serri, Shalom, ed. 1983. *Travel Thy Dove: Yemenite Jews in Israel* [In Hebrew.] Tel Aviv: ʿAm ʿOved.

Sharaby, Rachel. 2000. *Syncretism and Adaptation: The Encounter between a Traditional Community and a Socialist Society* [In Hebrew.] Tel Aviv: Cherikover.

Shay, Yaʿel, ed. 2006. *And This Is the Blessing*. [In Hebrew.] Nataniya, Israel: Association for Cultural and Social Preservation.

Shevet Ve'Am [Tribe and people, Hebrew]. 1954–60. 6 volumes. [In Hebrew.] Jerusalem: Israeli Directorship of the World Sephardic Federation.

Shohat, Ella. 1988. "Sephardim in Israel: Zionism from the Point of View of its Jewish Victims." *Social Text* 19–20:1–35.

Stoler-Liss, Sahlav. 1998. "Raising a Zionist Baby: An Anthropological Analysis of Parents' Guidebooks." [In Hebrew.] Master's thesis, Tel Aviv University.

———. 2003. "Mothers Birth the Nation: The Social Construction of Zionist Mother-hood in Wartime in Israeli Parents' Manuals." *Nashim* 6 (Fall): 104–18.

Tubi, Yoseef, ed. 1982. *I Will Rise in the Palm Tree* [In Hebrew.] Jerusalem: Ben Zvi Institute.

Twig, Ruth, ed. 2000. *Spanish Jews in Israel in the Test of Time: Essay Collection.* [In Hebrew.] Jerusalem: Hebrew University of Jerusalem.

Yehoshua, Ya'akov. 1965. *Childhood in Old Jerusalem.* [In Hebrew.] 6 volumes. Jerusalem: Reuven Mass.

INDEX

Page numbers in *italics* indicate illustrations. Entries beginning with numbers are located under the spelled-out number; for instance, "'48 Arabs'" will be found under "forty-eight."

'Abed Rabbo, Yasser, 10, 226n15
Abergel, Reuven, 234n26
Abu Lughod, Lila, 239–40n18
academia: agency and identity politics in, 24–25, 28; "Ashkenazi Academic Junta," 17–18; EWIC entry and, 31–35, 47–60, 73–74; Mizraḥi women's positions in, 18, 58, 232n20; Palestinian positions in, 227n22; professor as term of use in, 244n7; tenured market in, 131
ACRI (Association for Civil Rights in Israel), 231n10
Adiv, Udi, 234n26
Adler, Chaim, 230n9
affirmative action: academia and, 24, 28; Arab-Israeli borderzone and, 109–10; "Ashkenazi Academic Junta," 18, 245n10; bureaucracy as torture system as denying, 120–24, 170; bureaucratic logic as denying, 25, 89–90, 104, 108–10, 159, 170; communitas, 89, 107–10, 120; community advocacy or collective mind and, 33, 89–90, 105; court appointments and, 149; discrimination, impossible position of Mizraḥi Jews in fight for, 88, 89, 121–23; disenfranchisement of demo-

graphic majority, Bitton's perspective on, 86; ethnographies as denied, 97; GendeRace essence as denied, 28, 91, 170, 186; love for Jewish state and, 91; majoritarian agency, as denied by bureaucratic logic, 25, 89–90, 159; male judge appointments, 149, 246n20; minority agency and resistance, 89, 90, 104; negative communitas, 107–10, 120; racism and, 115; single mothers and, 24, 28, 75–80, 165. *See also* failure of Mizraḥi protest movements; identity politics
agency: academia and, 24–25, 28; Arab-Israeli borderzone and, 110, 174, 205; bureaucracy as torture system as denying, 120–24, 170, 173; bureaucratic logic as denying, 25, 89–90, 104, 110, 159, 170, 172; communitas and, 110, 120; community advocacy or collective mind and, 33, 89–90; ethnographies as denying, 97; GendeRace essence as denying, 28, 91, 170, 186, 208; love for Jewish state and, 24, 90, 110, 175; majoritarian agency, as denied by bureaucratic logic, 25, 89–90, 159; minority agency and resistance, 89, 90, 104, 206, 207; national security versus, 170; negative communitas and, 110, 120; single mothers and, 24–25, 75–80, 172, 175–76; subalternity and, 175. *See also* failure of Mizraḥi protest movements; identity politics

Bedouin: Egyptian Bedouin guerrillas, 166; military service in IDF by, 76, 230n4, 236n1; Mzeina Bedouin scholarship, 20; Palestinian identity *versus*, 76; scholarship on, 12; settlements and, 36, 76; single mothers' agency and, 75–77, 144; *Yishuv* era land sales by, 50

Begin, Menachem, 39, 64, 66, 240n22

Behar, Ruth, 96, 241n25

behemat bayit ktana (little domestic beast, or Yemeni girl), 53

"Beilin-'Abed Rabbo Flying Circus," 10, 226n15

Beit Ha'am (people's home, or community center), 46, 231n12

Beit Halachmi, Hanna, 32

belonging: desire of Mizrahim to belong to Israel's mainstream, 86–88; love for Jewish state and, 24, 90–93, 95, 109, 110; secular Ashkenazi-centric identity and, 87–88

Bennett, Naftali, 250–51n20

Bentham, Jeremy, 242n3

Berger, Peter L., 242n2

Bernardi, Claudia, 243n7

Bernstein Research Project, 26, 229n29, 229n31

Betzalel Art Academy, 59

Bialik, Haim Nachman, 163, 247–48n2

Biton, Charlie, 159

Black Panthers (Mizrahi), 66, 159, 180, 234n26. *See also* HaLo Nehmadim (New Black Panthers)

blondes: *blondinit* (woman with natural blonde or dyed blonde hair), 117, *118*; in Knafo protest, 5; as Mizrahi stereotype, 75; *sh'hordinit* (woman with natural dark dyed blond with exposed dark roots), 117, *118*

boarding school system. *See* forced boarding school system

Bohadana, Miri, *118*

bombings: at borders of Israel, 161; as diversion from protests/social unrest, 164, 166–67; of Gaza strip, 186, 188, *189*, 190, 215; of Iranian nuclear facilities, 172. *See also* suicide bombing

Bouazizi, Mohamed, 166–67

Boycott, Divestment, and Sanctions movement (BDS), 201, 205

Braverman, Avishay, 195–96

B'Tselem, 226n17

Budick, Sanford, 100

bureaucracy as cosmology: bureaucracy as torture system and, 103; bureaucratic logic and, 106, 172; "chosen people/chosen land" and, 81, 92–93, 101, 108, 119–20; description of, 23–24; Divinity of Chance and, 23–24, 28, 81, 93, 103, 106, 138, 228n27; Divinity of Jewish State and, 23, 28, 81–85, 95; GendeRace essence and, 93, 97, 119–20; military service in IDF and, 24; national security and, 168; Operation "Pillar of Cloud" or *'Amud 'Anan* and, 168, 199; pilgrimage and, 23, 81, 107, 176; ritual process and, 107

bureaucracy as torture system: agency as denied by, 120–24, 170, 173; bracketing of single mothers' lives as response to, 102, 120–21, 145; bureaucracy as cosmology and, 103; "chosen people/chosen land" and, 119–20, 124; communitas, negative, and, 107–10, 120; conflict resolution in context of, 27; court system and, 121–23, 127, 146–47; description of, 23, 80–81, 176–77; Divinity of Chance and, 23–24, 28, 81, 93, 103, 106, 138, 228n27; Divinity of Jewish State and, 28, 81, 95; documents as implements of torture and, 112–14;

ethno-religious nationhood and, 81; healing from trauma through creative art and, 124, 243n7, 244n11; inflictor-inflicted relationship and, 111–13; love for Jewish state and, 95, 109, 110; Manchester Extended-Case Study method and, 25–27; neoliberal economics and, 103, 173, 181; pain and, 28, 90, 103, 109–11, 172; plus-minus model of torture and, 110–11; plus-plus relationship of torture and, 111–13; as pre-discursive phenomenology, 26, 105, 111, 176; ritual process and, 25, 108, 113; scholarship on, 103, 209; subaltern theory of interrelationships between bureaucracy and torture, 29, 105, 109, 133; "tough love" and, 109; zone of repulsion and, 111–13, 114, 120, 121. See also bureaucracy as cosmology

bureaucratic infrastructure in Israel: Ashkenazi women's circumvention of, 105; citizenship requirements and, 24, 41, 73, 115, 238n9; GendeRace essence and, 24, 91–93, 115–17, 119–20; hierarchy of bureaucrats and, 105–6, 140; history of, 19–20; Judaization of Palestine under, 19–20; Mizraḥim in context of, 19–20, 106; placement clerks and, 134–37, 140; secularization/de-Arabization of Mizraḥim and, 20, 51, 87; social protests in 2011 to 2013 and, 165–67, 233n22, 239n17, 248n5 (ch. 6); warfare and bombings as diversion from protests/social unrest and, 164, 166–67, 178, 209. See also bureaucracy as torture system; bureaucratic logic; court system; Israeli Defense Force (IDF)

bureaucratic logic: agency as denied by, 25, 89–90, 104, 110, 159, 170, 172;

bracketing by bureaucrats and, 120–21; bureaucracy as cosmology and, 106, 172; bureaucrats' role in, 107, 111–12, 120–21; "chosen people/chosen land" and, 108–9, 124; classificatory criterion or categories in, 89–90, 104–7; communitas and, 89, 108, 113; deep structure and, 108, 110; Gaza and, 89, 104, 121; horizontal system within, 107–8, 121; Jews versus Goyim binary in context of, 89, 90, 104, 167, 208–9; liminal time-space and, 104, 106, 111; liminality and, 106, 108, 243n4; as monothetic, 89, 106, 112; mothers' endless cycle of adjustment to bureaucratic encounters and, 107, 113; principles of logic and, 110; rational and secular bureaucracy and, 104; ritual process and, 25, 89, 104–7, 111, 113, 209, 243n4; vertical system within, 107–8, 121, 123

Burke, Kenneth, 242n30
Bush, George W., 163

Cade, Toni, 143, 244n3 (ch. 5)
Camp David Accords, 228n26
Central Bureau of Statistics, 4, 84–85
Chetrit, Sami Shalom, 86
Child and Spouse Support Laws (1959 and 1972), 8, 41
children: abduction charges against single mothers and, 14–16; "anti-pediarchy" Ashkenazi practice and, 56–57; baby kidnappings and adoption of, 60, 88, 233n21; child support for single mothers and, 8–9, 42, 145; custody issues and, 14–17, 33, 225n11, 227n21; unconsented medical experimentation on, 60, 233n21. See also forced boarding school system
Chomsky, Noam, 110

Goren, Shosha, 69
Graeber, David, 209
Grafhoff, Richard, 242n2
Gruzinim, 3. *See also* post-Soviet Jews
guest workers, 11, 135
Gur, Rutie, 69
gvarot (ladies), 52, 69

Ḥad horit/horiyot (single mother/mothers, single parent/parents). *See* single mother/mothers
Hague Convention on the Civil Aspects of International Child Abduction, 14–16
Haimovich, Miki, 118
Ḥakimi, Tehila, 252n33
HaLo Neḥmadim (New Black Panthers), 179–85, 180, 188, 190, 197, 249n8
ḥalutzot (pioneers, feminine), 52
Ḥamas: bombings by, 166; *hudna* ceasefire and, 5, 12, 161; kidnappings by, 185–86; on Operation Protective Edge (Tzuk Eitan, Hebrew), 177; Palestinian refugee camps run by, 225n9; PLO coalition with, 178; removal from list of terrorist organizations, 190, 250n19; salary dispute with, 184–85; in War on Gaza, 188–91
Handelman, Don, 23–24, 89–90, 103–6, 172, 228n27, 229n31, 232n17, 242nn1–2
Hannibal Directive, 251n20
Ḥanukkah miracle, 163, 247–48nn1–2
Harari, ʿOvadia, 234n26
Harrison, Faye, 240n21, 241–42n28
Ḥasan, Roy, 252n33
Ḥassan Aḥmed ʿArman, Moḥammed, 250n14
Ḥatuka, Shlomi, 252n33
ha-Viskonsin (The Wisconsin), 137
Heart at East coalition, 179–80, 202, 248n5 (afterword)
"Hebrew as Step-Mother Tongue" project, 18–19, 20–22, 228n23

Hebrew language, 2, 7–8, 224–25n9, 224n7, 248n1
Hebrew University, 58, 147, 247n2
Hemo, David, 2
Hertzog, Esther, 32, 245–46n18
Herzfeld, Michael, 242n1
Herzl, Theodor, 47, 232n15
Ḥezbollah, 35, 43, 72–73, 164, 182, 193
hishtaknezut (Ashkenazification), 88, 117
Ḥok HaHesderim (Arrangements Law) amendment (2003): amendment to (2014), 181–82, 191, 192, 195–97; case note by Paz-Fuchs on, 142–43; description of, 9–10, 12, 164; income assurance and, 138; income augmentation and, 138; late capitalism and, 130; neo-conservative economics and, 9–10, 129; op-ed article on, 125–31; patriarchal institutions and, 126; single mothers' welfare payments and, 13–14, 80; social engineering policies, rehabilitation of heteronormative family and, 126, 130
hooks, bell, 157
hudna ceasefire, 5, 12, 35, 161, 226n18
human rights, 71, 78–79
Hurston, Zora Neale, 96, 241n27
Husserl, Edmund, 115, 244n9

identity politics: academia and, 24–25, 28; agency of, 3–4, 24–25, 28, 75–81, 172; contextual disconnection of, 205; cultural resistance and, 239n16; ethnic cleansing and, 159–60; GendeRace essence and agency of, 28, 91, 170, 186; intersectionality model, 91, 108–10, 239n18; "Israeliness" (secular Ashkenazi-centric identity), 87–88; Israelis, as term of use, 3, 87–88; multiplicities of, 110; prohibition of, 93; resistive, 90

—ultra-orthodox (*continued*)
Schnitt Committee recommendation and, 225n11; secular Ashkenazi-centric identity and, 87–88; Tender Age Doctrine and, 225n11
Joseph, Suad, 32, 73–74, 232n17
Judaism: circumcision rite, 47, 82, 232n15, 238n8; Ḥanukkah miracle, 163, 247–48nn1–2; Jewish state within Arab World, 28, 81, 108, 127; kosher dietary laws, 82, 237–38n7; Shabbat observance, 82, 237n6; *Yiddishkeit* (Eastern European shtetl Jewish way of life), 87
Judaization of Palestine, 19–20. *See also* ethno-religious nationhood; Palestinians; religion; secularization and de-Arabization of Mizraḥim; Zionism

Kabala ("acceptance by transmission" or mysticism in Judaism), 101, 145, 152, 245n8
Kaḥlon, Moshe, 199–200
Kanaaneh, Rhoda, 236n1
Kapferer, Bruce, 237n5, 242n2
kapo syndrome of Mizraḥim, 88, 106, 123
Katsav, Moshe, 116
Kavkazim/Kavkaziyot (Kavkazi), 3, 41. *See also* post-Soviet Jews
Kehilot Ashkenaz (Ashkenazi communities), 3
Keissar, ʿAdi, 252n33
Khait-Marelly, Orna, 224n6
kibbutz/kibbutzim (agricultural cooperative/s), 44, 50, 58, 68
Kleinman, Arthur and Joan, 243n6
Knafo, Vicky: ethnic background of, 1, 223n2; income for, 14, 162; march from Mitzpe to Jerusalem by, 1, 5; media and, 153–55, 230n9; peace process and, 162; photograph of Netanyahu with, 169; political party

recruitment and, 162, 168; stereotypic image of Mizraḥi women and, 117
Knafoland: end of encampment of, 161–62; funding for, 77; media and, 8, 12–13, 143, 153–55, 159, 230n9; photograph of, 15; post-Soviet Jewish support for, 42; sectarian support for, 76, 144–45, 150–51; single mothers agency and, 24–25, 75–80, 165; suicide bombing of Bus #2 effects and, 8, 27, 29, 161, 162, 164, 208; in Wohl Rose Park, 7. *See also* failure of Mizraḥi protest movements; Single Mothers March or Knafo protest (2003)
Krieger, Nancy, 23
Kuntsman, Adi, 239n15, 243n6

Labor Court, 148, 149
Labor Hill B-Jamusin, 182–84, 187, 198, 199, 201, 249n8
labor unions, 54, 163. *See also* employment; unemployment
Landau, Idan, 248n3 (afterword)
Landes, Dorit, 134
land-for-peace advocates, 62, 63, 198
Langer, Susanne, 242n2, 242n30
Lapid, Yair, 63, 196–97, 233n22
late capitalism, 106, 130
Lebanon: 1982 Lebanon War, 39, 64, 230n4; 2006 Lebanon War, 35, 43–44, 182, 192–93; *Fataḥland* on border in, 8, 39; Ḥezbollah activities against Israel from, 43, 72–73, 164; relocation of citizens from border near, 44
leftist politics: anti-Zionist left, 63, 64, 66, 69, 71; Ashkenazim and, 63–64, 68–69, 77, 195, 204–6; history of, 62–69; mass social protests in 2011 and, 165, 168, 233n22; Mizraḥi disenfranchisement and, 63–64, 77, 79; peace process and, 62, 63; political party recruitment of

secularization and de-Arabization of Mizraḥim, 20, 51, 87. *See also* ethno-religious nationhood; Judaization of Palestine

Selzer, Michael, 63–64, 233n23

separatist feminism, 244n2 (ch. 5)

Sephardim (Spaniards), 1, 48, 50, 53, 57–58, 60, 232n18

Serry, Robert H., 185

sexual assault: demands for sexual favors in return for welfare benefits, 116, 135, 177; rape of Yemeni domestic workers, 53; sexual harassment allegations, 116

SHABAK (Sherut Bitahon Klali, General Security Service), 111, 163, 166, 184, 243n8

Shadmi, Erella, 249n5

Shamai, Ilana, 69

Shami, Seteney, 31, 33, 44

Sharon, Ariel, 62, 64

SHATIL (*Sherutei Tmikhave Ye ʿutz leIrgunim*), 12–13, 70–71, 78. *See also* New Israel Fund (NIF)

Shatz, Boris, 59

Shazar, Zalman, 65

Shaʿer, Gilad, 185, 187, 250n15

Shifman, Pinkhas, 225n11

Shiknaz (Ashkenazim), 50. *See also* Ashkenazim

Shilansky, Dov, 240–41n22

Shiran, Vicki, 69, 71, 159, *180*

Shohat, Ella, 157–58

Shoshana, Avi, 242n1

Shoushan, Flora, 43, 230n9

Shoushan, Sami, 43, 230n9

Shubeli, Rafi, 33, 68, 146

"Silenced from All Directions" (Lavie), 228n23

Silman, Moshe, 167, *167*

Single Headed Families Law of 1992, 8, 41, 128

single mother/mothers (*Ḥad horit/horiyot*): academic publication for merit and promotion and, 31–35, 47–60, 232n17; agency of identity politics and, 24–25, 75–80, 172, 175–76; autoethnography and, 101; bracketing by, 102, 120–21, 145, 172; child abduction charges and, 14–16; child custody and, 14–17, 33, 225n11, 227n21; child support for, 8–9, 42, 145; cultural renaissance and, 207; data on, 126, 157; divorced single mother type and, 14–17, 40, 42, 127, 225n11, 227n21; *du raglit* or two-legged descriptor for, 38, 39; economic support for, 8–9, 40, 41, 42, 127, 129; *em had horit* or "single parent mother" and, 37; employment for, 36, 46, 130; etymology of single motherhood and, 37; forced boarding school system and, 20, 33, 58, 145, 148–49, 151, 162, 196; healing from trauma through creative art as luxury for, 124, 244n11; hip alternative single mothers type, 40, 127; *Ḥok HaHesderim* and, 13–14, 80; Ingber revolt by, 36–37, *37*; intra-Jewish racism or Ashkenazi-Mizraḥi racial divide and, 71–72; in middle-class, 144; Mizraḥi single mothers, 9, 22, 25, 28, 42, 75, 80–81, 90, 95, 102–9, 120, 122–24, 161, 171–73, 175, 181, 196, 207, 208; op-ed article on, 125–31; post-Soviet Jews and, 41; post-Soviet single mother types and, 40–42, 127, 144, 230n2; scholarship on, 22; sexual favors demanded in return for employment for, 116, 135, 177; social analysis of welfare system for, 100, 125; social engineering policies, rehabilitation of heteronormative family and, 126, 130; stereotypes, 39–42; talisman used

Tel Aviv (*continued*)
Ḥezbollah target, 35; job opportunities in, 5; as missile target, 73, 188, 191; Mizraḥi Women's Group, 69–70; *Pinuy-Binuy* municipal plan for, 183, 249n9; social welfare bureau of, 32; U.S. Consulate in, 16; White City, 38, 94, 134, 182, 188, 192, 230n7
tent movement, 237n2. *See also* Knafoland
tenured labor market, 131
Third World, 77, 97, 158, 236n32
Thorleifsson, Cathrine, 239n16
Thrift, Nigel, 101
Tisha B'Av, 45, 192
Tnuʿat ha-poʿelet (Women's Labor Movement), 52
torture: documents as implements of, 112–14; inflictor-inflicted relationship, 111–13; plus-minus model of, 110–11; plus-plus relationship of, 111–13; prison torture, 234n26; procedural torture, bureaucratic practice and, 25; victimhood narratives, 29, 95; welfare bureaucracy as system of, 23, 25, 26, 28, 80–81; zone of repulsion, 111–13, 114, 120, 121. *See also* bureaucracy as torture system
trauma: daily living, traumatization by, 112; documents and, 114; healing from trauma through creative art, 124, 243n7, 244n11; intergenerational transmission of, 110; pain and post-traumatic healing of, 110; psychological/psychoanalytical models of, 243n6; traumatic pain and bureaucracy as torture system, 110–11
travel abroad regulations, for single mothers, 34, 230n2
Turner, Edie (Edith), 243n5
Turner, Victor, 89, 243n4

ultra-orthodox Jews: as anti-Zionist, 56, 224n5; military service in IDF exemption for, 85; Mizraḥim *versus*, 224n5; motherhood and, 56; *Neturei Karta*, 84; population statistics for, 28, 84; Schnitt Committee recommendation and, 225n11; secular Ashkenazi-centric identity and, 87–88; Tender Age Doctrine and, 225n11
unconsented medical experimentation, by Ashkenazim on Mizraḥim, 60, 233n21
unemployment: of Ashkenazi women, 52; in Israeli hinterlands, 234n27; in Mizraḥi communities, 1, 72; overqualified for available jobs and, 19, 137; in Sderot, 190; of single mothers, 130; in West Bank and Gaza, 11. *See also* employment
United Kingdom: neo-conservative economics and, 129; U.S.-UK anthropological formula for publications and, 95–97, 172, 241–42nn27–28, 242n1; welfare reforms in, 126
United Nations (UN): 1947 UN resolution for division of Palestine, 51; Development Programme reports, 188; International Volunteer Day of, 73, 236n33
United States: affirmative action in, 246n20; child custody for single mothers in, 14, 227n21; civil rights movements in, 174; Consolidated Omnibus Budget Reconciliation Act of 1985 in, 9; feminism of color paradigm in, 19; IDF operations in context of politics in, 163, 168; Israel-Palestine conflict/divide as driver of foreign policy decisions, 173; media on democratic stability of Israel, 171; neo-conservative economics and, 129; nuclear treaty negotiations with Iran, 200; professor as term of use in, 244n7; *schwartze* or "black" as term of use in, 245n9;

Lightning Source UK Ltd.
Milton Keynes UK
UKHW01f0721250518
323200UK00001B/23/P